Ireland in the Bronze Age

Ireland in the Bronze Age
Proceedings of the Dublin Conference, April 1995

Edited by
John Waddell and Elizabeth Shee Twohig
for
The Office of Public Works

BAILE ÁTHA CLIATH
ARNA FHOILSIÚ AG OIFIG AN tSOLÁTHAIR.

DUBLIN
PUBLISHED BY THE STATIONERY OFFICE

ISBN 0-7076-2311-1

Sponsored by: The Office of Public Works

Typeset in Ireland by Tower Books, Ballincollig, Co. Cork
Cover Design by Kunnert & Tierney, Cork City
Printed by Shanway Press, Belfast

Le ceannach díreach ón
OIFIG DHÍOLTA FOILSEACHÁN RIALTAIS, TEACH SUN ALLIANCE.
SRÁID THEACH LAIGHEAN, BAILE ÁTHA CLIATH 2.
nó trí aon díoltóir leabhar.

To be purchased through any Bookseller, or directly from the
GOVERNMENT PUBLICATIONS SALE OFFICE,
SUN ALLIANCE HOUSE, MOLESWORTH STREET, DUBLIN 2.

Contents

List of Figures

List of Tables

List of Plates

List of Contributors

Professor Martín Almagro-Gorbea, Departmento de Prehistoria, Universidad Complutense, Ciudad Universitaria, 28040 Madrid, Spain.

Professor M. Baillie, Palaeoecology Centre, Queen's University, Belfast, BT7 1NN.

Professor Richard Bradley, Dept. of Archaeology, Whiteknights, PO Box 218, Reading, RG6 2AA, England.

Anna Brindley, Biologisch-Archaeologisch Instituut, Poststratt 6, 9712 ER Groningen, Netherlands.

Mary Cahill, National Museum of Ireland, Kildare Street, Dublin 2.

Humphrey Case, Pitt's Cottage, 187 Thame Road, Warborough, Wallington, Oxon, OX10 7DH.

Professor George Eogan, Dept. of Archaeology, University College, Dublin.

Dr. Alex Gibson, 2-3 Hen Domen Cottages, Hendomen, Montgomery, Powys SY15 6HB, Wales.

Dr. Jim Mallory, Dept. of Archaeology and Palaeoecology, Queen's University, Belfast, BT7 1NN.

Charles Mount, 18 Fox Hill, Wheaton Hall, Drogheda, Co. Louth.

Dr William O'Brien, Dept. of Archaeology, University College, Galway.

Dr. Greer Ramsay, Armagh County Museum, The Mall East, Armagh BT61 9BE.

Henrik Thrane, Fyns Oldtid-Hollnfgard, Hestehaven 201, Odense SO, Denmark.

Professor John Waddell, Dept. of Archaeology, University College, Galway.

Paul Walsh, Archaeological Branch, Ordnance Survey, Phoenix Park, Dublin 8.

Preface

As part of a Council of Europe initiative, Ireland is participating in a European campaign on the theme of **The Bronze Age: the First Golden Age in Europe**. The aim of the campaign is to promote the understanding of the archaeological heritage and its protection for future generations. The Irish contribution to this programme, implemented under the auspices of the Office of Public Works, centres on 1995 as **The Year of the Bronze Age.**

The Bronze Age in Europe was a time of considerable technological progress and witnessed important changes in social organisation, in the daily lives of ordinary peoples, in religious beliefs and artistic expression. Ireland shared in many of the changes recognised in Continental Europe at this time. The appearance of copper, bronze and gold objects shortly after 2500 BC saw this island participate in a technological revolution shared throughout most of Europe and, with abundant sources of copper and gold, Ireland emerged as one of the most prolific centres of metal production in this early period. The development of a trade in metals encouraged long-distance contact between Ireland, Britain and the Continent, connections which brought new cultural influences.

The Bronze Age in Ireland was also a time of population growth, novel funerary and ritual expression, agricultural progress and continued transformation of the landscape. A growing number of settlement sites have been identified, ranging from large hill-top enclosures to lake-side dwellings and many thousands of *fulachta fiadh* or burnt mounds are known today. Yet, in common with much of Europe, the Bronze Age is best known for its rich artefact record in metal, stone and ceramics, and indeed for the production of bronze weapons of war, as well as for the large number of sacred monuments dedicated to death and ritual.

The Irish programme was planned by a national committee under the chairmanship of Professor George Eogan. The committee secretary was Dr William O'Brien and members included Ms Mary Cahill, Dr Rhoda Kavanagh, Mr Eugene Keane, Dr Ann Lynch, Mr Conleth Manning, Dr Elizabeth Shee Twohig, and Professor John Waddell. Informal links were established with colleagues in Northern Ireland, notably Professor Derek Simpson, Dr Chris Lynn and Mr Richard Warner whose assistance is gratefully acknowledged. The committee proposed a series of events: a photographic exhibition, a lecture series, a conference, and the acquisition of a Bronze Age site or landscape.

These proposals were enthusiastically adopted by the Office of Public Works which generously agreed to provide the necessary financial support. The programme was announced on the 15th October 1994 by Mr Noel Dempsey, TD, Minister for State at the Department of Finance, who also launched the specially commissioned photographic exhibition on the Irish Bronze Age. This exhibition was designed by Dr Anna Brindley with the assistance of Ms Mary Cahill and Dr Ann Lynch. Three sets of the exhibition (two in English and one in Irish) are circulating to a large number of venues, including libraries, local museums and heritage centres, throughout the island. A series of lectures was proposed with the cooperation of most Irish workers in the realm of Bronze Age studies, and many local societies and clubs have organised lectures and field excursions as part of the Bronze Age theme. Artefacts from the period are currently on display in many museums, most notably in the National Museum of Ireland where there is a major exhibition of Bronze Age goldwork.

As a conservation measure to commemorate the Year of the Bronze Age, the Office of Public Works has purchased a major Bronze Age landscape at Mount Gabriel, near Schull in west Cork, which is one of the best preserved Bronze Age copper mining locations in Europe. The acquisition of this site is an important initiative at a time when many prehistoric monuments and landscapes are threatened through land reclamation and afforestation. Long after this Year of the Bronze Age has passed, this initiative will be a permanent memorial to the Council of Europe's Bronze Age campaign.

Finally, a major conference was hosted by the Office of Public Works. It was held in Dublin Castle from the 21st-23rd April 1995 and organised by Mr Eugene Keane and Ms Roseanne Meenan. The conference, on the theme of **Ireland in the Bronze Age**, was opened by Mr Michael D. Higgins, TD, Minister for Arts, Culture and the Gaeltacht, who acknowledged the role of the Council of Europe in fostering a greater public awareness of our common archaeological heritage leading to more general support for protective measures. He particularly welcomed Professor Gustav Trotzig, of the Central Board of National Antiquities in Stockholm, Chairman of the Council of Europe's Specialist Committee on the Bronze Age, who also addressed the Conference.

Some twenty-two speakers from Ireland and abroad reviewed a large number of issues, from Bronze Age chronology and environment, to settlement and economy, death and ritual, and Ireland's place in Bronze Age Europe. The contributions included reports from three of the Project Directors of the Discovery Programme, an innovative research programme which is, at present, addressing the problem of late prehistoric settlement in Ireland. Dr Eoin Grogan described the work of the North Munster Project including the late Bronze Age settlement evidence from Mooghaun hillfort; Ms Claire Cotter and Mr Martin Doody gave an account of the late Bronze Age settlements at Dún Aonghasa, Aran, Co. Galway, and Chancellorsland, Co. Tipperary, respectively. Accounts of their work to date will be found in the *Discovery Programme Reports*.

This publication of the proceedings of the Dublin Conference has been generously funded by the Office of Public Works. It is hoped the publication will illustrate the wide range of work now being undertaken on the Irish Bronze Age and illuminate a formative period in our common past when Ireland, Britain and the Continent were all parts of an older and very different political reality.

JW

Introduction

George Eogan

The Bronze Age ushered in a new stage in the long history of human endeavour. In all regions it was a time of widespread and often recurrent change which affected most aspects of life – commercial, economic, social and ritual. It was a time of far-flung connections and interrelated cultural enrichment. Amongst the countries of Europe, Ireland was a significant Bronze Age land. To a large extent this could be due to native supplies of gold and copper but also to the presence of a society with sufficient wealth to acquire objects, some of which were made from exotic materials. The term Bronze Age has been used loosely, not in a strict technological sense, for instance it incorporates the initial centuries of the metal age (before 2000 BC) when tools and weapons were made from copper. Nevertheless, it has become a useful generic term for a period that lasted for close to 2000 years in Ireland.

Interest in the Irish Bronze Age has a long history going back to the 17th century. Humphrey Case in the Hencken *Festschrift* (1977) has given us a fascinating account of one of the earliest recorded finds – two gold sun discs from Ballyshannon, Co. Donegal, only one of which has survived. These were discovered about 1690 as a result of an excavation, probably the first recorded excavation in Ireland. The surviving disc was one of the first objects to reach a public collection in either Britain or Ireland.

At the beginning, Bronze Age studies were largely confined to descriptions of artefacts, some being very inadequate. Field archaeology did not play a significant role. During the following centuries the number of finds that came to light and accounts of discoveries increased. Michael Herity's researches in the Minute Books of the Society of Antiquaries of London have revealed numerous records of finds made during the early decades of the 18th century (1969). In 1730 finds started to come to light during turf-cutting in the Bog of Cullen, Co. Tipperary, a site that yielded, mainly over the succeeding couple or so decades, a vast quantity of gold and bronze objects. Out of all of these, the only definite find that survives is a portion of one object, the terminal of a large 'dress-fastener' (Wallace 1938; Eogan 1983a, 155). The others, or at least most

of them, appear to have been melted down, a fate that was to befall so many objects, gold in particular, during the remainder of that and the following 19th century.

By the end of the 18th century private collections of antiquities, which included many items of Bronze Age date, were becoming a feature. One of the first collectors was Richard Pococke, Bishop of Ossory and later of Meath. But Pococke was not just a selfish collector, he had a scholarly approach to the material that he collected and in 1757 contributed a paper which is published in Volume 2 of *Archaeologia*. Another significant figure of the 18th century was Charles Vallancey. He also built up a collection including some splendid gold objects but also established a publication outlet, *Collectanea de Rebus Hibernicis*, which he edited. This ran to six volumes which appeared between 1770 and 1808 (Nevin 1993). As collectors Pococke and Vallancey had contemporaries and successors. Important collections were formed in Dublin by a Town Major, Henry Charles Sirr, and by the Dean of St Patrick's Cathedral, Henry Richard Dawson, but collectors were also active in other areas such as Redmond Anthony of Piltown, Co. Kilkenny, or John Windele of Cork (Cahill 1994).

Public collections were also getting under way notably by the Royal Irish Academy which was becoming the national repository for antiquities; its early acquisitions being two bar-twisted gold torcs from Tara acquired in 1839. These were promptly published by the distinguished antiquary George Petrie in Volume 1 of the Academy's *Proceedings* (1839). But from a much earlier period, from the commencement of its publications in 1785, antiquities, including objects of Bronze Age date, were being published. One of the earliest publications was an account of an urn from Kilranelagh, Co. Wicklow, which appeared in Volume 1 of the Academy's *Transactions*. Another important public collection was also being built up at this time, that was by the Belfast Museum.

Significant discoveries continued to be made. The previously mentioned bar-torcs from Tara were found in 1810, while a number of years later, in 1854, a vast hoard of over a hundred gold objects was found at Mooghaun, Co. Clare.

The first major publication of Irish archaeological artefacts was the Academy's catalogue of its collection of antiquities, including all its Bronze Age material, which was compiled by William Wilde and published between 1857 and 1862. This was an astonishing event in Bronze Age studies not only for Ireland but internationally as well. It still remains a standard work of reference (Wilde 1857, 1861, 1862). Subsequently, in 1890, the Academy transferred its collection to the newly established National Museum of Ireland (Mitchell 1985). Shortly afterwards George Coffey assumed responsibility for the collection of Irish Antiquities and later became Keeper. This appointment proved to be a significant event for Irish archaeology, especially for Bronze Age studies. His researches were comprehensive, amongst them being descriptive accounts of Bronze Age finds, not only metal finds but those from burials as well, but he was also a synthesiser and interpreter. It may not be generally realised that Coffey was a pioneer in the geographical approach to archaeological studies as his 1909 paper on the distribution of gold lunulae shows. The first overall review of the Irish Bronze Age was also the work of Coffey. This appeared in 1913 and in it he provided a synthesis of the period. As a result of Coffey's work one could no longer regard antiquities merely as antiquities, they assumed a new and significant role as documents of the past. Coffey's successor in the Keepership, E. C. R. Armstrong, continued Coffey's scholarly approach to Bronze Age problems, and one of his great achievements was the placing of the study of prehistoric gold ornaments on a scientific footing (Armstrong 1933). Throughout this century artefacts continue to play an important role in Bronze Age studies, of note being Seán P. Ó Ríordáin's pan-European study of halberds (1937). During the 1930s excavations and other forms of field-work were also becoming a feature, again the work of Ó Ríordáin on Beaker settlement sites and on ritual sites in the Lough Gur region of Co. Limerick is noteworthy (1951, 1954, Grogan and Eogan 1987). Hencken and Movius's excavation of the multiple cist cairn at Knockast, Co. Westmeath (1934), and the publication by Evans and Megaw of the pottery from the Mount Stewart Early Bronze Age burial cairn in Co. Down (1937), inaugurated a new and scientific stage in the study of Bronze Age burials. Excavation and other aspects of field-work were now assuming a very significant role in research in addition to artefact studies. County and regional surveys since the 1950s are providing a great deal of new evidence (e.g. Co. Down and Co. Louth) and for the early stage the

Megalithic Survey has enormously increased our knowledge of wedge-shaped tombs (de Valera and Ó Nualláin 1961, 1964, 1972, 1982, 1989). Ó Nualláin's work on the Munster stone circles, alignments and boulder burials has emphasised the importance of such sites in their regional setting (1978, 1984, 1988). John Waddell's evaluation of Early Bronze Age burials was the first national study of such monuments and their associated ritual (1970, also 1990). Of course artefactual studies continue to play a key role. The Colloquium on the Origins of Metallurgy held in Dublin in 1978 considered amongst other things the beginnings of Irish metallurgy (Ryan 1979), aspects of which have now been studied in greater detail by William O'Brien (1994).

For the Early Bronze Age bronze artefacts, the studies of Harbison are comprehensive (1969a and b) as are Kavanagh's studies of urns and pygmy cups (1973, 1976, 1977). Ó Ríordáin and Waddell have thoroughly published the Food Vessels (1993). The Later Bronze Age has been reviewed by Eogan (1964) who has also published a series of corpora (e.g. 1965, 1972, 1983). Technological studies such as those by Hartmann (1970, 1982) on gold or on early copper metallurgy by Coghlan and Case (1957) were significant.

Not only does research continue but considerable developments have taken place recently. The establishment of the Discovery Programme in 1991 has led to a major upsurge of research into problems of the Late Bronze Age and the Iron Age. This is a comprehensive research programme with particular emphasis on habitation and settlement. The initial results have made worthwhile contributions to our knowledge of that important but tantalising stage (*The Discovery Programme: Strategies and Questions*, Dublin, 1992, and *Discovery Programme Reports* 1, 1993 and 2, 1995).

Bronze Age societies were responsible for a series of major changes and advancements that took place over a period of a millennium and a half or so. These include major technological developments that involved metal-working, but also other media such as organic materials. The landscape was further opened up for agricultural purposes while a wider range of artefacts, both mundane and exotic, came into existence. Some of these items have localised distributions, yet the overall distribution shows that during its different stages Bronze Age society was integrated materially. But Irish Bronze Age people were also part of a wider culture. Irish items and materials were exported to other lands while Irish skills helped with the development of Bronze Age complexes abroad, for instance in areas such as south Scandinavia and the Low Countries (Butler 1963, 19; De Navarro

1950). Bronze Age people have left an indelible mark on Ireland, their achievements have made significant contributions to subsequent cultural development, the importance of which is being further highlighted by current and continuing research.

References

Armstrong, E. C. R. 1933. *Catalogue of Irish Gold Ornaments in the Collection of the Royal Irish Academy.* Dublin.

Butler, J. J. 1963. Bronze Age connections across the North Sea. *Palaeohistoria* 9, 1-286.

Cahill, M. 1994. Mr Anthony's Bog Oak Case of Gold Antiquities. *Proceedings of the Royal Irish Academy* 94C, 53-109.

Case, H. J. 1977. An early accession to the Ashmolean Museum. In V. Markotic (ed.), *Ancient Europe and the Mediterranean: Studies presented to Hugh Hencken,* 18-34. Warminster.

Coffey, G. 1909. The Distribution of Gold Lunulae in Ireland and North-West Europe. *Proceedings of the Royal Irish Academy* 27C, 25-58.

Coffey, G. 1913. *The Bronze Age in Ireland.* Dublin.

Coghlan, H. H. and Case, H. J. 1957. Early metallurgy of copper in Ireland and Britain. *Proceedings of the Prehistoric Society* 23, 91-123.

de Navarro, J. M. 1950. The British Isles and the Beginning of the Northern Early Bronze Age. In C. Fox and B. Dickens (eds), *The Early Cultures of North-West Europe,* 77-105. Cambridge.

de Valera, R. and Ó Nualláin, S. 1961, 1964, 1972, 1982, 1989. *Survey of the Megalithic Tombs of Ireland.* Vols. 1-5. Dublin.

Eogan, G. 1964. The Later Bronze Age in Ireland in the light of recent research. *Proceedings of the Prehistoric Society* 30, 268-351.

Eogan, G. 1965. *Catalogue of Irish Bronze Swords.* Dublin.

Eogan, G. 1972. 'Sleeve-fasteners' of the Late Bronze Age. In F. Lynch and C. Burgess (eds), *Prehistoric Man in Wales and the West,* 189-209. Bath.

Eogan, G. 1983a. *The Hoards of the Irish Later Bronze Age.* Dublin.

Eogan, G. 1983b. Ribbon Torcs in Britain and Ireland. In A. O'Connor and D. V. Clarke (eds), *From the Stone Age to the Forty-Five,* 87-126. Edinburgh.

Evans, E. E. and Megaw, B. R. S. 1937. The Multiple-Cist Cairn at Mount Stewart, Co. Down. *Proceedings of the Prehistoric Society* 3, 22-42.

Grogan, E. and Eogan, G. 1987. Lough Gur Excavations by Seán P. Ó Ríordáin: Further Neolithic and Beaker Habitations on Knockadoon. *Proceedings of the Royal Irish Academy* 87C, 299-506.

Harbison, P. 1969a. *The Daggers and Halberds of the Early Bronze Age in Ireland. Prähistorische Bronzefunde,* 6.1, Munich.

Harbison, P. 1969b. *The Axes of the Early Bronze Age in Ireland. Prähistorische Bronzefunde,* 9.1, Munich.

Hartmann, A. 1970. *Prähistorische Goldfunde aus Europa, Studien zu den Anfängen der Metallurgie* 3. Berlin.

Hartmann, A. 1982. *Prähistorische Goldfunde aus Europa II, Studien zu den Anfängen der Metallurgie* 5. Berlin.

Hencken, H. O'N. and H. L. Movius. 1934. The Cemetery-Cairn of Knockast. *Proceedings of the Royal Irish Academy* 41C, 232-84.

Herity, M. 1969. Early finds of Irish antiquities. *Antiquaries Journal* 49, 1-21.

Kavanagh, R. 1973. The Encrusted Urn in Ireland. *Proceedings of the Royal Irish Academy* 73C, 507-617.

Kavanagh, R. 1976. Collared and Cordoned Cinerary Urns in Ireland. *Proceedings of the Royal Irish Academy* 76C, 293-403.

Kavanagh, R. 1977. Pygmy Cups in Ireland. *Journal of the Royal Society of Antiquaries of Ireland* 107, 61-95.

Mitchell, G. F. 1985. Antiquities. In T. Ó Raifeartaigh (ed.), *The Royal Irish Academy: a bicentennial history 1785-1985,* 93-165. Dublin.

Nevin, M. 1993. General Charles Vallancey 1725-1812. *Journal of the Royal Society of Antiquaries of Ireland* 123, 19-58.

O'Brien, W. 1994. *Mount Gabriel. Bronze Age Mining in Ireland.* Galway.

Ó Nualláin, S. 1978. Boulder-Burials. *Proceedings of the Royal Irish Academy* 78C, 75-114.

Ó Nualláin, S. 1984. A survey of Stone Circles in Cork and Kerry. *Proceedings of the Royal Irish Academy* 84C, 1-77.

Ó Nualláin, S. 1988. Stone Rows in the South of Ireland. *Proceedings of the Royal Irish Academy* 88C, 179-256.

Ó Ríordáin, B. and Waddell, J. 1993. *The Funerary Bowls and Vases of the Irish Bronze Age.* Galway.

Ó Ríordáin, S. P. 1937. The Halberd in Bronze Age Europe. *Archaeologia* 86, 195-321.

Ó Ríordáin, S. P. 1951. Lough Gur Excavations: The Great Stone Circle (B) in Grange Townland. *Proceedings of the Royal Irish Academy* 54C, 37-74.

Ó Ríordáin, S. P. 1954. Lough Gur Excavations: Neolithic and Bronze Age Houses on Knockadoon. *Proceedings of the Royal Irish Academy* 56C, 297-459.

Ryan, M. (ed.). 1979. *The Origins of Metallurgy in Atlantic Europe.* Dublin.

Waddell, J. 1970. Irish Bronze Age Cists: a survey. *Journal of the Royal Society of Antiquaries of Ireland* 100, 91-139.

Waddell, J. 1990. *The Bronze Age Burials of Ireland.* Galway.

Wallace, J. N. A. 1938. The Golden Bog of Cullen. *North Munster Antiquarian Journal* 1, 89-101.

Wilde, W. 1857, 1861, 1862. *A Descriptive Catalogue of the Antiquities of Stone, Earthen and Vegetable Materials* (1857), *Animal Materials and Bronze* (1861), and *Gold in the Museum of the Royal Irish Academy* (1862). Dublin.

Radiocarbon, Chronology and the Bronze Age

A. L. Brindley

Abstract

About 600 radiocarbon dates are now available for the Irish Bronze Age. The aim of this contribution is to provide a general survey of these dates, to show where advances have been made and to indicate areas which should be looked at in the future. The dates are presented within the framework of the following phases: an introductory phase, an Earlier Bronze Age, a Transitional phase and a Later Bronze Age. These four phases have been identified chiefly to facilitate the discussion of the 2000 years of the Bronze Age as represented by the dates and are not meant to suggest discontinuity of cultural practices.

Introduction

Over the last decades, radiocarbon dating has led to a considerable reviewing of the Bronze Age. Arguably, its greatest contribution has been in allowing the recognition of far more evidence than was previously imaginable and integrating this into a vibrant and stimulating whole. This not only refers to the distinct elements of this period in Ireland, but also to their relationship to the European Bronze Age. For the first time, radiocarbon dating makes it possible to order the past not only vertically but also horizontally by means of establishing an absolute chronology.

The numbers of Bronze Age radiocarbon dates have increased steadily since the technique was employed to date a *fulacht fiadh* at Killeens, Co. Cork, and a trackway at Corlona, Co. Leitrim, and hundreds of Bronze Age samples have now been processed at various laboratories. These include a core of 280 specifically collected by Jan Lanting and this author and dated by conventional methods in Groningen and by AMS in Oxford. These samples were retrieved from the collections of the Ulster Museum and the National Museum of Ireland, or solicited from excavators. Specific topics were selected, such as the food vessel and urn accompanied burials, the *fulachta fiadh* cooking places, wedge tombs, and the trackways and logboats which yielded evidence of the period that otherwise would not have come to light. Samples from excavations are now dated as a matter of course and the bulk of the remainder have been dated in connection with large complexes such as Navan, Clogher, Ballynagilly, Lough Gur, and Dún Aonghasa. These samples have been processed at a number of different laboratories, the main ones being Groningen, Belfast,

Oxford and the former Dublin laboratory.

Radiocarbon samples are usually limited to charcoal, wood, bone and in a small number of important cases, soot or encrustations on pottery. Charcoal is the most widespread, but the most valuable are normally bone and soot because these are often integral to the object of the dating exercise and there is little or no age lapse between the two. The Irish Bronze Age is fortunate in having a series of well-defined cultural phenomena which have made the dating of some aspects of the period comparatively easy because an essential part of the construction of an absolute chronology is the identification of suitable sample contexts. There is, however, no single phenomenon which provides comparable samples from the beginning of the Bronze Age to its end which could provide a useful framework for the entire period.

In radiocarbon terms, the Irish Bronze Age corresponds to approximately the years 3900-2400 BP (Fig. 1). This represents some 2000 or so calendar years stretching from about 24/2300 BC to 400 BC or thereabouts. The 600 radiocarbon dates are spread relatively evenly over the entire period.

Major steps or plateaux in the shape of the calibration curve give rise to problems in dating. Because of these, radiocarbon dates tend to bunch at particular and predictable points. This occurs because a radiocarbon date which falls on a steep part of the curve has a much more limited calibrated range and thus yields a fairly precise calendar date. A date of 2650 BP without standard deviation calibrates nicely to about 850 BC, while the date 2500 BP calibrates to somewhere between 800 and 400 BC. For obvious reasons, samples which fall on the steep parts of the

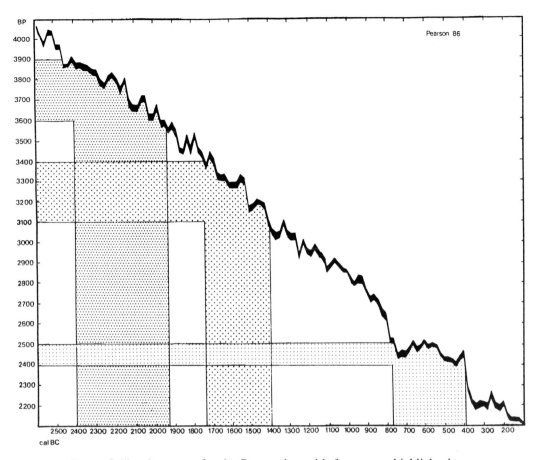

Fig. 1. Calibration curve for the Bronze Age with four stages highlighted.

curve are comparatively rare. What is more commonly seen is the influence of the plateaux which is shown by the clumping of radiocarbon results for a range of material at one particular radiocarbon date. Fortunately, most of the Bronze Age is characterised by a series of smaller steps with two large ones at either end. The effect of these smaller steps is negligible until one begins to speak in terms of a refined chronology of 20-30 years.

For the purposes of this article, the 2000 years of the Bronze Age have been broken up into four periods. These are identified on the basis of cultural changes but are not intended to suggest discontinuity on a grand scale; the phenomena discussed below show strong evidence of cultural integrity and continuity.

An *introductory phase* of about 300-400 (but possibly as much as 500) calendar years from about 3900-3600 BP during which initial development of all the main characteristics of the Bronze Age became established, down to the time when food vessels ceased to be the main ceramic type in graves.

An *Earlier Bronze Age* between 3600 and 3400 BP (some 200-300 calendar years) during which the single burials with pottery of the Vase Tradition and Collared Urns dominated the burial record.

A *Transitional phase* between 3400 and 3150 BP (about 200-300 calendar years) which is marked by the use of the cord-decorated and cordoned pottery as both domestic and funerary ware, the appearance of a visible settlement tradition and the exploitation of the Mount Gabriel mines.

Finally, a *Later Bronze Age* which starts at about 3000 BP or 1400/1200 cal BC and is characterised by large scale settlement, barrow burials and undecorated pottery. This period lasts between 600 and 1000 years.

1. *Introductory phase* (3900-3600 BP; *c.* 2350-2000/ 1950 BC).

Of the four periods, by far the most complicated is the first. This is a reflection of the various sources of the radiocarbon samples and the diversity of the cultural phenomena.

For most people, the appearance of Beaker Pottery and metallurgy in Ireland are synonymous and signify the beginning of the Bronze Age proper. Beaker Pottery is distinctive, widely distributed and occurs in various different contexts. It is also a means of linking developments in Ireland into the European Bronze Age. For these reasons, its dating is significant. In regard to the pottery, all the available dates are for early Beaker types. Radiocarbon dates for Beaker

Pottery are still comparatively few due chiefly to the absence of both well-preserved settlement sites and individual burials. The dates are derived from two main sources: charcoal in refuse pits and bone from multiple inhumation burials in wedge tombs. Samples from settlement contexts are often characterised by low association values and by the usually unknown age and source of the charcoal which is most often the material dated. The bone samples are from wedge tombs and represent actual burials of the period. They have no age lapse.

There is a clear discrepancy between the settlement dates and the burial dates which can be explained by a) the sample material and b) the shape of the curve at this point. The bone samples fall in the period 3800-3700 BP and can be reconciled with dates of 2250 and 2100 cal BC. The charcoal dates range from as early as 3980 BP and the majority fall before 3800 BP. These represent dates on the curve between 2400 to 2200 BC. This difference which may be as large as 200 years is probably less in most cases, perhaps as little as fifty years and represents the age of the charcoal and its uncertain determination and supports the correctness of the bone dates. The beginning of the Bronze Age in Ireland can therefore be placed fairly accurately somewhere between 2400 and 2300 BC.

This date is supported by the radiocarbon dates from the Labbacallee, Co. Cork, wedge tomb (Brindley and Lanting 1991/92) and by the radiocarbon dates which show conclusively that plain or very simply decorated Grooved Ware was used apparently in most if not all of this country when Beaker Pottery first appeared, with the Newgrange Grooved Ware/Bell Beaker hybrid illustrating the overlap of the two traditions nicely (Brindley, forthcoming, a and b). There are no dates for Neolithic material later than this, but there is plenty of evidence at this early stage for activities which are usually considered as Bronze Age. Perhaps the most reassuring are the dates for the mines and Beaker Pottery from Ross Island, Co. Kerry (O'Brien 1995, 24-7, and this volume). These show that a mining technology was already being employed to produce the raw material needed at this time.

Settlement evidence during this stage is scarce. No unambiguous domestic structures have been discovered and the limited evidence is confined to refuse pits and ploughed-out midden spreads. However, there are some typical indications of Bronze Age activity already appearing. The earliest dated *fulacht fiadh*, Ballynoe, Co. Cork, has a date of 3850±30 BP (GrN-11803) which places it around 2300 cal BC. Although *fulachta fiadh* are more characteristic of the following stages of the Bronze Age, they were apparently already being used at this early stage (Brindley *et al.* 1989/90).

One of the things that radiocarbon does particularly well is to reveal contemporary diversity and this is clearly demonstrated by the burial traditions of the first half of the Bronze Age. The evidence of both Beaker Pottery and radiocarbon dates show that wedge tombs were built exclusively at this time. Until AMS was developed, multiple burials were difficult to date because many of the individuals could not provide sufficient bone for conventional radiocarbon dating. Other problems with dating wedge tombs are the frequency with which they were disturbed and the relatively infrequent survival of unburnt bone. A series of radiocarbon dates from Lough Gur and Labbacallee supports the evidence of the Beaker Pottery found in these tombs (Brindley and Lanting 1991/2).

By comparison, the single burials of this stage have proved an excellent subject for dating purposes. The contexts are limited, easily definable and recognisable. The graves often contain highly decorated pottery of several different and distinct types which provide ample possibility for chronological, typological and regional study. There are also a small number of other associations (Waddell 1990; Ó Ríordáin and Waddell 1993).

The single burial 'tradition' is apparently highly diversified from its earliest manifestations. This in itself is surprising and one could speculate as to the social conditions which led to this. One possible explanation is that it reflects highly ordered and regulated social groups; another is a tolerance of multiple cults or ritual groups side by side. In any event, by 3850 BP, the practice of single burial (i.e. single interment, sometimes of several individuals) is recognisably a distinct characteristic of the Bronze Age. Early structural forms include the substantial above ground cist with covering cairn of Moneen, Co. Cork (Brindley *et al.* 1987/88), the cairn and cists of Grange, Co. Roscommon (Ó Ríordáin, forthcoming), the enlargement of the early Neolithic cairn of Poulawack, Co. Clare (Brindley and Lanting 1991/2) and the use of an apparently unmarked flat cemetery of cists at Straid, Co. Derry (Brannon *et al.* 1990).

The calibration curve for the Bronze Age is marked by a series of small steps or wiggles which are not significant for general dating purposes. However, the heavily decorated pottery which accompanies many single burials provides the means of penetrating within that broader chronology. Radiocarbon dates can best be interpreted in conjunction with a detailed typological analysis of the accompanying pottery and together provide a powerful dating tool – typochronology – capable of resolution of twenty years or so. Chronology of this detail is immensely valuable when applied to the dating of, for instance, unstratified settlement material and cemeteries but is applicable to any context yielding datable pottery. In fact, the very characteristic which makes single burials so suitable for radiocarbon dating, namely very closely defined contexts, has also contributed to making the associated pottery so difficult to understand. Early Bronze Age pottery is dominated by a series of apparently separate types. With few associations between these types, it has been difficult to make any headway using the conventional tools of cross-association, stratigraphy and typology. However, the complex decoration can be used to order the pottery on a typological basis, stressing the changes in the layout of the decoration and the popularity of individual elements as well as their development, and this typology can be used to interpret the radiocarbon dates. Although the differences between the various types of food vessels (and indeed the urns) have been stressed particularly on recent occasions (e.g. Ap-Simon 1969, Waddell 1976, Kavanagh 1973 and 1976), details of ornament are traceable across the various types. This is important because it is clear that bowl and vase food vessels were in contemporary use until about 3600 BP or perhaps slightly after. (During this period too, Beaker Pottery was still being used in wedge tombs.)

Narrow bands of simple elements characterize both the earliest bowls and vases. These bands increase in width some time around 3650 BP as the elements incorporated within them expand in size, evolving into bar chevron bands and other related motifs. Urns were added to the repertoire at about the same time as the enlarged motifs developed. These ultimately dominate the burial rituals of the subsequent two phases of the Bronze Age. By the end of the century, that is by about 3600 BP, the motif bands have evolved into floating panels of various forms. At this stage, the bowls disappear while the vases extend their repertoire and functions.

One of radiocarbon's great advantages is its ability to reveal evidence which would otherwise remain unrecognisable. The *fulachta fiadh* and trackways are examples of this. Routeways are not easily recognised as Bronze Age even though the tracks themselves are often well recorded. As a result of searches in the collections of the National Museum of Ireland and recent excavations in the midlands, some 100 samples of tracks have been dated, many proving to be of Bronze Age date (Brindley and Lanting, forthcoming). At the same time as the Ross Island mines were being exploited, the wedge tombs built and used and the funerary pottery was being formed and decorated, tracks were being constructed and used to cross Co. Longford bogs, at Annaghbeg via a track of finely made hurdle screens (Annaghbeg 2, 3770±40,

GrN-18360) and at Corlea on a track of transverse timbers some 2-2.5m wide (Corlea 6, 3860±25 BP, GrN-16008 and 3855±25 BP, GrN-16009), or on simple narrow paths such as through the townland of Derryoghill (Derryoghill 7, 3930±40 BP, GrN-16-006) (Raftery 1990). At the same time by a small lake now completely overgrown by peat, one of the largest logboats yet found in Europe was being made at Lurgan in Co. Galway. Until recently, it was difficult to imagine the extent of wood working and use during the early Bronze Age, but it is now possible to recognise massive logboats, extensive wood surfaced tracks, and even smaller items such as the polypod bowl from Tirkernaghan, Co. Tyrone (3960±100 BP, OxA-3031; Earwood 1991/2, 27-8) (Fig. 2).

This *introductory phase* witnesses the adoption of many of the characteristics of the Irish Bronze Age.

2. *Earlier Bronze Age* (3600-3400 BP; 2000/1950-1750/1700 BC).

After 3600 BP, the Bronze Age can be considered as fully underway. From this date onwards, the radiocarbon chronology is dominated by dates on charcoal and wood samples. This reflects both the decline in the practice of inhumation burial and the increasing numbers of *fulachta fiadh* and trackways and, later, settlements and the occurrence of many of these in waterlogged environments where conditions of preservation are good. The burial tradition becomes more homogenous with the passage of time, possibly reflecting slow but deep changes in social relationships.

From about 3590 BP the burial record is dominated by cremations placed in or accompanied by small vases, or covered by large Vase Urns, Encrusted Urns or Collared Urns. Occasionally, small accessory vessels, daggers and battle axes were left in the graves. The dates are almost exclusively on charcoal from the cremations but as these are remarkably clean, the number of samples is limited. Despite this and the problems of the charcoal's own-age, it is possible to recognise a typochronology of Vase and Encrusted Urn decoration which should be useful for refining dates and dating successive burial in cemeteries.

Apart from these burials, a significant contribution to this period has been made by the dating of *fulachta fiadh*, including those at Slatt Lower, Co. Laois, Clashroe, Co. Cork, Ballyremon Commons, Co. Wicklow, Ballylin and Raheen, Co. Limerick (Brindley *et al.* 1989/90). The dating of *fulachta fiadh* is important for a number of reasons: these monuments are not otherwise dateable; they are extremely common throughout large parts of the country and most importantly, the troughs in particular provide very suitable wood samples, while the mounds are composed of burnt stone and charcoal. *Fulachta fiadh* were used into the Late Bronze Age and are an important aspect of Bronze Age technology whether used for domestic or industrial purposes, or both. Their popularity at this time may have been connected with a greater awareness of the power of heat and hot stone technology in general, possibly heightened by its application to mining and metallurgical processes. These monuments are not only widespread but also occur in groups, some with as many as 150-200 *fulachta fiadh* (Buckley, pers. comm.). It is unlikely that, if they were used on such a widespread and apparently frequent basis, they would have been constructed far from contemporary settlements. They are therefore important indicators of settlement activity not only on a gross Bronze Age scale but could also, if dated in sufficient numbers in a defined locality, give a precise dating of activity in that area.

3. *Transition Phase* (3400-3150 BP; 1750/1700-15/ 1400 BC)

The period between about 1750 and 15/1400 BC is marked by the appearance of settlements of round houses and a further move towards an apparently homogenous burial rite. For the first time in several centuries domestic and funerary pottery are demonstrably of the same type.

Amongst the settlements can be considered the lake-edge site of Cullyhanna, Co. Armagh (Hodges 1958, 7-13, 3475±75 BP, UB-341; 3305±50 BP, UB-688), the site of Maigue on Carrigdirty Island in the Shannon estuary, Co. Limerick (O'Sullivan 1995, 9-10, 3300±25 BP, GrN-20976), the two houses at Meadowlands, Co. Armagh (Pollack and Waterman 1964, 31-57; 3325±75 BP, UB-474; 3265±80 BP, UB-473), and possibly also Moynagh Lough, Co. Meath (Bradley 1991, 11-12, fig. 4; 3460±35 BP, GrN-11442). Meadowlands, Cullyhanna and Maigue all produced evidence of circular wooden structures. Other evidence for contemporary activity is provided by the nine *fulachta fiadh* which have been dated to this period. Apart from the lacustrine and estuarine settlements, evidence for water-based activity is provided by the logboats from Ballyvoghan, Co. Limerick (3300±30 BP, GrN-18361), and Cloongalloon, Co. Mayo (3265±30 BP, GrN-18751), not forgetting the logboat of Teeronea, Co. Tipperary (3310±35 BP, GrN-15968) which was re-used as a *fulacht fiadh* trough (Lanting and Brindley, in press). For movement by foot across the bogs and marshes, there are at least twelve tracks of various types at Derryoghil including the 2m-wide Derryoghil 10 (Raftery 1990; 3295±40 BP, GrN-16566), and others at Corlona, Co. Leitrim (3255±40 BP, GrN-18377; previously dated 3395±170 BP, GrN-272), (Tohall *et*

al. 1955, 77-83), Clooncullaun, Co. Galway (3350±30 BP, GrN-14736) and Dromalught, Co. Kerry (3370±35 BP, GrN-14724) (Brindley and Lanting, forthcoming).

As regards ritual activity, there is some rather general evidence that stone alignments were being constructed at this time. Lynch's dates for Maughanasilly (3265±55, GrN-9280 and 3265±55 BP, GrN-8281) and Cashelkeelty, Co. Kerry (Lynch 1981, 66) and perhaps also Dromatouk fall into this period (Lynch 1981, 100), in each case, probably preceding nearby stone circles in construction and use. These herald the developments of the next period.

The burial record shows a continuation of the trend towards a fairly unified style of burial ritual. The cremations are either covered by the inverted urn or contained in it. These urns are chiefly cord and cordoned decorated urns although some Collared Urns of similar type were used for some time. A distinctive trend towards more limited ornament is clearly discernible. The earliest urns of this group have fully filled patterns and had already appeared by the end of the previous stage (*Earlier Bronze Age*). These were followed during the transitional phase by urns with only alternatively filled motifs, and finally linear cord decoration of a fairly simple kind (without motifs) was employed. These last are the forerunners of the domestic and funerary pottery of the subsequent and last stage of the Bronze Age which occasionally bear cord-impressed lines. Cord decorated pottery has been found on the settlement sites of this period (e.g. Meadowlands and Moynagh Lough) and it is clear that essentially domestic pottery was used in the burials.

In addition to occurring in both domestic and burial contexts, pottery of this type is also associated through the burials with a metal industry. At least fourteen graves included both cordoned urns and razors (Kavanagh 1991, 83). The razors occur in all but one case with alternatively filled motif decorated urns or simply decorated urns. This suggests that the custom of putting razors in graves had a limited currency, although of course the razors as a type had a longer life. Razors were made in two-piece stone moulds which helps to establish an absolute date for this technological attribute as well as for the likely date of the other bronze types which were made using the same two-piece stone moulds. Some of these moulds are large and include moulds for rapiers (especially those with trapezoidal hafting plates), spearheads (kite-shaped blades with loops on the socket) and rings. Palstaves, although not occurring on the same moulds, are also the product of two-piece moulds. Cord decorated pottery and these metal types have not been found together, but it appears that the younger types of Cordoned Urn were in use simultaneously with these objects.

One other artefact which would not have been recognised as Bronze Age without AMS radiocarbon dating is the bow from Drumwhinny, Co. Fermanagh (3220±70 BP, OxA-2426, Glover 323-7; Hedges *et al.* 1991, 129) (Fig. 2).

Finally, radiocarbon dates also shows that Mount Gabriel, Co. Cork, was one of the sources of metal for the industries of this period (Fig. 3). The excavation of the waterlogged Mines 3 and 4 provided a series of charcoal samples which show that these two mines were exploited between 1700 and 1500 BC (Brindley and Lanting 1994, 281-7). Other finds from the excavation include an assemblage of wooden artefacts, a wooden shovel, a pick, lighting chips and a withy, as well as the stone mauls to work the mines (O'Brien 1994, 144-62). Other mines on the mountain also belong to the same general period of exploitation.

4. *Later Bronze Age (3150-2400 BP; 15/1400-800/400 BC)*

There is a noticeable change in the radiocarbon evidence for the last part of the Bronze Age which reflects changes in both burial customs and the quantity and quality of settlement evidence. The later part of the Bronze Age is characterised by the occurrence of cremation burials deposited in pits with or without large undecorated containers of the types found on settlement sites. Amongst the main forms of burial are the apparently unenclosed groups of pits such as Mitchelstowndown North and enclosed groups such as Shanaclogh and Adamstown, Co. Limerick (Gowen 1988; Brindley, forthcoming, c). Most of the dates for ringbarrows and ringditches are on charcoal from the ditches or peat above or below the bank and cannot be considered as good direct dating for the actual burial; however, when considered collectively they indicate the general Late Bronze Age. Dates of these types are available from Ballybeen, Co. Down (Mallory 1984, 3), Beaghmore 10 (Pilcher 1969, 71) and Carnkenny, Co. Tyrone (Lynn 1973, 17-31), Pubble (Smith *et al.* 1981, 53-4) and Ballygroll (Williams 1981-2, 35), Co. Derry. The related monument at Reanascreena, Co. Cork (Fahy 1962) combines the elements of a ringbarrow with a stone circle and a central burial pit, while Drombeg, Co. Cork (Fahy 1959, 1-27) and Cashelkeelty, Co. Kerry (probably constructed between 2920±60 BP (GrN-9173) and 2665±50 BP (GrN-9172) (Lynch 1981, 66)) recumbent-stone circles with their burials, the Cooradarrigan boulder burial (3080±35 BP, GrN-15716, O'Brien 1994, 212-13) and probably the

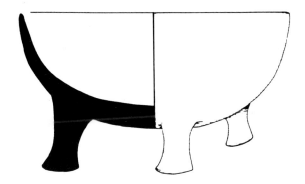

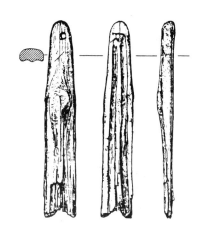

Fig. 2. Polypod wooden bowl (3960±100 BP, OxA-3031) and bow (3220±70 BP, OxA-2426). (Tirkernaghan, Co. Tyrone, after Earwood 1991/2, Drumwhinny, Co. Cavan, after Glover 1979.)

Beaghmore complex in Co. Tyrone represent particular aspects of the funerary and ritual tradition of the period.

Another important source of samples are the settlements of the period. Compared to the earlier Bronze Age, this period is marked by a surge in the number and variety of settlements although this upturn had already started during the preceding transitional phase. Settlements occur in a wide variety of environments, from lakeside sites such as Clonfinlough, Co. Offaly (Moloney 1993, 22), Knocknalappa, Co. Clare (Raftery 1942, 53-72), and Ballinderry 2, Co. Westmeath (Hencken 1942), to cliff edges such as Dún Aonghasa on Inishmore in Galway Bay (Cotter 1993), hilltops such as Haughey's Fort, Co. Armagh (Mallory 1991a and 1991b) and also comparatively hospitable places such as Drombeg (Fahy 1960) and Fota (O'Connell and Rutter 1993, 7; B. Cassidy, pers. comm.) Co. Cork, Curraghatoor and Ballyveelish North, Co. Tipperary (Doody 1987, 22-35; 36-42, 1993, 94) and Lough Gur, Co. Limerick (Cleary 1992, 31-2). These settlements consist of

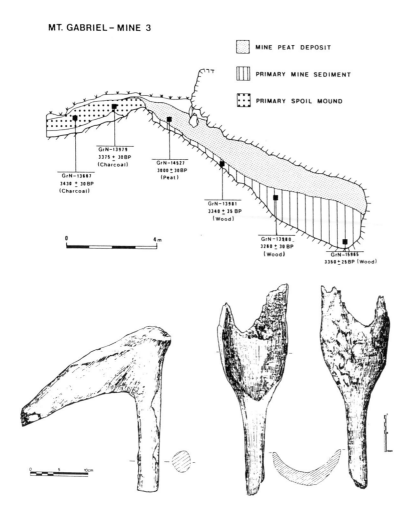

MT. GABRIEL – MINE 3

Fig. 3. Mount Gabriel, Mine 3, pick and shovel (after O'Brien 1994).

single or groups of round huts with diameters ranging from about 4m to 8-9m. The construction details vary from spaced posts as at Aughinish 2 (Kelly 1975), trench and posts as at Curraghatoor, post and wattle as at Clonfinlough and stone walls as at Dún Aonghasa and Drombeg). Some at least were floored, e.g. the paving at Dún Aonghasa and Drombeg, the platforms at Clonfinlough and Ballinderry. These structures may occur as apparently isolated and unprotected as at Drombeg and Fota, as single houses enclosed by a stone wall, as at Carrigillihy (O'Kelly 1951), Lough Gur and Aughinish, as groups of houses protected by a palisade on a lake edge as at Clonfinlough, protected by a ditch (parts of Curraghatoor), or as part of the large triple ditched enclosure of Haughey's Fort. The enclosing elements at Lough Gur and Aughinish were walls with a kerb on either side and a filling of field stones and soil. Some of the structures have central stone-built hearths, roasting ovens and troughs. Associated structures include *fulachta fiadh* as at Drombeg and Coarhamore (C. Walshe, pers. comm.).

Another aspect of these settlements is that some also show evidence of a long period of activity on the site. To some extent, this is difficult to identify from the finds alone as most of the pottery is not suscepti-

ble to fine typological division. These settlements show for the first time groups of people living together and possibly remaining at one location for more than one or two generations. This is also what is shown by the large concentrations of *fulachta fiadh* in some areas and contrasts with most of the earlier settlements which are represented by small quantities of material usually of a single generation. Apart from these settlements, *fulachta fiadh* from counties Kilkenny, Kerry, Cork, Tipperary, Wicklow, and Mayo also bear witness to the period (Brindley *et al.* 1989/90).

If the radiocarbon evidence for settlement activity for the later Bronze Age is to be compared to that of the earlier stages, several aspects should be taken into account. First of all, how real is the upsurge in settlement evidence? This may be not so much evidence for growth in population and settlement, just the better survival of that evidence. Secondly, the timespan allotted here to the later Bronze Age is far longer than any of the preceding phases, but even if the whole of the Bronze Age is divided into two periods, the contrast remains. However, when settlement dates are looked at more closely, there does appear to be a decrease in the number of settlements after 2800 BP. This is also the time when *fulachta fiadh* decline in numbers and it is tempting to view the two as being in some way related. This may be a reflection of the relatively steep part of the calibration curve between 2800 and 2500 BC.

Another aspect of the period are the thirty-eight trackways which have been dated to it. These large numbers probably represent the better preservation of tracks at deeper levels in the bogs but not so deep that they are rarely found, perhaps the intensification of communications and possibly the growth of wetlands, although this last is unlikely as most of these bogs were already in existence.

Another source of information for this period are tools and weapons, in particular those with the advantageous characteristic over their predecessors of sockets and especially those that were apparently deliberately deposited in wet environments. Sockets sometimes contain remnants of their wooden hafts which provide a useful source of samples, although until AMS was developed these were normally too small for dating by conventional means. For this reason, only small numbers of spears and axes have been dated. There are also two indirect dates for Class 4 swords from Littleton A, Co. Tipperary (2720±90 BP, OxA-2449, for peat immediately above the track on which the sword was found: Brindley and Lanting 1990) and Island MacHugh, Co. Tyrone (nearby palisade date of 2770±80 BP, HAR-6821, Ivens *et al.* 1986, 99; Simpson 1986, 103). There are also radiocarbon dates for the wooden shield-former from Cloonlara, Co. Mayo (3150±90 BP, OxA-3228 Hedges *et al.* 1993, 316), a wooden vessel from Carrickmore, Co. Tyrone (2550±85 BP, UB-2434, Williams 1983, 150-1) and a wooden cauldron from the Grainger collection (Earwood 1989/90, 44) (Fig. 4). Of perhaps greater interest are wooden objects which without radiocarbon dating would not have been placed in this period. These include an unlocalised wooden yoke (A 1911.373, 2660±60 BP, OxA-2428, Hedges *et al.* 1991, 129), the first indisputable evidence for traction, although the construction of large and wide bog tracks suggests that traction played a role in transportation since at least the end of the Neolithic.

The contribution of radiocarbon to the Later Bronze Age is different to that of the Early Bronze Age. Until the advent of this dating technique, the Later Bronze Age consisted almost entirely of metal types. Large parts of the country seemed to be wastelands on the various distribution maps which were a main source of evidence for the period. The many individual sites referred to draw attention to the enormous geographical spread of dates now becoming available where before practically nothing was known of either the settlement or burial record. Without

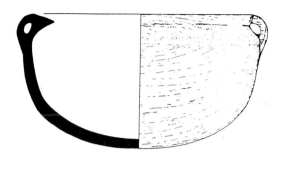

Fig. 4. Wooden cauldron (OxA-2745±70, OxA-2427) and vessel (2550±85 BP, UB-2434). (Grainger collection after Earwood 1989/90 and Carrickmore, Co. Tyrone, after Williams 1983.)

radiocarbon dates, it is likely that many would still regard these sites as undatable or assign much of this material to the later stages of the Neolithic, so great has been the influence of Lough Gur.

It is difficult to pinpoint the end of the Bronze Age in the same way as it has been possible to identify its beginning. The long plateau at 2400 BP represents 400 actual years. Only dendrochronology will be able to sort out this period with any chance of success. After this plateau, the evidence begins to change again. The first distinctive and new elements to appear amongst the dates are the linear earthworks of the Black Pig's Dyke, Co. Monaghan (Walsh 1987, 9), the Doon of Drumsna, Co. Leitrim (Lanting *et al.* 1991, 56) and the Dorsey, Co. Armagh (Lynn 1991-92, 66 and 75), all acceptably Iron Age. A little later the first extended inhumation burials appear. Few characteristic Bronze Age traits can be distinguished, although it is clear that some of the large settlements continued in use, some perhaps earning the term complex, and extending to cover a whole landscape, such as Navan. Ringbarrows and ditches continued too for some time, for instance Dathi's Mound (Glenballythomas), Co. Roscommon (Waddell 1987/88) while others include amongst their grave goods distinctive Iron Age types such as iron objects and blue glass beads (Raftery 1981, 180-202).

Finally, where are the next radiocarbon dates to come from? For a start, the wedge tombs remain an ambiguous element in the Bronze Age. Identification of wedge tombs with fresh bone, such as probably exist in the limestone areas of Co. Clare, and the AMS dating of their multiple inhumations is an obvious and relatively accessible target. As regards pottery, emphasis should be directed towards dating soot or burnt matter adhering to pottery. Deposits of this kind are not uncommon from Cordoned Urns onwards. At this stage in our knowledge, charcoal samples of uncertain age are unlikely to add to what is already known, but samples with no own-age and absolute certainty of association can add significant detail. Leather and wooden artefacts from bogs are also an important source, once more because of AMS dating. Many existing artefacts have been treated and are irredeemably contaminated. Several groups of artefacts in particular require dating at the moment, such as leather shoes and deer traps. There is no reason why these should belong exclusively to the early historic period.

References

ApSimon, A. M. 1969. The Earlier Bronze Age in the North of Ireland. *Ulster Journal of Archaeology* 32, 28-72.

Bradley, J. 1991. Excavations at Moynagh Lough, Co. Meath. *Journal of the Royal Society of Antiquaries of Ireland* 121, 2-26.

Brannon, N. F., Williams, B. B. and Williamson, J. L. 1990. The salvage excavations of Bronze Age cists, Straid Townland, County Londonderry. *Ulster Journal of Archaeology* 53, 29-39.

Brindley, A. L. (forthcoming, a). Sequence and dating in the Grooved Ware Tradition. In R. Cleal and A. MacSween (eds), *Grooved Ware in Context*.

Brindley, A. L. (forthcoming, b). Irish Grooved Ware. In R. Cleal and A. MacSween (eds), *Grooved Ware in Context*.

Brindley, A. L. (forthcoming, c). Radiocarbon dates from the gas pipeline excavations. In M. Gowen (ed.), *5000 Years in the Pipeline*. Dublin.

Brindley, A. L. and J. N. Lanting. 1990. Concerning the boat, the track and the sword. *Archaeology Ireland* 4 (4), 6.

Brindley, A. L. and J. N. Lanting. 1991/92. Radiocarbon Dates from the Cemetery at Poulawack, Co. Clare. *Journal of Irish Archaeology* 6, 13-17.

Brindley, A. L. and J. N. Lanting. 1991/92. Radiocarbon Dates from Wedge Tombs. *Journal of Irish Archaeology* 6, 19-26.

Brindley, A. L. and J. N. Lanting. 1994. The radiocarbon chronology of Mines 3 and 4, Mount Gabriel. In W. F. O'Brien, *Mount Gabriel. Bronze Age Mining in Ireland*, 281-7. Galway.

Brindley, A. L. and J. N. Lanting (forthcoming). Radiocarbon dates for Irish trackways.

Brindley, A. L., J. N. Lanting and W. G. Mook. 1987/88. Radiocarbon dates from Moneen and Labbacallee, County Cork. *Journal of Irish Archaeology* 4, 14-20.

Brindley, A. L., J. N. Lanting and W. G. Mook. 1989/90. Radiocarbon Dates from Irish *Fulachta Fiadh* and other Burnt Mounds. *Journal of Irish Archaeology* 5, 25-33.

Cleary, R. M. 1992. Knockadoon Hill, Lough Gur. In I. Bennett (ed.), *Excavations 1991, Summary Accounts of Archaeological Excavations in Ireland*, 31-2.

Cotter, C. 1993. Western Stone Fort Project. In *Discovery Programme Reports 1 Project Results 1992*, Dublin.

Doody, M. 1987. Ballyveelish and Curraghatoor. In R. M. Cleary, M. F. Hurley and E. A. Twohig (eds), *Archaeological excavations on the Cork-Dublin Gas Pipeline (1981-82)*, 22-42. Cork.

Doody, M. 1993. Bronze Age Settlement. In E. Shee Twohig and M. Ronayne (eds), *Past Perceptions: The Prehistoric Archaeology of South-West Ireland*, 93-100. Cork.

Earwood, C. 1989/90. Radiocarbon Dating of Late Prehistoric Wooden Vessels. *Journal of Irish Archaeology* 5, 37-44.

Earwood, C. 1991/92. A Radiocarbon Date for Early Bronze Age Wooden Polypod Bowls. *Journal of Irish Archaeology* 6, 27-8.

Fahy, E. M. 1959. A Recumbent-stone Circle at Drombeg, Co. Cork. *Journal of the Cork Historical and Archaeological Society* 64, 1-27.

Fahy, E. M. 1960. A Hut and Cooking-place at Drombeg, Co. Cork. *Journal of the Cork Historical and Archaeological Society* 65, 1-17.

Fahy, E. M. 1962. A Recumbent-stone Circle at Reanascreena South, Co. Cork. *Journal of the Cork Historical and Archaeological Society* 67, 59-69.

Glover, W. 1979. A Prehistoric Bow fragment from Drumwhinny Bog, Kesh, Co. Fermanagh. *Proceedings of the Prehistoric Society* 45, 323-7.

Gowen M. 1988. *Three Irish Gas Pipelines: New Archaeological Evidence in Munster*. Dublin.

Hedges, R. E. M., R. A. Housley, C. R. Bronk Ramsey and G. J. van Klinken. 1991. Radiocarbon Dates from the Oxford AMS system: Datelist 12. *Archaeometry* 33 (1), 129.

Hedges, R. E. M., R. A. Housley, C. R. Bronk Ramsey and G. J. van Klinken. 1993. Radiocarbon Dates from the Oxford AMS system: Datelist 17. *Archaeometry* 35 (2), 305-26.

Hencken, H. O'N. 1942. Ballinderry Crannog No. 2. *Proceedings of the Royal Irish Academy* 47C, 1-79.

Hodges, H. W. M. 1958. A Hunting Camp at Cullyhanna Lough near Newtown Hamilton, Co. Armagh. *Ulster Journal of Archaeology* 21, 7-13.

Ivens, R. J. A., D. D. A. Simpson and D. Brown. 1986. Excavations at Island MacHugh 1985 - Interim Report. *Ulster Journal of Archaeology* 49, 99-103.

Kavanagh, R. M. 1973. The Encrusted Urn in Ireland. *Proceedings of the Royal Irish Academy* 73C, 507-617.

Kavanagh, R. M. 1976. Collared and Cordoned Urns in Ireland. *Proceedings of the Royal Irish Academy* 76C, 293-403.

Kavanagh, R. M. 1991. A Reconsideration of Razors in the Irish Earlier Bronze Age. *Journal of the Royal Society of Antiquaries of Ireland* 121, 77-104.

Kelly, E. 1975. Aughinish Island. In T. G. Delaney (ed.), *Excavations 1974, Summary Accounts of Archaeological Excavations in Ireland*, 20-1.

Lanting, J. N., and A. L. Brindley. (in press). Radiocarbon Dates for Logboats. *Journal of Irish Archaeology* 7.

Lanting, J. N., A. Brindley, V. Buckley and T. Condit. 1991. Preliminary Carbon 14 dates from the Doon of Drumsna. *Emania* 9, 66.

Lynch, A. 1981. *Man and Environment in S.W. Ireland. British Archaeological Reports (British Series)* 85. Oxford.

Lynn, C. J. 1973. The Excavation of a Ring-cairn in Carnkenny Townland, Co. Tyrone. *Ulster Journal of Archaeology* 36, 17-31.

Lynn, C. J. 1991-92. Excavations at the Dorsey: Earthworks in Dorsy and Tullynavall, County Armagh, 1977. *Ulster Journal of Archaeology* 54-5, 61-77.

Mallory, J. P. 1984. The Long Stone, Ballybeen, Dundonald, County Down. *Ulster Journal of Archaeology* 47, 1-4.

Mallory, J. P. 1991a. Excavations at Haughey's Fort: 1989-1990. *Emania* 8, 10-26.

Mallory, J. P. 1991b. Further Dates from Haughey's Fort. *Emania* 9, 66.

Moloney, A. 1993. *Excavations at Clonfinlough, County Offaly. Irish Archaeological Wetland Unit Transactions 2.* Dublin.

O'Brien, W. F. 1994. *Mount Gabriel. Bronze Age Mining in Ireland.* Galway.

O'Brien, W. F. 1995. Ross Island - the beginning. *Archaeology Ireland* 9 (1), 24-7.

O'Connell, P. and Rutter, A. E. 1993. Fota Island, Carrigtwohill. In I. Bennett (ed.), *Excavations 1992, Summary Accounts of Archaeological Excavations in Ireland*.

O'Kelly, M. J. 1951. An Early Bronze Age Ringfort at Carrigillihy, Co. Cork. *Journal of the Cork Historical and Archaeological Society* 56, 69-86.

Ó Ríordáin, B. (forthcoming). Excavation report, Grange, Co. Roscommon.

Ó Ríordáin, B. and J. Waddell. 1993. *The Funerary Bowls and Vases of the Irish Bronze Age.* Galway.

O'Sullivan, A. 1995. Marshlanders. *Archaeology Ireland* 9 (1), 9-10.

Pilcher, J. R. 1969. Archaeology, Palaeoecology, and 14C Dating of the Beaghmore Stone Circle Site. *Ulster Journal of Archaeology* 32, 73-90.

Pollack, A. J. and D. M. Waterman. 1964. A Bronze Age Site at Downpatrick. *Ulster Journal of Archaeology* 27, 31-57.

Raftery, B. 1981. Iron Age Burials in Ireland. In D. Ó Corráin (ed.), *Irish Antiquity*. 173-204. Cork.

Raftery, B. 1990. *Trackways through time. Archaeological Investigations on Irish Bog Roads, 1985-1989.* Dublin.

Raftery, J. 1942. Knocknalappa Crannog, Co. Clare. *North Munster Antiquarian Journal* 3, 53-72.

Simpson, D. D. A. 1986. A Late Bronze Age Sword from Island MacHugh, Co. Tyrone. *Ulster Journal of Archaeology* 49, 103-4.

Smith, A. G., C. Gaskell Brown, I. C. Goddard, A. Goddard, G. W. Pearson, and P. Q. Dresser. 1981. Archaeology and environmental history of a barrow at Pubble, Loughermore townland, County Londonderry. *Proceedings of the Royal Irish Academy* 81C, 29-66.

Tohall, P., H. de Vries and W. van Zeist. 1955. A trackway in Corlona Bog, Co. Leitrim. *Journal of the Royal Society of Antiquaries of Ireland* 85, 77-83.

Waddell, J. 1976. Cultural Interaction in the Insular Early Bronze Age: some ceramic evidence. In S. J. de Laet (ed.), *Acculturation and continuity in Atlantic Europe mainly during the Neolithic period and the Bronze Age. Papers presented at the IV Atlantic Colloquium, Ghent 1975*, 284-95. Bruges.

Waddell, J. 1987/88. Excavation at 'Dathi's Mound', Rathcroghan, Co. Roscommon. *Journal of Irish Archaeology* 4, 23-36.

Waddell, J. 1990. *The Bronze Age Burials of Ireland.* Galway.

Walsh, A. 1987. Excavating the Black Pig's Dyke. *Emania* 3, 5-12.

Williams, B. B. 1981-2. A Prehistoric Complex at Ballygroll and Mullaboy, County Londonderry. *Ulster Journal of Archaeology* 44 and 45, 29-46.

Williams, B. B. 1983. A wooden bucket from near Carrickmore, Co. Tyrone. *Ulster Journal of Archaeology* 54-55, 150-1.

Irish Beakers in their European Context

Humphrey Case

Abstract

The chronology of the Beaker period is best understood in quarter-millennium phases. The European origins of the pottery were before the mid-3rd millennium BC. Although owing much to Corded Ware, they should be sought in south-west Atlantic Europe. Versions of the austere Atlantic prototype were spread through much of Europe around the mid-3rd millennium BC; but local variants were rapidly developed. Irish early Beaker pottery, spanning the second half of the 3rd millennium fairly closely, is among those variants which show much inter-regional reaction. Together with its associations, it can be related partly to the primeval Atlantic tradition and partly to developments in north-west Europe, including Britain. It also has strong regional character. Later Beaker developments in Ireland, during the fourth quarter of the 3rd millennium BC, can be related to those in Britain and overlap with the development of Irish Bowl pottery. Beaker pottery represents a basic craft, with production of pots for everyday life. It was spread in seasonal movements, the purpose of which was at least partly a search for resources.

Chronology

Some hundreds of radiocarbon results must now exist on a European scale for the bell-beaker period; Pape listed 112 in 1979. They are unevenly distributed geographically (few for example in central Europe: Forenbaher 1993), but a far from insignificant number are from Ireland and Britain. Pape listed 33 in 1979; probably four times as many exist now. How can a researcher use this mass of data? First of all, accept its limitations. Much more may be unpublished, since *radiocarbon's* date-lists have shrunk in recent years, but I know of no dendrochronologically associated results, no well-stratified Beaker series suitable for Bayesian statistical analysis (e.g. Litton and Buck 1995, 16) and no truly replicate series of results suitable for averaging in the strictest sense. The corpus consists of routine determinations, some recent but many ranging from early days in radiocarbon dating.

Thus, interpretation involves problems. First, uncertainties as to laboratory procedures: for example, Baillie (1985, 19) warned that published standard deviations should be multiplied, some up to three times. Secondly, the samples dated involve many uncertainties. Relevance of even widely-accepted dates to the specified archaeological phenomena may be problematic (e.g. Kinnes *et al.* 1991, 36). Most results in the corpus are charcoal-derived, with implied doubts about timber age and residuality; and

bone (e.g. Irthlingborough 1, Northants, cf. UB-3148, OxA-2084-2087: Davis and Payne 1993), seed and even organic pot-residues could all be residual, although with lesser degrees of likelihood. The uncertainties involved in using some results even as *terminus post quem* are such that an extreme position is sometimes discussed: that all determinations made before, say, 1985 (when the problems may have become better understood) should be ignored. But this seems analogous to an irrational view suggesting the same for all archaeologically excavated data from before say 1950. British Beaker-period charcoal results (some pre-1985) show no appreciable age-offsets relative to short-lived material, and no significant age-offset from bone results (Kinnes *et al.* 1991, 38 and fig. 4). The view taken here is that charcoal determinations point generally in the right direction and that the present corpus of results is usable within broad limits.

Beaker-period chronology is not inscribed in tables of stone; precise dates given to individual events would be meaningless. The present corpus should be used in a more modest effort, familiar in archaeological reasoning, to define broad phases which appear more likely than not to be correct. Baillie advised (1985, 20) that it was generally not possible using non-dendro dates to argue in calendrical terms of one or two centuries. What system of phasing is appropriate then for the Beaker period as a useful working hypothesis?

Since publication of the 1986 consensus tables

(Stuiver and Becker 1986; Pearson *et al.* 1986) most researchers have adopted the so-called *Intercept Method*, displaying calibrated age-spans at two standard deviations. Take an example from the southern English Beaker period: 3930 ± 80 BP (OxA-1874) provides an age-span of 2860-2145 BC. But this is an insignificant and misleading conclusion. The span of over 700 years relates to a period unlikely to have lasted anywhere more than a millennium (often apparently less) or to have begun long before 2500 BC and it is in fact discontinuous with breaks of 160 and 10 years before 2500 BC and one of 30 years after.

Researchers have tended to overlook that radiocarbon results are best expressed not as simple age-spans but as Gaussian or normal distributions, as Smith and Willis (1961/2) indicated more than thirty years ago. But the calibration curve is non-linear and interaction between them thus often produces a multimodal distribution, as Kinnes and his collaborators indicated, when advocating an alternative *Probability Method* of display (Kinnes *et al.* 1991, 37-8) - a display intended to show clearly the variation in probability within the age spans and enable comparisons to be made more easily (Needham and Ambers 1994, 231; cf. Brindley and Lanting in O'Brien 1994, 282-4).

In an example of 37 British beaker-associated human bone determinations (Kinnes *et al.* 1991, fig. 3, excluding SRR-453), the major degrees of probability can be seen, even where comparatively large standard deviations are concerned, to fall within or quite closely around quarter-millennium spans (as emphasised in Case 1993, fig. 1), permitting concise verbalisations, thus 'around the mid-3rd millennium BC' in the example quoted above (OxA-1874). Encouraged too by the assertion that higher probabilities are encountered around the intercept ages (Stuiver and Pearson 1993, 5), I have applied approximate quarter-millennium spans from figures given in the 1986 consensus tables (ignoring outliers) to the mass of European bell-beaker results and defined these spans in terms such as 'second quarter of the 3rd millennium BC', 'around the mid-3rd millennium', or 'around the turn of the 3rd and 2nd millennia BC', and so on.

I am encouraged also by the fact that applying the same rough-and-ready method to the widespread and likewise routine dates for the preceding but somewhat overlapping Corded Ware period would not give a greatly different result as to its duration and, to some extent, phases from that revealed by the solidly dendro-based chronologies for what seems to have been a central part of the period around the Swiss Lakes, *c.* 2700-2400 BC (Strahm 1991b; Hardmeyer 1991; Wolf 1991).

I have used the 1986 consensus data throughout,

assuming that the 1993 revisions (Stuiver and Pearson 1993; Stuiver and Becker 1993) would not significantly modify my scheme within its broad limits. I have made whatever allowances possible in each instance for the problems of interpretation set out above and have not averaged results.

The European Background

Corded Ware and bell-beakers: geographical and chronological ranges

Finds of bell-beakers extend from Norway (Slettabø, Ogna: Skjølsvold 1977) to Morocco (Souville 1977) and from the Lisbon region (e.g. Fig. 5, nos 1 and 2) to Budapest (Kalicz-Schreiber 1976) and the Upper Vistula (Wojciechowski 1987). This is a greater extent than that of the partly overlapping Corded Ware, which lies further into eastern Europe but has a westward boundary more or less at the Rhine and a southern one at the Alps. Corded Ware appears to emerge more or less throughout its range in the first quarter of the 3rd millennium BC (summary in Strahm 1991c) and to have survived in some form or another into the third quarter and possibly in places into the fourth (below). Its use plainly overlapped with that of bell-beaker pottery in some regions (e.g. Jutland, Jensen 1972; the Lower Rhine, Lanting and van der Waals 1976; Bohemia, Moucha 1992; Moravia, Dvořák and Šebela 1992).

In most areas where radiocarbon results are available, bell-beaker pottery appears around the mid-3rd millennium BC with similar apparent suddenness to that of Corded Ware. But its persistence may have varied considerably; in Britain it apparently survived into the second quarter of the 2nd millennium BC (Case 1993, fig. 1).

An early austere bell-beaker tradition

British evidence provides a warning that typologically apparently quite early vessels may survive late (e.g. Brean Down, Somerset, Case 1993, 262 and references; Radley 4660, Oxon., *loc. cit.* and information Alistair Barclay; Berwick St John, Wilts., Case 1995a, 1 and references). But recurrent among the forms appearing around the mid-3rd millennium BC on a European scale are austere more or less overall-zonally decorated beakers, often comb-impressed, sometimes shell or cord-impressed or incised. The wide occurrence of this early tradition indicates its strength, appearing for example in Portugal (Fig. 5, nos 1 and 2); Spain (Harrison 1980, 140); western France (Fig. 5, nos 3-8, 10); Ireland (Fig. 11, nos 1-3, 6); Britain (Fig. 15; Case 1993, fig. 16, nos 1, 4, 7, 8); the Low Countries (Fig. 6, nos 1, 2);

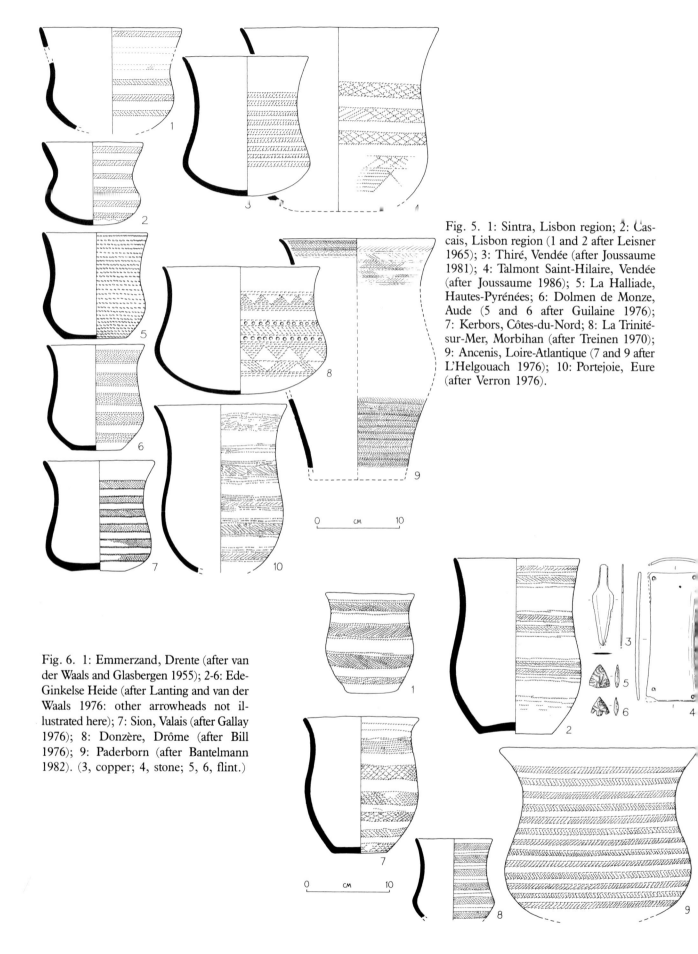

Fig. 5. 1: Sintra, Lisbon region; 2: Cascais, Lisbon region (1 and 2 after Leisner 1965); 3: Thiré, Vendée (after Joussaume 1981); 4: Talmont Saint-Hilaire, Vendée (after Joussaume 1986); 5: La Halliade, Hautes-Pyrénées; 6: Dolmen de Monze, Aude (5 and 6 after Guilaine 1976); 7: Kerbors, Côtes-du-Nord; 8: La Trinité-sur-Mer, Morbihan (after Treinen 1970); 9: Ancenis, Loire-Atlantique (7 and 9 after L'Helgouach 1976); 10: Portejoie, Eure (after Verron 1976).

Fig. 6. 1: Emmerzand, Drente (after van der Waals and Glasbergen 1955); 2-6: Ede-Ginkelse Heide (after Lanting and van der Waals 1976: other arrowheads not illustrated here); 7: Sion, Valais (after Gallay 1976); 8: Donzère, Drôme (after Bill 1976); 9: Paderborn (after Bantelmann 1982). (3, copper; 4, stone; 5, 6, flint.)

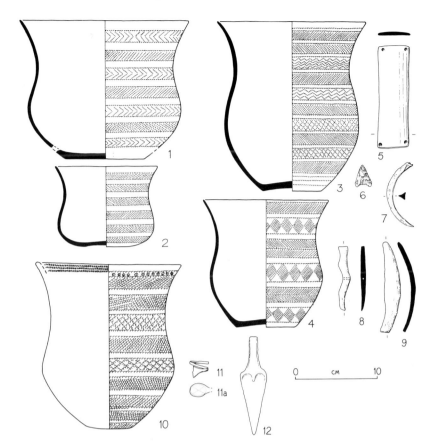

Fig. 7. 1 and 2: Kuřim I, Moravia (flint unillustrated here); 3-9: Ledce II, Moravia (1-9 after Dvořák 1992); 10-12: Praha-Bubeneč (after Hájek 1966: 11 and 11a not to scale). (5, stone; 6, flint; 7, boar's tusk; 8 and 9, bone; 11 and 11a, silver; 12, copper.)

the Rhineland (Fig. 6, no. 9); the Rhône area (Fig. 6, nos 7, 8); north Italy (Fig. 8, nos 1, 2) and central Europe (Figs 7, nos 1-4, 10). Included in this broad tradition are well-known more strictly definable variants, such as Maritime (Figs 5, nos 1, 2, 6; 6, nos 1, 8; 7, no. 2) and all-over-corded beakers (Fig. 5, no. 5).

Corded ware, transitional types and the origin of bell-beakers

Most scholars favour the so-called Dutch model (based on Lanting and van der Waals 1976) of bell-beakers derived *in situ* from Corded Ware at the Lower Rhine. The general sequence argued by the Dutch authors (partly following van der Waals and Glasbergen 1955 and Butler and van der Waals 1966) is convincing: Corded Ware → Corded Ware/bell-beaker transitional types (AOO, held to include the all-over-corded variant) → bell-beakers, starting with Maritimes. The detailed typological scheme is plausible too on paper (as summarised in Lanting and van der Waals 1976, fig.1); but confronted by the pots themselves, the Maritime beakers have always seemed to me an intrusively inspired production rather than a systemic development.

Also, Maritime beakers seem rare at the Lower Rhine. No Maritime beaker phase appears at recently-excavated settlement sites in North Holland dating to the second quarter of the 3rd millennium BC, where large assemblages of Corded Ware and putative

transitional types contain no sherds which are clearly bell-beaker. Bell-beaker sherds seem absent from the well-known mid-3rd millennium BC assemblage from Aartswoud, and to appear only at the similarly-dated thinly-stratified De Veken II (information Dr W. J. H. Hogestijn).

Contrastingly in Atlantic Europe, Maritime beakers are widespread, and numerous on individual sites (e.g. Zambujal, central Portugal: Kunst 1987); and radiocarbon results suggest an earlier appearance there than at the Lower Rhine. My approximation (Case 1993, 248) dating them at the Lower Rhine to the third quarter of the 3rd millennium BC may have been too cautious, in view of a subsequent result from De Veken II. A better approximation may be around the mid-3rd millennium BC. However, they seem emphatically second quarter of the 3rd millennium BC in Iberia. Five results from Zambujal point that way and are held to mark the climax and end of the popularity of beakers on that site (Harrison 1988; also Kunst 1987, *passim*). As confirmation, three results from Atalayuela, central Spain (Harrison 1988 and references) provide a second quarter date for the Ciempozuelos type of beaker, generally stratified later than the Maritime type in Spain. Other radiocarbon results (below – and others summarised in Case 1977) help to confirm the presence of the bell-beaker in Atlantic and Mediterranean Europe in the second quarter of the 3rd millennium BC.

I propose therefore a modification to the Dutch

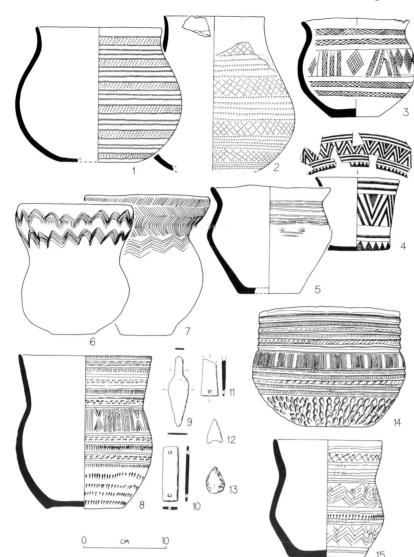

Fig. 8. 1 and 2: Monte Covolo, Brescia (after Barfield 1977); 3-5: Myrhøj, Jutland (after Jensen 1972); 6 and 7: Gårslev, Jutland (after Hvass 1988/9); 8-13: Lunterse Heide (after Butler and van der Waals 1966); 14: Apeldoorn, Gelderland (after van der Waals and Glasbergen 1955); 15: Molenaarsgraaf, Western Netherlands (after Louwe Kooijmans 1974). (9, copper; 10 and 11, stone; 12 and 13, flint.)

model: that in an early Corded Ware phase, perhaps around the turn of the first and second quarters of the 3rd millennium BC, Corded Ware influence extended beyond its apparent frontier at the Rhine into Atlantic Europe, sparking off the development of the bell-beaker there, in the same way as its influence spread southwards across the Alps, sparking off the development of the Remedello and Rinaldone cultures before the mid-3rd millennium BC in north and central Italy. The transitional beaker types at the Lower Rhine (AOO; cf. Fig. 5, no. 9) can then be seen as second quarter imitations of the new pottery style which had been developed in the West, and to have been joined eventually around the mid-3rd millennium BC by truer renderings (e.g. Fig. 6, no. 1).

Some contacts are evident between the Corded Ware frontier and the West around the mid-3rd millennium BC or earlier. *Grand-Pressigny flint* in AOO beaker association at the Lower Rhine (Lanting and van der Waals 1976, 13-14, 67) is complimentary to the AOO type beaker from the Loire at Ancenis, Loire-Atlantique (Fig. 5, no. 9). Other evidence is less conclusive but points the same way. Similar flint in Swiss

Corded Ware-related association (Strahm 1972/3) is accompanied by bone pins of Corded Ware (and sometimes later) affinity which occur in late Artenacian context in the French Centre-West (Joussaume 1981, 398; Strahm 1979, 57-8). *Cord-impressed sherds* occur in similar association in western France (Joussaume 1981, 404). Further south in the Aude, similarly impressed sherds in layer 2c, Font Juvenal (Guilaine *et al.* 1980) could be referable chronologically to an early Corded Ware phase, in view of the radiocarbon results associated with the succeeding layer 2b with bell-beaker sherds (4190±90, 4160±90 BP; MC-567, MC-568).

Shaft-hole stone implements are a feature of the north and west French Neolithic and a few have been recorded in single graves (e.g. Bailloud 1964, 349; Joussaume 1981, 404; Roussot-Larroque 1983, 200). The well-known *bipennes* are a distinctly regional type and an origin in some way associated with Corded Ware battle axes seems unlikely, fragments having been found in Peu-Richardien or equivalent association (Joussaume 1981, 353); but Roussot-Larroque (1983, 199) has seen a resemblance in some others in central and western France to H type axes – a type associated with Corded Ware and transitional types of beaker at the Lower Rhine (Lanting and van der Waals 1976, 14; cf. Hvass 1992, 222). Many of the shaft-hole implements are of Breton amphibolite, and two well-known Breton copper battle axes (Briard 1965, 52-4, fig. 11, nos 2 and 3) may be part of a related exchange cycle, the example from Trévé, Côtes-du-Nord, being possibly of Corded Ware affinity.

The west French coastal region from the Morbihan southwards was an important area of interaction around the mid-3rd millennium BC or earlier, with its Maritime beakers and distribution of bone tortoise-buttons and copper Palmela points of south-east French and Iberian affinity and of gold and copper generally (Joussaume 1981, 500-1, 504-13). I suggest that in the second quarter of the 3rd millennium BC a Corded Ware fashion for a beaker-like pot was transmitted thence to Iberian potters, who became the first makers of Maritime beakers.

The stone wristguard (Figs 6, no. 4; 7, no. 5; 8, no. 10, 11; 9, no. 2), the V-button and the tanged copper knife (Figs 6, no. 3; 7, no. 12; 8, no. 9), recurrent associations with bell-beakers in their European range, appear likewise earliest in the west Mediterranean (Case 1977, 117 and references). The copper knives show features which can be seen more or less throughout their range: hollow-ground cutting edges and crimped edges to the tang to retain the haft (e.g. Joussaume 1981, fig. 232, no. 3; Butler and van der Waals 1966, fig. 10, no. 6; Case 1966, fig. 10, no. 2, fig. 11, no. 6. This paper: Fig. 6, no. 3; Fig. 7, no. 12).

Beaker pottery: regional variants

The Maritime beaker then became the prototype for bell-beaker developments throughout their European range. Made first in south-west Europe before the mid-3rd millennium BC, imitations spread rapidly and were transformed and incorporated into a great variety of often profusely but less emphatically zonally decorated assemblages. Harrison (1988) recognised nine such regional groups in Spain and Portugal in developments beginning before the mid-3rd millennium BC; among other sources, some contribution seems possible from the so-called *Kerbblattverzierte* pottery, with incised chevron decoration, earlier than bell-beaker pottery at Zambujal but probably overlapping with it (Kunst 1987). Other profusely decorated assemblages with similarly early origins are from the French Pyrenees, the Languedoc and Provence (Guilaine 1976) and some of the Mediterranean islands (Waldren and others in Waldren and Kennard 1987). French Atlantic and northern coastal assemblages (summaries in Joussaume 1981, L'Helgouach 1984)

adhere more closely to an austere tradition. Notice also vessels with horizontal cordons near the rim in the coastal settlement assemblages of the Centre West; and marginal to these assemblages the occurrence of beakers with cord impressions in uniform zones (all-over-corded, e.g. Fig. 5, no. 5) or in combination with other impressions (Fig. 5, no. 7). Western France seems as likely an area as any for the origin of the cord-impressed bell-beaker.

To some limited extent it is possible to see increasing complexity of decoration from south to north along the Atlantic fringe (cf. Zambujal, Kunst 1987, figs 47-9; French Centre West, Joussaume 1981, figs 222-4; Brittany, *loc. cit.*, fig. 225).

The southern British group D (Case 1993, 260-3; Case 1995a) dates possibly from around the mid-3rd millennium BC, and can be seen mainly as an unusually long-lasting development of the same Atlantic tradition into the 2nd millennium BC. Variations in the same tradition in the third quarter of the 3rd millennium BC can be seen in the region of the Rhône (Fig. 6, no. 7; Gallay 1976, Bill 1976) and in north Italy (Fig. 8, no. 1; Barfield 1976, 1977, 1984); and to some extent in numerous regional groups east of the Rhine into Central Europe distinguished however by a possibly early tendency for broad bands of decoration, including panels (Fig. 9, nos 1, 4) some with the so-called flag motif (Fig. 9, no. 1).

This same tendency, together with quite considerable decorative variety including horizontal ribs and finger-nail and finger-tip impressions (Fig. 8, nos 8, 14, 15) can be seen at the Lower Rhine in the locally developed Veluwe beakers (van der Waals and Glasbergen 1955; Lanting and van der Waals 1976; Louwe Kooijmans 1974, 171-339).

A generally still more marginal development can be seen in Jutland, where later Corded Ware traditions persisted (Hvass 1986, 1992). Included with these are the so-called curved beakers with convex necks or inturned rims (occurring in the islands but also central and north Jutland), dating from the Groundgrave period (e.g. Fig. 8, nos 6, 7) but contemporary in the Uppergrave period in the third quarter of the 3rd millennium BC with tubs, mostly small, some with characteristic bell-beaker decoration (Fig. 8, no. 4), which themselves persisted into the fourth quarter. True bell-beakers, showing broad band and panel motifs of Lower Rhenish and central European affinity appear (Fig. 8, no. 3; Myrhøj, north Jutland, probably here fourth quarter) and beaker lookalikes (Fig. 8, no. 5), alongside the prevalent tubs decorated in bell-beaker style (Fig. 8, no. 4).

In north Britain, beaker group B (Case 1993, 254-9) dating possibly from the mid-3rd millennium BC

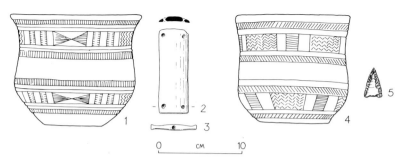

Fig. 9. 1-3: Weimar, Bachstrasse; 4 and 5: Löbnitz, Stassfurt (1-5 after Behrens 1973). (2, stone; 3, bone; 5, flint.)

(4060±80 BP: HAR-6630 on bone from burial IR 340, Heslerton, north Yorkshire: Powesland *et al.* 1986, 98) has affinities in Jutland and at the Lower Rhine. It shows the basic west European repertoire combined with, if not overwhelmed by, traits of later north-west European Corded Ware and transitional Corded Ware/bell-beaker pottery (such as zig-zags, herringbones, fringes and inturned and straight necks), together with later bell-beaker traits (such as broad bands of decoration and big geometrical motifs including panels). Group B beakers were associated in graves by the fourth quarter of the 3rd millennium BC with stone battle axes and flint daggers, which can be related to south Scandinavian Uppergrave/Late Neolithic types (Case 1993, 259).

Traits shared in common across the North Sea (but possibly somewhat earlier) can also be seen in the rectilinear arrangements of ribs and grooves on the Jutish tubs (e.g. Hvass 1986, figs 3, 4) and on Grooved Ware tubs of eastern and especially north-eastern England (e.g. Manby 1974, figs 17-21).

Ireland

Earlier developments

In contrast to north Britain, evidence for earlier developments in Ireland (defined collectively as Group A in Case 1993, 248-54) is mostly from non-grave assemblages. These include (Fig. 10): Ballynagilly, Co. Tyrone (ApSimon 1976 and personal information); Newgrange, Co. Meath (O' Kelly *et al.* 1983; Sweetman 1985, 1987); Knowth sites B, C, D, Co. Meath (Eogan 1984); Monknewtown, Co. Meath (Sweetman 1976); Dalkey Island, Co. Dublin, earlier phase (Liversage 1968); Longstone, Cullen, Co. Tipperary (Peter Danaher, personal information); Knockadoon, Lough Gur, Co. Limerick, sites C, D, K, J, L and 10 (Ó Ríordáin 1954; Grogan and Eogan 1987); Moneen, Co. Cork, phase 1 (O'Kelly 1952).

The best beaker-associated radiocarbon sample from Newgrange (no. 3, a charcoal sample well sealed under the cairn slip: O'Kelly *et al.* 1983, 15, fig. 4b) suggests a date in the third quarter of the 3rd millennium BC. Whether a date around the mid-3rd millennium BC (Case 1993, 254 where sample GrN-10629 from Moneen phase 1 is incorrectly des-

cribed as bone) exaggerates the age of early developments in Ireland remains an open question. Other dates from Newgrange and elsewhere suggest the survival of characteristic early features to the fourth quarter of the 3rd millennium BC (e.g. Monknewtown: 3810±45 BP, UB-728).

Irish pottery, like much beaker pottery in northern Europe, has a threefold aspect: affinity with the Atlantic mainstream of development; a strong mixture of eastern influence, from north Britain, the north-west European Corded Ware legacy and from central Europe; as well as its own regional character.

Strong *Atlantic affinity* can be seen in the simple zonal decoration (Fig. 11, nos 1-6) and motifs, for example ladder (Fig. 12, no. 6) and criss-cross (Fig. 11, no. 1) patterns and simple diamonds (Fig. 11, no. 3) and chevrons (Fig. 12, nos 1, 2), and a minor component of cord impressions (but see below). Recurrent neck cordons (Figs 11, nos 7, 8; 12, no. 3) are very characteristic of the settlement pottery of central western France (Joussaume 1981, 1986 (ed.), *passim*).

Pottery traits which show *eastern affinities*, from north Britain and further afield, include zig-zags (Figs 11, no. 4; 12, no. 10), fringes (Fig. 11, nos 3-5), multiple chevrons (Fig. 12, no. 7) and inturned necks (Figs 11, no. 8; 12, no. 5), which can be related to Corded Ware and the mid-3rd millennium BC transitional types of pottery discussed above. Herringbone motifs (Figs 11, no. 2, 6; 12, no. 5) are probably best similarly related; they seem rare in Atlantic Europe. Similarly, inner rim decoration (Fig. 12, nos 8, 9) which has a wide range (e.g. Figs 5, no. 9; 8, no. 2) including from the Lower Rhine to central Europe (Fig. 7, no. 10), and may appear everywhere early in beaker-association; it is also a common Grooved Ware trait. Double cord impressions (Fig. 12, no. 8 and as at Ballynagilly and the wedge-tomb Cashelbane, Loughash, Co. Tyrone: Case 1993, fig. 7, no. 2; Davies and Mullin 1940, pot C) have late Corded Ware affinities. Footed bowls at Newgrange (O'Kelly *et al.* 1983, fig. 25) and possibly the Longstone, Cullen (and cf. a wooden example from Tirkernaghan, Co. Tyrone, radiocarbon dated around the mid-3rd millennium BC: Earwood 1991/2) are an early, widespread and persistent Corded Ware type. Ermine decoration (Figs 11, no. 4; 12, nos 1, 2, 6)

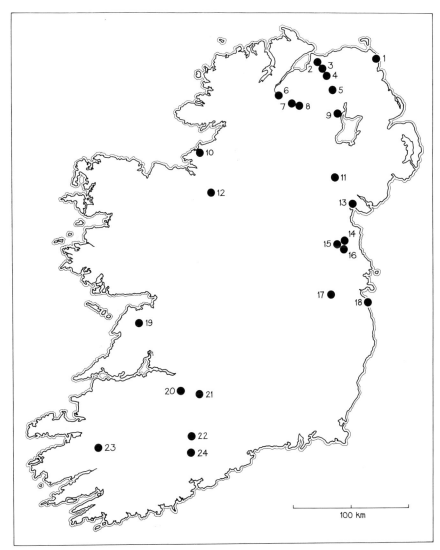

Fig. 10. 1: Goodland; 2: Largantea; 3: Gortcorbies; 4: Kilhoyle;
5: Fallahogy; 6: Tirkernaghan;
7: Loughash, Giant's Grave;
8: Loughash, Cashelbane; 9: Ballynagilly; 10: Creevykeel; 11: Corran;
12: Moytirra; 13: Ballyedmonduff;
14: Monknewtown; 15: Knowth;
16: Newgrange; 17: Furness;
18: Dalkey Island; 19: Poulawack;
20: Lough Gur area; 21: Cullen;
22: Labbacallee; 23: Ross Island;
24: Moneen.

has emphatically north British parallels, and is matched on presumably fourth-quarter Veluwe beakers
at the Lower Rhine (Fig. 8, no. 8). Panel decoration
(Fig. 12, no. 4; and at Newgrange and Lough Gur
D) is similarly matched (Fig. 8, nos 8, 14) and in
Jutland (Jensen 1972, fig. 53), and may be similarly
dated in north Britain (Keabog 1: 3730±60 BP,
GU-1123) but possibly dated earlier in central Europe
(Fig. 9, nos 1, 4) where the best result from the Löbnitz grave appears to be 3805±50 BP (Bln-1447). The
context of radiocarbon sample no. 5 at Newgrange
(4050±40 BP; GrN-6344), possibly to be associated
with the panel-decorated sherd, may not be totally
reliable, having come from near the edge of the cairn
slip (O'Kelly *et al.* 1983, fig. 4b).

Finger-nail and finger-tip impressions have sometimes been claimed as showing north-west European
connections with British beaker pottery. Sparse arrangements of finger-nail impressions (Fig. 11, no.
7), possibly mostly zonal and including the so-called
crow's foot pattern (Grogan and Eogan 1987, fig. 53,
no. 2188a), recur on Irish earlier beaker pottery, but
not apparently in great quantity. They have been

recorded in all the British beaker groups and here
and there in western Europe (Case 1993, 244). Finger-
nail impressions seem common in British later
Neolithic pottery.

Relationships with north Britain are emphasised by
the close connections of Irish early beaker
developments with Grooved Ware of north British affinity (Case 1993, 251-4). A Grooved Ware assemblage
was in isolation at the recently-excavated wooden
structure at Knowth (Eogan and Roche 1994), but
Grooved Ware occurs several times in beaker association. Although not so noted at Ballynagilly (ApSimon
1976), it was present as a minor element at Knowth
D (Eogan 1984, e.g. fig. 115, no. 3727) and at Lough
Gur D; it appears conspicuous at Cullen, and at
Newgrange to be represented by about a quarter of
the pottery assemblage (judging by Cleary in O'Kelly
et al. 1983, and personal examination), with its
presence at Newgrange emphasised by elements in
the flint assemblage (Eogan and Roche 1994, 328),
including presumably the petit tranchet arrowheads
(Lehane in O'Kelly *et al.* 1983, 146-50).

Grooved Ware and beaker pottery appear to have

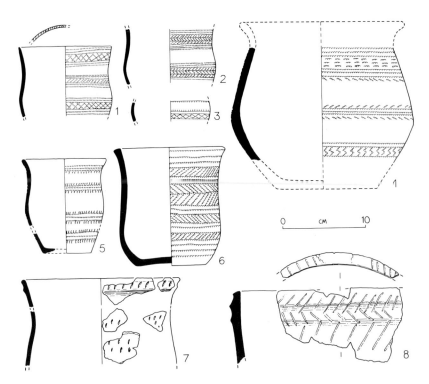

Fig. 11. 1-3: Moytirra (after Madden 1969); 4 and 5: Newgrange (after O'Kelly *et al.* 1983); 6-8: Dalkey Island (after Liversage 1968).

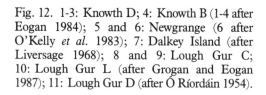

Fig. 12. 1-3: Knowth D; 4: Knowth B (1-4 after Eogan 1984); 5 and 6: Newgrange (6 after O'Kelly *et al.* 1983); 7: Dalkey Island (after Liversage 1968); 8 and 9: Lough Gur C; 10: Lough Gur L (after Grogan and Eogan 1987); 11: Lough Gur D (after Ó Ríordáin 1954).

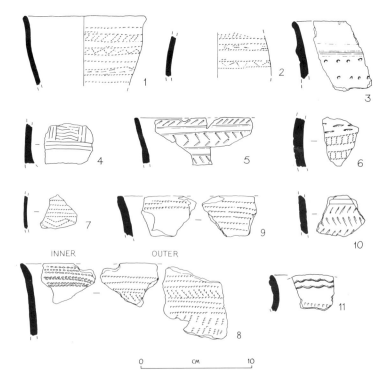

been separate entities at Newgrange, although showing interaction (cf. Case 1993, fig. 5, nos 5 and 4); other examples of the reaction of Grooved Ware on beaker pottery may be superlative sherds from Lough Gur D (Ó Ríordáin 1954, 396; Case 1993, fig. 6, no. 6) and the mosaic-hatching on some sherds from Cullen.

There is no conclusive evidence that Grooved Ware was earlier than beaker pottery at Newgrange, unlike at Knowth apparently (Eogan and Roche 1994, 328). The best stratified Grooved Ware associated radiocarbon result (3990±40 BP, GrN-6343; sample 4, O'Kelly *et al.* 1983, 15, fig. 4b) can be approximated as around the mid-3rd millennium BC, possibly somewhat earlier than the nearby beaker-associated sample 3 (above).

Finally, Irish beaker pottery shows strong *regional character*; motifs seem more often incised than comb- or shell-impressed (reversing the trend in Atlantic Europe generally); and, being unusually well-represented in non-grave assemblages, can be seen to have many features of regional rather than wide significance, such as jabbed (Fig. 12, no. 3), stamped, whipped-cord (e.g. Newgrange; Case 1993, fig. 7, nos 4, 5, 3 respectively) and apparently barbed-wire impressions (Knowth D; Eogan 1984, fig. 113, no. 3246a) and false-relief (Fig. 12, no. 11 and at Ballynagilly).

Later developments in Ireland

Throughout Britain, in the fourth quarter of the 3rd millennium BC, beaker pottery styles developed from those of north British group B became dominant (Case 1993, 256-9; Case 1995a), although never entirely supplanting the more austere group D in southern Britain. This was a very formative epoch, which saw not only the currency in southern Britain of the northern-derived flint daggers and battle axes but also the use of tin-bronzes and much activity in barrow building and around monuments (Case 1995a). The British pottery shows regional variations, but recurrent features include not only inturned rims but also strong emphasis on broad bands of decoration, panels and vertical and floating motifs; incised decoration is prominent, as well as comb- and cord-impressions and a great variety of other impressions, including dense finger-nail and finger-tip impressions, sometimes in relief patterns.

A similar stage can be seen to some extent in Ireland, notably stratified above earlier beaker developments at Dalkey Island, Co. Dublin (Liversage 1968, 154-7, 160-1, 164; this paper, Fig. 13, nos 1, 2, 4 and possibly 11; and cf. multiple cordons and finger-nail relief-pattern on Veluwe beaker, Fig. 8, no. 14). It can be seen (Fig. 13, no. 3) at Moneen,

Co. Cork, probably to be related to the massive central cist of phase 2 (O'Kelly 1952; Brindley and Lanting 1987/8, 3755±30 BP, GrN-11904), and to have been associated with the rebuilding with stone of the Great Circle, Lough Gur, Co. Limerick (Ó Ríordáin 1951, e.g. fig. 5, pl. XII and personal study); and it seems apparent in Wedge Tombs further north, for instance at Ballyedmonduff, Co. Dublin (Ó Ríordáin and de Valera 1952), at Largantea, Derry (Fig. 13, nos 5, 6; Herring 1938) and the Giant's Grave, Loughash, Co. Tyrone (Fig. 13, nos 8-10; Davies 1939). As in southern England, pottery forms related to earlier types (e.g. Fig. 13, no. 7) did not vanish, and assemblages with earlier traditions may have continued alongside the intrusive developments.

This later beaker decorative repertoire (especially broad decorative bands, verticality, flag and floating ornament; and including possibly false-relief, Fig. 13, no. 11) was a major contribution to the very varied decorative range of Irish Bowls (Ó Ríordáin and Waddell 1993), which may have begun to replace beaker pottery, for example at Dalkey Island (Liversage 1968, 157), at site 10, Lough Gur (Grogan and Eogan 1987, 461) and the Great Circle (Ó Ríordáin 1951, 61), in a major way during the fourth quarter of the 3rd millennium BC (radiocarbon results associated with Bowls and Vases in Ó Ríordáin and Waddell 1993, 37; and additional ones in Hedges *et al.* 1993, 313). Beaker pottery may have been used to some extent in Ireland to the end of the 3rd millennium BC (grave 6, Poulawack, Co. Clare; Hencken 1935, 204, sherd fig. 9a, personal examination; Brindley and Lanting 1991/2a, 16), but it does not appear to have survived into the 2nd millennium BC as in Britain.

Some Irish beaker-associated objects, activities and contexts

Stone wristguards

A western contribution to the early Irish Beaker culture can be seen in two-hole stone wristguards (e.g. Fig. 8, nos 10, 11), characteristic of Western France (Joussaume 1981; L'Helgouach 1984), prevalent in Ireland (Harbison 1976) and in beaker-related association in the cist burial at the foot of the monolith at the Longstone, Furness, Co. Kildare (Macalister *et al.* 1913), and at Cullen, Co. Tipperary, and possibly in the Corran hoard, Co. Armagh (Case 1966, 165). Contrastingly, the four-hole wristguard, a prevalent central European type (Figs 7, no. 5; 9, no. 2), occurring at the Lower Rhine (Fig. 6, no. 4) and throughout Britain, is rarer in Ireland (Harbison 1976) and western France (Birocheau and Large 1986).

Flint arrowheads

Flint arrowheads suggest a more even balance

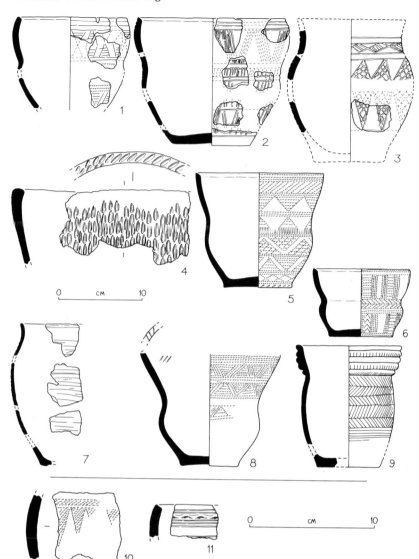

Fig. 13. 1, 2, 4 and 11: Dalkey Island (after Liversage 1968); 3: Moneen (after O'Kelly 1952); 5-7: Largantea (partly after Herring 1938 and Clarke 1970); 8-10: Giant's Grave, Loughash (partly after Davies 1939).

between west and east. The barbed-and-tanged type (e.g. Fig. 6, no. 6; in Ireland, e.g. Newgrange, O'Kelly *et al.* 1983, fig. 64; Lough Gur D, Ó Ríordáin 1954, fig. 41, no. 1) being typically western in beaker association (Joussaume 1981, 502; L'Helgouach 1984, 66; but cf. at the Lower Rhine, Lanting and van der Waals 1976, 68-70); and the prevalent hollow-based type (e.g. Lough Gur L, Grogan and Eogan 1987, fig. 4, no. 197; Lough Gur D, Ó Ríordáin 1954, fig. 41, no. 12) being characteristically eastern (Figs 7, no. 6; 10, no. 5; 8, no. 12; and at Myrhøj, Jutland, Jensen 1972, fig. 23). Green (1980, fig. 55) mapped both types in Ireland.

Metals

Copper metallurgy appears to reproduce the relative western and eastern contributions seen in early pottery developments. Beaker-associated copper extraction at Ross Island, Co. Kerry (O'Brien, this volume) began during the third quarter of the 3rd millennium BC and may have continued during the fourth quarter (radiocarbon results in O'Brien 1994, 230). Irish early copper products, typically flat axes but including

tanged knives, appear to show a relatively minor primeval technological stage, modified by a later rather prolonged so-called impact phase (Case 1966). Primeval-looking products, typically straight-sided thick-butted flat axes (Case 1966, fig. 4, no. 1), adapted for a club haft, are of pan-European type but can be matched like the tanged knives in central Western France (Joussaume 1981, figs 234, 232) and Iberia. In contrast, the techniques of the impact phase show relationships more emphatically eastwards. These relationships are likely to have begun earlier than the mature central European Early Bronze Age (which I emphasised in 1966). It may not be far-fetched to relate the curved sides characteristic of Irish copper flat axes to northern English Late Neolithic heirloom Seamer type flint axes (discussed in Manby 1974, 95-6, 98; fig. 42). And the split haft to which thin-butted impact phase Irish copper flat axes seem adapted occurs in Corded Ware association (Behrens 1973, f.p. 192, hafting a stone adze), if not earlier. As a possible eastern contribution, note also a hollow based flint arrowhead from Ross Island (O'Brien 1995, 26).

Tin-bronzes and some later forms of axes, especially Harbison's Ballyvalley type (Harbison 1969), are best related to later Beaker and other developments in the fourth quarter of the 3rd millennium BC.

Gold shows a somewhat less clear-cut pattern. British radiocarbon results (Radley 4a, Oxon., information Alistair Barclay; Chilbolton, Hants., Russel 1990) suggest that early Irish production (of so-called basket earrings, diadems, plaques, type A discs: Case 1977) began in the third quarter of the 3rd millennium BC. Diadems and gold generally have western associations (Joussaume 1981; L'Helgouach 1984) but the earrings and discs show some eastern affinities (earrings: cf. Fig. 7, no. 11, 11a and Butler and van der Waals 1966, 62). Production of lunulae from northern Irish gold (information from Richard Warner) may be related to later Beaker and other developments in the fourth quarter of the 3rd millennium BC. The decorative motifs of lunulae can be compared to those of north British beakers (Taylor 1970, pl. xiii).

Burial practice

Irish practice (by inhumation and cremation) appears to follow a western tradition of burial in collective tombs. Cist, pit and barrow-associated burials seem even rarer than in the French Atlantic coastal region (Joussaume 1981, 467-75; L'Helgouach 1984, 61-2). Examples are Gortcorbies cairn, Derry (May 1947, 17), Poulawack 6, Co. Clare (above) and the Longstone, Furness, Co. Kildare (Macalister *et al.* 1913); the massive central cists at Moneen, Co. Cork (O'Kelly 1952) and Cullen, Co. Tipperary, are other possible examples. Burial at the foot of a monolith as at Furness has interesting parallels in Britain (e.g. North grave, Cairnpapple, West Lothian, Piggott 1947/8, 88-90; Gulval, Cornwall, Russell and Pool 1964) and in western France (Avrillé, Vendée, of fourth quarter date, Bénéteau *et al.* 1992).

There seems no evidence for burial in Court Tombs, which were occasionally visited (Herity 1987, *passim*; the few sherds include those possibly from a large vessel at Creevykeel, Co. Sligo, *loc. cit.*, fig. 42, C40). A cremation burial came from the passage of Passage Tomb 15 , Knowth, Co. Meath (Eogan 1984, 308-12).

Contrastingly, burials by inhumation and cremation have been repeatedly recorded from Wedge Tombs, monuments which it seems reasonable to assume were initiated by beaker-users. Recent radiocarbon results (Brindley and Lanting 1991/2b) suggest a major period of use in the fourth quarter in a span from around the turn of the third and fourth quarters of the 3rd millennium BC into the 2nd millennium. This span seems generally consistent with later Beaker finds from Largantea (Fig. 13, nos 5, 6), Giant's Grave, Loughash (Fig. 13, nos 8, 9)

and Ballyedmonduff (Ó Ríordáin and de Valera 1952), and with other finds extending into the full Bronze Age (a summary list in Case l969b, 22). But it seems unlikely to indicate the start of beaker-associated activity in Ireland.

Earlier beaker pottery, comparable to that from Ballynagilly, came from the wedge tomb Cashelbane, Loughash, Co. Tyrone (personal examination and e.g. Case 1993, fig. 7, no. 2), suggesting a date in the third quarter of the 3rd millennium BC. And it seems legitimate to doubt whether the construction of monumental tombs was among exceptionally early beaker-associated activities (below). Leask and Price (1936, 88) noted that the condition of the basal burial D in the east chamber at Labbacallee, Co. Cork (which provided the earliest radiocarbon result at that monument: 3805±45 BP, GrN-11359; Brindley and Lanting 1987/8, 16) suggested that it had been moved, presumably from temporary interment or exposure elsewhere.

Walsh (this volume) has stressed the difficulty of re-entering the completed tombs. The comparative ease with which a capstone could be moved at Labbacallee (Leask and Price 1936, 81) may have been exceptional, although the practice has been suggested elsewhere (West Kennet, Wilts.: Case 1995a, 10). Characteristic chamber-deposits in Wedge Tombs seem disturbed and difficult to read; but at Cashelbane, Loughash, Davies and Mullin (1940, 150) considered the Food Vessels to have been secondary deposits in chamber II, and the span of finds at that tomb especially does suggest a sequence of deposits. Such a sequence would be comparable to the apparent sequences of burials on barrow surfaces, within ring-barrows and in shaft graves in north Britain (as at Heslerton, North Yorkshire; Powesland *et al.* 1986); and the so-called cists within the chambers at Largantea (Herring 1938, 171), Ballyedmonduff (Ó Ríordáin and de Valera 1952) and the Lough Gur megalith (Ó Ríordáin and Ó hIceadha 1955) recall somewhat those at the base of the shaft at Rudston 62, East Yorkshire (Greenwell 1877, 234-45; Kinnes and Longworth 1985 and references).

How was Beaker pottery spread?

The nature of the problem

Traditional studies of beakers as grave pottery have led to a widely held opinion that they represented a specialised production. However, viewing grave and settlement pottery together emphasises that beakers were generally part of a basic craft, which made a range of goods for everyday life (Case 1995b). Its products ranged from cups (Grogan and Eogan 1987, 381) and other small pots, through characteristically decorated smaller beakers (Figs 5, nos 2, 5-7; 6, nos 1, 8; 7, no. 2; 11, nos. 1, 5, 6; 13, no. 6) some of which may indeed have served as drinking vessels; to larger examples (e.g. Figs 5, nos 3, 8, 10; 6, no. 2; 7, no. 1; 11, no. 4), some of which seem unlikely drinking vessels (e.g. Figs 5, no. 4; 6, no. 9); to large vessels of approximately beaker shape which are unlikely to have been for other than storage (e.g. probably Figs 11, no. 8; 13, no. 4). And included in the repertoire were other large and small pots of which the Beaker affiliation appears less obvious (e.g. Figs 12, no. 1; 13, no. 9) or even slight (Case 1993 figs 5, nos 7, 8; 13, nos 5, 7).

Petrological analyses of pottery give further insights. Those on Irish beaker pottery (Cleary 1980 and in O'Kelly *et al.* 1983, 112-14; Brindley in Eogan 1984, 331-46) have been pioneering in an admirably empirical tradition. Similar studies have now been published for Britain (to references in Case 1995b, add Parker-Pearson 1990) and central Europe (Rehman *et al.* 1992) and been reported for Iberia (Richard Harrison in correspondence); and have now been undertaken on Irish Bowl and Vase pottery (Sheridan in Ó Ríordáin and Waddell 1993, 45-75). The results so far all point the same way: the pottery was locally made. Little suggests that it was systematically traded over long distances. The evidence appears to favour an ethnographically derived model of limited regional distribution from occasional household or semi-specialised production (brief selection from a large literature in Case 1995b).

If so, how then did potters, exponents of a basic craft producing goods for local consumption, for everyday life as well as special occasions, become aware of each other's products over such very wide areas in Europe (including some with quite demanding access) and so apparently rapidly at the start of the bell-beaker period? And continue to influence each other in such variety?

Movement and resources

Exploitation of resources is conspicuous in the 3rd millennium BC archaeological record; it is seen for example in early Beaker association with metalworking at Zambujal, Portugal (Kunst 1987, 197), with metal-extraction at Ross Island, Co. Kerry (O'Brien, this volume) and with horses at Budapest (Kalicz-Schrieber 1976).

I suggest that the bell-beaker, like the Corded Ware beaker before it, became widely familiar through being the small general purpose pot used by small groups seeking exchanges and resources, in *seasonal movements* (of the kind suggested in Case 1969a), to and fro from their home bases. The beaker's exotic associations such as copper and gold objects, some plainly not locally made, could be seen as among the goods exchanged and imitated.

Complex movements of this kind, over very many seasons around the mid-3rd millennium BC and early in its third quarter, could have led to local versions of the bell-beaker spreading across Europe, and becoming rapidly imitated in larger forms and incorporated in a great variety of regional styles, themselves with varying local traditions. Similar reactions between such local groups would have continued through the second half of the 3rd millennium BC; and some movements into new territories (including exchanges of kin) are always a possibility.

Finally, doubts are sometimes expressed as to whether voyages across the North Sea and to some extent in the Atlantic, as implied here, were feasible in the 3rd millennium BC. Only coasting or voyages within sight of land are considered possible. But such views seem conditioned by familiarity with large powered ships with modern navigation equipment.

However, those who have handled small muscle-propelled craft in Atlantic seas, such as off the west of Ireland, will need no reminding of their seaworthiness or that the open sea is often a safer place than coastal waters, which can be most unpredictable and extremely dangerous. The North Sea has been crossed in kayaks in recent times, and navigation without instruments is well known to be feasible. (Discussion of possibilities open to Neolithic and Bronze Age seafarers in Case 1969a, 178-80 and references; Case 1969b, 7; Green *et al.* 1970; Waddell 1991/2.)

Acknowledgements

Arthur ApSimon, Peter Danaher and Brian O'Kelly generously showed me finds from Ballynagilly, the Longstone, Cullen and Newgrange before publication; similarly Willem-Jan Hogestijn and Alistair Barclay gave me unpublished information. My debt is great to colleagues at the Ulster Museum and the National Museum of Ireland over many years for giving me access to finds and information on them. I am grateful to Sam Howison for mathematical advice and to Laurence Barfield, Anthony Harding and Christian Strahm for information. Mike Tite kindly commented on a draft of the section on chronology. Nick Griffiths made the drawings.

References

ApSimon, A. M. 1976. Ballynagilly and the beginning and end of the Irish Neolithic. In S. J. De Laet (ed.), *loc. cit.*, 15-30.

Baillie, M. G. L. 1985. Irish dendrochronology and radiocarbon calibration. *Ulster Journal of Archaeology* 48, 11-23.

Bailloud, G. 1964. *Le Néolithique dans le Bassin Parisien.* Paris.

Bantelmann, N. 1982. *Endneolithische Funde in rhenisch-westfälischen Raum.* Neumunster.

Barfield, L. H. 1976. The cultural affinities of Bell Beakers in Italy and Sicily. In J. N. Lanting and J. D. van der Waals (eds), *loc. cit.*, 307-22.

Barfield, L. H. 1977. The Beaker Culture in Italy. In R. Mercer (ed.), *Beakers in Britain and Europe, British Archaeological Reports International Series* 26, 27-49. Oxford.

Barfield, L. H. 1984. The Bell Beaker Culture in Italy. In J. Guilaine (ed.), *loc. cit.*, 129-39.

Behrens, H. 1973. *Die Jungsteinzeit im Mittelelbe-Saale-Gebiet.* Berlin.

Benéteau, G., Cros, J-P., and Gilbert, J-M. 1992. L'enclos campaniforme à monolithe(s) des Terriers à Avrillé, Vendée. *Gallia Préhistoire* 34, 259-88.

Bill, J. 1976. *Die Frühphase der Glockenbecherkultur in Ost-Frankreich.* In J. N. Lanting and J. D. van der Waals (eds), *loc. cit.*, 333-49.

Birocheau, P. and Large, J. M. 1986. Un fragment réutilisé de Brassard d'Archer aux Chatelliers de Vieil-Auzay (Vendée): description et relations. In R. Joussaume (ed.), *loc. cit.*, 105-12.

Briard, J. 1965. *Les dépôts bretons et L'Age du Bronze Atlantique.* Rennes.

Brindley, A. L., Lanting, J. N. and Mook, W. G. 1987/8. Radiocarbon dates from Moneen and Labbacallee, County Cork. *Journal of Irish Archaeology* 4, 13-20.

Brindley, A. L. and Lanting, J. N. 1991/2a. Radiocarbon dates from the cemetery at Poulawack, Co. Clare. *Journal of Irish Archaeology* 6, 13-17.

Brindley, A. L. and Lanting, J. N. 1991/2b. Radiocarbon dates from Wedge Tombs. *Journal of Irish Archaeology* 6, 19-26.

Buchvaldek, M. and Strahm, Ch. (eds). 1992. *Die Kontinentaleuropäischen Gruppen der Kultur mit Schnurkeramik.* Prague.

Butler, J. J. and van der Waals, J. D. 1966. Bell Beakers and Early Metal-Working in the Netherlands. *Palaeohistoria* 12, 41-139.

Case, H. J. 1966. Were Beaker-people the First Metallurgists in Ireland? *Palaeohistoria* 12, 141-77.

Case, H. J. 1969a. Neolithic explanations. *Antiquity* 43, 176-86.

Case, H. J. 1969b. Settlement-patterns in the North Irish Neolithic. *Ulster Journal of Archaeology* 32, 3-27.

Case, H. J. 1977. An early accession to the Ashmolean Museum. In V. Markotic (ed.), *Ancient Europe and the Mediterranean: Studies presented in honour of Hugh Hencken*, 18-34. Warminster.

Case, H. J. 1987. Postscript: Oxford International West Mediterranean Bell Beaker Conference, In W. H. Waldren and R. C. Kennard (eds), *loc. cit.*, 115-27.

Case, H. J. 1993. Beakers: Deconstruction and After. *Proceedings of the Prehistoric Society* 59, 241-68.

Case, H. J. 1995a. Some Wiltshire Beakers and their Contexts. *Wiltshire Archaeological and Natural History Magazine* 88, 1-17.

Case, H. J. 1995b. Beakers: loosening a stereotype. In Kinnes, I. and Varndell, G. (eds), *'Unbaked Urns of Rudely Shape': Essays on British and Irish Pottery for Ian Longworth.* Oxford, 55-67.

Clarke, D. L. 1970. *Beaker Pottery of Great Britain and Ireland,* vols 1 and 2. Cambridge.

Cleary, R. M. 1980. *The Late Neolithic/Beaker period Ceramic Assemblage from Newgrange, Co. Meath – a study.* University College, Cork, M.A. thesis.

Davies, O. 1939. Excavations at the Giant's Grave, Loughash. *Ulster Journal of Archaeology* 2, 254-68.

Davies, O. and Mullin, J. B. 1940. Excavation of Cashelbane Cairn, Loughash, Co. Tyrone. *Journal of the Royal Society of Antiquaries of Ireland* 70, 143-63.

Davis, S. and Payne, S. 1993. A barrow full of cattle skulls. *Antiquity* 67, 12-22.

De Laet, S. J. (ed.). 1976. *Acculturation and Continuity in Atlantic Europe. Dissertationes Archaeologicae Gandenses* 16. Bruges.

Dvořák, P. 1992. *Die Gräberfelder der Glockenbecherkultur in Mähren,* vol. 1. Brno.

Dvořák, P. and Šebela, L. 1992. Beziehungen zwischen Schnurkeramik und Glockenbecherkultur in Mähren. In M. Buchvaldek and Ch. Strahm (eds), *loc. cit.*, 99-107.

Earwood, C. 1991/2. A radiocarbon date for Early Bronze Age Wooden Polypod Bowls. *Journal of Irish Archaeology* 6, 27-8.

Eogan, G. 1984. *Excavations at Knowth,* vol. 1. Dublin.

Eogan, G. and Roche, H. 1994. A Grooved Ware wooden structure at Knowth, Boyne Valley, Ireland. *Antiquity* 68, 322-30.

Forenbaher, S. 1993. Radiocarbon dates and absolute chronology of the central European Early Bronze Age. *Antiquity* 67, 218-56.

Gallay, A. 1976. The position of the Bell-Beaker Civilisation in the chronological sequence of Petit-Chasseur (Sion, Valais, Switzerland). In J. N. Lanting and J. D. van der Waals (eds), *loc. cit.*, 279-306.

Green, C., Bellwood, P., Hammond, N. and Case, H. J. 1970. Neolithic comments. *Antiquity* 44, 105-14.

Green, H. S. 1980. *The Flint Arrowheads of the British Isles. British Archaeological Reports, British Series* 75. Oxford.

Greenwell, W. 1877. *British Barrows.* Oxford.

Grogan, E. and Eogan, G. 1987. Lough Gur excavations by Seán P. Ó Ríordáin: further Neolithic and Beaker habitations on Knockadoon. *Proceedings of the Royal Irish Academy* 87C, 299-506.

Guilaine, J. 1976. La civilisation des vases campaniformes dans le Midi de la France. In J. N. Lanting and J. D. van der Waals (eds), *loc. cit.*, 351-70.

Guilaine, J. (ed.). 1984. *L'Age du Cuivre Européen: Civilisations à vases campaniformes*. Paris.

Guilaine, J., Vacquer, J., Gasco, J. and Banie, P. 1980. Le Néolithique recent-final et le Chalcolithique de L'abri de Font-Juvenal (Aude). In J. Guilaine (ed.), *Le Groupe de Véraza et le fin des temps Néolithiques*, 13-16. Paris.

Harbison, P. 1969. *The Axes of the Early Bronze Age in Ireland. Prähistorische Bronzefunde*, 9.1 Munich.

Harbison, P. 1976. *Bracers and V-perforated buttons in the Beaker and Food Vessel Cultures of Ireland. Archaeologia Atlantica Research Report 1*, Bad Bramstedt.

Hardmeyer, B. 1991. Zusammenfassung der Chronologie in der Ostschweiz. In Ch. Strahm (ed.) 1991a, *loc. cit.*, 127-8.

Hájek, L. 1966. Die älteste Phase der Glockenbecherkultur in Böhmen und Mähren. *Památky Archeologické* 57, 210-41.

Harrison, R. J. 1980. *The Beaker Folk: Copper age archaeology in Western Europe*. London.

Harrison, R. J. 1988. Bell Beakers in Spain and Portugal: working with radiocarbon dates in the 3rd millennium BC. *Antiquity* 62, 464-72.

Hedges, R. E. M., Houseley, R. A., Bronk Ramsey, C., and van Klinken, G. J. 1993. Radiocarbon dates from the AMS system: date list 17. *Archaeometry* 35, 305-26.

Hencken, H. O'N. 1935. A cairn at Poulawack, County Clare. *Journal of the Royal Society of Antiquaries of Ireland* 65, 191-222.

Herity, M. 1987. The finds from Irish Court Tombs. *Proceedings of the Royal Irish Academy* 87C, 103-281.

Herring, I. J. 1938. The cairn excavation at Well Glass Spring, Largantea, Co. Londonderry. *Ulster Journal of Archaeology* 1, 164-88.

Hvass, L. 1986. Enkeltgravskulturens regionalgrupper i Vejle Amt. In Ch. Adamsen and K. Ebbesen (eds), *Stridsøksetid i Sydskandinavien*, 108-25. Copenhagen.

Hvass, L. 1992. Die Einzelgrabkultur in Jütland, Dänemark. In M. Buchvaldek and Ch. Strahm (eds), *loc. cit.*, 221-8.

Hvass, L. and S. 1988/9. Et gravkammer fra enkeltgravskulturen. *Kuml* 1988/9, 57-75.

Jensen, J. A. 1972. Myrhøj. 3 hustomter med klokkebaegerkeramik. *Kuml* 1972, 61-122.

Joussaume, R. 1986. Campaniforme de la Republique 2 à Talmont-Saint-Hilaire (Vendée). In R. Joussaume (ed.), *loc. cit.*, 55-65.

Joussaume, R. 1981. *Le Néolithique de l'Aunis et du Poitou occidentale dans son cadre atlantique*. Rennes.

Joussaume, R. (ed.). 1986. *Cultures campaniformes dans le Centre-Ouest de la France*. La-Roche-sur-Yon.

Kalicz-Schreiber, R. 1976. Die Probleme der Glockenbecherkultur in Ungarn. In J. N. Lanting and J. D. van der Waals (eds), *loc. cit.*, 183-215.

Kinnes, I., Gibson, A., Ambers, J., Bowman, S., Leese, M. and Boast, R. 1991. Radiocarbon dating and British Beakers. *Scottish Archaeological Review* 8, 35-78.

Kinnes, I. A. and Longworth, I. H. 1985. *Catalogue of the excavated prehistoric and Romano-British material in the Greenwell Collection*. London.

Kunst, M. 1987. *Zambujal: Glockenbecher und Kerbblattverzierte Keramik aus den Grabungen 1964 bis 1973*. Mainz.

Lanting J. N. and van der Waals, J. D. (eds). 1976. *Glockenbechersymposion Oberried 1974*. Bussum.

Lanting, J. N. and van der Waals, J. D. 1976. Beaker culture relations in the Lower Rhine basin. In J. N. Lanting and J. D. van der Waals (eds), *loc. cit.*, 1-80.

Leask, H. G. and Price, L. 1936. The Labbacallee Megalith, Co. Cork. *Proceedings of the Royal Irish Academy* 43C, 77-101.

Leisner, V. 1965. *Die Megalithgräber der Iberischen Halbinsel: der Westen*, 3. Berlin.

L'Helgouach, J. 1976. Les relations entre le groupe des vases campaniformes et les groupes néolithiques dans l'Ouest de la France. In J. N. Lanting and J. D. van der Waals (eds), *loc. cit.*, 439-51.

L'Helgouach, J. 1984. Le groupe campaniforme dans le Nord, le Centre et l'Ouest de la France. In J. Guilaine (ed.), *loc. cit.*, 59-80.

Litton, C. D. and Buck, C. E. 1995. The Bayesian approach to the interpretation of archaeological data. *Archaeometry* 37, 1-24.

Liversage, G. D. 1968. Excavations at Dalkey Island, Co. Dublin, 1956-1959. *Proceedings of the Royal Irish Academy* 66C, 53-233.

Louwe Kooijmans, L. P. 1974. *The Rhine/Meuse Delta: Four Studies on its prehistoric occupation and Holocene geology*. Leiden.

Macalister, R. A. S., Armstrong, E. C. R. and R. Ll. Praeger. 1913. On a Bronze-Age interment with associated standing-stone and earthen ring near Naas, Co. Kildare. *Proceedings of the Royal Irish Academy* 30C, 351-60.

Madden, A. C. 1969. The Beaker wedge tomb at Moytirra, Co. Sligo. *Journal of the Royal Society of Antiquaries of Ireland* 99, 151-9.

Manby, T. G. 1974. *Grooved Ware Sites in Yorkshire and the North of England*. British Archaeological Reports. British Series 9. Oxford.

May, A. McL. 1947. Burial Mound, Circles and Cairn, Gortcorbies, Co. Londonderry. *Journal of the Royal Society of Antiquaries of Ireland* 77, 5-22.

Moucha, V. 1992. Die Schnurkeramik und die Glockenbecherkultur in Böhmen. In M. Buchvaldek and Ch. Strahm (eds), *loc. cit.*, 81-7.

Needham, S. and Ambers, J. 1994. Redating Rams Hill and reconsidering Bronze Age enclosure. *Proceedings of the Prehistoric Society* 60, 225-43.

O'Brien, W. 1994. *Mount Gabriel. Bronze Age Mining in Ireland*. Galway.

O'Brien, W. 1995. Ross Island - the beginning. *Archaeology Ireland* 9, 24-7.

O'Kelly, M. J. 1952. Excavation of a cairn at Moneen, Co. Cork. *Proceedings of the Royal Irish Academy* 54C, 121-59.

O'Kelly, M. J., Cleary, R. M. and Lehane, D. 1983. *Newgrange, Co. Meath, Ireland: the Late Neolithic/Beaker period settlement*. British Archaeological Reports. International Series 190. Oxford.

Ó Ríordáin, B. and Waddell, J. 1993. *The Funerary Bowls and Vases of the Irish Bronze Age*. Galway.

Ó Ríordáin, S. P. 1951. Lough Gur excavations: The Great Stone Circle (B) in Grange Townland. *Proceedings of the Royal Irish Academy* 54C, 37-74.

Ó Ríordáin, S. P. 1954. Lough Gur excavations: Neolithic and Bronze Age houses on Knockadoon. *Proceedings of the Royal Irish Academy* 56C, 297-459.

Ó Ríordáin, S. P. and de Valera, R. 1952. Excavation of a megalithic tomb at Ballyedmonduff, Co. Dublin. *Proceedings of the Royal Irish Academy* 55C, 61-81.

Ó Ríordáin, S. P. and Ó hIceadha, G. 1955. Lough Gur excavations: the megalithic tomb. *Journal of the Royal Society of Antiquaries of Ireland* 85, 34-50.

Pape, W. 1979. Histogramme neolithischer 14C-Daten. *Germania* 57, 1-51.

Parker-Pearson, M. 1990. The production and distribution of Bronze Age pottery in south-west Britain. *Cornish Archaeology* 29, 5-32.

Pearson, J. W., Pilcher, J. R., Baillie, M. G. L., Corbett, D. M. and Qua, F. 1986. High-Precision 14C measurement of Irish oaks to show the natural 14C variations from AD 1840-5210 BC. *Radiocarbon* 28, 911-34.

Piggott, S. 1947/8. The excavations at Cairnpapple Hill, West Lothian, 1947-48. *Proceedings of the Society of Antiquaries of Scotland* 82, 68-123.

Powesland, D., Haughton, C. and Hanson, J. 1986. Excavations at Heslerton, North Yorkshire. *Archaeological Journal* 143, 53-173.

Rehman, F., Robinson, V. J. and Shennan, S. J. 1992. A neutron activation study of bell beakers and associated pottery from Czechoslovakia and Hungary. *Památky Archeologické* 83, 197-211.

Roussot-Larroque, J. 1983. Le 'reseau' du Néolithique final: mutations économiques et interrelations ouest-est et est-ouest en France et dans quelques régions voisines. *Godišnjak* 21, 185-220.

Russel, A. D. 1990. Two Beaker burials from Chilbolton, Hampshire. *Proceedings of the Prehistoric Society* 56, 153-72.

Russell, V. and Pool, P. A. S. 1964. Excavation of a Menhir at Try, Gulval. *Cornish Archaeology* 3, 15-26.

Skjølsvold, A. 1977. *Slettabøboplassen*. Stavanger.

Smith, A. G. and Willis, E. H. 1961/2. Radiocarbon Dating of the Fallahogy Landnam Phase. *Ulster Journal of Archaeology* 24 and 25, 16-24.

Souville, G. 1977. La civilisation du vase campaniforme au Maroc. *L'Anthropologie* 81, 561-77.

Strahm, Ch. 1972/3. Les fouilles d'Yverdon. *Jahrbuch der Schweizerischen Gesellschaft für Ur- und Frühgeschichte* 57, 7-16.

Strahm, Ch. 1979. Les épingles de parure en os du Néolithique final. In H. Camps-Fabrer (ed.), *L'industrie en os et bois de cerf durant le Néolithique et l'age des métaux*, 47-84. Paris.

Strahm, Ch. (ed.) 1991a. *Die kontinentaleuropäischen Gruppen der Kultur mit Schnurkeramik. Die Chronologie der regionalen Gruppen: Zusammenfassungen.* Freiburg i. Br.

Strahm, Ch. 1991b. Die Chronologie der schweizerisch-sudwestdeutschen Schnurkeramik. In Ch. Straum (ed.), *loc. cit.*, 122-6.

Strahm, Ch. 1991c. Schlussfolgerungen. In Ch. Strahm (ed.), *loc. cit.*, 142-4.

Stuiver, M. and Becker, B. 1986. High-precision decadal calibration of the the radiocarbon time scale, AD 1950-2500 BC. *Radiocarbon* 28, 863-910.

Stuiver, M. and Becker, B. 1993. High-precision decadal calibration of the radiocarbon time scale, AD 1950-6000 BC. *Radiocarbon* 35, 35-65.

Stuiver, M. and Pearson, G. W. 1993. High-Precision bidecadal calibration of the radiocarbon time scale: AD 1950-500 BC and 2500-6000 BC. *Radiocarbon* 35, 1-24.

Sweetman, P. D. 1976. An earthen enclosure at Monknewtown, Slane, Co. Meath. *Proceedings of the Royal Irish Academy* 76C, 25-72.

Sweetman, P. D. 1985. A Late Neolithic/Early Bronze Age pit circle at Newgrange, Co. Meath. *Proceedings of the Royal Irish Academy* 85C, 195-221.

Sweetman, P. D. 1987. Excavation of a Late Neolithic/Early Bronze Age site at Newgrange, Co. Meath. *Proceedings of the Royal Irish Academy* 87C, 283-98.

Taylor, J. J. 1970. Lunulae reconsidered. *Proceedings of the Prehistoric Society* 36, 38-81.

Treinen, F. 1970. Les poteries campaniformes en France. *Gallia Préhistoire* 13, 53-107, 263-332.

Verron, G. 1976. Acculturation et continuité en Normandie durant le Néolithique et les Ages de métaux. In S. J. De Laet (ed.), *loc. cit.*, 261-83.

Waals, J. D. van der and Glasbergen, W. 1955. Beaker types and their distribution in the Netherlands. *Palaeohistoria* 4, 5-46.

Waddell, J. 1991/2. The Irish Sea in prehistory. *Journal of Irish Archaeology* 6, 29-40.

Waldren, W. H. and Kennard, R. C. (eds). 1987. *Bell Beakers of the Western Mediterranean*. British Archaeological Reports, International Series 331. Oxford.

Wojciechowski, W. 1987. The Bell Beaker Culture in Southern Poland: Origin and Evolution. In W. H. Waldren and R. C. Kennard (eds), *loc. cit.*, 685-99.

Wolf, C. 1991. Die Chronologie der Schnurkeramik der Westschweiz. In Ch. Strahm (ed.), *loc. cit.*, 129-34.

Dendrochronology and the Chronology of the Irish Bronze Age

M. G. L. Baillie

Abstract

Dendrochronology offers the possibility to provide a precisely dated framework for the archaeology of the Bronze Age. By specifying dates at which human activity is well represented in the archaeological record and by identifying notable environmental events in the records of oak growth it is possible to make a start on the construction of that framework. This paper seeks to specify some of the marker dates associated with the Bronze Age in Ireland and to demonstrate that the dates themselves are represented in widely separated regions of the northern hemisphere. These observations suggest that at least some aspects of Irish Bronze Age chronology may be understandable in a much wider context.

Introduction

Radiocarbon dating is the most widely used chronometric method in archaeology. In the 1960s the radiocarbon method was calibrated when Suess (1970) derived conventional radiocarbon ages for known-age samples of bristlecone-pine wood derived from the long bristlecone chronology, constructed by Ferguson at Tucson (Ferguson 1969). As a direct result of the controversy associated with this original 'Suess' calibration – was it applicable in the Old World and were the short term variations, or 'wiggles' real or merely statistical artefacts – it was decided to explore the possibility of repeating the calibration exercise by constructing a long oak tree-ring chronology in Ireland; providing low-altitude, Old World wood samples for subsequent radiocarbon measurement. Thus, Jon Pilcher and myself, working with a series of research assistants, (including Jennifer Hillam, Vic Buckley and Dave Brown, among others) set out to build a six-thousand-year oak chronology. Following conventional wisdom, we overlapped the ring patterns from living trees to timbers from historic buildings, to archaeological samples and ultimately back into prehistoric, sub-fossil or bog oaks. It quickly became apparent that the secret of successful chronology construction lay in the production of well-replicated, robust 'site' chronologies.

Site chronologies could be many hundreds, occasionally more than one thousand, years in length and this had the effect of radically simplifying the chronology building process. As an example, the chronology of the last two millennia was not produced by finding a dozen successive overlaps between 250-year oak ring patterns, rather it required only four robust 'site' units and the consolidation of three key overlaps. The main units were the Teeshan chronology (13 BC to AD 896), the Dublin chronology (AD 855 to AD 1306), the Hillsborough/Coagh/Gloverstown chronology (AD 1360 to AD 1716) and the modern oak chronology (AD 1649 to present); working out the linkages between these robust units occupied most of the 1970s (Baillie 1982). A similar approach was taken to the construction of the long sub-fossil oak chronology. In total some thousands of oaks of all ages were sampled to provide the necessary building blocks. In the end only some 1500 individual ring patterns were required to produce the 7272-year Belfast chronology announced in 1984 (Pilcher *et al.* 1984).

Although the Irish long chronology is capable of standing alone as an internally replicated chronology unit, it is important to recognise that the work was not carried out in isolation. While the Irish chronology was being constructed, workers in Germany (at Köln, Stuttgart and Göttingen) were also building oak chronologies. By 1984 they had also produced at least one independent chronology back to 4000 BC (Leuschner and Delorme 1984). The existence of the independent Irish and German chronologies allowed a final level of checking, namely tertiary replication – replication between the results of totally independent workers. It was possible to demonstrate significant cross linkages from the Irish to the Germany chronology, step-wise via long sections of English chronology. In other words, we can date sections of English oak chronology independently against either Irish or German chronologies and obtain the same dating. This replication underpins all oak dendrochronology in northern Europe. If anyone wishes to contest these chronologies – if an attempt is made to move one of them – all of them must be moved!

This brief survey documents the construction of the long tree-ring chronologies which represent the underlying chronological background for this paper. With a continuous year-by-year record of mean oak growth for Ireland for over seven millennia, it has been possible to date some archaeological oak timbers directly; thus some calendrical dates have been introduced into the archaeological record. In addition it has been possible to identify a series of natural events, mostly catastrophic downturns in tree-growth, which effectively break up time and introduce chronological 'marker' horizons (Baillie 1991). Some of this information is brought together here to introduce a firm chronological backdrop to studies of the Bronze Age in Ireland. It must also be remembered that the Irish tree-ring work (and that of Bernd Becker in Germany) provided the precisely-dated wood samples for the high-precision calibration of the radiocarbon timescale (work conducted in Belfast by Gordon Pearson and in Seattle by Minze Stuiver (Pearson and Stuiver 1986; Stuiver and Pearson 1986)). These calibration results allow the best available conversion of raw radiocarbon dates into estimates of real age. Obviously, both in its own right, and as the standard which underpins radiocarbon calibration, dendrochronology has to be at the forefront of discussions of chronology relating to the Bronze Age.

The Bronze Age 2354 BC to 430 BC

The substance of this paper is to provide a series of real, historical-quality dates which serve to delineate the two millennia which encompass the Bronze Age in Ireland. These dates serve as a starting point for chronological refinement and are merely the first dates to make themselves apparent from dendrochronological study (it has to be remembered that precisely dated tree-ring chronologies have only been available in Europe since the early 1980s). As time goes on, more archaeological dates will become available across Europe; it will eventually be possible to make comparisons from Ireland to Anatolia and from Scandinavia to Northern Italy. In addition, a more refined understanding of environmental conditions will become available to complete the backdrop for the study of all human activity.

The dates are not listed in chronological order, but in an order which attempts to make clear how they have become apparent. Most have already been published in various forms, but this article draws

them together and attempts to provide a wider setting.

948 BC

One considerable advantage of dendrochronology is that both archaeological dates and environmental information can be derived from the same tree-ring data sets. Thus, both types of information are dated with the same resolution and direct comparisons can be made between the two. As an example, we can observe a severe reduction in the number of surviving bog oaks from the 10th century BC (see Fig. 14).

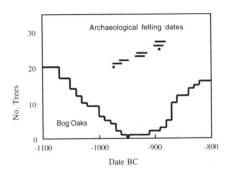

Fig. 14. The notable depletion in Irish bog oaks in the 10th century BC, plotted with the felling dates (or ranges) of a cluster of archaeological sites and timbers.

These natural samples are drawn from a number of bog locations in the north of Ireland, so this is not simply a local phenomenon. Just at the time of the reduction in bog oaks we have a whole cluster of archaeological structures providing dendrochronological dates. This clustering was apparent even in the mid-1980s (Baillie 1985) and now consists of more than twice as many sites (the dates relate to a spectrum of objects and structures from trackways and proto-crannogs to dug-out boats). It really isn't clear just what the full significance of this is. It could be that environmental pressure, such as increased wetness, caused oaks to have a difficult time on bog surfaces and at the same time people were building structures in contexts where they survive for us to study – so it might be a wet period. However, an alternative hypothesis is that the juxtaposition of archaeological construction with reduced bog trees might have been due to people cutting down the trees – a possible sign of increased population pressure and favourable environmental conditions. Obviously, we would like to know the answers, though this example with alternative explanations shows just how difficult resolution may be. What is clear is that the available evidence focuses attention on the 10th century BC and the available observations demand an explanation.

On the other hand, it is apparent from this dating exercise that we have an isolated episode of archaeological activity showing up in the record of surviving timbers. The next cluster of archaeological tree-ring dates is not until the 2nd century BC. Earlier, we have another cluster between 1520 BC and 1480 BC. So, the act of dating a series of archaeological oak structures, collected essentially at random, is a non-random distribution of tree-ring dates; we now know that there is something significant about the later 10th century BC and the period just around 1500 BC.

Widespread environmental events

In 1984 LaMarche and Hirschboeck pointed out a significant frost-ring event in American bristlecone pines in the annual growth ring for 1627 BC and suggested that (a) this probably related to the effects of a major volcanic eruption and (b) that eruption might be Santorini (Thera) in the Aegean. Subsequently, extremely narrow growth rings were observed in Irish bog oaks in the 1620s BC with the event starting in 1628 BC. So Irish oaks were affected at the same time as the bristlecone pines.

Following up this observation, of something going on in 1628 BC, it was discovered that a series of these 'narrowest ring' events in the Irish oak record coincided with a series of strong acid layers in the Greenland icecap (Baillie and Munro 1988). Acid in Greenland ice is the smoking gun of large explosive volcanic eruptions. These coincidences indicated for the first time that the prehistoric Irish trees were responding to the environmental effects of large volcanic eruptions. Now obviously this was an interesting finding. (People on this island do not consider themselves to be in the front line of volcanic activity – the finding that in the past trees had been severely affected by the environmental downturns associated with large explosive eruptions raises many questions about what may have happened to human populations at those same times.) For the purposes of this paper we can isolate four environmental events, three of which are apparently related to volcanic activity.

2345 BC

The earliest of the four takes place at a time which must be very close to the beginning of the Bronze Age in Ireland. This is the so-called Hekla 4 volcanic eruption. It shows up as an extremely narrow band of rings, beginning in 2354 BC and reaching lowest

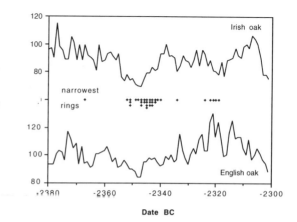

Fig. 15. Irish and English bog oak chronologies showing the growth reductions around 2350 BC. It is of interest that the major cluster of 'narrowest rings' (centred on 2345 BC in oaks from south of Lough Neagh) fall at a time when the majority of trees are already recovering.

growth – the narrowest rings – at 2345 BC (Fig. 15). It is apparent that trees in Lancashire also show reduced growth at the same time, reinforcing the view that this is a widespread event. While the event was very apparent in the ring-width patterns, it was a surprise to discover a highly unusual growth defect in one of the samples from the Motorway complex (trees which grew in the fenlands just to the south of Lough Neagh). The sample shows a change in the character of growth, from normal ring porous to diffuse porous – an anomaly which lasts for about a decade and which could be consistent with the tree being inundated. So, there is clear evidence for an environmental event affecting oak growth generally and trees near Lough Neagh specifically. However, the evidence in this case is not limited to the oaks themselves.

Tephrochronology involves the identification and dating of microscopic volcanic glass shards and their use as marker horizons in ancient deposits. Recent work has indicated that Hekla 4 tephra, which can be specifically identified to that Icelandic volcano on chemical grounds, is found in numerous Irish peat bogs at 2310 ± 20 cal BC (Pilcher *et al.* forthcoming). The dating exercise used a series of high-precision radiocarbon measurements on stratified peats across the Hekla 4 layer and it is likely that the date given above is correct in absolute terms to within a half century. So the implication may well be that the narrow growth rings and associated tree-ring effects after 2354 BC are directly due to the environmental effects of Hekla 4.

Now that raises interesting questions. Because the radiocarbon dates associated with this event would be almost indistinguishable from radiocarbon dates for the earliest section of the Beaker period, it becomes possible to ask if the Hekla 4 event was in any way related to the arrival of the first metal users in Ireland? It is also known that pine pollen disappears from pollen spectra in the north of Ireland just a few centimetres above this event in most pollen diagrams (Hall *et al.* 1994). Is it possible that the demise of pine is linked to the arrival of those same metal-using people? We may be beginning to see the start of the Bronze Age in some sort of wider context, involving a package of

(a) environmental events

(b) the arrival of at least a new technology and

(c) the disappearance of a species (pine) which had been present in Ireland for millennia.

This sort of package is suggestive that humans were almost certainly involved in the demise of pine trees in Ireland. However, irrespective of the pine issue, it is clear that some interesting things took place in the 24th century BC. The evidence is indelible and is not going to go away. I would suggest that this is a classic 'marker date' i.e. a date which will show up on a regular basis in studies of various kinds.

It has to be noted that Warner (1990) sees the 2354 BC to 2345 BC event as very close to one of only four major disasters recorded in the *Anno Mundi* section of the Irish Annals. One of these references bears the date AM 2820 (which Warner interprets as '2380 BC') and says 'Nine thousand . . . died in one week. Ireland was thirty years waste' (i.e. to 2350 'BC'). A coincidence perhaps? In fact, although Warner draws attention to the human aspect of catastrophe in the Annals, it transpires that things are even more curious. The Annals go on to say that in 'about AM 2859 and after' (i.e. '2341 BC' and after) 'lakes erupted'. Of course we know that these ancient annals have no basis in fact – or do they? Incredibly, there is an even more bizarre coincidence.

While we are talking about innundation of oaks at the south of Lough Neagh (in Co. Armagh) in the period 2354 BC to 2345 BC (dated by totally independent dendrochronology), an earlier scholar with Armagh connections, namely Archbishop Ussher, worked out the date of the biblical Flood to be 2349 BC (see King James Bible)! There are several things which could be said about these coincidences, two of which seem appropriate. The first is a question: did the scholars who worked up the *Anno Mundi* section of the Irish Annals in fact use the same Biblical sources as Ussher to derive their chronology? Indeed, is it possible that the various scholars came into direct contact somewhere in Donegal? If they did, then the prehistoric sections of the Annals are probably as compromised as critics suggest. The second point is merely amusing; maybe all those aged farmers who said the bog oaks were 'all washed down in The Flood' weren't so completely wrong after all.

430 BC

If 2354 BC defines a date at, or close to, the beginning of the Bronze Age, then 430 BC can be used to mark a date not far from its end. This date was not discovered as part of the volcanic story but came about as follows. In the early 1990s a classical research student from New Zealand enquired about environmental change in Greece in the 4th and 5th centuries BC. The answer, of course, was that very little is known about the climate of those centuries and no relevant dendrochronological or dendroclimatological reconstruction had been attempted within the Mediterranean area. However, attention having been drawn to this time window, it was possible to make some observations on the basis of the radiocarbon calibration work cited above. In the middle of the first millennium BC there is a major radiocarbon anomaly. Just at 400 BC on the tree-ring scale we observe a very rapid enrichment of radiocarbon activity in the Belfast measurements (and in the independent Seattle calibration measurements on German oak (Stuiver and Becker 1986)). In lay terms, just at 400 BC radiocarbon dates suddenly become younger; jumping from 2445 ± 18 BP to 2280 ± 15 between 410 BC and 390 BC (Pearson *et al.* 1986). This radiocarbon enrichment is interesting because, for the radiocarbon dates to become rapidly *younger*, more radiocarbon must have been produced in a relatively short time. For *more* radiocarbon to be produced, more cosmic radiation must reach the upper atmosphere of the earth – for that to happen, it is almost certain that the Sun has to become quiet and the solar wind has to 'drop off'. Physicists interested in understanding Sun–Earth relationships would automatically be interested in trying to observe if around this period, *c.* 400 BC, there were any clear environmental effects on planet Earth.

Fig. 16 shows graphically what is happening in a European oak chronology, and in an independent American bristlecone-pine chronology, across the 400 BC period (because of the nature of dendrochronology, we can look at chronologies from different parts of the world in precise time control). It is quite clear that there is an episode of growth enhancement in both species from around 460 BC until 430 BC. Suddenly, between 430 and 420 BC both species show a dramatic growth reduction. This observation is very surprising for several reasons. First, there is no expectation that trees growing 10,000 km apart *should* show similar ring width characteristics. Second, these trees are of different species and, while the oaks grow at low altitude, the bristlecone pines grow above 3000 m. For these chronologies to show such similar responses implies a very widespread environmental effect.

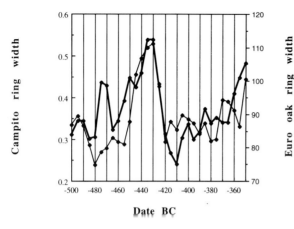

Fig. 16. The curious growth surge in both European oaks (heavy line) and American bristlecone pines from Campito Mountain from 460 BC to 430 BC, and the synchronous abrupt decline in ring width in the 420s BC shortly before a significant radiocarbon enrichment around 400 BC.

So, at the very least it can be said that there is a widespread effect in northern hemisphere trees within a few decades of the inferred 'quiet Sun' event. The case for direct cause and effect is not proven, but it seems clear that towards the end of the 5th century BC something significant is going on. It would seem that 430, the year after which this notable reduction in ring width takes place, is as good a fixed point to delimit the end of the Bronze Age as 2354 BC was to delimit its beginning. It is perhaps worth noting that in ancient history the Peloponnesian wars were taking place at just this time and the plague of Athens dates to 430 BC.

So Irish dendrochronology has produced three fixed dates, at 2345 BC, 948 BC and 430 BC, which help to provide the starting point for tightening up Bronze Age chronology. To these we can add the cluster of archaeological dates which occur around 1500 BC. To complete the framework we can add additional information on the volcanic events at 1628 BC and 1159 BC. It can then be demonstrated how these dates may well fit into a wider pattern which could force an overall tightening of world chronology.

1628 BC

The interest in the 1628 BC event was triggered by the possibility that it might relate to the Bronze Age eruption of Thera in the Aegean. In fact, whether or not Thera is involved, the event is real and its effects are widespread. We have already noted the frost ring event in bristlecones in 1627 BC and the narrowest ring event in Irish oaks. It is also possible to demonstrate clear signs of reduced growth in the only English chronology covering the period, and in several

German chronologies (Baillie 1990). It can definitely be stated that there was a major volcanic eruption which had effects around the northern hemisphere in 1628 BC and succeeding years.

More recently, workers in Tucson have identified frost-ring effects in two, new, foxtail-pine chronologies from the Sierra Nevada (Caprio and Baisan, pers. comm. 1993), while in Anatolia an anomalous growth surge in drought regime trees has now been observed at a date within 25 years of 1640 BC. As will be noted below, other evidence makes it virtually certain that this is the same event as that observed in 1628 BC in Irish, English and German oaks. It is also increasingly likely that this 1628 BC volcano was Thera, in the Aegean.

Given the widespread nature of this environmental event it would be surprising if it had *no* effect on the Bronze Age human population of Ireland.

1150 BC

The other event in the Irish oaks, and the one which stands out most clearly in the bog oak record, spans 1150 BC. This is a protracted event which starts in 1159 BC and lasts for 18 years, many trees recovering from 1141 BC. Now, understanding the nature of such tree-ring effects is difficult. For example, archaeological timbers which grew across this period do not show the 18-year effect so dramatically, however most are affected in some way and in extreme cases it is clear from reaction-wood that trees were blown over while others were defoliated. What is not in doubt is that the 12th century BC was an interesting period in ancient history – it marks among other things the beginning of the Greek Dark Age *c.* 1200 to *c.* 800 BC – and falls close to the beginning of the Third Intermediate Period in Egypt. There is a case for asking just what was going on.

Again there is quite a bit of evidence for environmental change and a strong case for the involvement of volcanoes, possibly including at least one 'local' Icelandic volcano, in this case Hekla 3 (Baillie 1989a). However, this brings me to an important point about the study of ancient chronology. If we want to understand the nature of these events in detail we need to know what was happening in the archaeological record, in Ireland and elsewhere, to complement the information from the tree-rings. Here we run into an international problem. It is incredibly difficult to tie down the calendrical dates of archaeological sites other than those which produce timbers for dendrochronological dating.

These difficulties are well illustrated by results from recent excavations in Ireland where hill forts are providing dating evidence which places them somewhere at the end of the 2nd millennium BC.

Consider the following scenario:

(a) Irish oaks indicate that something unpleasant happened around 1150 BC.

(b) We find some Irish hill forts dating to this general period of the Bronze Age.

It seems reasonable to postulate that the construction of at least some hill forts in Ireland may have been a direct response to the environmental effects of the mid-12th century. In order to test that postulation it would be necessary to date the construction and occupation of some hill forts very exactly. However, the difficulty in dating any prehistoric archaeological site (including hill forts) has already been noted.

Let us consider the case of Haughey's Fort, near Navan in Co. Armagh, excavated by Jim Mallory. This hill fort is delineated by three massive concentric ditches. Constructing this fort was a very considerable undertaking. If we look at the radiocarbon dates from the initial Haughey's Fort excavations we see that all ten dates cluster within 75 radiocarbon years - between 2923±50 BP and 2850±20 BP (Mallory 1991); we should note in this case what a good method radiocarbon is. Unfortunately, in order to convert these dates to estimates of real age they have to be calibrated and it is here that difficulties are experienced. The calibration curve is relatively flat at this period and as has been pointed out by Warner in a detailed analysis of the dates:

> . . . occupation at Haughey's Fort began before about 1080 BC and ended after about 1100 BC. The minimum period of occupation was around or slightly after 1100 BC (within the century after Hekla 3). The occupation span could have been up to 150 years anywhere between about 1250 and 950 BC (with the proviso that the span should include 1100 BC) . . . Haughey's Fort dates therefore to around 1100 BC and perhaps, though we doubt it, into the late 13th or the early 10th centuries (Warner 1994, 69).

So, although the site could have been constructed just after 1150 BC, it could also have been constructed and occupied anywhere between 1250 BC and 950 BC. This evidence makes it difficult to test the postulation that Haughey's Fort was constructed and occupied just after 1150 BC (we should not forget that there is a piece of oak from the bottom of the inner ditch at Haughey's Fort which has a highly qualified 'possible' dendro-date of '1150-1116 BC or later' (Baillie and Brown 1991)).

However, for the sake of argument, let us hypothesise that Haughey's Fort was constructed and occupied in the half-century following 1150 BC. The

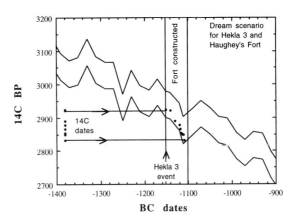

Fig. 17. The 'dream scenario' wherein the ten radiocarbon dates from Haughey's Fort, Co. Armagh, can be shown to be *not inconsistent with* construction and occupation of the fort in the half-century following the so-called Hekla 3 environmental event 1159-1141 BC.

hypothesis itself is perfectly reasonable given that we know there was an environmental downturn centred on 1150 BC which may have affected the whole northern hemisphere; insular north-west Europe may well have been significantly affected. In human terms, populations may have been forced to move from more marginal land to areas of better soil; there may have been population pressure; there may have been a real stimulus for the construction of massive fortified settlement by those who could control populations and resources - possibly those who could control populations through resources. On this hypothesis, Haughey's Fort (and Mooghaun with an embarrassingly similar radiocarbon date - Grogan and Condit 1994) may have been constructed at or just after the middle of the 12th century BC. Fig. 17 shows the 'dream scenario' with all the radiocarbon dates fitting the calibration curve in the second half of the 12th century BC. Now, of course, this dream scenario cannot be sustained in scientific terms, because, as pointed out above, an alternative explanation exists where the dates might be smeared through several centuries between 1250 BC and 950 BC. However, there are interesting ways of using English to cover such eventualities. It is possible to make the following statement which is avowedly true.

> The radiocarbon evidence from Haughey's Fort (and Mooghaun) is not inconsistent with the scenario that the 1150 BC environmental event caused the construction of massive fortified settlements in Ireland.

Obviously a statement containing a double negative is inherently weak. However, the tone of the statement is positive - aims at a solution - in comparison with the more grudging tone of a purist who might say 'the radiocarbon evidence doesn't support the scenario'. At least we now have a hypothesis for testing even though it is clear that we have a long way to go in chronological refinement before a definitive answer can be provided.

Future possibilities

One great advantage of dendrochronology, ice-core work, tephrochronology, etc. is that new evidence is coming on line all the time. For example, as noted above, Peter Kuniholm, who is working on a long prehistoric tree-ring chronology for the eastern Mediterranean, has studied ring patterns from Anatolia across the 2nd millennium BC. The chronology has been tied down to within 25 years in real time using radiocarbon wiggle-matching techniques. He can now report that there are two notable positive growth anomalies which begin exactly 469 years apart and which fall in the later-17th and mid-12th centuries respectively (Kuniholm, Kromer and Manning, pers. comm. 1995). Readers will note that two of the environmental dates listed above, those at 1628 BC and 1159 BC, start exactly 469 years apart. It seems certain that cooler/wetter conditions in Anatolia foster growth in trees which normally experience severe summer drought; hence the positive growth anomalies in that area. Thus these Mediterranean observations concur with the evidence for climatic downturn seen in the Irish oaks.

To extend the picture, Fig. 18 shows a provisional temperature reconstruction for Fennoscandia for the bulk of the Bronze Age (after Briffa 1994). The chronology is not absolutely dated but is highly

constrained by radiocarbon evidence; the dates being supplied by Briffa. Reference to Fig. 18 shows how several of the events which have just been discussed fall in or around periods of significant temperature reduction in Fennoscandia. I would point out particularly the nineteen year gap in the 12th century BC. (The gap is known to be 19 years because a Finnish chronology bridges the period and specifies the gap length.)

These Anatolian and Fennoscandian records typify the way in which our understanding of the past is beginning to improve. We are beginning to see the widespread nature of some events; we are beginning to see hints of the close juxtaposition of environmental change and some effects on human populations as witnessed through the archaeological record.

Wider considerations

Having suggested the significance of Fig. 18, it seems appropriate to look at an even wider context. Fig. 19 shows that both the Shang Dynasty in China and the New Kingdom in Egypt can (with minimal movement) be fitted to the dates of the Irish tree-ring events in the 17th and 12th centuries BC. (Traditional dates for the Shang are 1617-1122 BC, the New Kingdom 1570-1085 BC.) It is tempting to suggest that the same hemispheric environmental events delimit these great episodes of civilisation. Certainly this hypothesis cannot be lightly dismissed for the simple reason that experts on both civilisations admit that the dynasties themselves are not precisely dated (Kitchen 1991; Chang 1980), i.e. there is nothing to stop these robust dynasties conforming to the Irish tree-ring dates (see Baillie 1989b). Chronologically, the bottom line is this. There is a finite possibility that a series of extremely widespread environmental events, which were caused apparently by explosive volcanic eruptions, may allow the unification of world chronology in the 2nd millennium BC. However, even if that turns out not to be the case; even if Briffa's Fennoscandian chronology, when independently dated, *fails* to show the same events as the Irish oak chronology; even if the Shang Dynasty and the Egyptian New Kingdom *fail* to conform to the 1628 BC and 1159 BC events, the very act of proving those failures will have improved Bronze Age chronology immeasurably. What is not in doubt is the fact that all Bronze Age studies in Ireland will ultimately have to fit around the marker dates 2354 BC; 1628 BC; 1159 BC; 948 BC and 430 BC.

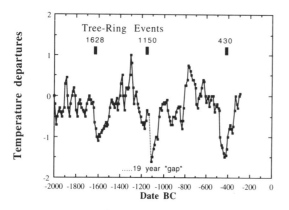

Fig. 18. Three of the Irish tree-ring marker dates, mentioned in the text, plotted with a new Fennoscandian temperature reconstruction by Briffa (1994). Note (a) that the Fennoscandian chronology is floating by up to ± 50 years and (b) the 19-year gap in the Fennoscandian chronology in the 12th century BC (cf. the 18-year narrow band in the Irish oaks).

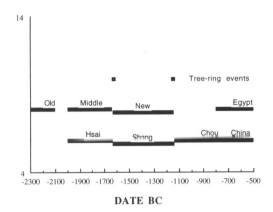

Fig. 19. The two Irish narrowest-ring events at 1628 BC and 1159 BC plotted with the main sections of the Egyptian and Chinese dynastic chronologies. For the purposes of this figure the Egyptian New Kingdom has been moved back in time by 70 years; the Chinese Shang dynasty back by 13 years.

Acknowledgements

This research was in part supported by the EC Environment Research Programme (contract: EV5V-CT94-0500, Climatology and Natural Hazards). The author wishes to thank Richard Warner for kindly reading an earlier version of this paper at the Dublin Bronze Age Conference 21 April 1995 and for useful discussions on many of the issues dealt with in the paper.

References

Baillie, M. G. L. 1982. *Tree-Ring Dating and Archaeology.* London.

Baillie, M. G. L. 1985. Dendrochronology and Radiocarbon Calibration. *Ulster Journal of Archaeology* 48, 11-23.

Baillie, M. G. L. 1989a. Hekla 3 - just how big was it? *Endeavour* 13, No. 2, 78-81.

Baillie, M. G. L. 1989b. Do Irish Bog Oaks Date the Shang Dynasty? *Current Archaeology* 117, 310-13.

Baillie, M. G. L. 1990. Irish Tree-Rings and an Event in 1628 BC. In D. A. Hardy (ed.), *Thera and the Aegean World III* Vol. 3, The Thera Foundation, London, 160-6.

Baillie, M. G. L. 1991. Marking in Marker Dates; towards an archaeology with historical precision. *World Archaeology* 23, 233-43.

Baillie, M. G. L. and Brown, D. M. 1991. A Dendro-date from Haughey's Fort? *Emania* 8, 39-40.

Baillie, M. G. L. and Munro, M. A. R. 1988. Irish tree-rings, Santorini and volcanic dust veils. *Nature* 332, 344-6.

Briffa, K. R. 1994. Mid and late Holocene climate change: evidence from tree-growth in northern Fennoscandia. In B. M. Funnell and R. L. F. Kay (eds), *Palaeoclimate of the Last Glacial/Interglacial Cycle.* Special Publication no. 94/2, NERC, London, 61-5.

Chang, K-C, 1980. *Shang Civilization.* London.

Ferguson, C. W. 1969. A 7104-Year Annual Tree-Ring Chronology for Bristlecone Pine, Pinus Aristata, from the White Mountains, California. *Tree-Ring Bulletin* 29, 2-29.

Grogan, E. and Condit, T. 1994. New hillfort date gives clue to Late Bronze Age. *Archaeology Ireland* 8 (2), 7.

Hall, V. A., Pilcher, J. R. and McCormac, F. G. 1994. Icelandic volcanic ash and the mid-Holocene Scots pine (*Pinus sylvestris*) decline in the North of Ireland; no correlation. *The Holocene* 4, 79-83.

Kitchen, K. A. 1991. The Chronology of Ancient Egypt. *World Archaeology* 23, 201-8.

LaMarche, V. C. Jr and Hirschboeck, K. K. 1984. Frost Rings in Trees as Records of Major Volcanic Eruptions. *Nature* 307, 121-6.

Leuschner, von H. H. and Delorme, A. 1984. Verlangerung der Göttinger Eichenjahrringchronologien für Nord- und Suddeutschland bis zum Jahr 4008 v. Chr. *Forstarchiv* 55, 1-4.

Mallory, J. P. 1991. Further dates for Haughey's Fort. *Emania* 9, 64-5.

Pearson, G. W., Pilcher, J. R., Baillie, M. G. L., Corbett, D. M. and Qua, F. 1986. High-Precision 14-C Measurement of Irish Oaks to Show the Natural 14-C Variations from AD 1840 to 5210 BC. *Radiocarbon* 28, 911-34.

Pearson, G. W. and Stuiver, M. 1986. High-Precision Calibration of the Radiocarbon Time Scale, 500-2500 BC. *Radiocarbon* 28, 839-62.

Pilcher, J. R., Baillie, M. G. L., Schmidt, B. and Becker, B. 1984. A 7272-Year Tree-Ring Chronology for Western Europe. *Nature* 312, 150-2.

Pilcher, J. R., Hall, V. A. and McCormac, F. G. (in press). Dates of Holocene Icelandic volcanic eruptions from tephra layers in Irish peats. *The Holocene.*

Stuiver, M. and Becker, B. 1986. High-Precision Decadal Calibration of the Radiocarbon Time Scale, AD 1950-2500 BC. *Radiocarbon* 28, 863-910.

Stuiver, M. and Pearson, G. W. 1986. High-Precision Calibration of the Radiocarbon Timescale AD 1950-500 BC. *Radiocarbon* 28, 805-38.

Suess, H. E. 1970. Bristlecone Pine Calibration of the Radiocarbon Timescale from 5200 BC to the Present. In Olsson, I. U. (ed.), *Radiocarbon Variations and Absolute Chronology*, 303-9. New York.

Warner, R. B. 1990. The 'Prehistoric' Irish Annals: Fable or History. *Archaeology Ireland* 4 (1), 30-3.

Warner, R. B. 1994. Emania Varia I. *Emania* 12, 66-72.

Ross Island and the Origins of Irish-British Metallurgy

William O'Brien

Abstract

The arrival of copper-bronze metallurgy was an important development, both in economic and social terms, in the Neolithic to Bronze Age transition in Ireland. The rapid spread of the new technology owed much to the availability of raw material, with the result that Ireland emerged as one of the most prolific metal producers in Bronze Age Europe. This paper examines the appearance of the first copper objects in Ireland during the final Neolithic period, c. 2500-2000 BC, with particular emphasis on the source of that metal. Analytical studies have long hinted at an early focus of production in Munster where early copper axe forms and hoard deposits have been found. An important source of early copper metal has recently been identified at Ross Island, Killarney, where the discovery of early Beaker pottery offers a new insight into the origins of Irish metallurgy.

Metal is often regarded as the defining feature of the Bronze Age, a period of prehistory first conceived by 19th-century antiquarians as a technological leap forward in human progress. The Bronze Age in Europe was marked by a widespread adoption of copper-alloy metallurgy after 2000 BC, which followed on from an earlier use of copper in the Neolithic, extending back in some regions to the fourth millennium BC. The appearance of metal has always been considered important in the social and economic development of prehistoric peoples in Europe. While the new technology did ultimately lead to more efficient tool-kits in activities as diverse as agriculture and warfare, the earliest use of metal cannot be seen in solely utilitarian terms. It is widely acknowledged that metal played an important social role for human societies undergoing change towards the end of the Stone Age.

Early opinion on the origin of European metallurgy focused on one centre of innovation, the Near East, from where the new technology spread out to the 'barbarian' peoples of Europe. Through radiocarbon dating we now know that metallurgy was independently developed in the Balkans and Iberia as early as 4000 BC. Copper axes were circulating in northern Europe, in firmly Neolithic contexts, by the fourth millennium BC (Randsborg 1979). While similar examples may have reached Ireland and Britain as early as 3000 BC, metallurgy - the ability to apply heat to the reduction of copper minerals and make metal - does not appear in this part of Europe until possibly as late as 2500 BC. While late in European terms, Ireland was to emerge as a prolific metal producer in the Bronze Age, a development most commentators

attribute to an obvious availability of copper ore sources.

The origins of Irish metallurgy have long been debated, assuming considerable significance for Bronze Age researchers in Britain because of supposed connections with the earliest use of metal on that island. Research has centred on typological and scientific studies of the relevant copper and bronze objects, in particular the all-important copper axe horizon. These studies identified an early focus of production in Munster where there is a high recovery of early copper axe forms and hoard deposits. This copper axe production has been linked to a distinctive metal composition, believed to derive from arsenical copper deposits in the Cork-Kerry region. One such source appears to have been Ross Island, Killarney, where copper mining in the period 2400-2000 BC has recently been correlated with users of early Beaker pottery. This paper will explore the technological implications of the Ross Island discovery for our understanding of the earliest copper metallurgy in both Ireland and Britain.

Diffusion or Independent Development?

As with the study of megalithic tombs, the spread of metallurgy has often been regarded as the product of a single historical process, linked to the movements of a particular ethnic group from a single region of origin. In Atlantic Europe, much attention in this regard has focused on metal objects associated with the circulation of Beaker pottery, with the 'Beaker Folk' as one of the prime movers in the early west European metallurgy. Scholars are still divided as to the social significance of Beaker material culture and whether innovations like metallurgy should be linked to the migration of ethnic groups or to the small-scale movement of people, ideas and objects through trade and other exchange mechanisms.

Copper-bronze metallurgy is a complex technology in terms of raw material supply, ore reduction and metal fabrication. It demands an ability to locate and extract mineral ores, to control furnace processes often at high temperatures and, in many cases, to articulate long-distance trade-exchange networks to procure raw materials like tin. Not surprisingly, the introduction of metallurgy in many regions of Europe has been linked to external stimulus, yet in an effort to link the diffusion of this technology to the movement of one or more groups of 'people', scholars may have underestimated the potential for innovation which existed within indigenous Late Neolithic societies for innovation. Was the development of metallurgy totally beyond those societies and their immediate descendants who built the great megalithic tombs of Atlantic Europe, who had some 2000 years of experience in ceramic technology and who engaged in long-distance exchange for hard rocks and other exotic materials in the Late Neolithic period? Clearly we must view the arrival of the first metal objects to Ireland against a background of widespread contact between Stone Age peoples living on the western fringe of Europe in the early third millennium BC.

At present, there is little support for an independent *invention* of metallurgy in Ireland or Britain. In the absence of any significant supply or use of native (naturally occurring pure) copper, it is clear that the development of metallurgy in these two islands must have followed a different course than that evident in the Near East. While invention seems unlikely, it may be possible to talk in terms of an independent *development* of metallurgy once the *idea* was introduced (see Needham 1979 for discussion on possible mechanisms behind the introduction of metallurgy to Britain and Ireland). Most commentators in the past have favoured outside stimulation in the transmission of this complex technology to explain why metallurgy rapidly took off in Ireland and at such an apparently sophisticated level. At the same time, it would be premature to rule out the possibility that native peoples could have independently developed the technology once exposed to the idea abroad.

This question of diffusion versus independent discovery has recently been considered by Paul Craddock who argues that the earliest extractive metallurgy in regions like Ireland and Britain consisted of a primitive, poorly reducing, non-slagging technology. This technology was of a type developed independently by the earliest metal-producing cultures in different parts of Europe (Craddock 1995). The discontinuous spread of this new technology resulted mainly from the uneven spread of copper ore sources, with each region having to independently develop its own metallurgical expertise. The stylistic similarity of early metal artefacts over much of Europe suggests that these developments were not carried out in total isolation and that, in effect, we are looking at the spread of an idea through the movement of objects. Craddock goes on to conclude:

> The evidence, tentative though it is, and probably always will be, suggests that the working of metalliferous deposits was developed locally, often by people who did not realise the full potential of the resources they had to hand for centuries, even millennia. They evolved primitive extractive processes that had long been abandoned in more recent advanced parts of the world. The isolation may not have been total, thus the more advanced regions may have unwittingly promoted the exploitation of metals in new areas, not by deliberate prospection, but by the metal artefacts themselves as the potent, if mute, ambassadors for the new material (Craddock 1995, 144-5).

This interpretation is directly opposed to a widely held view that metallurgy was first introduced into Britain and Ireland by Beaker-using immigrants from the Continent. Instead of a search for metal by conquistador-like 'Beaker Folk', the initiative here is given to the indigenous inhabitants of these two islands and their contacts with metal-using groups on the Continent. At issue is the significance we attach to the movement of Beaker pottery and related material along Atlantic Europe in the third millennium BC.

Who were Ireland's first metallurgists?

This particular question has long taxed Irish prehistorians and was the focus of much debate in the Fifth Atlantic Colloquium meeting, held in Dublin in 1978. Discussion here centred on a concern with geographical origins and cultural identity (Ryan 1979). A subsequent review (Sheridan 1983) sought to explore some processual aspects of this earliest metallurgy, namely why this innovation was adopted and what social function metal played in these Final Neolithic societies. With strong Beaker connections, this is indeed a fertile ground for new theoretical

Pl. 1. An early metal hoard from Knocknagur, Co. Galway. This deposit contains copper axe forms considered typical of the earliest Beaker-inspired metal production in Ireland (Courtesy National Museum of Ireland).

approaches, however progress has been hampered by long-standing problems of context and chronology.

The study of the earliest metallurgy in Ireland has long been object-oriented, focused on some 3000 or so copper, bronze and gold artefacts from the period 2500-1500 BC. The copper-bronze production is marked by a limited number of types, principally axeheads, halberds and daggers, whose stylistic development in this period can be followed through typology (Burgess 1979; 1980). The background to the discovery of these objects is well known (Harbison 1969; 1979), with the great majority lacking secure archaeological contexts, helpful associations or radiocarbon dates. There are virtually no settlements in Ireland of the Final Neolithic/Early Bronze Age period which allow us to view the production, consumption and deposition of this rich metalwork record. The poor quality of this data-base is a particular problem when assessing the earliest stages of metal use on this island.

For the latter, the focus of research has long centred on the copper axe horizon which marks the earliest phase of large-scale metal production. Through typology and associations, scholars like Humphrey Case, Colin Burgess, Peter Harbison and Peter Northover have traced three stages in the early development of Irish metallurgy, namely:

1. The introduction of copper metallurgy from the Continent, marked by the appearance of trapezoidal thick-butted copper axes which began to be produced here. These earliest copper axe forms are typified by the example present in the Castletownroche hoard from Co. Cork (Burgess Stage 1).

2. Metallurgy is quickly adopted with the emergence of an insular form of the Castletownroche series axes, namely the curved-sided Lough Ravel series. Case (1966) referred to this stage as an Impact Phase, when Irish metallurgy was strongly influenced by Continental Beaker technology ultimately rooted in central Europe. This influence is apparent in the appearance of the thin butted copper axe (Type Growtown) and tanged copper knives. The examples contained in the Knocknagur hoard from Co. Galway (Pl. 1) are typical of this early horizon of insular production (Burgess Stage 2).

3. Development of a new form of copper axe with curved sides and thin butt (Type Ballybeg), and the introduction of halberds and rivet-notched knives. The Frankford hoard from Co. Offaly is the type-find from this phase (Burgess Stage 3).

The development of the copper axe is finally overtaken some time between 2200 and 2000 BC with the appearance and rapid adoption of tin-bronze, as seen in the distribution of Killaha-Migdale axes across Ireland and Britain (Burgess Stage 4). It is thus possible to distinguish an early use of unalloyed copper prior to 2200 BC, though this is generally regarded as the introductory phase of the Early Bronze Age and not as a distinct Copper Age or Chalcolithic horizon (see Brindley, this volume).

Case (1966) believes that the Knocknagur and Frankford stages of the copper axe horizon can be securely linked to his Impact Phase of early Irish metallurgy, when the influence of Continental technology was very strong and probably linked to the arrival of Beaker metallurgists. This Beaker contribution to copper axe production in Ireland is evident through dagger connections with Beaker burials in southern Britain. In terms of origins, the difficulty lies with the affinities of what he terms the Archaic Phase, namely the hypothetical Castletownroche stage marked by the appearance and production of trapezoidal copper axes of Continental type in Ireland. Trapezoidal copper axes are widely known across Europe in both Beaker and pre-Beaker contexts and their influence in the earliest stage of Irish metallurgy raises the possibility of pre-Beaker metallurgy here (Sheridan 1983). While the Irish trapezoidal axe form may be paralleled on the Continent, no examples made from imported metal have been identified in Ireland. The Irish axes from this stage are few in number and cannot be reliably dated or linked to a precise Continental origin.

As well as the study of artefact form and distribution, scientific analysis of metal compositions has played an important role in our understanding of the earliest Irish metallurgy. Various analytical programmes have addressed this area, beginning in the 1950s with the work of the Ancient Mining and Metallurgy Committee (Coghlan and Case 1957; Coghlan *et al.* 1963), and continuing with the Stuttgart (Junghans, Sangmeister and Schröder 1968), Oxford (Allen *et al.* 1970; Northover 1980; 1982) and British Museum (Craddock 1979) programmes in recent decades. This work began with the spectrographic analysis of some one hundred Early Bronze Age axeheads, daggers and halberds by Coghlan and Case, who identified what was believed to be a distinctive early Irish metal. They argued that this composition, so-called Group 1 metal marked by high levels of arsenic, antimony and silver, was derived from the *fahlerz* (tetrahedrite-tennantite) series of copper ores.

A programme of ore analysis subsequently identified the copper deposits of Cork and Kerry as one possible source of this early metal type (Coghlan *et al.* 1963). Case (1966) linked the presence of arsenical copper ore in that region to the discovery of a large number of early copper axe forms and hoard deposits. Both Case and more recently Northover (1980; 1982) have argued that this Munster-based 'industry' was the primary source of early copper metal in Ireland, a supply which carried on into the earliest bronze-using period. This interpretation has recently been strengthened by the discovery of a Copper Age mine in Killarney, associated with both the exploitation of *fahlerz* copper ore and the users of early Beaker pottery.

Ross Island

The Ross Island early copper mine is located on the eastern shore of Lough Leane, the largest of the Killarney lakes in Co. Kerry. The site has a long history of mining, beginning in Final Neolithic/Copper Age times and concluding with large-scale industrial operations in the early 19th century AD. Of particular interest is the evidence for copper mining in the period 2400-2200 BC which can be linked to the use of early Beaker pottery in this site. The site is currently the subject of a multi-disciplinary research programme, established in University College, Galway, in 1992 and funded by the Office of Public Works through the Royal Irish Academy.

Mining in the 18-19th centuries at Ross Island uncovered a series of primitive 'Danes Mines', associated with the use of fire-setting and of stone hammers in rock extraction. While much of this record was subsequently destroyed, recent investigation has confirmed that a large cave-like opening and an underlying mine in the western part of this site are of Bronze Age date (Pl. 2). A similar age is suspected for primitive mine evidence associated with the 'Blue Hole', a large open-cut working in the Eastern Mine area. These mine workings are located in a copper-rich horizon of the Lower Carboniferous limestone associated with calcite veining.

The archaeological investigation at Ross Island is currently focused on a work camp site, located on a level escarpment immediately next to Bronze Age workings in what is known as the Western Mine area. Excavation here has uncovered spreads of crushed mineralised limestone, associated with stone hammers and anvil blocks. The foundation traces of at least four hut structures have been identified, together with animal bone food waste, sherds of Beaker pottery and a small quantity of worked flint. Of particular interest is the discovery of pit features connected with on-site metallurgy, the first such find from any early Irish or British copper mine.

Radiocarbon dates are now available for charcoal, wood and animal bone residues associated with primitive copper mining at Ross Island (Table 1). These point to an early phase of mining linked to the use of Beaker pottery in the period 2500-2000 BC. At present Ross Island is the oldest copper mine known in north-western Europe and the first metal source to be identified from the early Beaker copper-using phase. The chronology of this mine, its connection with the use of Beaker pottery, the type of metallurgy practised and the subsequent history of the copper produced are all highly relevant to any discussion on the origins of Irish–British metallurgy.

Chronology

Any consideration of the earliest copper-bronze metallurgy in Ireland must confront the absence of

Pl. 2. Beaker period copper mine at Ross Island, Killarney.

independent chronology for this rich artefact record. There are no radiocarbon dates or securely stratified contexts for either the copper axe horizon or the earliest bronze axes (Killaha series). Instead, scholars have been forced to rely on typological analysis and the study of hoard-grave associations to build a chronological framework (e.g. Harbison 1969; Burgess 1979, 1980). Relying largely on axe development and associations, these typologies provide a basic ordering of overlapping metalworking traditions which are sometimes referred to as 'industries'. In the case of the early copper axe horizon in Ireland, this sequence is tenuously linked to absolute chronology through dagger connections with the Beaker grave sequence in southern Britain (Burgess 1980, figs. 1-3).

Recent radiocarbon results from Ross Island provide the first independent dating evidence for metal production in Ireland in the Final Neolithic/copper-using period (Table 1). The earliest mining identified in this site centres on 3900-3800 BP (2500-2200 BC; five determinations), continuing down to 3600 BP (2200-1800 BC; four determinations). Ross Island is significantly earlier than the operations on Mount Gabriel, Co. Cork which date to the latter part of the

Early Bronze Age, c. 1700-1500 BC (O'Brien 1994). The Ross Island production also pre-dates copper mining in Britain where recent radiocarbon results from six sites in mid- and north-Wales indicate copper mining beginning between 2000 and 1800 BC at the earliest (Dutton and Fasham 1994; Timberlake 1994).

While there is no independent chronology for the earliest copper-bronze metalwork in Ireland, radiocarbon dates are available for copper and gold objects from Beaker graves in southern Britain (Northover, forthcoming). These results indicate an early use of unalloyed copper between 2500 and 2100 BC, marked by tanged copper daggers and the very early find of copper wire and strip rings from Grave 919, Barrow Hill, Oxfordshire. Northover concludes that the earliest copper use in southern Britain may be placed between 2500 and 2100 BC, overlapping with the inception of tin-bronze use c. 2200-2100 BC. The British radiocarbon results shed light on the chronology of what Case (1966) referred to as the Impact Phase of early Irish-British metallurgy marked by technical innovation introduced by Beaker-using people from the Continent. Three important hoard associations, namely Knocknagur, Co. Galway, Whitespots, Co. Down and Frankford, Co. Offaly, connect the tanged copper

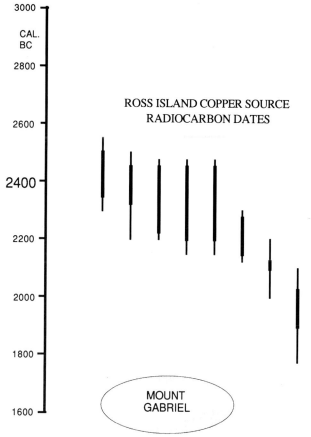
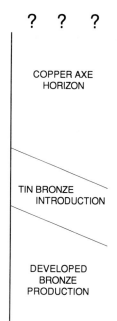

Fig. 20. A broad chronology for the inception of metallurgy in Ireland, together with radiocarbon dates for the earliest phase of copper extraction at Ross Island (one and two sigma calibration).

dagger, radiocarbon dated to between 2200 and 2000 BC in Britain, to both thick- and thin-butted copper axe production in Ireland, as well as to Irish halberds and awls. This implies that copper mining at Ross Island between 2500 and 2000 BC must have supplied metal to both the early copper-using phase and to the earliest use of tin-bronze (Killaha-Migdale phase). We can reasonably conclude that the earliest copper mining at Ross Island, *c.* 2500-2200 BC, pre-dates the inception of tin-bronze and must therefore be connected with the early copper axe horizon in both the Knocknagur and Frankford stages (Fig. 20). While the Ross Island chronology remains to be refined, this

site may be safely regarded as the first copper mine to be discovered in Ireland and Britain which dates to the short-lived 'Copper Age' at the inception of metallurgy.

Early Sulphide Metallurgy

With likely links to the early copper axe horizon, the level of metallurgical expertise evident in the Ross Island production is highly relevant to any discussion on the origins of Irish metallurgy. Using ore and metal analyses, Coghlan and Case (1957) argued that

Table 1: Radiocarbon dates for Beaker period copper mining at Ross Island (two-sigma calibration)

GrN-20224 3910±40 BP	Wood charcoal	2562-2298 BC
GrN-19628 3875±45 BP	Wood charcoal	2492-2204 BC
GrN-19624 3845±40 BP	Wood charcoal	2460-2202 BC
GrN-19626 3830±35 BP	Wood charcoal	2456-2148 BC
GrN-19627 3820±35 BP	Wood charcoal	2454-2146 BC
GrN-19622 3765±25 BP	Wood charcoal	2286-2136 BC
GrN-20223 3730±40 BP	Wood charcoal	2282-2034 BC
GrN-19621 3690±30 BP	Waterlogged wood	2192-1984 BC
GrN-19623 3580±50 BP	Bone collagen	2128-1776 BC

production of the earliest copper and bronze in Ireland was based on the use of sulphide ore from a zone of secondary enrichment probably occurring in the upper part of vein-style mineralisation. They argued that high levels of arsenic, antimony and silver present in this metal point to a source rich in *fahlerz*, so-called 'grey' copper ore in the tetrahedrite-tennantite mineral range. This *fahlerz* ore thus constituted the primary source of metal used in the bulk of all copper and early bronze production in Ireland. The exploitation of this *fahlerz* ore was felt to be a high temperature process, involving a roasting procedure followed by furnace smelting and crucible refining (*op. cit.* 93-4).

Coghlan and Case concluded that the ability to exploit primary sulphide ore at such an early date in Ireland reflected the introduction of metallurgy at a high technological level, most probably introduced by Beaker-using people '. . . connected ultimately with the technologically advanced central European area' (Case 1966, 168). They argued that the origin of this sulphide extraction process lay in the metal technology of west-central European Beaker groups like the Saxo-Thuringian complex and the Elbe-Saale metal industry, a view supported by the strong Wessex-Middle Rhine element in the earliest Irish Beaker pottery (Clarke 1970, 97). Others have argued for a Beaker-hosted introduction of metallurgy ultimately derived from Iberia or Brittany (see Sheridan 1983 for discussion).

Opposed to this Beaker introduction is a recent suggestion that the earliest copper-bronze metallurgy in Ireland and Britain was a simple, low-temperature process, essentially non-slagging and based on a supply of secondary copper minerals. Such a process would better explain the apparent absence of copper smelting slag in the insular Bronze Age and the low levels of iron in the earliest copper-bronze metalwork (Craddock 1990; 1995). The early use of sulphide ore has similarly been questioned by researchers in the University of Bradford who proposed a model of early extractive metallurgy based on the reduction of secondary copper arsenate minerals at low temperatures (Pollard *et al.* 1990; Budd 1993).

Recent investigations of Bronze Age copper mines in both Britain and Ireland have revealed operations in a variety of different geological settings, with variable supply of oxidised and sulphide mineralisation. Some sources stress the use of oxidation zone minerals, most notably the Great Orme in north Wales (Lewis 1994), Alderly Edge in England (Gale 1990) and the Mount Gabriel-type workings in Co. Cork. A recent study of the latter concluded that the earliest metallurgy in south-west Ireland may have been solely based on a supply of rich oxidised mineralisation from

quartz-sulphide veins (O'Brien *et al.* 1990; O'Brien 1994). It was suggested that this supply of secondary copper mineral was gradually depleted as the Early Bronze Age progressed, forcing local metallurgists to turn to poorer sources of oxidised mineralisation, most notably sedimentary copper-beds of the type found on Mount Gabriel. It was argued that low-grade deposits like the latter were probably used due to an inability to exploit primary sulphide ore, a process which only developed later on in the Bronze Age. This model, together with the Bradford research cited above, questioned Coghlan and Case's belief that the earliest copper metal used in Ireland and Britain was derived from sulphide ores. It is now possible, with the discovery of an early metal source in Killarney, to address the question of ore supply and early sulphide metallurgy directly.

Current research indicates two zones of mineralisation within the copper-rich horizon of Lower Carboniferous limestone at Ross Island, both of which may be linked to ancient copper mining. The Western Mine is located on strata-bound mineralisation, occurring within fine-grained bioclastic limestones with extensive calcite veining. This mineralisation is disseminated through the 'Blue Limestone' to a depth of between 13 and 18m when it is sharply cut off by a thrust plane. It consists mainly of finely mixed chalcopyrite and grey (*fahlerz*) copper ores, the latter dominated by tennantite rich in arsenic. This ore is well represented in spoil deposits associated with the primitive mine workings and is also a major constituent of ore processing in the adjacent Beaker work camp. Primitive mine workings in this area, radiocarbon dated to before 2000 BC, can be directly linked to the extraction of this chalcopyrite/*fahlerz* ore. Examination of this mineralisation, through outcrop inspection, shallow and deep drilling, as well as in residual spoil form, has not revealed a significant zone of oxidation in this ore-body. With the absence of even minor secondary copper mineralisation at surface, we may rule out the possibility that the early miners at this location were targeting malachite or any other secondary copper mineral.

In the eastern part of the Ross Island mine, there appears to be a more complex mineralogy associated with the 'Blue Hole', a large open-cut working which appears to be structurally controlled. Once again, the mineralisation is dominated by sulphide ore, including zones of fine-grained chalcopyrite and pyrite, galena and sphalerite, as well as minor amounts of grey (*fahlerz*) copper ore. While the history of this particular mine working is unclear, there are indications of primitive extraction comparable to those in the Western Mine area. The mineralisation of this 'Blue Hole' deposit is more complex than that of the Western

Mine and may have included some oxidation zone mineralogy, though this is not likely to have been significant.

Further details on ore mineralisation in this site must await research currently being undertaken by Robert Ixer in the University of Birmingham. Nevertheless, with the discovery of a Beaker copper mine and work camp in the Western Mine area at Ross Island, we can now confirm that the ability to process primary sulphide ore existed in Ireland during the early copper-using period, *c.* 2500-2000 BC. Archaeological evidence strongly points to the mixed chalcopyrite/*fahlerz* ore as an important source of metal at that time. Reduction of this sulphide ore is likely to have produced copper with significant levels of arsenic, most probably the type of metal (Case's Group 1) used in the copper- and earliest bronze-using period in Ireland. This conclusion supports Coghlan and Case's belief that the earliest metallurgy in Ireland was at least partly based on the exploitation of sulphide ores and not exclusively on the use of secondary copper mineralisation as suggested above.

This is supported by the recent discovery of pit features and sediments connected with on-site metallurgy in the Beaker work camp on Ross Island. No firm conclusions can be drawn while the excavation and analysis of these residues is underway, however the evidence would appear to be consistent with technology required to reduce sulphide ore at a high temperature. While the archaeological evidence may remain equivocal on this point, there is no denying the copper source available to early copper miners in this site, a resource base dominated by sulphide ore. Analysis of the Ross Island metallurgical residues and experimental smelting presently underway in the University of Bradford will hopefully throw further light on this sulphide ore reduction process.

The use of sulphide ore at an early stage in the Irish-British Bronze Age is also supported by recent investigations at Cwmystwyth and other early copper mines in mid-Wales (Timberlake 1994). Mining at Cwmystwyth was certainly underway by 1800 BC and appears to have targeted the copper sulphide, chalcopyrite, for extraction. Opposed to this is the evidence that secondary copper minerals, principally malachite, were also exploited from early on in the insular Bronze Age, for example at Mount Gabriel in west Cork (O'Brien 1994) and the Great Orme in north Wales (Lewis 1994). Together, these sites indicate an ability to adapt to different types of mineralisation from early on in the Bronze Age, an adaptation caused both by the natural occurrence of the copper ores and their availability as determined by technological constraints and resource ownership.

Arsenical Copper

The processes used to reduce *fahlerz* copper ore to metal at Ross Island are highly relevant to a long-standing debate on the significance of arsenical metal in the European Copper Age. This debate has centred on whether arsenical copper was deliberately produced and the manner in which this was achieved. A small amount of arsenic in copper metal will act as a deoxidant in casting and will also result in increased strength and toughness along hammered work edges. In considering the production of their Group 1 metal in Ireland, Coghlan and Case (1957) concluded that this was achieved through conscious selection of arsenical copper ores, most notably *fahlerz* deposits of the type identified in several of the Cork-Kerry mines.

The arsenic content of copper and earliest bronze in Ireland has received considerable attention, mainly as a marker element in source characterisation. However, metallographic studies carried out on these axes, daggers and halberds do not emphasise the importance of this element in the quality of metal produced. The analyses of Allen *et al.* (1970) and more recently of Northover suggest that this arsenic content was not fully exploited in terms of improved edge hardness (Northover 1989, fig. 13, 6). This conclusion is supported by metallographic studies on arsenical copper elsewhere, most notably Budd's examination of Eneolithic copper from Austria (Budd 1991; Budd and Ottaway 1991). Budd (1993) has gone on to argue that arsenical copper may not have been intentionally produced, but may instead be a function of a particular smelting process and ore type. Budd and co-researchers in the University of Bradford have proposed that the arsenic content of early Irish-British metal may have derived from the use of secondary copper arsenate minerals from the zone of oxidation, in a low-temperature process which would yield arsenic contents similar to those in finished metalwork (typically 1-5% max.). The arsenic content allows these secondary copper minerals to be smelted in bonfire-type installations, at temperatures as low as 700 degrees centigrade.

Ongoing research at Ross Island does not support this conclusion, principally because secondary copper arsenates are almost totally absent from the mineralisation observed in both bedrock and spoil form at this Copper Age metal source. While the process modelled by the Bradford team may be viable in a laboratory environment, it is doubtful whether secondary copper arsenate minerals, which are relatively exotic and of minor occurrence, could ever have been targeted as a specific ore resource by Bronze Age miners. These minerals are almost totally absent

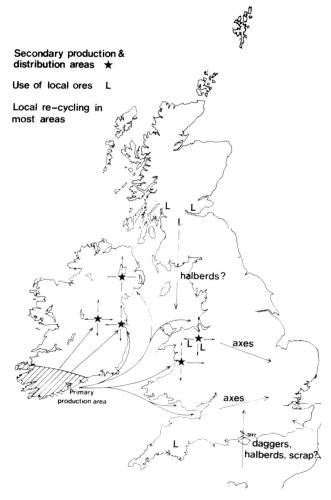

Secondary production &
distribution areas ★

Use of local ores L

Local re-cycling in
most areas

Fig. 21. The organisation of metal-working in
the insular copper-using period (Northover
1982).

from Bronze Age copper mines examined to date in
Ireland or Britain. Opposed to this is the discovery
of a Copper Age mine at Ross Island, almost certainly
connected to the extraction of *fahlerz* and other
sulphide ores containing arsenic.

Early Copper in Britain

The significance of this arsenical copper in Ireland
also lies in its possible contribution to the earliest
metal use in Britain. Both Case and Northover have
argued that copper axes, typologically connected to
the primary Irish industry, constitute the earliest examples of copper metal to appear in Highland Zone
Britain. This has recently been challenged by Budd
and co-researchers in the University of Bradford who
question the existence of this Irish primary industry
and its contribution to the beginnings of metal use
in Britain (Budd *et al.* 1992). It is now possible to
address these questions directly with the recent
discovery of a Copper Age metal source in south-west
Ireland.

Coghlan and Case (1957) argued that by using
artefact analyses it was possible to identify three distinctive sources of early copper metal in Britain. The first,

Group 1 metal, was marked by high levels of arsenic,
antimony and silver which they believed to be Irish
in origin. Group 3 metals are very different, marked
by high levels of nickel and believed to be Continental in origin. Both of these compositions are
represented in the copper dagger series associated with
Beaker graves in southern Britain, pointing to two
external sources of copper metal at that time. A third
composition, Group 2, was partly residual from the
latter two metal sources, but was also believed to mark
the exploitation of British copper sources at a later
date in the Early Bronze Age.

Recent research by Peter Northover broadly supports the conclusion that Irish metal, marked by a
distinctive arsenic-antimony-silver composition, not
only supplied some of the copper used in southern
British Beaker graves, but was also the first metal to
circulate in western and northern Britain (Fig. 21).
Northover (forthcoming) estimates that as much as
80% of the early copper axes in Highland Zone
Britain are made from this distinctive composition,
which together with typological links strongly point
to an Irish origin. He believes that this Group 1 metal
also fuelled the earliest bronze production in Britain,
declining in importance around 1900 BC when other
metal compositions begin to appear. It is highly

significant that the currency of this arsenical metal between 2500 and 1900 BC coincides closely with radiocarbon-dated exploitation of the Ross Island mine. The appearance of new metal compositions after 1900 BC may be taken to reflect the emergence of new copper mines exploiting different types of copper ore, among them Mount Gabriel in Ireland, Cwmystwyth and the Great Orme in Wales, and probably Alderly Edge in England.

This raises the question of whether Ross Island could have been the *sole* source of copper in the early Beaker period in Ireland. Unfortunately, our understanding of production levels at this site between 2500 and 2000 BC is limited by recent mine disturbance and lake-flooding of the primitive workings. With recorded sales of over 3000 tons of dressed copper ore at the Swansea smelters in the early 19th century, there can be little doubt that Ross Island was rich in copper ore. What is significant about the 19th-century production is that all of this ore was raised from a surface horizon extending down to between 13 and 18m in depth – well within the technological range of the Bronze Age miner. There can be little doubt that Ross Island could have supplied the level of metal use suggested by the present stock of Beaker period metalwork in our museums. Such a dependence on a single rich source may in turn explain the apparently homogenous metal composition in circulation at that time. However, there are several other ore deposits in the Cork-Kerry region and beyond which could have yielded metal of this type and it would be premature to discount this possibility in view of the highly skewed archaeological record of early mining today.

Conclusions

Many scholars in the past have defined Ireland's place in the Bronze Age in terms of an ability to supply metal. This model of core-and-periphery probably owes more to the perceived colonial status of this island in recent centuries than to any reality in Bronze Age times, when the great bulk of metal produced was almost certainly destined for domestic consumption. Having said that, the movement of people, of ideas and of objects along the Atlantic seaways in Final Neolithic times is undeniable and provides a starting point for our consideration of the origins of Irish metallurgy. All indications at present are that the knowledge of metallurgy was introduced into Ireland, probably in the mid-third millennium BC, by those same shadowy groups connected with the spread of Beaker pottery.

On chronological and compositional grounds, it is almost certain that Ross Island supplied metal to make thick-butted Lough Ravel series copper axes in

Ireland. The contribution of this site to the initiation of copper axe production, in particular to the putative Castletownroche stage, is less clear. The difficulty here lies with the lack of securely dated contexts for the earliest copper axe forms, which continue to belong to '. . . an industry with indefinite cultural or geographical affinity' (Case 1966, 168). While the earliest contacts with Continental metal may have occurred prior to 2500 BC, it seems reasonable on both chronological and metallurgical grounds to argue that copper mining underway by 2400-2300 BC at Ross Island was connected with the earliest metal production in these islands.

While the bulk of arsenical (Group 1) metal in Ireland was probably produced using sulphide ores from sources like Ross Island, recent metallographic studies now question whether this was a deliberate process. Is it possible that the arsenic content of this early Irish metal simply reflects the exploitation of a particular ore source, namely Ross Island? Could this mine have supplied the bulk of metal produced in Ireland in the period 2500-2000 BC, gradually being surpassed by the emergence of other copper mines in Ireland and Britain after 2000 BC? The prevalence of early arsenical metal may thus reflect the importance of one particular source, namely Ross Island, which dominated early copper production in Ireland for a period of several centuries. The arsenic content in metal derived from this mine may be entirely fortuitous and may reflect the ability to process a particular type of copper ore, using expertise learned on the Continent. In light of the Ross Island results, we are now closer to evaluating the opinion offered by Coghlan and Case almost forty years ago:

> Our conclusion about techniques is that the earliest metallurgists in Ireland were very skilled. Not only could they select the right deposit, hand-pick, wash and concentrate the ore; they could control the roasting, smelting and possibly refining process in a very competent way (1957, 97).

It remains to be seen whether this ability to process sulphide ore was developed independently within Ireland or was introduced as part of a complete technological package from the Continent. Ross Island has the potential to address many long-standing problems in this area of research. It is to be hoped that analysis of the Beaker pottery assemblage will shed some light on the geographical context of this early metallurgy, both in terms of foreign stimulus and indigenous contribution. Does the apparent absence of Late Neolithic ceramics in this site strengthen the case for an intrusive Beaker metallurgy? Are these miners working to a technological level first developed on the Continent? Or is the earliest metallurgy in Ireland of the type envisaged by Craddock, natives experimenting with very primitive processes in an attempt to imitate those first 'mute ambassadors' from the Continent? The ongoing research at Ross Island will hopefully shed light on these and many other research questions central to the origins of Irish metallurgy.

References

Allen, I. M., Britton, D. and Coghlan, H. H. 1970. *Metallurgical Reports on British and Irish Bronze Age Implements and Weapons in the Pitt-Rivers Museum.* Oxford.

Budd, P. 1991. Eneolithic Arsenical Copper: Heat Treatment and the Metallographic Interpretation of Manufacturing Processes. In Pernicka, E. and Wagner, G. A. (eds), *Archaeometry '90.* Heidelberg.

Budd, P. 1993. Recasting the Bronze Age. *New Scientist,* October 26th.

Budd, P. and Ottaway, B. 1991. The Properties of Arsenical Copper Alloys: Implications for the Development of Eneolithic Metallurgy. In Budd, P. *et al.* (eds), *Archaeological Sciences '89.* Oxford.

Budd, O., Gale, D., Pollard, A. M., Thomas, R. G. and Williams, P. A. 1992. The Early Development of Metallurgy in the British Isles. *Antiquity* 66, 677-86.

Burgess, C. 1979. The Background of Early Metalworking in Ireland and Britain. In Ryan, M. (ed.), *The Origins of Metallurgy in Atlantic Europe, Proceedings of the Fifth Atlantic Colloquium,* 207-47. Dublin.

Burgess, C. 1980. *The Age of Stonehenge.* London.

Case, H. J. 1966. Were Beaker-people the first metallurgists in Ireland? *Palaeohistoria* 12, 141-77.

Clarke, D. L. 1970. *Beaker Pottery of Great Britain and Ireland.* Cambridge.

Coghlan, H. H. and Case, H. J. 1957. Early Metallurgy of Copper in Britain and Ireland. *Proceedings of the Prehistoric Society* 23, 9 1-123.

Coghlan, H. H. *et al.* 1963. A Note on Irish Copper Ores and Metals. In *Ores and Metals, A Report of the Ancient Mining and Metallurgy Committee, Royal Anthropological Institute.* 1-33.

Craddock, P. T. 1979. Deliberate Alloying in the Atlantic Bronze Age. In Ryan, M. (ed.), *The Origins of Metallurgy in Atlantic Europe. Proceedings of the Fifth Atlantic Colloquium,* 369-85. Dublin.

Craddock, P. T. 1990. Copper Smelting in Bronze Age Britain: Problems and Possibilities. In Crew, P. and Crew, S. (eds). *Early Mining in the British Isles,* 69-71. Snowdonia.

Craddock, P. T. 1995. *Early Metal Mining and Production.* Edinburgh.

Dutton, A. and Fasham, P. 1994. Prehistoric Copper Mining on the Great Orme, Llandudno, Gwynedd. *Proceedings of the Prehistoric Society* 60, 245-86.

Gale, D. 1990. Prehistoric stone mining tools from Alderly Edge. In Crew, P. and Crew, S. (eds), *Early Mining in the British Isles,* 47-8. Snowdonia.

Harbison, P. 1969. *The Axes of the Early Bronze Age in Ireland. Prähistorische Bronzefunde* 9.1. Munich.

Harbison, P. 1979. Who were Ireland's First Metallurgists? In Ryan, M. (ed.), *The Origins of Metallurgy in Atlantic Europe. Proceedings of the Fifth Atlantic Colloquium,* 97-105. Dublin.

Junghans, S., Sangmeister, E. and Schröder, M. 1968. *Studien zu den Anfängen der Metallurgie.* Berlin.

Lewis, A. 1994. Bronze Age Mines of the Great Orme. In Ford, T. D. and Willies, L. (eds), *Mining before Powder.* Peak District Mines Historical Society Bulletin 12: 3, 31-6.

Needham, S. 1979. The Extent of Foreign Influence on Early Bronze Age Axe Development in Southern Britain. In Ryan, M. (ed.), *The Origins of Metallurgy in Atlantic Europe. Proceedings of the Fifth Atlantic Colloquium,* 265-93. Dublin.

Northover, J. P. 1980. Bronze in the British Bronze Age. In Oddy, W. A. (ed.), *Aspects of Early Metallurgy.* British Museum Occasional Paper 17, 63-70. London.

Northover, J. P. 1982. The Exploration of the Long-Distance Movement of Bronze in Bronze and Early Iron Age Europe. *Bulletin of the Institute of Archaeology* 19, 45-72.

Northover, J. P. 1989. Properties and use of Arsenic-Copper Alloys. In Hauptmann, A. *et al.* (eds), *Old World Archaeology,* 111-18. Bochum.

Northover, P. forthcoming. The Earliest Metalwork in Southern Britain. To be published in the Proceedings of the International Symposium on *The Beginnings of Metallurgy,* Bochum, April, 1995.

O'Brien, W. 1994. *Mount Gabriel. Bronze Age Mining in Ireland.* Galway.

O'Brien, W., Ixer, R. and O'Sullivan, M. 1990. Copper Resources in Prehistory: an Irish Perspective. In Crew, P. and Crew, S. (eds), *Early Mining in the British Isles,* 30-5. Snowdonia.

Pollard, A. M., Thomas, R. G. and Williams, P. A. 1990. Experimental Smelting of Arsenical Copper Ores: Implications for Early Bronze Age Copper Production. In Crew, P. and Crew, S. (eds) *Early Mining in the British Isles,* 72-4. Snowdonia.

Randsborg, K. 1979. Resource Distribution and the Function of Copper in Early Neolithic Denmark. In Ryan, M. (ed.). *The Origins of Metallurgy in Atlantic Europe.* Proceedings of the Fifth Atlantic Colloquium. Dublin, 303-18.

Ryan, M. (ed.). 1990. *The Origins of Metallurgy in Atlantic Europe. Proceedings of the Fifth Atlantic Colloquium.* Dublin.

Sheridan, A. 1983. A Reconsideration of the Origins of Irish Metallurgy. *The Journal of Irish Archaeology* 1, 11-19.

Timberlake, S. 1994. Evidence for Early Mining in Wales. In Ford, T. D. and Willies, L. (eds), *Mining before Powder.* Peak District Mines Historical Society Bulletin 12: 3, 133-43.

Middle Bronze Age Metalwork: Are Artefact Studies Dead and Buried?

Greer Ramsey

Abstract

With the publication of detailed catalogues of bronze artefacts, criticism has been levelled at their over-emphasis on typology and classification and their failure to integrate the metalwork into a wider context. The study of Middle Bronze Age metalwork highlights these issues. By necessity it requires the examination of large numbers of single finds, the end result of which could be another subjective classification scheme adding little to our overall knowledge of the period. It also raises the issues of the most appropriate way to subdivide the Bronze Age and whether the Middle Bronze Age is a valid entity. Conversely it is very misleading to think that the major categories of metal objects have all been examined and published in accessible form; this is clearly not the case. For example, the entire spearhead series has only received cursory attention. As regards the concept of the Middle Bronze Age, it is suggested in this article that as long as various limitations are perceived, it remains an appropriate and useful term. Rather than relegating traditional artefact studies to a subsidiary role, the need to record and carefully examine bronze objects remains of paramount importance for increasing our understanding of the period. These points are illustrated by reference to three artefacts types considered diagnostic of Middle Bronze Age metalwork: flanged axes/palstaves; dirks/rapiers and looped spearheads. For these three categories of objects a detailed visual inspection, catalogue and typological study has been undertaken: this examined issues including function, the origin and development of types and regional diversity. A number of these conclusions are summarised to highlight the value of this type of research.

Introduction

We should not forget that the crushing routine of collecting, collating and publishing artefacts is by no means over. Unfortunately few have emerged in recent years prepared to stick to the grind of gaining familiarity with the material. For many young workers an early sortie into Bronze Age metalwork, resulting in a small regional survey or publication of a hoard, has been followed by an abrupt change of tack.

(Burgess and Coombs 1979, i)

At the time of writing in 1979, Burgess and Coombs emphasised the need for continuing research into bronze metalwork, as many of the major categories of artefacts had not been examined in detail. A similar situation existed in Ireland regarding the need for further work. Despite important papers which discussed the general range of Middle and Late Bronze Age artefact types (e.g. Eogan 1962, 1964), more detailed studies were confined to the publication of swords (Eogan 1965) and the *Prähistorische Bronzefunde* catalogues by Harbison (1969) on Early Bronze Age halberds, axes and daggers. Despite this work the entire spearhead series had not been comprehensively

examined, neither had Middle Bronze Age flanged axes and palstaves, or Late Bronze Age socketed axes. In terms of quantity this represented the majority of surviving bronze objects.

This lack of research may reflect reservations about the traditional methodologies for studying metalwork. These have concentrated on detailing typologies and arranging types into chronological sequences. This approach is open to criticism specifically regarding the replicability and usefulness of classification schemes and the subjectivity of divisions. To a large extent this has made artefact studies like the *Prähistorische Bronzefunde* series unfashionable, particularly because of their failure to comment on wider issues. Undoubtedly the crushing routine of data collection and the complexity of the material may also have been contributing factors.

In recent years, and rightly so, there has been an attempt to move away from typological studies and examine the social trends of the Bronze Age, setting the metalwork into an integrated context. The most recent example of this approach is the section on the Bronze Age in the book by Cooney and Grogan (1994), where the metalwork is examined primarily from a depositional perspective.

The study of Middle Bronze Age metalwork highlights the dichotomy between these two approaches. By necessity it requires the examination of large numbers of single finds, which are not associated with burials or settlements, the concern being that it could result in another subjective classification scheme which adds little to our knowledge. However without this type of study the data which allows depositional patterns to be examined would not be available, neither would the foundations be in place upon which future work could develop and expand. It is important to remember that the discovery of metal represents one of the great watersheds in Irish prehistory. This required a new range of skills and an ability to exploit different types of raw materials. These changes were driven by the desire to manufacture bronze artefacts whose shape and form altered through time. Given the effort required to procure the raw materials necessary to manufacture bronze and gold objects, the skills needed to produce them, and the importance attached to metal work in society, it is clear that the ability to produce metal objects represents the key element which distinguishes this period from what had gone before, and from what was to follow.

The relevance of the traditional artefact study, as illustrated particularly by the publications of Eogan, should not be underestimated, and the comments made by Burgess and Coombs some fifteen years ago are as appropriate now as they were then. The information derived from examining large numbers of objects should be used to increase our knowledge and understanding of the social and economic aspects of the period rather than detracting from it, and for the Middle Bronze Age, bronze artefacts are the inevitable starting point. As Burgess and Coombs stated (1979, i) '. . . artefacts are the "stuff", the "facts", of our discipline, and everything else is inference'.

Is there a Middle Bronze Age?

Before going on to illustrate the value and range of information that can be revealed by examining bronze artefacts, it is necessary to discuss the nature of the subdivisions within the Bronze Age. For any period in prehistory archaeologists have introduced and imposed modern terms aimed at breaking down into meaningful form a collection of material to provide it with a descriptive label. This label should have some common level of understanding of what constitutes its component parts, whether they represent artefact, burial or settlement evidence. For the Bronze Age many subdivisions and descriptive labels have

been applied, some of which are not universally agreed, which has given rise to questioning whether the Middle Bronze Age is a valid entity.

Traditionally the Bronze Age has been divided into three periods: Early Bronze Age, Middle Bronze Age and Late Bronze Age. These divisions are based upon a study of burial types, pottery and metalworking traditions. Other formats have opted for a simple Earlier-Later division, e.g. Megaw and Simpson (1979), relegating the Middle Bronze Age to a phase within a Later Bronze Age. As a result this reduces the significance of the Middle Bronze Age as a period with a separate and clear identity.

One reason for Megaw and Simpson's treatment of the Middle Bronze Age may relate to the fact that it is identified primarily by a range of metal artefacts which are rarely associated with burials or settlements. This makes it difficult to gauge whether this Middle Bronze Age metalworking horizon was accompanied by other changes in society which would strengthen its case to be viewed as a distinct period. This dilemma also reflects varying opinions over isolating when the major changes in the Bronze Age are perceived to have occurred.

Megaw and Simpson favour a major break just after the decline of the Wessex culture. This marks the beginning of their Later Bronze Age. Although Eogan has also recognised certain changes in Irish metalwork which begin to appear at this time, more significant developments are believed to have occurred later in the millennium during the Bishopsland period (1962, 57). These include the arrival of the sword which marks the beginning of the Late Bronze Age in Ireland (Eogan 1962, 59). While Eogan does use the term 'Middle Bronze Age' in reference to metal types which begin to appear in Ireland at a time contemporary with the end of the Wessex culture, he questions the significance of their impact on society by emphasising a degree of continuity with Early Bronze Age metal types (Eogan 1962, 46).

These alternative schemes illustrate the difficulties of attempting to draw dividing lines typologically and chronologically between possible industrial phases, which in themselves seem indicative of change. In reality it is unlikely that there will ever be only one agreed way to subdivide the Bronze Age, as different criteria could be used, but because of the large quantity of metal artefacts it is natural and indeed necessary to try and create some logical order for them which is why a chronological framework exists.

In theory it is necessary for the divisions to appear rigid, rather like the drawers in a filing cabinet. While there may be arguments over the number of drawers and their names, there seems to be general consensus on the sequence or relative order in which certain artefacts occur and evolved. The axe series developed through flat and flanged axes to palstaves and socketed axes, while the chronological position of daggers, in relation to dirk/rapiers and swords, is firmly established. When the order of development for an artefact type has been established and its relative order in a chronological sequence compared to other artefact types clarified, arguments over divisional names become less significant. In practice the disadvantages of drawing hard and fast boundary lines between phases becomes evident, particularly if artefacts are found with material belonging to different chronological periods which is often the case. To over-compartmentalise the Bronze Age is to suggest that changes were geographically and chronologically synchronous and places the material in a strait-jacket from which it is hard to escape. As long as their limitations are perceived, the labels attached to the Bronze Age should aid our understanding of the period rather than confuse it.

Taking into account these problems, it is recognised that in metalworking terms changes take place in the development of daggers, axes and spearheads, giving rise to a new range of dirks/rapiers, looped spearheads and flanged axes/palstaves, some of which are represented in the Killymaddy moulds from Co. Antrim (Coghlan and Raftery 1961). This Killymaddy phase marks the start of the Middle Bronze Age which probably begins between 1600 and 1500 BC. It is bounded at its other end by the emergence of swords, socketed axes and peg-holed spearheads, as well as the increased use of personal ornaments. Some of these changes take place in the opening phase of the Bishopsland period, while others occur towards its end (Eogan 1962). For this reason and for those expressed previously, combined with the complexities of dating metalwork, it remains difficult and perhaps unnecessary to attempt to suggest a fixed chronological point by which time all these changes were in place. If forced to do so then a date between 1200 and 1000 BC may be the most appropriate.

To attempt to discuss Irish metalwork without using the term 'Middle Bronze Age' simply creates confusion rather than clarifies it and if only for this reason it should be retained. The word 'middle' emphasises a stage of development seen as intermediary between the objects produced towards the beginning of the second millennium and those manufactured towards its end. This can be seen typologically as well as technologically. In terms of metalworking the Middle Bronze Age smiths mastered the skill necessary to produce long castings, particularly with cores. They created a greater variety of forms than had been available previously, yet did so using the medium of the stone mould as in the Early Bronze Age. Towards

the end of the second millennium typological changes, such as the adoption of the socketed axe, and the arrival of the sword, are significant landmarks, mirrored by a development in technology away from casting in stone moulds to the use of clay. This represented a significant break with the past and was accompanied by increasing expertise in gold and sheet bronze work. In addition, it may well be that other changes took place during the Middle Bronze Age. These would include a decline in the frequency of burials associated with pottery of the food vessel, cordoned, encrusted urns and collared urn traditions, and an increasing frequency of metalwork from 'wet' locations. For these reasons the traditional division of the Bronze Age into three periods is retained, with the Middle Bronze Age viewed as a separate entity.

When Eogan first defined the characteristic features of the Middle Bronze Age he described three artefacts as the leading weapons in use: 'palstaves, rapiers and socket-looped spearheads . . .' (Eogan 1962, 45). Although dirks/rapiers were subsequently published by Burgess and Gerloff (1981), the nature of the flanged axe/palstave series had not been fully explored. Neither had the relationship of side looped spearheads to the basal and protected looped groups, all of which are seen to have had their origin in the Middle Bronze Age (for a detailed discussion of chronology see Ramsey 1989). With the total surviving number of dirks/rapiers, flanged axes/palstaves and the three types of spearheads approaching 2500 examples, the need to examine this large body of material in the manner of a catalogue and typological study seemed a prerequisite to further work. This is particularly the case as only 16 of these artefacts are from hoards, none survive from burials and only a few have tentative settlement links. The value and necessity of such an approach and the need to re-examine and look at primary material provides valuable insights into the origin of certain types, their regional diversity and function. This can be demonstrated by summarising a few selected observations concerning the three artefact types mentioned by Eogan, which formed part of a more comprehensive study (Ramsey 1989). Hopefully this will demonstrate that Middle Bronze Age artefact studies are alive and well!

Spearheads

One common denominator recognised by all archaeologists studying Bronze Age spearheads is the modification to the hafting mechanism, involving first the use of a tang, then socket with differing loop types, and finally the adoption of rivets to secure the

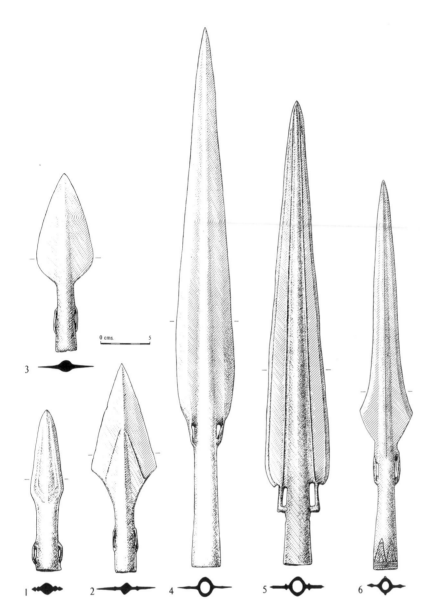

Fig. 22. 1. Early Bronze Age end looped spearhead (UM 278.1964). 2. Middle Bronze Age 'kite' shaped side looped spearhead (UM A7.1972). 3. Middle Bronze Age 'leaf' shaped side looped spearhead, Edenvale, near Connor, Co. Antrim (UM 292.1934). 4. Middle Bronze Age 'leaf' shaped basal looped spearhead, Toome, Co. Antrim (UM A202.1965). 5. Middle Bronze Age 'triangular' shaped basal looped spearhead (UM GC 4013). 6. Middle Bronze Age side looped spearhead, Gara type (NMI W26).

haft. The simplistic division into looped and rivet hole groups was recognised at an early stage by Coffey (1894, 487) and marks a change in the hafting arrangement which distinguishes Middle Bronze Age looped spearheads, and the majority of Early Bronze Age spearheads, from those of the Late Bronze Age.

The predominant type of Early Bronze Age spearhead is the end looped variety (Fig. 22, no. 1). Although no specific study of these spearheads has been published, they appear to be relatively standardised which is an unusual feature of certain categories of Irish metalwork. The presence of loops, which developed in the Early Bronze Age, sets apart the Irish and British series from Western Europe, suggesting a rejection of outside influence and emphasising a distinct local evolution in spearhead design. The loops' function was to provide an aperture through which binding could be secured and tied around the shaft.

The socket of the Early Bronze Age spearhead did

not penetrate into the blade but stopped at its base. In order to create a stronger grip on the shaft the socket could be extended into the blade area. This is a feature of the Middle Bronze Age spearhead series, which along with modification to the blade shape and position of the loops, provide the main typological distinctions between Early Bronze Age and Middle Bronze Age spearheads.

There are over 600 Middle Bronze Age side looped spearheads from Ireland. The most diagnostic Irish form are those with 'kite' shaped blades and blade-rib decoration. This decoration is set at a right angle running from the blade base towards the midrib (Fig. 22, no. 2). These are spearheads of the Knockanearla, Cashel and Maryborough types of which there are over 300 examples and some 16 surviving moulds (Ramsey 1989, 93). The low frequency in Britain of spearheads with 'kite' shaped blades and blade-ribs suggests that they were influenced by Irish smiths if not manufactured by them. Rowlands lists 14 'kite' shaped spearheads of probable Irish origin of which seven are illustrated (Rowlands 1976a, pl. 37). Davey lists two further examples (Davey 1973, 79, fig. 15, no. 115, 163), while the potential number from Scotland is greater at 25 (Coles 1963-64, 105, fig. 9). While leaf shaped side looped spearheads are also known from Ireland (Fig. 22, no. 3) they are more typical of the British series. As regards Continental associations, the find from Finistère, in France, is interesting, as it is a distinctly Irish Knockanearla type (Briard and Mohen 1983, fig. 1).

These typological variations and differing frequencies point to significant regional variations between the British and Irish side looped series, which include exclusively Irish types such as Larkfield spearheads (Ramsey 1989, 95). It is also apparent that Ireland had a greater variety of side looped spearheads than Britain which may be significant in discussing the origin of basal and protected looped spearheads.

Basal looped spearheads

As the name suggests, the diagnostic feature of these spearheads is the position of the loops set at the base of the blade. When examined in detail, two types of blade exist. Those with a leaf shaped form whose loops tend to be incorporated within the overall shape of the blade (Fig. 22, no. 4); and those with triangular shaped blades with loops projecting from the blade base (Fig. 22, no. 5). Basal looped spearheads are considered to have originated in Ireland or Britain, with some notable concentrations throughout Europe, particularly France (O'Connor 1980, list 20, map 13; Ramsey 1989, 97).

Evans's (1881, 327) concept that basal looped spearheads originated as the result of fusion between Continental leaf shaped forms and indigenous looped spearheads remains a popular theory and has been supported by Coles (1963-64, 110) and Eogan (1964, 268). The precise details of this hybridisation are not clearly explained and neither is there any evidence for dated imported spearheads. What seems a more likely explanation for their development is a modification to the position of the loops on side looped spearheads, in conjunction with changes in blade shape and dimensions.

One reason for experimenting with the position of the loops may relate to preventing damage. For example, the Knockanearla type has 29 spearheads with damaged loops (Ramsey 1989, 56). In addition, if the loops became bent and it became necessary to renew the binding, the aperture may have needed reopening. If not carried out carefully this hot and/or cold hammering may have fractured the loop, rendering

it useless. By moving the loops up the socket, close to the blade base, they would be afforded greater protection and be less likely to get caught or broken. In the Larkfield type the loops are in such a position (Fig. 23, no. 7) and in the Gara type (Ramsey 1989, 65) a number are attached to the blade by a small flange of metal (Fig. 22, no. 6). A natural culmination of this process is the amalgamation of loop and blade giving basal looped spearheads.

It has been stated on a number of occasions that the likely place of origin for the basal looped spearhead is Ireland (Rowlands 1976a, 57; Smith 1959, 179). This is based on the argument that Irish basal looped spearheads are more varied than British examples, which suggests a possible degree of experimentation and earlier evolution. In addition, the greater variety of side looped spearheads from Ireland, some of which are likely to have played a part in their development, is also a contributing factor.

Rowlands (1976b) listed 184 basal looped spearheads in his catalogue, while the number from Ireland must be now approaching *c.* 150. This does not suggest a significant imbalance between the two regions as did the number of 'kite' shaped, blade-ribbed spearheads. In contrast, the number of basal looped spearheads from Scotland is lower compared with Ireland and southern Britain. Coles lists 21 examples from Scotland and suggests that the main sphere of influence may have been southern England (Coles 1963-64, 108). If the basal looped spearhead did originate in Ireland, which is a distinct possibility, it seems unlikely that the majority of British examples were Irish imports, with joint centres of production being more probable. Certainly in the Late Bronze Age, Dainton style spearheads, which are essentially basal looped spearheads with unperforated loops, were being cast in England (Needham 1980).

Protected looped spearheads

The loops on these spearheads are set well within the blade, above the blade socket junction, and may have a raised ridge on their outer edge sometimes referred to as a 'protective plate' (Fig. 23, no. 8). Typologically they form a very tight homogenous group. The imbalance in the number of spearheads between Ireland and Britain and the similarity in design to Larkfield spearheads (Fig. 23, no. 7), from which they may have evolved, strongly suggests that they originated in Ireland. Rowlands (1976a, 61) lists only two protected looped spearheads from southern Britain. Ten examples are noted from northern England (Burgess 1968, 22), and a further three are referenced from Scotland by Coles (1963-64,

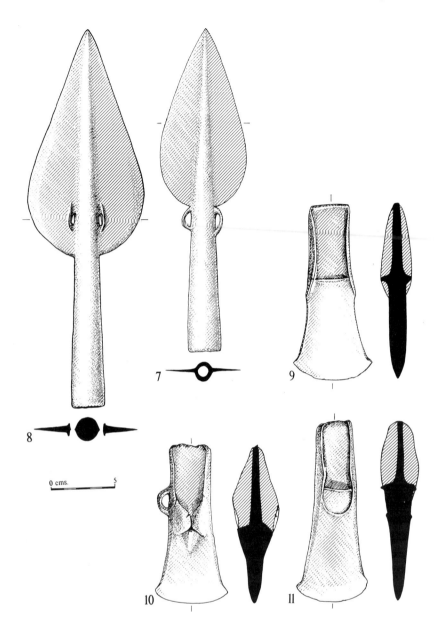

Fig. 23. 7. Middle Bronze Age side looped spearhead, Larkfield, Co. Leitrim (NMI 1941.330). 8. Middle Bronze Age protected loop spearhead, R. Bann, Co. Antrim (UM L.33.1934). 9. Middle Bronze Age flanged axe (UM 111.1958). 10. Middle Bronze Age 'wing' flanged axe (UM 500.1937). 11. Middle Bronze Age primary shield pattern palstave (UM 6-98.3895s).

141-5). The number of protected looped spearheads from Ireland is now approaching *c.* 40. As far as can be certain only one protected loop spearhead is known from the Continent, found in dredging the river l'Isle, Dordogne, France (Briard and Mohen 1983, 143, fig. 2). The greater number of protected loop spearheads from Ireland and their similarity to Larkfield side loop spearheads, seems to confirm the suggestion that they are an Irish invention.

Function

The design of the spearhead, with a comparatively effective hafting mechanism compared to the axe and dirk/rapier, gave it the potential to be an effective weapon. Rowlands (1976a, 192) lists an example of a Bronze Age burial from Tormarton, on the Gloucestershire–Wiltshire border, with the remains of

blade tips from two side looped spearheads embedded in the lumbar vertebrae and pelvis of the victim. From Queenford farm, near Dorchester, are the remains of a pelvis pierced by a large spearhead, with part of the blade broken off. It was probably a basal looped spearhead but this is not certain (Rowlands 1976a, 193). Ehrenberg (1977, 23) references a further example from France of a spearhead lodged in the vertebrae. These examples are significant because of the lack of associated Middle Bronze Age metalwork with human remains from Ireland and they demonstrate that the spear was a useful weapon.

The possibility that some spears were intended to be used for throwing, and others thrusting, has been suggested by Coombs as evidenced by the use of 'long' and 'short' spears used as javelin and lance as represented on bronze situlae from the Adriatic. The Irish sagas have also warriors carrying, throwing and thrusting spears (Coombs 1975, 74). The size

Table 2: Middle Bronze Age spears: summary statistics of weight (gms) and length (mm) for Middle Bronze Age side looped, basal looped and protected looped spearheads

	Side looped group		Basal looped group		Protected looped group	
Weight	16gms	min	32gms	min	78gms	min
	91gms	mean	236gms	mean	287gms	mean
	387gms	max	726gms	max	860gms	max
Length	49mm	min	96mm	min	120mm	min
	138mm	mean	276mm	mean	263mm	mean
	501mm	max	685mm	max	610mm	max

difference within, and between, groups, may be indicative of a functional difference, which must also include the possibility that not all spears were intended to be practical fighting weapons. Coffey attacked the idea of migrating loops being responsible for the direct evolution of basal and protected looped spearheads and argued that if they represented an improvement in design their frequency would be greater than side looped spearheads (Coffey 1894, 499). While the movement in the position of the loops may have influenced the evolution of basal and protected looped spearheads, it does not necessarily follow that basal and protected looped spearheads were designed to be more effective fighting weapons which may be reflected by an increase in numbers. The substantial difference in length between the side looped group, compared to the protected and basal groups, may be indicative of a functional difference (Table 2). In addition the quality of workmanship and the extreme length of some basal and protected looped spearheads may preclude a practical military role.

This is most vividly demonstrated by the five basal looped spearheads of the Tempo type (Ramsey 1989, 74) which are among the finest castings of the Bronze Age (Fig. 22, no. 5). These are all possibly from the same workshop and are of a type not found in Britain. The quality of finish must have been reflected in their being valued as prestige objects, regardless of whether they were used as fighting weapons. It is also interesting to note that Tempo spearheads occur in two out of the three Irish hoards containing basal looped spearheads, which may be a further indication of their importance (Eogan 1983, 259, 298). The basal looped spearhead from Pyotdykes, Angus, with gold decoration at the mouth of the socket is also compatible with the interpretation that certain basal looped spearheads were regarded as luxury items (Coles *et al.* 1964, pl. 17). Similar arguments apply to the function of the protected loop group. The

possibility that the loops were no longer practical, the symmetry of the blade, and quality of finish, seem indicative of prestige artefacts. Coles (1963-64, 110) shared this view of the protected loop group.

Axes

Unlike the classification of spearheads, which fall into a number of well-defined groups based upon loop type, Middle Bronze Age axes present difficult typological problems. The complexity of existing classifications, their wide range of shapes and confused descriptive terminology, has highlighted many limitations of traditional typological work. These problems are recognised by Schmidt and Burgess (1981, 76):

> Short-flanged axes epitomise a problem peculiar to Irish/British metalwork and one which provides such a contrast to the Continental material, namely the remarkable variability of their form, offering a bewildering permutation of features which make coherent classification very difficult. The subdivisions presented here are the end-product of innumerable reworkings spreading back over several years, and the writers realise how subjective their results are and the room for further work that still exists.

This pertinent statement clearly expresses the writers' frustration in coping with the wide variety of shapes found among Middle Bronze Age axes, a problem even more evident within the Irish series. In practice it is extremely difficult to classify with recurring regularity, either stylistically or statistically, the component variables which make up a Middle Bronze Age flanged axe or palstave. For example, subdivisions based upon the relative heights of flanges have resulted in terminological confusion as illustrated by Coles in reference to Butler (1963). '. . . The problem with calling these axes "high-flanged" is that certainly in Scotland there are "higher-flanged" axes. Butler's "high-flanged" axes are, for Scotland, equivalent to our low flanged class!' (Coles 1963–64, 84). Coles's attempts to divide axes on the type of flange, either convex or angled, runs into the problem that the correlation between flange type and other attributes, such as decoration or blade shape, is low.

Even if the component parts which make up an axe could be classified satisfactorily, they rarely group easily into types. Given the almost infinite permutations for classifying axes whether on flange shape, any combination of blade shapes, decoration, stop type or loop, the search for a widely accepted classification scheme is difficult and perhaps even a fruitless exercise. With 'flanged' axes, 'haft flanged' axes, 'wing flanged' axes, 'high flanged' axes, 'low flanged' axes and 'palstaves', the scope for terminological confusion and vague value judgements is endless. Is it possible to delve below this typological quagmire and make some sense of the Middle Bronze Age axe series?

Flanged axes and palstaves

Perhaps the obvious starting point is to attempt to distinguish between a flanged axe and a palstave. Although many opinions have been expressed in the literature defining the difference between the two, an agreed definition is still not available (Ramsey 1989, 106ff). The basic distinction relates to the treatment of the flanges and the stop. On a flanged axe the flanges extend beyond the stop, curving back into the sides of the axe (Fig. 23, no. 9). On a number of occasions they may be hammered or bent over the septum floor which gave rise to the term 'wing flanged' axe (Fig. 23, no. 10). This can be viewed as a specific attempt to gain a secure grip on the wooden haft with the flanges bent over it. On axes where the flanges were not worked in this fashion, the term 'haft flanged' axe has been used. Conversely with a palstave the flanges are fused with the stop and do not extend beyond it unless merging into a decorative motif (Fig. 23, no. 11).

It seems clear that the experimentation and evolution which took place among the Middle Bronze Age axe series was mainly an attempt to secure a better grip on the wooden haft. The increased height of Middle Bronze Age flanges, contrasting with Early Bronze Age forms, allowed them on occasion to be worked over the handle, while the general function of flanges was to reduce sideways movement within the haft,

hence steadying the axe. A further characteristic feature of Middle Bronze Age flanged axes is the increasing height of the stop, making it a more effective wedge for the wooden haft to brace against. The fusing of flange and stop seems a logical step if the wooden haft does not extend beyond the septum and it is this fusing which distinguishes the essential elements of a palstave from a flanged axe.

Bearing in mind that these basic distinctions are open to interpretation, and that the following figures may vary slightly, they still point to a significant imbalance between the proportion of flanged axes to palstaves between Britain and Ireland. Using the definitions preferred here (Ramsey 1989, 109), Rowlands (1976) lists some 300 flanged axes and 700 palstaves, while in Ireland the pattern is reversed with over 700 flanged axes and over 400 palstaves. While the development of the Irish palstave parallels southern British lines, in that it has an equivalent to the primary shield pattern group and the transitional series (Ramsey 1989, 176ff), the Irish palstave remains typologically insular compared with Britain, and is less standardised in design. This includes distinct Irish traits like the undercut or shoe stop which acts as a type of socket for the haft (for illustrations of stop types see Schmidt and Burgess 1981, 20).

The previous discussion, and these regional variations, allow us to examine several important questions. These concern the possible explanations to account for the greater number and variety of flanged axes in Ireland compared to England; and in particular why Middle Bronze Age flanged axes and palstaves are so typologically diverse when contrasted with other material.

The reason for Ireland's having a greater variety and frequency of flanged axes than Britain, and its possible implications, raise complex typological and chronological issues (Ramsey 1989, 177ff). These relate in particular to the date and place of origin of the palstave. While it is clear that hafting improvements have influenced features of flanged axe and palstave design, it does not necessarily follow that the palstave originated as an end result of an evolutionary series of changes to flange and stop arrangements. Taking this argument to its extreme, it could require that the date of origin of the Middle Bronze Age palstave was later than that of the majority of Middle Bronze Age flanged axes. It is clear from British and Continental evidence that the palstave can be dated to the opening phase of the Middle Bronze Age, while some have even suggested an overlap with the previous Early Bronze Age flanged axe series (Needham 1979, 290). This makes it difficult to maintain a long evolutionary design sequence, from Middle Bronze Age flanged axe to Middle

Bronze Age palstave. In addition the early arrival of the palstave in England and Wales could account for the lower frequencies of flanged axes from these areas. However this is not to deny the flanged axe a role in palstave design, as it seems quite clear that the primary shield pattern palstave had its origins in flanged axes with similar styled decoration (Butler 1963, 51).

As no shield pattern palstaves occur in Irish hoards, their chronology remains uncertain. The earliest Irish association of a palstave is in the Bishopsland hoard (Eogan 1983). If the palstave did arrive in Ireland at a later date than in Britain, in conjunction with the insularity of the Irish series, this could be taken as evidence that Ireland played a subsidiary role in palstave development. By necessity this would require a longer dependence on the flanged axe, which may account for their greater variety and numbers in Ireland.

This hypothesis has a number of problems. The Irish hoard evidence does not prove that the primary shield pattern palstave was definitely a late introduction. With British evidence placing it to the opening phase of the Middle Bronze Age, it is possible that it also occurred in Ireland at this time, giving a dual tradition of flanged axe and palstave production.

Similarly the place of origin of the palstave is uncertain. Rowlands considered Ireland and southern England as possible areas, favouring East Anglia (Rowlands 1976a, 28) while Schmidt and Burgess opted for Wales in preference to Ireland (1981, 119). One common denominator considered of prime importance for palstave evolution is the existence of antecedent axe forms, with an atmosphere of experimentation a significant factor (Schmidt and Burgess 1981, 119). The axes considered to be the prototypes for the development of the primary shield pattern palstave are flanged axes with shield decoration which are well known from Ireland (Ramsey 1989, nos 252-345). If the flanged axe played a significant part in the evolution of the palstave, then Ireland's position may have been influential because no other region in Britain has such a range of flanged axes as well as palstaves.

If it were not for the significance that other writers attach to the role of the flanged axe in the evolution of the palstave, the insularity of the Irish series, although paralleling changes in England, could be taken as evidence of a secondary role in palstave development. This could have included a longer dependence on the flanged axe and the introduction of the palstave from elsewhere. Conversely it is equally plausible that such individualistic traits as the shoe stop of Irish palstaves and the wide range of flanged axes are indicative of an innovative industry that gave the 'idea' of the palstave to Britain, where it was manufactured and paralleled in production by similar axes in north western France.

At present it is not clear when the palstave first appeared in Ireland and where it originated from. Given the low frequency of Irish hoards it is not possible to resolve these chronological issues. The insularity of Irish designs, contrasting with the close links between southern England and France, suggests a subsidiary role in later developments and perhaps even hints that the origin of the palstave rests elsewhere.

Function

Function may help provide an explanation for the degree of variability among Middle Bronze Age axes, in that both flanged axes and palstaves may have been used for a range of tasks. The evidence from Corlea trackway, Co. Longford, clearly demonstrates that from an early date (to within a decade of 2259 BC), bronze or copper axes were used to cut wood (Moloney *et al.* 1993, 73). With the increasing number of trackways dated to varying periods throughout the Bronze Age and the staggering quantities of wood from sites such as Flag Fen (Pryor 1991), it is clear that flanged axes and palstaves must have served a woodworking function, although not all were capable of cutting down trees. In addition to this purpose there seems no reason to dismiss the possibility that they could have served as general cutting and chopping tools for other materials besides wood.

Whether the suggestion that a number of axes may have served a non-utilitarian function is applicable to Middle Bronze Age forms, as argued for Early Bronze Age axes, is more difficult to ascertain (Ramsey 1995). However, Middle Bronze Age axes do show massive variations in size (52mm to 192mm) and weight (44gms to 903gms), with a notable change from light surface decoration to cast forms, particularly below the stop. What significance to attach to the meaning of this decoration, or to unravel the complex social function of axes throughout prehistoric society, is partly conjecture, though it is clear that these functions can be complex and unexpected (Sharp 1952).

The possibility that some of these flanged axes and palstaves could have served as weapons, as well as tools, is also feasible and they are often referred to as both (Eogan 1962). The depictions in rock art from Fossum, Sweden, appear to show axes being used as weapons, even if they are ritual or stylised representations (Coles and Harding 1979, pl. 24). It is difficult to believe that in times of trouble or necessity these axes would not be lifted in anger or used in hunting along with the spear.

If this multiplicity of functions is a correct interpretation then their manufacture may not have been subject to tight controls in terms of design, with production and casting taking place in a number of dispersed workshops. Any notion that they were subject to the control of specialist weapon smiths does not seem appropriate. While it is much easier to view a number of spearheads or rapiers as objects valued primarily for their appearance, as opposed to a functional value, it should be remembered that the average weight of a Middle Bronze Age flanged axe (370gms), or palstave (313gms), is significantly higher than that for spearheads or dirks/rapiers. These axes were therefore not insignificant in terms of the amount of metal required to cast them, and a saving was clearly made with the adoption of the socketed axe.

Conversely, to place a value on an artefact simply by thinking of it in terms of bullion leaves little place for the skill of the metalworker or the social significance attached to the object within its own cultural horizon. Given that Middle Bronze Age axes display a much wider range of shapes than perhaps any other type of bronze artefact, the interpretation that they served a variety of functions rather than one specialist purpose best matches the archaeological record. This can be combined with a degree of experimentation in hafting arrangements, not experienced to the same extent among other artefacts, so adding to the potential for a greater range of shapes.

Dirks and rapiers

The major reference work on dirks and rapiers by Burgess and Gerloff (1981) is an invaluable source of material. However, a closer and more detailed examination of these artefacts reveals a number of important observations which do not appear to have been given sufficient attention in that publication (Ramsey 1993). This relates in particular to damage caused to the butt area which provides a valuable insight into the function of these weapons and has implications for classification. It also graphically illustrates that rewards can still be gained from a careful visual inspection of objects.

Burgess and Gerloff classified dirks and rapiers into four groups on the basis of blade cross section. These four groups were further subdivided into 17 types and 21 variants on the shape of the butt, and whether the butt contained rivet holes (Pl. 3) or notches (Pl. 4). The butt is the area over which an organic handle was placed, though these handles rarely survive. On examining the illustrations in their corpus the general impression of damage to this butt area is inescapable.

This ranges from irregular shaped edges, through fractured and torn rivet holes, to severe damage, where the original shape of the butt is obliterated.

One reason for the damage to the butt area is that the rivet holes were placed close to the butt edge, often in the area of thinnest metal (Pl. 5). Side strain could lever the rivets out of the rivet holes and render the haft useless. A recently discovered dirk from the river Blackwater, in Co. Armagh, demonstrates that the rivet holes were not part of the original casting process but were created after the weapon had been removed from the mould (Ramsey *et al.* 1991-1992, no. 8). As a result of butt damage it is often difficult to distinguish between butts originally manufactured with side notches and notches resulting from torn rivet holes. If the damage is restricted to one side of the butt only, there may be one intact rivet hole and one notch, in which case it is clear that originally there were two rivet holes (Pl. 6). However, with other examples it is difficult to tell whether the notches are deliberate cast features or result from rivet hole damage.

As mentioned previously, this has profound implications for classification because dirks and rapiers are separated into different types based on the shape of the butt and whether they have rivet holes or notches. That damage of this nature may have been considerably widespread can be gauged by reference to the Cutts type, all of which have notched butts except for one example (Burgess and Gerloff 1981). The fact that one Cutts dirk survives with one intact rivet hole and one broken rivet hole creating a notch (Pl. 7) raises the possibility that others could have rivet holes (Pl. 8). If we are prepared to concede this as a possibility the wisdom of any classification that relies heavily upon the details of butt shape is suspect.

It seems clear that Burgess and Gerloff's first three groups were all manufactured with rivet holes and that any examples with notches resulted from damage. With Group 4 dirks there is a mixture of those with rivet holes, those with cast notches, and those with notches as secondary features. Unfortunately, because of continued rivet hole damage, it is not always clear which notches are cast and which are secondary features.

For reasons explained elsewhere, it is possible to haft a notched dirk (Ramsey 1993, 130). The advantage this may have had is that the notches could be cast directly from the mould as they are essentially only two semi-circular indentations on opposite sides of the butt. This seems a more attractive proposition than the more laborious task of drilling rivet holes. However, this modification, given the chronological position of Group 4 dirks, may have come too late, as the dirk and rapier were about to compete with the sword.

Pl. 3. Dirk butt, showing rivet holes placed very close to its edge. Keeran, Co. Fermanagh (UM 968.1937; Burgess and Gerloff 1981, no. 227).

Pl. 4. Example of a dirk with a notched butt (UM A118.1974; Burgess and Gerloff 1981, no. 761).

Pl. 5. Dirk butt, showing the fragility of the rivet holes. Mulawornia, Co. Longford (NMI W67; Burgess and Gerloff 1981, no. 391).

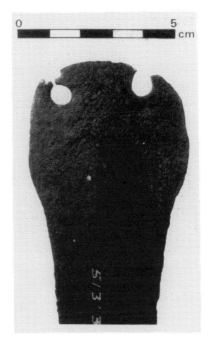

Pl. 6. Dirk butt, showing one torn rivet hole forming a notch and the other in the process of fracturing (UM 513.1937; Burgess and Gerloff 1981, no. 110).

Function

Taking into consideration the limitations of the hafting arrangement, the susceptibility of the butts to damage from side strain and the size and shape of the blade, it seems most probable that these weapons were best suited to a stabbing action. Inevitably they would have been used in a manner to which they were less suited, such as a slashing action, putting pressure on the haft and increasing the potential for damage. Their use in this fashion, whether intentional or accidental, must account for the high percentages of

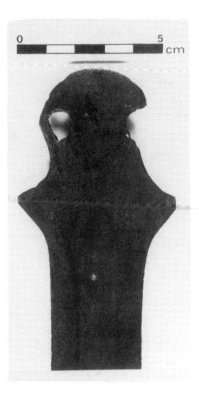

Pl. 7. Cutts dirk with a damaged butt showing only one intact rivet hole (NMI 1897.165; Burgess and
Gerloff 1981, no. 779).

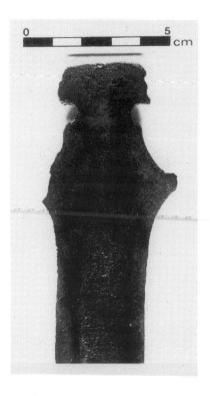

Pl. 8. Cutts dirk with two notches set in a damaged
butt. R. Bann, Cutts, Co. Derry (NMI W97; Burgess
and Gerloff 1981, no. 766).

damage. Nevertheless, it still seems surprising that
they did not attempt to strengthen the butt area. This
weakness becomes particularly apparent when
measured against the skill necessary to manufacture
the Lissane rapier (Burgess and Gerloff 1981, no.
387). Technically it is extremely difficult to cast an
object of this length (80cm), particularly as it has a
fluted blade. That these problems were overcome, as
evidenced in the flawless appearance of the blade,
contrasts with the almost complete disregard paid to
securing an effective handle. Only if this rapier fulfilled a social function, in terms of display or prestige,
rather than ever being designed as a fighting weapon,
could such a weak hafting arrangement as it exhibits
be tolerated. This interpretation parallels the function of Ommerschans 'rapiers', where their huge size,
weight, and absence of rivet holes renders them
useless as weapons (Coles and Harding 1979, 315).

With the arrival of the flanged-hilted sword, marking a radical improvement in weapon design, the hafting weakness of the dirk/rapier was exposed as it was
not capable of securing a handle to a heavier and more
powerful blade. It remains surprising that the technique of joining handle and blade as part of one casting
was not perceived prior to the arrival of the sword,
a solution which seems so obvious when viewed in
the light of later developments.

Conclusion

As the majority of Middle Bronze Age metal objects are not from burials, hoards or settlements, a
combination of these factors has forced us to study
individual objects in detail and to rely upon typology
and classification more than we would like. This is
particularly evident given the difficulty of trying to
tie the metalwork into an independent chronology.
The end result of this approach should be to provide
a corpus of material which can be used to expand
upon and address other issues. One danger in this
process is that classification may become an end in
itself, resulting in a failure to consider other issues.

In terms of metalworking, as examined through
three artefacts considered characteristic of the Middle Bronze Age, different trends and patterns were
highlighted. There seems little doubt that Ireland had
a flourishing spearhead manufacturing industry, producing a wide variety of side looped spearheads, some
of which can be recognised as distinctly Irish products in British contexts. Irish smiths also developed
the protected looped spearhead, a type easily recognised when it occurs outside the country.

With the Middle Bronze Age axe series, an increased degree of insularity is evident, both through the
greater number of flanged axes and the retention of

individualistic traits such as the shoe stop, characteristic of the Irish palstave series. The wide variations in the shape and form of Middle Bronze Age axes seems best appreciated if they are viewed as multipurpose implements.

Although dirks and rapiers were previously published by Burgess and Gerloff (1981) and show similar trends of development in Britain and Ireland, a more thorough examination of their hafting arrangements allows a greater appreciation of their function when contrasted with the sword. It also points to problems with previous classification schemes which rely too heavily on butt shape as a distinguishing feature, as the butt was evidently prone to alteration.

It is important to remember that artefacts were designed to serve a purpose, their manufacture involved ore extraction, casting and ancillary processes; they functioned within a social system whether or not they served as tools, weapons or ritual objects. A primary purpose of archaeology must be an attempt to discover the function of artefacts and the process of their manufacture and development. While the primary motive for their manufacture was not to conform to neat classification schemes or provide archaeologists with dating sequences, without the basic effort involved in gaining familiarity with bronze artefacts, including the more difficult areas of classification and chronology, an opportunity for a fuller appreciation of developments within the Bronze Age is lost.

The conclusions presented here are based upon what is often seen as a traditional approach to examining metalwork. Such an approach still has a significant part to play in Bronze Age research, emphasising the point that metalwork studies are not quite dead and buried.

Acknowledgements

I would especially like to thank Deirdre Crone of the Ulster Museum for providing the illustrations for this paper, Michael McKeown for photographs from the Ulster Museum, Mary Cahill for help with photographs from the National Museum, Dr Michael Avery, Queen's University, Belfast, Sinead McCartan, Ulster Museum, for comments on the text and Professor George Eogan, University College, Dublin, for advice on chronology.

References

Briard, J. and Mohen, J-P. 1983. *Typologie des objets de l'Age du Bronze en France: Fascicule II: Poignards, hallebardes, pointes de lance, pointes de flèche, armement défensif*, 135-45. Paris.

Burgess, C. B. 1968. *Bronze Age Metalwork in Northern England c. 1000-700 BC* Newcastle-Upon-Tyne.

Burgess, C. B. and Coombs, D. G. (eds.) 1979. *Bronze Age Hoards: Some Finds Old and New. British Archaeological Reports (British Series)* 67, i-vii. Oxford.

Burgess, C. B. and Gerloff, S. 1981. *The Dirks and Rapiers of Great Britain and Ireland. Prähistorische Bronzefunde* 4.7. Munich.

Butler, J. J. 1963. Bronze Age Connections across the North Sea. *Palaeohistoria* 9, 1-286.

Coffey, G. 1894. Notes on the Classification of Spear-Heads of the Bronze Age found in Ireland. *Proceedings of the Royal Irish Academy* 3, 486-510.

Coghlan, H. H. and Raftery, J. 1961. Irish Prehistoric Casting Moulds. *Sibrium* 6, 223-44.

Coles, J. M. 1963-64. Scottish Middle Bronze Age Metalwork. *Proceedings of the Society of Antiquaries of Scotland* 97, 82-156.

Coles, J. M., Coutts, H. and Ryder M. L. 1964. A Late Bronze Age Find from Pyotdykes, Angus, Scotland, with associated Gold, Cloth, Leather and Wood Remains. *Proceedings of the Prehistoric Society* 30, 186-98.

Coles, J. M. and Harding A. F. 1979. *The Bronze Age in Europe*. London.

Coombs, D. G. 1975. Bronze Age Weapon Hoards in Britain. *Archaeologia Atlantica* 1, 49-81.

Cooney, G. and Grogan, E. 1994. *Irish Prehistory: a social perspective*. Bray.

Davey, P. J. 1973. Bronze age metalwork from Lincolnshire. *Archaeologia* 104, 51-127.

Ehrenberg, M. R. 1977. *Bronze Age Spearheads, from Berkshire, Buckinghamshire and Oxford*. British Archaeological Reports (British Series) 34. Oxford.

Eogan, G. 1962. Some Observations on the Middle Bronze Age in Ireland. *Journal of the Royal Society of Antiquaries of Ireland* 92, 4-60.

Eogan, G. 1964. The Later Bronze Age in Ireland in the light of recent research. *Proceedings of the Prehistoric Society* 30, 268-351.

Eogan, G. 1965. *Catalogue of Irish Bronze Swords*. Dublin.

Eogan, G. 1983. *The Hoards of the Irish Later Bronze Age*. Dublin.

Evans, J. 1881. *The Ancient Bronze Implements, Weapons and Ornaments of Great Britain and Ireland*. London.

Harbison, P. 1969. *The Daggers and the Halberds of the Early Bronze Age in Ireland. Prähistorische Bronzefunde* 6.1. Munich.

Harbison, P. 1969. *The Axes of the Early Bronze Age in Ireland. Prähistorische Bronzefunde* 9.1. Munich.

Moloney A. *et al.* 1993. *Irish Archaeological Wetland Unit, Transactions: Volume 1. Survey of the raised bogs of County Longford*. Dublin.

Megaw, J. V .S. and Simpson, D. D. A. 1979. *Introduction to British Prehistory*. Leicester.

Needham, S. P. 1979. The Extent of Foreign Influence on Early Bronze Age Axe Development in Southern Britain. In M. Ryan (ed.), *The Origins of Metallurgy in Atlantic Europe: Proceedings of the Fifth Atlantic Colloquium*, 265-93. Dublin.

Needham, S. P. 1980. An assemblage of Late Bronze Age

metalworking debris from Dainton, Devon. *Proceedings of the Prehistoric Society* 46, 177-215.

O'Connor, B. 1980. *Cross-Channel Relations in the Later Bronze Age. Part II*. British Archaeological Reports (International Series) 91 (ii). Oxford.

Pryor, F. 1991. *Flag Fen Prehistoric Fenland Centre.* London.

Ramsey, G. 1989. Middle Bronze Age Weapons in Ireland. Unpublished Ph.D Thesis, Queen's University, Belfast.

Ramsey, G., Bourke, C. and Crone, D. 1991-1992. Antiquities from the River Blackwater I, Bronze Age Metalwork. *Ulster Journal of Archaeology* 54-5, 139-49.

Ramsey, G. 1993. Damaged Butts and Torn Rivet Holes: The Hafting and Function of Middle Bronze Age 'Dirks' and 'Rapiers'. *Archaeomaterials* 7, 127-38.

Ramsey, G. 1995. Bronze Age Metalwork. *Archaeology Ireland* 9, no. 1, 14-17.

Rowlands, M. J. 1976a. *The Organisation of Middle Bronze Age Metalworking. Part 1. Discussion*. British Archaeological Reports (British Series) 31. Oxford.

Rowlands, M. J. 1976b. *The Organisation of Middle Bronze Age Metalworking. Part II. Catalogue and Plates. British Archaeological Reports (British Series)* 31. Oxford.

Schmidt, P. K. and Burgess, C. B. 1981. *The Axes of Scotland and Northern England. Prähistorische Bronzefunde* 9.7. Munich.

Sharp, L. 1952. Steel axes for Stone Age Australians. In E. H. Spicer (ed.), *Human Problems in Technological Change*, 69-90. New York.

Smith, M. A. 1959. Some Somerset Hoards and their Place in the Bronze Age of Southern Britain. *Proceedings of the Prehistoric Society* 25, 144-87.

Later Bronze Age Goldwork from Ireland – Form, Function and Formality

Mary Cahill

Abstract

One of the most striking features of the Irish Later Bronze Age is the contrast between ornaments produced in sheet gold and those produced from bars or ingots. Sheet gold objects are notable for their originality of form and their relatively small numbers while the numbers of penannular ornaments of bracelet, dress-fastener and other forms run to many hundreds. A group of exceptionally heavy gold ornaments which take the form of dress-fasteners has been identified. The presence of so many heavy gold objects in the Irish record suggests that rich sources of gold were available and that these objects may represent concentrations of wealth and status or temporal or spiritual power. This paper discusses some aspects of the form this material takes and suggests a possible function-related differentiation between certain categories of object.

The Dowris phase, named after the largest hoard of Later Bronze Age bronze metalwork known from Ireland, is conventionally dated 900-600 BC. It was a period of major resurgence in the production of goldwork in Ireland. By far the greatest number of gold objects from the Irish record can be dated to this period. Due to the nature of discovery of gold ornaments in Ireland, which is characterised principally by the lack of association with burial, workshop or settlement sites, it is difficult to define close date brackets or function for this material. Unlike the preceding Bishopsland phase when the forms of object being produced can be paralleled with similar objects from Britain and the Continent, the Dowris period is notable for a number of new products which are known only from Ireland. These innovations are mostly confined to objects of fine, decorated sheet gold.

Another significant development was the conscious commitment of large quantities of gold to the production of a single object. This phenomenon must have resulted both from the availability of rich sources of raw materials and from social or cultural imperatives of a compelling nature. In this paper, I propose to discuss some aspects of the form this material takes and to suggest a possible function-related differentiation between certain categories of material.

During the Dowris period two principal types of goldwork were produced:

(i) objects made from sheet gold (including foil) and

(ii) objects made from cast or hammered bars and ingots.

Less than thirty objects of sheet gold survive (not including individual gold beads) whereas several hundred objects of bar or ingot work exist. Objects made substantially of gold wire, called lock-rings, are also known. Wire may be used also either as an embellishment or as a structural component in the construction of complex pieces.

Associations and Find Circumstances

Gold objects may be found in hoards or as single finds. Hoards may contain objects made solely of gold or a combination of objects of gold and other materials such as bronze tools, weapons and ornaments or necklaces of amber beads. Both sheet and bar gold are found together in hoards. Certain types of objects seem to have been produced in pairs. These include lock-rings, boxes and the recently recognised 'reels' or 'spools'. Finds come from both dryland and wetland sites.

Sheet gold

Sheet gold products are limited in number, type and distribution and include a range of objects from very small bi-conical and cylindrical beads of fine sheet gold (e.g. Cruttenclough, Co. Kilkenny; NMI W34-47) to heavy gauge, large (grapefruit-sized) beads (e.g. Tumna, Co. Roscommon; NMI W28-32, 1975:231, 1990:81 and BM 39.3-27.1), from fine sheet collars such as Ardcrony, Co. Tipperary (NMI W16), to foil-coverings for objects produced in other

Pl. 9. Gold Collar, Ardcrony, Co. Tipperary.

Pl. 10. Detail, Gold Collar, Ardcrony, Co. Tipperary.

Pl. 11. Detail, Gold Collar, Ardcrony, Co. Tipperary.

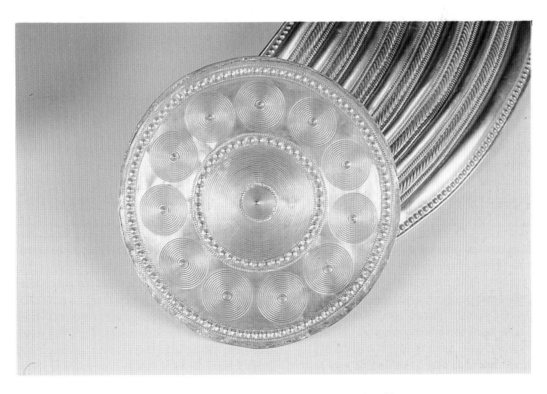

Pl. 12. Detail, Gold Collar, Gleninsheen, Co. Clare.

media such as the bulla from the Bog of Allen, Co. Kildare (NMI W265) or the sunflower pins from Ballytegan, Co. Laois (NMI 1967: 2-3). Decorated fine sheet gold objects and objects composed chiefly of wire (lock-rings) are the most technically difficult to produce and require very high levels of skill – they are the work of mastercraftsmen – yet they survive in very small numbers, almost in an inverse proportion to the level of skill required to produce them. The question arises as to how such levels of skill were attained and sustained. The maker of the Ardcrony gorget, for example, must have produced many other fine objects of sheet gold.

The principal ornament type is the large gold collar, called a gorget (Pl. 9). Eight substantially complete collars and one fragment of a collar survive. The collars are decorated by concentric ribbing alternating with panels of rope-moulding which is produced by a combination of repoussé and chasing techniques (Pl. 10). The terminals are formed from double discs which are usually attached to the collar by means of stitching with gold wire (Pl. 11). Each terminal consists of an upper and a lower disc held together either by lapping the edge of the lower disc over the upper disc or by attaching a length of C-sectioned tubing to the circumference of both discs. Only the upper discs are exposed to view. They are decorated with patterns of finely stamped concentric circles, round or conical bosses and raised herring-bone or rope patterns (Pl. 12). The lower discs of the terminals are obscured and are decorated with much simpler patterns, often poorly executed and incomplete (Pls 11 and 13).

The presence of a small pierced hole on either side of the inside upper edge of the collar suggests that a cord or light chain which would hold the collar in position across the back of the neck was originally present. The collar from Borrisnoe, Co. Tipperary (NMI W17) retains a gold wire link in one of the holes. Closely related to the collar terminals, in terms of their structure and decoration, are two other types of ornament whose functions remain unexplained. These are sealed 'boxes', which normally occur in pairs and the recently identified 'reels' or 'spools' which also seem to have been intended to function in pairs. Three pairs of boxes and one single find survive while two pairs and two fragmentary single finds of reels are known. The same gold working techniques and decorative patterning are used to produce boxes, reels and collar terminals. However, the mechanical sealing of the boxes which was achieved by the same techniques used to join the discs of the gorget terminals to one another, means that they were not intended to be opened on impulse and renders the interior and its contents inaccessible except by

the deliberate and damaging removal of one of the closing discs. The pair from Ballinesker, Co. Wexford (NMI 1990: 65-6; Pl. 15) each contained two small gold balls and one unlocalised pair (NMI W274, 275 and W277, 278) may each have contained a gold bracelet.

The Ballinesker hoard (Cahill 1994, 21-3) also contained one complete and one half reel (NMI 1990: 67-8). These objects were folded in antiquity and their form was revealed during the course of conservation (Pl. 14). The identification of this new type has led to the recognition as the component parts of reels, four large gold double discs (only two of which survive; NMI L1963:2 and MMNY 47.100.14) found near Enniscorthy, Co. Wexford in the late eighteenth century. The unprovenanced piece (NMI W276) described by Sir William Wilde (1862, 86-7) as 'not the least curious and as yet one of the most inexplicable specimens . . . the hat-shaped gold plate', can also now be identified as the back plate of a large reel. The reels or spools are of more complex construction than the boxes but maintain the same essential features in terms of technique of manufacture and decoration. Each face is made up of two discs, upper and lower, in the same way that gorget terminals are made. However, they differ in that, from the centre of each lower disc, is a projecting collar, which may be worked up from the disc or added as a separate piece, one fitting into the other. One example, Cashel, Co. Tipperary (NMI W306), also contained small gold balls. The reels are especially close to the collar terminals, sharing, in the case of the Ballinesker specimens, the same tendency to apply a poorly developed pattern of ornamentation to the back/lower disc, using simple, repetitive patterns confined to one or two motifs.

As the number of motifs used is very restricted, the main difference between the exposed/outer face of one object and another, whether box, reel or gorget terminal, is the variation in the spatial arrangement of the motifs – an arrangement which maintains a consistent pattern of concentricity which evolves from the positioning of the central boss as the primary motif.

Decorated foil was used to cover a range of objects made from other materials. These include sunflower pins, penannular rings (including ring money and the decorated foil-covered, penannular rings referred to as crescent-shaped bullae by Armstrong (1920, 93)), and the purse or heart-shaped objects also called 'bullae' (Eogan, forthcoming). The rings and bullae are often finely decorated with geometric motifs, drawn from a very limited repertoire, but in the case of the purse-shaped bullae also includes concentric circles. Enigmatic forms such as the decorated penannular rings and bullae survive only in small numbers. While the purse-shaped forms are capable of being suspended, it is not known if this was their primary purpose.

Distribution

The distribution of sheet gold ornaments is largely confined to the counties adjoining the lower reaches of the River Shannon in the south west (counties Clare, Limerick and Tipperary) but there are also significant occurrences in the south east in Co. Wexford. A 'trail' of related material can be plotted by a midland corridor towards the north-east through Westmeath, Cavan and Armagh. However, the predominant northern object types are the foil-covered purse-shaped bullae and the decorated foil-covered crescent-shaped rings.

Cast or Hammered Bar Goldwork

Within this category is a great variety of material ranging from small plain solid rings, sleeve-fasteners, plain and decorated rings with or without terminals, many of which might have been worn as bracelets, and fibulae or dress-fasteners. Eogan (1994) lists over three hundred and seventy objects from Ireland (not including ring-money) which come under this heading. The discussion which follows deals only with a small specialised group of twenty, very large, dress-fasteners and together with the conclusion is, in part, derived from a fuller study of these objects which is in press (Cahill, forthcoming).

Dress-fasteners are formed of two equally sized, conical or sub-conical terminals joined at their apices by a curved bar which may be solid or hollow. The terminals may lie in a fully horizontal position or they may be slightly inclined. They vary greatly in size and weight.

Amongst the objects conventionally assigned to this category is a group of exceptional objects which while generally conforming to that description must, because of their extreme size and weight, be considered as something more than the ordinary class of dress-fastener. Of the twenty examples recorded, only two complete objects, near Clones, Co. Monaghan (NMI L1963:1; Pl. 16) and Castlekelly, Co. Galway (NMI W122) and two fragmentary examples, Bog of Cullen, Co. Tipperary (Birmingham 283'64) and Clohernagh, Co. Tipperary (NMI R4025) survive. The remainder of the group are known from replicas, antiquarian drawings and descriptions. No entirely satisfactory name has yet been assigned to

these objects. Amongst the terms used in the past have been 'patera' (or double patera), an archaic antiquarian term suggesting a vessel. The term 'fibula with horizontal discs' which implies a functioning garment pin (as does the more recently used 'dress-fastener') has also been used. Some recent authors have preferred the less prejudicial term 'cup-ended ornament', which avoids any functional implications. However, until a more tenable explanation of their function has been defined it is unlikely that an acceptable terminology can be devised. In the present discussion the term 'Clones type dress-fastener' or 'super dress-fastener' has been used in order to distinguish this group from other forms of cup-ended ornament.

While accepting that this group is essentially an exaggerated form of the smaller dress-fasteners of the type well-known from hoards such as Mountrivers, Co. Cork (NMI 1908:8-9) their extreme size and weight necessitate their consideration as exceptional products commissioned to serve specific demands within the framework of Later Bronze Age society in Ireland.

As already mentioned a group of twenty super-dress-fasteners have so far been identified. They vary in size from 18.00cm to 28.00cm in maximum length. The minimum weight of objects in this group is 311 grammes (10 oz Troy) while the maximum weight is 1353 grammes (43½ oz). Both plain and decorated examples are known and as is the case with sheet gold work the range of decorative motifs is limited. Decoration, in its simplest form, is confined to a series of concentric, raised ribs on the terminals. The ribbing is present on both the internal and external surfaces. The number of ribs varies but the positioning is always immediately inside the rim of the terminal. Further elaboration of the piece may take the form of incised decoration using a limited repertoire of motifs including hatched triangles, hatched lozenges, zig-zags, bands of cross-hatching and groups of lines. This type of decoration is normally placed against the innermost rib on the terminal, internally or externally. The area around the junction of the bow and the terminals may also be decorated. The reason for decorating this area is most probably to disguise any remaining traces of the bow/terminal joins which have not been obliterated by polishing. Exceptionally, on the example from near Clones, Co. Monaghan, a motif consisting of a punched dot centrally set in a series of compass-drawn, incised, concentric circles is used to decorate the outer surface of the terminals. This is a unique use of both this motif and technique within this group of objects. A comparable use of a similar motif and technique can be seen on a pair of unprovenanced sheet gold boxes (Eogan 1983, 176-7

Pl. 13. Detail, Gold Collar, Borrisnoe, Co. Tipperary.

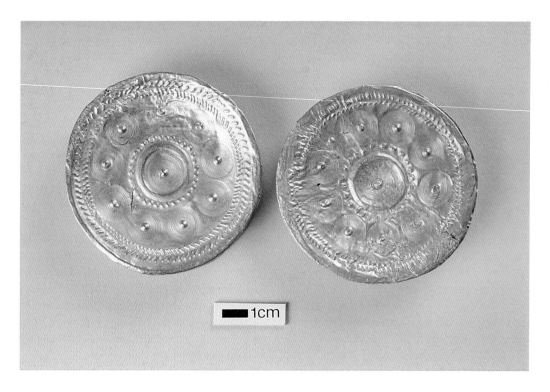

Pl. 14. Pair of Gold Boxes, Ballinesker, Co. Wexford.

Pl. 15. Gold Reel, Ballinesker, Co. Wexford.

Pl. 16. Gold Dress-fastener, near Clones, Co. Monaghan.

and pl. 6) and on the purse-shaped bulla from the hoard from Arboe/Killycolp, Co. Tyrone (Eogan 1983, 159 and fig. 88a) as well as the face-plates of the lock-ring from Cooper's Hill, Alnwick, Northumberland (Eogan 1969, 122-3 and fig. 3).

Apart from the exceptional size of objects in this group, the most outstanding feature is the weight of the individual specimens which range between 311g and 1353g. The determining factor of gross weight is whether the bow is hollow or solid. The three specimens with solid bows all weigh over 1000g - near Clones, Co. Monaghan, near Dunboyne, Co. Meath (NMI D955 - replica) and a lost, unprovenanced example. The remainder of the group all weigh between 311g and 746g. Within the range of gold ornaments known from the Irish record this type is by far the heaviest and in the more exceptional cases shows an extravagance unmatched at any other period. The total reckonable weight of this group amounts to 9.54kg or 306.71oz Troy.

The number of other objects of solid, cast or hammered bar work of Dowris phase date, from Ireland, which compare in terms of the amount of gold consciously committed to one object is comparatively small. They include a plain penannular bar with expanded ends from Cooga Lower, Co. Limerick (NMI R2599; previously recorded as Kilcommon, Co. Tipperary; 878.24g/28oz 4dwt 17gr); the decorated bracelet from a hoard from 'near New Ross', Co. Waterford (NMI 1896:1; 542.5g/17oz 8dwt 20gr); a decorated bracelet from near Lurgan, Co. Armagh (NMI 1875:54; 398.46g/12oz 16dwt 4gr) and a large ring with a smaller ring attached from Mooghaun, Co. Clare (NMI W27; 365.15g /11oz 14dwt 19gr). When sheet gold products are taken into consideration, there are only two objects of exceptional weight. These are the collar said to be from Co. Clare (NMI W21; 514.1g/16oz 10dwt 13gr) and the dismantled collar from Gorteenreagh, Co. Clare (NMI 1948:320-5), the component parts of which weigh 358.43g/11oz 10dwt 11gr. The average weight of a gorget is approximately 223.32g/7oz 3dwt 14gr. In simple terms this means that an object such as the dress-fastener from near Dunboyne, Co. Meath, could have provided the raw material for six to seven gorgets. When compared to the average quantity of gold used for the lunula of the Earlier Bronze Age (30-60g), the 'near Dunboyne' specimen would have represented an unparalleled resource, given that it could have provided between twenty to forty lunulae depending on the amount of metal allowed to each object.

Distribution

The distribution of super dress-fasteners is scattered in a broad band through the middle of the country with specimens recorded from the extreme north-east in Co. Antrim to the south coast at Youghal, Co. Cork. There are two small concentrations, one in Co. Galway where three examples are recorded and another in the west Tipperary/north Cork/Limerick area where six are known. There are no recorded examples from the north-west, south-west or south-east.

Discussion

When viewed as a whole it may be seen that three different types of ceremonial artefact can be distinguished in the classes of material which have been discussed.

1. Ostentatious personal ornament: objects worn perhaps for a time by a specific person before being ritually concealed. Sheet gold collars which are elaborately decorated and spectacular in appearance belong to this class. It is also apparent that of the nine surviving examples, six were folded before deposition perhaps in an act of ritual mutilation, possibly to signify that these objects had, in some sense, been decommissioned.

2. Objects of purely votive or ritual purpose: these include bullae, decorated crescent-shaped rings, boxes and reels. These are severely restricted in terms of numbers and are of no obvious utilitarian purpose. However, many of them are elaborately decorated and skilfully made, presumably to serve in ceremonial display. As the outer surfaces of both boxes and reels are decorated with patterns which incorporate raised elements, some of which are in quite high relief - the most extreme example being the central conical bosses on the reels (h. 1.00cm) from near Enniscorthy, Co. Wexford - it seems plausible to suggest that these objects were intended to be viewed from each side (i.e. to stand on edge rather than to be placed with one decorated face down). There is also a marked tendency for boxes and reels to occur as paired sets which suggests that they were intended to be viewed and to function together.

3. Objects of overt power, rank or status such as the Clones-type dress-fasteners which have been discussed above. These retain the form of smaller, more utilitarian types but in their grossly exaggerated form are incapable of being worn and have assumed new functions of both a symbolic and a real nature. They may have functioned as physical representations or concentrations of power and wealth. They may have been used as symbols of authority to exert territorial control or have been intended for deposition as dedicatory or propitiatory offerings. They may have been seen to be capable of exerting a supernatural power in the way that reliquaries of the Early Medieval

period were regarded as powerful entities in themselves which were capable of affecting the life and well-being of those who offended certain conventions (this need not apply exclusively to dress-fasteners). It may also be significant that these are all single object depositions (perhaps with one exception) although some may have been consigned to the ground in areas where multiple deposits of material (i.e. multiple episodes of concealment) took place, such as at the Bog of Cullen, Co. Tipperary, and other locations, rather than as a single-episode of hoard deposition. The 'power of place' should not be disregarded in this context as there can be little doubt that it is the combination of place, object and ceremony which defines the essential character and significance of the act of concealment.

Conclusion

The singular nature of much of the Irish goldsmiths' repertoire clearly indicates that they were reacting to a demand for highly specialised sheet and bar gold products, many of which must have been imbued with hidden symbolism. The presence in Ireland of such a large number of Dowris period gold ornaments suggests that substantial sources of raw materials were available. However the location of these sources is not known. Both access to and supply of the raw materials must have been well organised and controlled. The maintenance and support of highly skilled groups of craftsmen requires the ability to manage the process through many stages, from supply and preparation of raw materials to the provision of workshops, food and housing and assumes that strict regulatory procedures were enforceable.

It may also suggest that gold was not simply a commodity to be bartered or traded in the normal way but that its production at source was to serve the needs that society demanded of it whether that need was a hierarchical prerequisite or a religious dogma. It is a notable feature of the Irish record, for example, that so few cup-ended ornaments occur in bronze. This was not because bronze was in short supply but that it seems not to have been considered an appropriate material. The complete absence of any known association with burials or other monuments for objects of this type has been noted many times. Their purpose was therefore other than that of grave goods although many were intended to be purposely discarded in non-funerary contexts. This argument reflects the idea suggested by Barrett and Needham (1989, 136) that the production of a certain type of object may have been 'instigated in anticipation of its ultimate destiny'. This does not mean that all

goldwork was intended, solely, for the purpose of ritual deposition but perhaps it does allow the consideration that certain types of product were restricted conventionally in terms of function and numbers produced. These objects cannot be consigned to the category of decorative assets. Likewise, contrary to Hawkes's view (1963, 235) that very heavy objects are a form of bullion, the discovery at Gahlstorf, Lower Saxony, buried in a ceramic vessel (in a non-funerary context), of a gold cup-ended ornament of Irish type, weighing 475g/15oz 5dwt 10gr, supports the idea that these objects were deliberately manufactured to serve special purposes. Clones-type dress-fasteners represent, in effect, a society which could afford to devote large quantities of an extremely hard-won resource to a single object whenever that demand had to be satisfied. Bullion was far more likely to have been present in the form of ingots or bars which are unlikely to have survived. Antiquarian sources testify to the presence of heavy, plain bars of gold which must represent the raw materials.

Sheet gold objects, whose distribution is more markedly concentrated than the bar gold, constitute a small group of very highly specialised and formalised types of peculiarly Irish origin. While sharing a common background with European metalwork in terms of technique and some decorative elements, the forms differ greatly, suggesting an innovative response by Irish goldsmiths to Continental influence while at the same time meeting the needs of their own society. This may relate to Ireland's relatively isolated position *vis-à-vis* mainland Europe. The amount of goldwork produced in Ireland during the Later Bronze Age has always been the subject of much discussion and questioning. Antiquarian sources reveal that what has survived is but a fraction of what originally existed. Ongoing research into the nature of relationships between Later Bronze Age monuments and the find places of significant metalwork types is showing that, in spite of the problems caused by the lack of orthodox archaeological associations between the two types of evidence, we can begin to understand how this very important body of material can contribute to a fuller appreciation of the complexity of Later Bronze Age society and ritual in Ireland.

References

Armstrong, E. C. R. 1920. *Catalogue of Irish Gold Ornaments in the Collection of the Royal Irish Academy.* Dublin.

Barrett, J. C. and Needham, S. P. 1989. Production, Circulation and Exchange: Problems in the Interpretation of Bronze Age Bronzework. In J. C. Barrett and I.

Kinnes (eds), *The Archaeology of Context in the Neolithic and Bronze Age: Recent Trends*, 127-40. Sheffield.

Cahill, M. 1994. Beads, Bobbins and . . . Notions. *Archaeology Ireland* 8, no. 1, 21-3.

Cahill, M. forthcoming. Large Gold Dress-fasteners of the Irish Later Bronze Age. In M. Ryan (ed.), *Irish Antiquities – A Memorial Volume for Dr J. Raftery*. Dublin.

Eogan, G. 1969. 'Lock-Rings' of the Late Bronze Age. *Proceedings of the Royal Irish Academy* 67C, 93-148.

Eogan, G. 1983. *Hoards of the Irish Later Bronze Age*. Dublin.

Eogan, G. 1994. *The Accomplished Art – Gold and Goldworking in Britain and Ireland during the Bronze Age*. Oxford.

Eogan, G. forthcoming. Heart-Shaped Bullae of the Irish Late Bronze Age. In M. Ryan (ed.), *Irish Antiquities – A Memorial Volume for Dr J. Raftery*. Dublin.

Hawkes, C. F. C. and Clarke, R. R. 1963. Gahlstorf and Caister-on-Sea – Two finds of Late Bronze Age Irish Gold. In I. Ll. Foster and L. Alcock (eds), *Culture and Environment: Essays in Honour of Sir Cyril Fox*, 193-250. London.

Wilde, W. R. 1862. *Catalogue of Gold Ornaments in the Collection of the Royal Irish Academy*. Dublin.

Haughey's Fort and the Navan Complex in the Late Bronze Age

J. P. Mallory

Abstract

Among the monuments of the Navan Complex are a number of sites that may be ascribed to the Late Bronze Age. These comprise phases of occupation at the main monument, Navan Fort, the ritual site of the King's Stables, and Haughey's Fort. The latter is a trivallate hillfort which was occupied during the centuries around 1100 BC. The site has yielded some artefactual evidence and an impressive quantity of organic remains pertaining to the environment and economy of the Late Bronze Age settlement. The virtually exclusive crop would appear to have been barley while the major livestock were cattle and pigs. Although architectural features have been uncovered in the interior of the site, there are problems in ascribing the structures to purely secular or ritual functions. It is suggested that Haughey's Fort and the adjoining King's Stables may have served as the main tribal centre (political, ritual or both) during the centuries about 1100 BC but that after a century or two, power had shifted elsewhere to emerge most spectacularly at Navan Fort in the first centuries BC.

The Navan Complex of sites, which lies *c.* 3km west of Armagh, is traditionally identified with Emain Macha, the capital of the Ulaid reflected in early Irish literary and (pseudo-) historical sources (Mallory 1987). The most recent published survey of the Navan Complex (Fig. 24) records the existence of some 46 actual or possible sites ranging from such substantial surface monuments as Navan Fort to a considerable number of more ephemeral crop marks (Warner 1994a). Of this list, only a handful of sites have seen excavation, some of which have yielded evidence for Bronze Age occupation, pertaining especially to the Late Bronze Age. That associated with Navan Fort has seen preliminary publication (Lynn 1986, 1991, 1992, 1994) and the full account of the excavations of this site is expected in the near future (Lynn, forthcoming).

Briefly, the work undertaken so far at Navan has revealed evidence for Bronze Age occupation under the Site B mound sometime after the initial Neolithic settlement. This is attested by the presence of plough marks in the soil that accumulated over a series of Neolithic pits. Subsequently, a circular structure of timber posts, set at about 4m intervals, was constructed to enclose an area *c.* 39m across (Fig. 25). The timber structure was surrounded by a ditch some 5m wide and 1m deep whose diameter was *c.* 45m. The ditched enclosure revealed an entrance on the east. Although the circular structure and the ditch would appear to be contemporary with one another a radiocarbon date from one of the post-pits and two

from the ditch do not overlap even at two standard deviations: the timber post date falls broadly in the period *c.* 1600-1200 cal BC (see Appendix date no. 1 [henceforth D-1]) while the ditch has yielded two dates in the range *c.* 900-550 cal BC (D-2a-b; Mallory and Warner 1988). Artefactual evidence from the area of the enclosure has also yielded Bronze Age material, e.g. a socketed axe, the wing tip of a chape and a bar toggle, which may be broadly set to *c.* 8th-7th centuries BC.

There is also evidence for subsequent activity during the terminal Bronze Age into the Iron Age with the construction of a series of circular huts adjoined by larger circular enclosures (Fig. 25). The pattern of radiocarbon dates for these figure-of-eight structures has suggested occupation from about the mid 4th century BC into the Iron Age (Warner 1994b, 66). The ditch enclosing Navan Fort has not been excavated but a sample of organic material obtained from coring the base of the ditch (Weir 1989) yielded a date of *c.* 750-400 cal BC (D-3). Excepting the terminal Bronze (?) Age figure-of-eight structures, for which both 'secular' (Lynn 1991) and 'ritual' (Wailes 1990) interpretations have been presented, almost all other architectural evidence relating to the Late Bronze Age suggests ritual structures, i.e. the timber ring (Site B) with its corresponding shallow ditch and the hengiform Navan enclosure (Simpson 1989). Much the same comments could be directed at the King's Stables, the artificial pool which lay less than 1 km to the west of Navan Fort. Here Chris Lynn

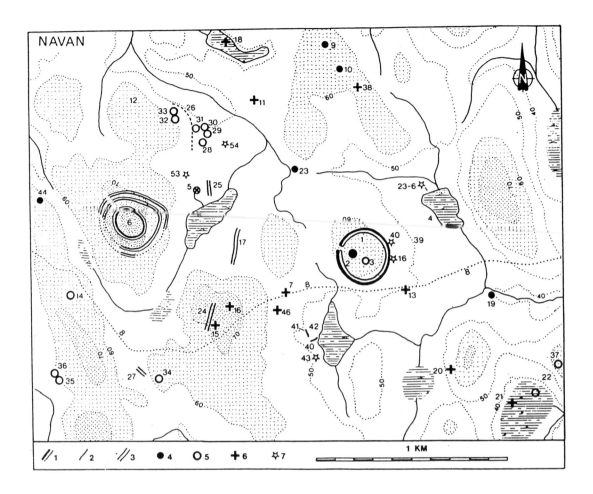

Fig. 24. Plan of the Navan Complex (after Warner 1994a). The Bronze Age sites mentioned in the text include site numbers 1 (Site B, Navan Fort), 2 (ditch, Navan Fort), 5 (King's Stables), 6 (Haughey's Fort) and 17 (Creeveroe ditches).

(1977) uncovered the remains of moulds, partially articulated animal bones, red deer antler, and the front portion of the skull of a young male. The structure has so far defied secular explanation and is most easily interpreted as a deliberate attempt to create a pool of water into which offerings might be made. Charcoal from the original ground surface underlying the earthen bank have yielded a date of *c.* 1100-800 cal BC (D-4) while organic samples extracted from the base of the King's Stables have yielded dates in the broad range *c.* 1400-400 cal BC (D-5a-b).

So far then the evidence for activity in the Navan complex would appear to associate better with ritual behaviour than with secular occupation (assuming that one can make such a distinction during the Bronze Age). This is further emphasised by most of the remaining unexcavated sites which include ten ring-ditches (destroyed barrows?), seven linear ditches, and an assortment of stone rings (?passage tombs), mounds, skeletal remains and later medieval monuments. The only site that presented a case for actual prehistoric settlement was Haughey's Fort.

Haughey's Fort

Haughey's Fort is a Late Bronze Age hillfort which has seen four seasons of excavation (1987, 1989, 1990, 1991). The fort is trivallate and comprises an elliptical outer ditch which measures some 340 x 310m in diameter (Fig. 26 [Tr. 12], Pl. 17). Twenty-five metres upslope is the middle ditch (Tr. 11) and a further 55m upslope is the innermost ditch (Tr. 5) which encloses an area measuring *c.* 150 x 140m in diameter.

Although few traces of an earthen bank survive near any of the ditches, it may be argued that we are nevertheless dealing with the remains of a truly defensive site, i.e., a hillfort. All three ditches are approximately V-shaped in section (Pl. 18) and measure *c.* 2.3 to 3.2m in depth which fits both the morphology and the minimum depth for a defensive enclosure. The excavated ditch sections indicate the movement of material from upslope into the ditches which supports the prior existence of earthen banks, possibly with some stone revetment, at least in the case of the innermost ditch. Moreover, what would appear to be

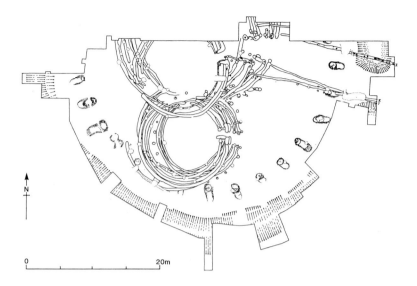

Fig. 25. Navan, Site B (after Lynn 1986). The ring ditch and internal circle of posts date to the Late Bronze Age; the 'figure-of-eight' timber structures are set to the terminal Bronze Age/Early Iron Age.

a small palisade slot was uncovered just beyond the lip of the innermost ditch. The ditches and the palisade slot have all produced broadly contemporary radiocarbon dates within the range of *c.* 1300-900 BC (D6a-c – D-9).

The innermost ditch is waterlogged and has yielded an impressive quantity of faunal (mammals, insects) and floral (wood, seeds) remains. These organic remains provide evidence for the initial erection of the defences and the subsequent abandonment of the site. The evidence from the former derives from a series of samples of short-lived organic remains (twigs, etc.) from the base of the ditch which permitted the application of high-precision dating. This revealed that the infilling of the innermost ditch began in the period *c.* 1160-1042 cal BC (D-6a-c; Mallory 1994). A sample extracted from 1m above the base of the ditch yielded a high precision date of 1047-941 BC (D-6d). By this time the quantity of *Sambucus* (elder) had risen to about 75% of all wood remains and the evidence for artefacts had become insignificant. At a further height of 0.30m, by which time the evidence for pollen suggested forest regeneration around the site, a high precision date yielded a range of 841-806 cal BC (D-6e). This all suggests that the defences of Haughey's Fort were probably established about 1100±50 BC and that abandonment of the site had probably occurred within a century, possibly less.

Settlement

Approximately 300m² of the interior of Haughey's Fort have been investigated so far which

would represent less than 2% of the total area enclosed by the innermost ditch. Numerous features have been uncovered which in general resolve themselves into four the following interpretative classes:

a. Stake holes: an assortment of small stake holes, particularly dense in the western area of the excavation, which do not reveal any clear structural patterns. These stake holes have yielded so little charcoal that it has been impossible to obtain a date for them.

b. Stockade line (Fig. 27, Pl. 19): three lines of stake holes and small post holes running in an arc from north to southeast. The larger post holes (0.25m diameter and set at intervals of 0.80m to 1m) could be traced for a length of at least 15m, possibly as much as 30m (Mallory 1991, 15-18), and would appear to have formed either a series of hurdles or a unitary structure. Radiocarbon dates from two of the posts (Fig. 27 [Fts 86, 112]) fell within the range *c.* 1250-900 BC (D11-D12). Parallel to this arc of posts were two lines of stakes (*c.* 0.14m diameter) running along the western side of the post row. Small quantities of charcoal were recovered from ten of the posts (Fig. 27 [Fts 207 to 110]) and combined to provide the very unexpected (and highly problematic) date of *c.* 2450-1550 BC (D-10). Given the fact that the stake holes are parallel with the larger post-built stockade, the wide variation in dates for the two structures remains unexplained. The larger alignment of post-holes bears a certain generic resemblance to the Bronze Age stockade excavated at Cullyhanna Lough in south Armagh (Hodges 1958).

c. Large pits: two possible lines of pits were uncovered in the centre and eastern part of the excavation (Fig. 27, Pl. 19). These pits measure about 1m

Pl. 17. Aerial view of Haughey's Fort. The three ditches are indicated with arrows.

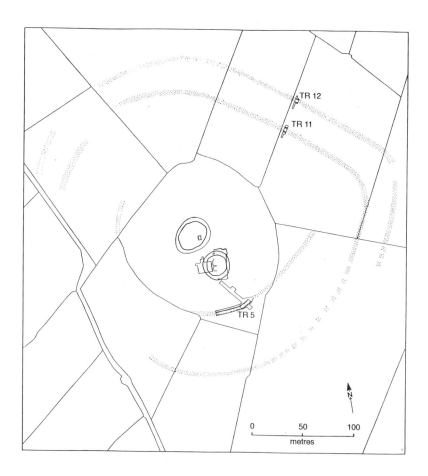

Fig. 26. Plan of Haughey's Fort. The outer ditch was sectioned at Tr. 12, the middle at Tr. 11, and the innermost ditch at Tr. 5. The two circular 'enclosures' observed through aerial photographs are only approximately positioned.

Pl. 18. Section of the innermost ditch (Tr. 5).

Pl. 19. View of the stockade line and the 'inner' row (Fts 70-43-48-75) of deep pits.

Fig. 27. A simplified plan of the interior of Haughey's Fort with some of the features mentioned in the text. The larger stockade alignment includes Fts 86 and 112; the smaller stake hole alignment that received radiocarbon dating includes Fts 207 and 110. Large pits, identified as possible post-pits, are to be seen in two rows, an inner row comprising Fts 70-43-48-75 and an outer row (Fts 27 7-267-268).

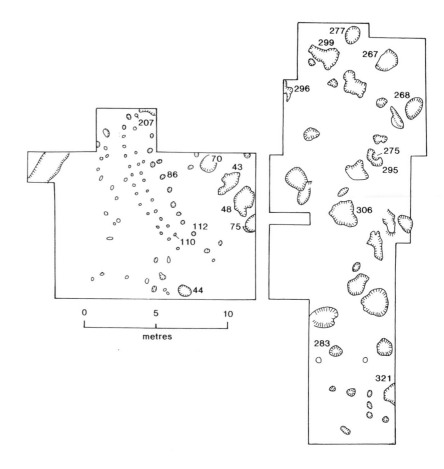

or more in depth and at least a metre in diameter. Although they suggested the possibility of a series of large post holes, there was considerable evidence against this: there were no traces of post-pipes to be seen in the sections and the pits revealed quantities of Late Bronze Age coarse wares, carbonised grain and even fragments of gold and bronze which all suggested that they had been filled with occupation debris. The function of the pits remained uncertain until 1994 when further evidence was revealed from aerial photographs. An archaeological survey (remote sensing) team from California State University, Long Beach, and Boston University enhanced a series of vertical aerial photographs which suggested that the interior of Haughey's Fort included two double ring structures (cf. Mallory 1988, 6). The location of one of these (Fig. 26) appears so close to that of the large pits excavated that it argues that the aerially documented post rings and the large pits may be the same. To account for the evidence of excavation it is most tempting to conclude that the pits derive from a double timber-ring structure which was subsequently dismantled, the timbers being removed from their post-pits, after which settlement debris accumulated in the pits. A radiocarbon date from one of the pits has revealed a date of 1260-910 cal BC (D-17).

d. Pits: a number of pits which do not apparently serve a structural purpose and whose contents (pottery, carbonised grain and hazel nut shells, burnt bone, fragments of quern stones, metal artefacts, etc.) and radiocarbon dates (*c.* 1250-900 cal BC; D-13-D-16) indicate Late Bronze Age occupation broadly contemporary with that of the ditches and post-pits.

e. Later pits: there is some evidence for Iron Age occupation on the site as indicated by the discovery of some fragments of iron and later glass beads in a few of the pits. Feature 299 (Fig. 27), for example, was an irregularly shaped pit, which yielded a small iron 'strap' (Mallory 1991, fig. 14.6). Two charcoal samples from this pit were dated in the range *c.* 400-200 BC (D-20) and define the latest evidence for occupation at Haughey's Fort, roughly contemporary with the figure-of-eight structures at Navan.

Environment and Economy

The environment of the Navan complex has been systematically studied by D. A. Weir (1987, 1993, 1993a, 1994), especially as it may be interpreted through pollen samples obtained from Loughnashade, about 1 km east of Haughey's Fort. These studies revealed a series of clearance episodes during the

Bronze Age which culminated in the period *c.* 1400-1000 BC. At this time there was a major reduction in elm, hazel, ash and oak coincidental with a peak in the charcoal suggesting a major clearance phase. The increasingly open landscape appeared to be primarily for grassland but evidence for cereals, present since *c.* 1760 BC, rose to reach levels of *c.* 6% which are among the highest known from Irish prehistoric sites (Weir 1994, 175). That there was considerable emphasis on arable agriculture is underscored by the recovery of large quantities of carbonised barley from the pits at Haughey's Fort. Preliminary analysis indicates that the cereal samples are free of contaminants and may indicate that the grain was processed off-site before its consumption at Haughey's Fort. Although the cereal remains are uniformly of barley, pollen from both rye and flax were observed in the Bronze Age levels of the lake cores.

The major clearance phase ended by *c.* 1000 BC, a time broadly coincidental with other indications for the abandonment of Haughey's Fort. There was a recovery first by hazel scrub but by *c.* 850 BC, ash and elm began to expand again as well and grass values fall from 27% to 16%. The rise in the lake level at Loughnashade for this period suggests deteriorating climatic conditions which may have prompted the abandonment of Haughey's Fort or at least a greater reliance on pastoral rather than arable subsistence in the region although the latter was not entirely abandoned, at least in the vicinity of Loughnashade. By about 600 BC there is again evidence for a major clearance but this would have occurred long after the abandonment of Haughey's Fort.

Additional botanical evidence was obtained from analysis of both wood and seed remains from the lower levels of the interior ditch, i.e. for the period *c.* 1100-900 BC. The wood remains consist of worked wood employed by the occupants of the site and naturally occurring shrubs and trees which were either disposed of in the ditches or, most certainly in the later periods, had been part of the arboreal 'reclamation' of the site. A preliminary account of the wood has been published (Hawthorne 1991) but there also exists a more thorough analysis of the wood remains (Neill, forthcoming). Maire Neill made 2486 identifications from several stratified samples of over 57kg of wood. The primary species identified was elder (*Sambucus*) which accounted for 51% of all wood remains. This, however, is misleading in that the main rise of elder occurred coincidental with the apparent abandonment of the site and, as Neill observes, elder was regarded in early Irish literature as a marker of an abandoned settlement. More important was *Prunus*, which comprises both wild cherry and blackthorn, the latter of which is quite efficient in

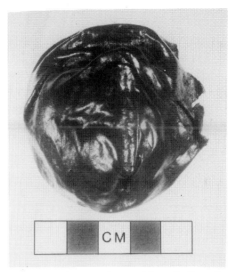

Pl. 20. Three thousand year-old apple from base of inner ditch (Tr. 5).

forming defensive hedgerows and whose distinguishing thorny shoots could be identified on a number of occasions. *Prunus* comprised 33% of the wood remains recovered. Other species were infrequently recorded: hazel (*Corylus*) at 6%, ash (*Fraxinus*) at 4%, alder (*Alnus*) at 2%, hawthorn (*Crataegus*) at 1.7% and under 1% were oak (*Quercus*), holly (*Ilex*), willow (*Salix*) and birch (*Betula*). Hazel was employed for the production of long rods but Neill's analysis finds no certain evidence for deliberate coppicing.

Large quantities of macro-botanical samples were also recovered and a preliminary report has been published (Weir and Conway 1988) while a more extensive provisional report has also been prepared (Ó Cathmhaoil 1992). The evidence of the seeds augments the impression provided by the analysis of the wood remains. Arboreal seeds are present with elder at about 6% and blackthorn at least present but the primary contributors to the seed remains were nettles (*Urtica*) at 26%, followed by dock (*Rumex*) at 20%, chickweed (*Caryophyllaceae*) at 18% and water dropwort (*Oenanthe*) at 15% (Weir and Conway 1988). There was moderate evidence for plantain (*Plantago lanceolata*), buttercup (*Ranunculus acris*), blackberry (*Rubus*) and traces also of thistles (*Cirsium*), knotgrass (*Polygonum*), and rushes (*Juncus*). Pollen extracted from the ditch suggests that the base was waterlogged because of the high percentages of water dropwort (*Oenanthe*) and reeds (*Phragmites*) while the evidence from Ó Cathmhaoil's examination of the seeds similarly supports such a reconstruction as one can witness the percentages of rushes, set at about 20% in the lower levels, descend to 0% in the later levels. Finally, one of the most surprising organic discoveries from the basal layers of the layers of the ditch was an apple (Pl. 20) some 3000 years past its 'sell by' date.

A quantity of faunal remains were recovered from the excavations and a summary report of the first three seasons of excavation has been published (McCormick 1988, 1991, 1994). According to these reports, the primary remains belong to cattle (Minimum Number of Individuals [MNI] is 29), followed by pig (MNI 14) and only small traces of sheep/goat (MNI 4), horse (MNI 2) and dog (MNI 4). The only evidence for hunted mammals were the remains of a single red deer, a fox and traces of wild pig. These remains were subsequently augmented by the excavation of a substantial section of the waterlogged ditch in 1991 and an unpublished report of the faunal remains exists (Murphy 1992). The new report augments the minimum number of individuals (in 1991 the MNI for the two primary species was 42 cattle and 25 pig but these figures will require adjusting against the previously excavated remains from adjacent areas of the inner ditch). The cattle are identified as short horned with variable stature with some attaining a withers height of 129.5cm which is comparable to the very large cattle excavated in the Early Bronze Age levels at Newgrange. The pigs were large with some up to 78cm at the shoulders. Evidence for sheep and goat was minimal with at least one of the three ovicaprids identified as goat. This included the horn core of a male that measured 344mm, substantially larger than that found in later historic sites (the evidence of prehistoric sites is silent) such as medieval Waterford where the largest goat horn measured only 280mm. The emphasis on large animals is also seen in the dog remains where several skulls comprise the largest canine skulls known from prehistoric Ireland. Measurements suggest heights of *c.* 63 and 65cm for some of the dogs. The repeated emphasis on animals of large stature has been invoked as one of the criteria by which one might identify a royal site (Warner 1988) on the argument that royalty would either be engaged in the selective breeding of larger animals or the recipients of very large animals as prestige gifts, e.g. the two exceptionally large bulls of the *Táin*.

Finally, the interior ditch also yielded the remains of an insect death assemblage which has provided additional evidence for the environment during the infilling of the ditches. A preliminary report (Anderson 1989) identified 185 individuals comprising 85 species of beetle which reflects a fairly high degree of diversity. Predictably, some of the species such as *Agabus chalconotus/unquicularis* and *Stenus* are generally associated with water or at least wetland areas which correlate well with the pattern of waterlogging found in the ditch while a variety of *Geotrupes/Aphodius* (dung beetles) best associates with decaying animal and plant remains. *Bracypterus glaber, Cidnorhinus*

Pl. 21. View of reverse side of small gold stud indicating manner by which it might be attached.

quadrimaculatus and *Ceuthorhynchus pollinarius* have life-cycles that closely or exclusively involve nettles (*Urtica*), the remains of which were well represented in the ditch sediments. One species (*Patrobus assimilis*) would normally select for colder environments and provides the only evidence from the assemblage of somewhat colder conditions than those prevailing at present.

Artefacts

Artefacts were recovered from the pits and post-holes in the interior of the sites and from the ditches, particularly from the waterlogged layers of the interior ditch. These ranged from metallic (gold, bronze), stone, glass, ceramic and objects fashioned from organic materials (wood, boar tooth).

Gold

Small traces of gold were recovered from nine contexts in the interior of the site. These generally comprised deep pits, including presumably post-pits, and the gold was discovered after flotation when the dried residue was examined. The objects were almost microscopic in size and generally consisted of small fragments of gold leaf or gold wire. One complete object was recovered in the form of a gold stud (Pl. 21) about 4.5mm in diameter and weighing less than *c.* 0.083gm. The finds might be explained as small fragments of industrial waste, intended to be utilised in the ornamentation of some object or perhaps to be melted down and reshaped into something else. Alternatively, the fragments may merely be part of other objects fashioned in wood or textile that had become separated or all that survives of a previously gold-decorated object. The gold stud derived from a possible post-pit which contained charcoal and the radiocarbon date for this sample yielded a calibrated date of *c.* 1260-910 BC (D-17), i.e. a date contemporaneous with the ditches surrounding the site.

Bronze

Five pieces of bronze were recovered, primarily from the deep pits. These comprised a fragment of what would appear to have been a bracelet (Pl. 22), three rings (Pl. 23), and an unidentified fragment of a larger object, possibly the terminal of an ornament. Several pieces of iron were also discovered but in pits that yielded clearly Iron Age dates, i.e. *c.* 400-200 cal BC.

Glass

Glass beads from Iron Age contexts (*c.* 400-200 BC) and possibly Late Bronze Age contexts were recovered.

Stone

The largest stone object recovered during the excavations was a cup-and-ring marked block of sandstone (Fig. 28) found in a shallow pit. The stone is carved with a double ring with a groove running from the centre to the outer edge of the stone. On typological grounds, such an ornamented stone should date to the later Neolithic or Early Bronze Age (van Hoek 1988). But as a portable object (requiring

Pl. 22. Fragment of possible bronze bracelet.

perhaps four or five people to carry it) it could obviously have been brought onto the site from somewhere else and need not reflect the earliest evidence for occupation at Haughey's Fort. The stone was found in a pit, charcoal from which dated to *c.* 1250-900 BC (D-18-19).

A small number of quern stones were recovered from both the interior of the site and the innermost ditch. Predictably, these were saddle querns and rubbers. Two stone pendants (Pl. 24) were recovered, one a lignite bracelet from the outermost ditch and the other a perforated piece of fossilised wood from one of the large pits.

Tooth

A broken but evidently perforated boar tusk (Pl. 24) was recovered from the outermost ditch.

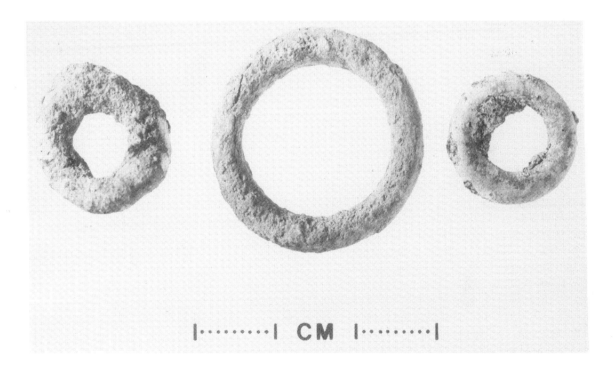

Pl. 23. Three bronze rings recovered from pits at Haughey's Fort.

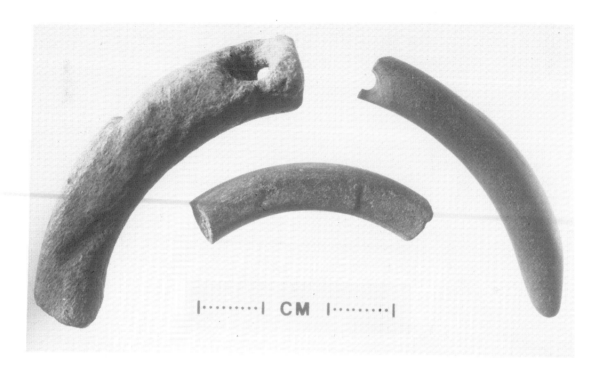

Pl. 24. Upper left - perforated pendant of fossilised wood; lower centre - fragment
of jet bracelet; upper right - boar tooth pendant.

Ceramics

Slightly less than a thousand sherds (*c.* 19.7kg) of pottery have been recovered from Haughey's Fort and these have been examined as the subject of a B.A. thesis (Boreland 1993). The pottery was generally classic Late Bronze Age coarse or flat-rimmed ware with large basaltic inclusions. The sherds provided sufficient evidence for the full reconstruction of seven vessels although the remains of a total of about 57 vessels were recovered. The reconstructed forms range from *c.* 30cm to 40cm in height with rim diameters of *c.* 23cm to 32cm. Although popularly known as 'flat-rimmed' ware, this described only about 11% of the rims examined and the majority were rounded or with an internal bevel. Analysis of the charred organic deposits on the interior of the vessels employing a Scanning Electron Microscope suggested that the sooty deposits were produced by a cellulose material derived from plants rather than animals. The study suggested that tree-bark accounted for the cellulose deposits. A more recent study employing a lipid test-kit (Quinn and McCormick, forthcoming) has found positive traces of the meat or skins of cattle in the sooty deposits.

Wood

The wood recovered from the interior ditch not only reflected the prevailing environment during the period of the occupation of the site and subsequent infilling of the ditch but also preserves a number of the structural artefacts of the site (Neill, forthcoming). Oak, ash, alder and hazel were all deliberately employed in the manufacture of implements or in structural timbers. Examination of over a hundred hazel poles failed to reveal any positive evidence for coppicing. Alder was also employed in the manufacture of poles. Split-wood oak was used for structural purposes while there were two handles, both in excess of 60cm, manufactured from ash (Fig. 29cm, Pl. 25cm). It is probable that they were originally hafts for a bronze axe or similar implement. Three fragments of a poplar bowl were also uncovered in the interior ditch.

Interpretation

Haughey's Fort is still in the process of excavation and any interpretations, published in the past or presented here, are extremely provisional. Indeed, as the excavations have progressed and the dating evidence has expanded, attempts to assess the role of Haughey's Fort within the landscape of the Navan complex has seen frequent changes. For example, it was initially suggested that Haughey's Fort may have been the secular component of the Navan Complex, a sort of defensive refuge serving the basic population while Navan Fort occupied the position of ritual and political centre of the complex. Such a neat

Pl. 25. Handle (0.62m) of tool carved from ash infill of inner ditch. Note also large dog skull, pig mandible and other fragment of worked wood.

division between the sacred and the profane, however, has been considerably upset by the evidence of radiocarbon dating that indicates that the main floruit of Haughey's Fort preceded most of the activity so far uncovered at Navan Fort. The possible reinterpretation of the large pits in the interior of Haughey's Fort as post-pits for two large double-ringed enclosures has also challenged the interpretation of a purely secular Haughey's Fort. The one argument still supportive of envisaging Haughey's Fort as primarily an occupation site is the presence of the three ditches whose sections still conform to the expectations of a hillfort rather than ritual enclosure (as the henge-like external bank and internal ditch might suggest for Navan Fort). But it must also be admitted that the type of circular dwellings that one might expect in the Late Bronze Age from other sites have yet to emerge from the Haughey's Fort excavations.

It is time now to attempt a chronological review of the evolution of Haughey's Fort.

Neolithic

The evidence for Neolithic occupation is marginal in the extreme and consists solely of a polished stone axe and a possible (conjectural) date for the cup-and-ring marked stone. No clearly identifiable flint implements or ceramics attributable to the Neolithic, the primary evidence one might expect from Neolithic occupation, have been recovered so far. There is therefore no solid evidence for Neolithic settlement

at Haughey's Fort approaching that known from the excavations at Navan Fort (Site B).

Early/Middle Bronze Age

Although there is one radiocarbon date (D-10) which would fall in the period *c.* 2450-1500 BC, this derives from no less than 10 stake holes, each of which contributed a very small quantity of comminuted charcoal. The validity of the dates may be suspect for two reasons. There are no other remains from this period (unless the cup-and-ring marked stone be so assigned) that might substantiate such early settlement at Haughey's Fort. More importantly, the dates are much earlier than those extracted from two post holes parallel with the line of stake holes that set this

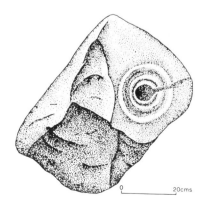

Fig. 28. Cup-and-ring marked stone from Ft 275.

Fig. 29. Handle (0.62m) of tool carved from ash.

stockade alignment to *c.* 1250-900 BC (D-10-D11). On archaeological grounds it is very difficult not to associate the different rows of stake holes and posts and the very marked discrepancy in radiocarbon dates between two of the lines is a serious problem.

Late Bronze Age

The primary occupation of Haughey's Fort dates to the Late Bronze Age. The pattern of radiocarbon dates for the various ditches suggests an initial occupation of *c.* 1100±50 BC (Mallory 1994) and there are no grounds as yet to order the sequence of the ditches, all of the dates suggesting broadly contemporary construction. Similarly, the features discovered within the site might also all be assigned to this same general period. Although settlement might have been protracted over a period of as much as two or three centuries (taking the broadest parameters of the radiocarbon dates), it is also quite possible that Haughey's Fort saw only a short period of occupation before it was abandoned. According to the botanical evidence from the inner ditch, this may have occurred already by *c.* 1050-950 BC (D-6d). As the dates for Haughey's Fort are broadly identical with the basal layer of the King's Stables, it is probable that the two sites were not only chronologically contemporary but also related in social terms, i.e. the community that constructed Haughey's Fort is likely to have also established the King's Stables. The

interrelationship between the two has been very recently strengthened by a small excavation prompted by a visit of the 'Time Team' which resulted in the discovery of a possible entrance-way through the middle ditch, aligned towards the King's Stables. Another result of the Time Team's visit was the test trenching of parallel ditches in Creeveroe townland (Fig. 24). These uncovered remains of coarse ware pottery which would also be compatible with a Late Bronze Age date.

Iron Age

The inner ditch sediments indicate that by the 9th century there is no evidence for human activity in the immediate vicinity of Haughey's Fort (Mallory 1994). Subsequent activity does appear in the form of several irregular pits containing artefacts compatible with an Iron Age date, e.g. fragments of iron, glass beads. Radiocarbon dates were obtained from two levels of the same pit and both fell within the range *c.* 400-200 BC.

Problems

The most superficially attractive interpretation at present is one which envisages Haughey's Fort as the primary focus of settlement and power for the Navan area during the period *c.* 1100 BC. There was then a subsequent shift to the east in the focus of settlement or prestige with the (re-)occupation of Navan. During the main floruit of activity at Navan, i.e. *c.* 400-100 BC, Haughey's Fort only saw transitory occupation. Whether this shift involved the same population as that earlier settled at Haughey's Fort is difficult to determine (Mallory 1994) and, on strictly architectural and artefactual grounds, there is no compelling reason to presume continuity although it may well have existed. Nevertheless, there are two aspects of Haughey's Fort that may require adjustments to any theory proposed.

It is now not entirely certain that the interior of Haughey's Fort represented purely secular settlement. The possibility that it contained two large circular timber enclosures – on the order of 25-30m across – suggests that Haughey's Fort, defended although it might be, was primarily the focus of ritual activities. The absence so far of any clearly vernacular Late Bronze Age architecture, presumably circular buildings in the range from 8 to 12m in diameter, does little to confirm the hypothesis that the site was a major defended settlement in which a variety of social and economic functions were undertaken.

Secondly, the suggestion that Haughey's Fort was a ritual site is to some extent further strengthened by the evidence from Navan Fort where it is easier to apply a ritual interpretation to many of the features than a secular, e.g. the 40m structure of the Iron Age, the similarity of the figure-of-eight structures at Navan with those of the larger (ritual?) buildings at Dún Ailinne. Both Haughey's Fort and Navan Fort may have been more broadly integrated into a landscape where primary settlement was dispersed about the two monuments. In this light, the food remains recovered from Haughey's Fort may be more properly interpreted as the food debris from occasional feasting and the relatively pure barley might be seen as the product of farmers living around but not on the site. In this light, it is not settlement that might have shifted but rather the ritual or political centre of a ruling dynasty. To what extent any of these theories remains creditable will depend on the further seasons of excavation that are planned for Haughey's Fort and other sites of the Navan Complex.

Appendix

Bronze Age Radiocarbon Dates from the Navan Complex (Calibrations quoted at 2 s.d.)

NAVAN FORT

D-1. Post-pit within ring ditch of Site B.
UB 974 charcoal 3140±90 BP 1620-1215 cal BC

D-2. Primary silting of ring-ditch of Site B.
a. UB 188 charcoal 2628±50 BP 900-770 cal BC
b. UB 979 charcoal 2615±75 BP 910-540 cal BC

D-3. Navan Fort ditch (extracted from pollen core)
UB 3091 organic 2420±40 BP 766-398 cal BC

KING'S STABLES

D-4. Old ground surface covered by earthen bank forming perimeter of King's Stables.
UB 2123 charcoal 2765±75 BP 1122-800 cal BC

D-5. Silt from the bottom of the pool at the King's Stables.
a. UB 2124 twigs 2585±80 BP 900-429 cal BC
b. UB 2157 twigs 2955±45 BP 1374-1024 cal BC

HAUGHEY'S FORT

Ditches

D-6. Samples from innermost ditch at Haughey's Fort.
a. UB 3050 wood 2923±50 BP 1300±990 cal BC
b. GrN 15480 wood 2855±40 BP 1158-916 cal BC
c. UB 3606 wood 2915±16 BP 1212-1042 cal BC
d. UB 3608 wood 2845±16 BP 1047-941 cal BC
e. UB 3607 wood 2666±16 BP 841-806 cal BC

D-7. Sample from bottom of the middle ditch at Haughey's Fort.
UB 3388 charcoal 2852±55 BP 1254-900 cal BC

D-8. Sample from lens of charcoal in outermost ditch.
UB 3387 charcoal 2889±27 BP 1205-998 cal BC

D-9. Palisade trench (Ft. 370) on inner edge of inner ditch.
UB 3605 charcoal 2923-16 BP 1252-1052 cal BC

Internal stockade

D-10. Accumulated sample from ten post-holes along central alignment (stockade) in interior of site.
UB 3877 charcoal 3591±147 BP 2454-1539 cal BC

D-11. Post-hole (Ft 112) on inner-line of stockade.
UB 3878 charcoal 2824±37 BP 1093-904 cal BC

D-12. Post-hole (Ft. 86) on inner-line of stockade.
UB 3879 charcoal 2920±43 BP 1266-999 cal BC

Internal features

D-13. Large hearth (Ft. 2) filled with coarse ware pottery and burnt bone.
GrN 15481 charcoal 2865±25 BP 1124-943 cal BC

D-14. Deep pit (Ft. 3) with coarse ware pottery, burnt bone, burnt stones.
GrN 15482 charcoal 2920±25 BP 1256-1032 cal BC

D-15. Large pit (Ft. 4) with carbonised barley, burnt bone and sherds of coarse ware pottery.
a. UB 3049 charcoal 2833±55 BP 1199-848 cal BC
b. GrN 15483 charcoal 2850±20 BP 1126-919 cal BC

D-16. Hearth (Ft 14) with sherds of coarse ware pottery and burnt bone.
GrN 15484 charcoal 2850±35 BP 1126-919 cal BC

D-17. Deep pit (Ft. 267) = probable post-pit from double post-ring.
UB 3386 charcoal 2877±60 BP 1260-910 cal BC

D-18. Large and shallow pit (Ft. 275) containing cup-and-ring marked stone.
UB 3880 charcoal 2872±47 BP 1255-918 cal BC

D-19. Pit (Ft. 295) underlying that of Ft 275 containing cup-and-ring marked stone.
UB 3881 charcoal 2962±47 BP 1381-1029 cal BC

Iron Age contexts

D-20. Pit (Ft. 299) with iron strap and glass beads.
a. UB 3384 charcoal 2253±26 BP 394-209 cal BC
b. UB 3385 charcoal 2221±26 BP 386-198 cal BC

Acknowledgements

I would like to thank Chris Lynn for reading an earlier draft of this paper.

References

Anderson, R. 1989. Haughey's Fort: Analysis of an Insect Death Assemblage. *Emania* 6, 37-42.
Boreland, D. 1993. Haughey's Fort: A Comparative Study of Late Bronze Age Pottery. Unpublished B.A. Thesis,

Queen's University, Belfast.

Hawthorne, M. 1991. A Preliminary Analysis of Wood Remains from Haughey's Fort. *Emania* 8, 34-8.

Hodges, H. 1958. A Hunting Camp at Cullyhanna Lough, near Newtown Hamilton, County Armagh. *Ulster Journal of Archaeology* 21, 7-13.

Lynn, C. 1977. Trial Excavations at the King's Stables, Tray Townland, Co. Armagh. *Ulster Journal of Archaeology* 40, 42-62.

Lynn, C. 1986. Navan Fort: A Draft Summary of D. M. Waterman's Excavations. *Emania* 1, 11-19.

Lynn, C. 1991. Knockaulin (Dún Ailinne) and Navan: Some Architectural Comparisons. *Emania* 8, 51-6.

Lynn, C. 1992. The Iron Age Mound in Navan Fort: A Physical Realization of Celtic Religious Beliefs? *Emania* 10, 33-57.

Lynn, C. 1994. Hostels, Heroes and Tales: Further Thoughts on the Navan Mound. *Emania* 12, 5-20.

Lynn, C. (forthcoming). *D. M. Waterman's Excavations at Navan Fort.* Belfast.

McCormick, F. 1988. Animal Bones from Haughey's Fort. *Emania* 4, 24-7.

McCormick, F. 1991. The Animal Bones from Haughey's Fort: Second Report. *Emania* 8, 27-33.

McCormick, F. 1994. Faunal Remains from Navan and Other Late Prehistoric Sites in Ireland. In J. P. Mallory and G. Stockman (eds), *Ulidia: Proceedings of the First International Conference on the Ulster Cycle of Tales,* 181-6. Belfast.

Mallory, J. P. 1987. The Literary Topography of Emain Macha. *Emania* 2, 12-18.

Mallory, J. P. 1988. Trial Excavations at Haughey's Fort. *Emania* 4, 5-20.

Mallory, J. P. 1991. Excavations at Haughey's Fort: 1989-90. *Emania* 8, 10-26.

Mallory, J. P. 1994. The Other Twin: Haughey's Fort. In

J. P. Mallory and G. Stockman (eds), *Ulidia: Proceedings of the First International Conference on the Ulster Cycle of Tales,* 187-92. Belfast.

Mallory, J. and Warner, R. 1988. The Date of Haughey's Fort. *Emania* 5, 36-40.

Murphy, E. 1992. The Animal Bones Recovered from the Inner Ditch of Haughey's Fort 1991. Unpublished MSS., Dept of Archaeology, Queen's University, Belfast.

Neill, M. (forthcoming). Analysis of Wood Remains from Haughey's Fort. *Emania* 14.

Ó Cathmhaoil, S. 1992. A Preliminary Report on the Seeds from the Bronze Age Ditch at Haughey's Fort, Co. Armagh. Unpublished MSS., Dept of Archaeology, Queen's University, Belfast.

Quinn, S. and McCormick, F. (forthcoming). Analysis of Lipid Residues on Pottery from Haughey's Fort. *Emania.*

Simpson, D. D. A. 1989. Neolithic Navan? *Emania* 6, 31-3.

van Hoek, M. A. M. 1988. The Prehistoric Rock Art of County Donegal (Part II). *Ulster Journal of Archaeology* 51, 21-47.

Wailes, B. 1990. Dún Ailinne: A Summary Excavation Report. *Emania* 7, 10-21.

Warner, R. B. 1988. The Archaeology of Early Historic Irish Kingship. In S. T. Driscoll and M. R. Nieke (eds), *Power and Politics in Early Medieval Britain and Ireland,* 47-68. Edinburgh.

Warner, R. 1994a. The Navan Complex: New schedule of sites and finds. *Emania* 12, 39-44.

Warner, R. 1994b. *Emania* Varia I. *Emania* 12, 66-72.

Weir, D. A. 1987. Palynology and the Environmental History of the Navan Area. *Emania* 3, 34-43.

Weir, D. A. 1989. A Radiocarbon Date from the Navan Fort Ditch. *Emania* 6, 34-5.

The Dating of Timber Circles: New Thoughts in the Light of Recent Irish and British Discoveries

Alex Gibson

Abstract

Recent work on timber circles both in Ireland and Britain has shed important light on the dating of the class, resulting in the modification of the chronological scheme proposed by the writer in 1994. Middle and Late Bronze Age dates for timber circles have extended the British sequence, allowed the re-interpretation of some British sites and have gone some way towards filling the gap between the Early Bronze Age sites and the Iron Age circles of Navan and Knockaulin. It is now possible that there may be an unbroken sequence of timber circle construction lasting almost three millennia.

Two Irish sites (Navan and Knockaulin) warrant special mention as they do not fit the chronology suggested above . . . These circles, despite their superficial resemblance to the British sites, warn against over-reliance on typological similarity (Gibson 1994, 206-7).

These words, written only in 1993, illustrate the uncertainty and confusion with which the present writer viewed the Irish timber circles at Navan and Knockaulin. The similarity in form of these Irish sites to the British corpus, even to the extent of the hypothetical reconstructions by Irish scholars (Wailes 1990; Lynn 1991; 1993) was difficult to explain given the apparent chronological hiatus between the two islands: the British circles could be seen to extend from *c.* 3000-1500 cal BC and, over a millennium later, strangely similar sites appeared in the Irish Iron Age.

The confusion was not lessened by the fact that Irish discoveries contemporary with the British material were also being made. Ballynahatty with its abundant Late Neolithic Grooved Ware associations was under excavation (Hartwell 1994) and its subsequent suggested reconstruction bore a striking and comforting resemblance to those suggested for Sarn-y-bryn-caled and contemporary British circles (Gibson 1992; 1994, 211-12). At Knowth, a single circle had also been recently excavated, once more associated with a substantial Grooved Ware assemblage (Eogan and Roche 1993; 1994). The two Newgrange circles with their Beaker associations and confirmatory radiocarbon dates were already well known (Sweetman 1985; 1987).

Two other sites were known from Ireland but had their own dating problems. A multiple timber circle at Raffin Fort had recently been recognised (Newman 1993) and had a *terminus ante quem* of the later Bronze Age since it was overlapped by building A which dated to that period. Then there was the putative 'henge' at Lugg which had little to date it other than 'Iron Age' sherds from post hole 17 (Kilbride-Jones 1950) though this find need also have been no more than a *terminus ante quem*.

At Raffin, future excavation may resolve the date of the timber circle (Newman, pers. comm.) but at Lugg, despite a recent re-assessment of the pottery assemblage and its re-allocation to the Later Bronze Age (inf. Helen Roche), the dating of the monument is largely unresolved. With its external ditch, Lugg bears more resemblance to British Later Bronze Age ringworks than to the henge monuments with which it was originally compared. Nevertheless, the timber circle and cardinally orientated avenue can be paralleled in Britain in the third and second millennia BC. Unfortunately the charcoal sample still present in the Lugg archive in the National Museum of Ireland is unlabelled and any date obtained from it would do little to rectifiy the site chronology. Thus even in Ireland, the sites of Navan and Knockaulin appear to stand chronologically apart from other morphologically similar monuments.

At this point another player enters the stage: continuity. Piggott, in 1968, had stressed the similarity of certain aspects of Iron Age religion with observances made in the Neolithic and Bronze Age record: henges and *temenoi*, ritual pits and *bothroi*, cursus monuments and *Viereckschanzen*. This probable continuity has also been demonstrated at stone circles (Burl 1983) where instances of orientation on solar directions at the time of the major Celtic festivals are common. In timber circles, in so far as orientations

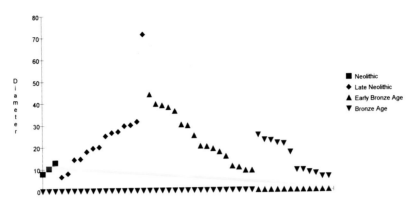

Fig. 30. Chronology of Neolithic and Early Bronze Age timber circles.

can be positively discerned in a circle, the nature of the superstructure of which is unknown, cardinal orientations are frequently found (Gibson 1994, 200). From such cardinal orientations, solstice and equinoctial events may be readily observed. In the Netherlands, Beex (pers. comm.) has convincingly demonstrated the equinoctial sunrise orientation of many of the timber circle-barrows of the south-west of the country. Further north, at Zwolle Ittersumersbroek (de Jong and Wevers 1994), two circles appear to have possible connections with solar risings approximating to major dates in the 'Druidic' calendar: 21st December (winter solstice), 21st June (summer solstice), 21st March and 21st September (equinoxes), 1st May (Beltane) and 1st November (Samain). It is fair to point out, however, that some of these orientations at Zwolle depend on assumed post positions within a post hole palimpsest environment but research at the site continues and it is possible that other circles in the excavated area may have been recognised (de Jong, pers. comm.).

Since 1993, however, recent discoveries have been made which prompt a re-assessment of timber circle chronology. Principal amongst these is the discovery of a possible double circle of substantial posts at Haughey's Fort (Mallory, this volume). This circle has an estimated diameter of some 25m and has been dated by radiocarbon to 1260-910 cal BC. Meanwhile, in Britain, at Ogden Down, a double circle with a diameter of *c.* 16m has produced a radiocarbon date of 1125-992 cal BC (inf. M. Green and R. Bradley) and is thus broadly contemporary with Haughey's Fort. Complementary dates from other contexts suggest that this single date is reliable.

These two sites extend the suggested sequence (Gibson 1994) to the first millennium but there is still a considerable gap between these sites and the two Iron Age sites which began the discussion. At Standlake 20, however, a ring ditch with external post circle, like Ogden Down, was assigned to the Early Bronze

Age by analogy with other British and Dutch sites (Catling 1982). Early Iron Age pottery in the ditch was suggested to belong to a secondary use of the monument despite its occurrence low in the ditch silts. An Iron Age date for the monument was entertained but considered unlikely in view of the apparent lack of parallels, both by Catling and by the present writer. The extension of the timber circle sequence, however, makes the Iron Age date of Standlake 20 much easier to accept and this site may well represent the link between the Bronze Age sites and Knockaulin and ultimately Navan.

These recent discoveries and re-assessments do not alter significantly the chronological sequence suggested in 1994 (Fig. 30) but do extend it by a millennium (Fig. 31). Knockaulin and Navan still stand out by virtue of their size, but gradually the lacuna between these sites and their Neolithic and Bronze Age predecessors seems to be closing. Future discoveries on both sides of the Irish Sea may do more to refine the sequence and further our understanding of the direct ancestry of Navan and Knockaulin.

Acknowledgements

The writer has benefited from discussions with Richard Bradley, Humphrey Case, Martin Green, Chris Lynn, Jim Mallory and Conor Newman to whom he extends his thanks. Mary Cahill and staff of the National Museum of Ireland allowed access to the Lugg archive and thanks are due to Helen Roche for sharing her opinions on the Lugg assemblage.

References

Burl, H. A. W. 1983. *Prehistoric Astronomy*. Princes Risborough.

Catling, H. W. 1982. Six ring-ditches at Standlake. In H.

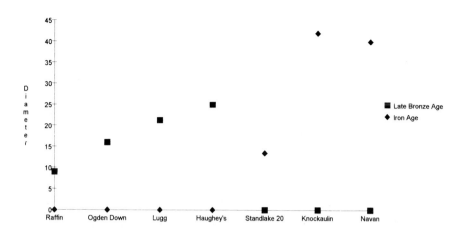

Fig. 31. Chronology of Later Bronze Age and Iron Age timber circles.

J. Case and A. W. R. Whittle (eds), *Settlement Patterns in the Oxford Region: Excavations at the Abingdon Causewayed Enclosure and other Sites*, 88-102. Council for British Archaeology Research Report No. 44. London.

Eogan, G. and Roche, H. 1993. Neolithic ritual at Knowth? *Archaeology Ireland* 7 (4), 16-18.

Eogan, G. and Roche, H. 1994. A Grooved Ware wooden structure at Knowth, Boyne Valley, Ireland. *Antiquity* 68, 322-30.

Gibson, A. M. 1992. The timber circle at Sarn-y-bryn-caled, Welshpool, Powys. Ritual and sacrifice in Bronze Age mid-Wales. *Antiquity* 66, 84-92.

Gibson, A. M. 1994. Excavations at the Sarn-y-bryn-caled cursus complex, Welshpool, Powys, and the timber circles of Great Britain and Ireland. *Proceedings of the Prehistoric Society* 60, 143-223.

Hartwell, B. 1994. Late neolithic ceremonies. *Archaeology Ireland* 8 (4), 10-13.

Jong, J. de and Wevers, H. 1994. Cirkels en zonnenkalendars in Zwolle-Ittersumerbroek. In Clevis H. and de Jong, J. (eds), *Archeologie en Bouwhistorie in Zwolle 2*, 74-93. Zwolle: Gemeente Zwolle, sectie Monumentenzorg.

Kilbride-Jones, H. E. 1950. The excavation of a composite early Iron Age monument with 'henge' features at Lugg, Co. Dublin. *Proceedings of the Royal Irish Academy* 53C, 31 1-332.

Lynn, C. 1991. Knockaulin (Dún Ailinne) and Navan, some architectural comparisons. *Emania* 8, 51-6.

Lynn, C. 1993. Navan fort – home of gods and goddesses? *Archaeology Ireland* 7 (1), 17-21.

Newman, C. 1993. The show's not over until the fat lady sings. *Archaeology Ireland* 7 (4), 8-9.

Piggott, S. 1968. *The Druids*. London.

Sweetman, P. D. 1985. A late neolithic/early bronze age pit circle at Newgrange, Co. Meath. *Proceedings of the Royal Irish Academy* 85C, 195-221.

Sweetman, P. D. 1987. Excavation of a late neolithic/early bronze age site at Newgrange, Co. Meath. *Proceedings of the Royal Irish Academy* 87C, 283-98.

Wailes, B. 1990. Dún Ailinne: a summary excavation report. *Emania* 7, 10-21.

After MacWhite: Irish Rock Art
in its International Context

Richard Bradley

Abstract

Almost fifty years ago MacWhite pioneered the study of Irish rock art in relation to the petroglyphs of Continental Europe. He did so by treating the individual motifs as if they were portable artefacts. This paper argues that such comparisons are more informative if they are concerned with the rules by which different design elements were drawn together in a single composition. It illustrates this approach through a series of studies comparing the prehistoric rock carvings of Ireland, Britain and north-west Spain. This approach supports MacWhite's original contention that strong links existed between all three areas. In addition, it seems likely that these carvings played a significant role in the organisation of the landscape in Atlantic Europe. Rock art provided a resource rather like Beakers or early metalwork which owed some of its importance to its international character. At the same time, it was employed in quite specialised ways from one region to another.

To talk of a 'Bronze Age Campaign' raises the question of scale. Certain features of the European Bronze Age have an international character, like Bell Beakers, daggers and axes, but that does not identify their full significance. The same types of metalwork might be used in different ways from one area to another, just as Beakers themselves could be made in regional styles. Their roles seem easy to recognise, yet this material resists a single interpretation. These objects had a part to play in daily life, yet each seems to have been deposited according to local traditions. Both can be thought of as resources that owed their importance to their international character. Such resources might be employed in a whole range of social transactions according to the conventions of those who adopted them.

The evidence of prehistoric rock art presents some of the same problems, but in this case the basic material is not so clearly understood. There is disagreement over its chronology (Burgess 1990; Morris 1990). Are the rock carvings in Ireland Neolithic or Bronze Age in date, or were they created during both periods, as I shall argue here? Did they form part of an international phenomenon, like bronze axes or Beaker ceramics, and how closely were they related to those in other parts of Europe? Like the widely distributed artefacts of the same period, might their roles have differed from one region to another?

Almost fifty years ago Eoin MacWhite was confident that he could answer such questions (MacWhite 1946). Irish rock art belonged to a wider tradition. It provided evidence of long distance links extending between Ireland, northern Britain and the Iberian peninsula. Such contacts could be demonstrated by studying the distribution of individual motifs, following the same methods as those used to analyse portable artefacts. MacWhite distinguished between two different styles of rock carving extending along the Atlantic coastline. One was associated with megalithic tombs, whilst the other, which he termed the Galician style, was found in the open air. Each included a different group of motifs, but both of them dated from the Bronze Age.

Half a century later we can make fewer assumptions of this kind. Some revisions are necessary because of changes of chronology. Passage tombs, for instance, are no longer dated to the Bronze Age. Other changes have affected our interpretation of material culture. It is quite wrong to think of art styles as a passive reflection of long distance contacts; they may well have played a more active role in social life (Tilley 1991). In view of our growing experience in studying pottery and metalwork, we need to begin our investigation from a different standpoint.

I can best illustrate the limitations of the traditional approach by considering a site in Co. Kerry. Derrynablaha is located in the main concentration of rock art in south-west Ireland and contains one of the most thoroughly studied groups of carvings anywhere in the country. It was first discussed by Anati in 1963, and at one time it seemed to provide the evidence by which Irish rock art could be dated. Most recently it has been investigated again by Avril Purcell, whom I must thank for showing me the site and for much

90

valuable information.

The earliest study did not document the full extent of the rock art; nor did it discuss the relationship of different carvings to one another. Instead Anati took a most individual line. Far from recording the largest decorated surface, he extracted only those elements that he identifed as a human figure. This was only the starting point for an interpretation that has become more fantastic over the years, and in a recent publication he identifies this design as 'a spirit emanating sexual energy' (1993, 144).

Anati published a second motif on the site, suggesting that it resembled a Bronze Age shield. This caught the attention of John Coles (1965) who argued that here was a way of dating at least one element in Irish rock art. Again this illustrates the dangers of considering a single motif out of context, for Anati's record of the design eventually proved to be wrong (Shee and O'Kelly 1971). The most diagnostic feature of that shield had never existed in the first place, leaving us with an abstract motif that can be paralleled at other rock carvings in Ireland.

The same point is illustrated in a recent study by van Hoek (1990) who has devoted an entire article to this type of motif. He describes no less than 61 different versions whose distribution extends from Ireland to Spain, and traces their diffusion along the Atlantic coastline. Although his article was published as recently as 1990, this is the method that MacWhite had used fifty years ago. Instead of treating the carved surface as a coherent composition, he considered the design elements in complete isolation. Later in life MacWhite developed an interest in historical linguistics (MacWhite 1956), and this might have suggested an alternative approach, for the motifs are simply the vocabulary out of which the compositions were created. It would have been more useful to study the grammar according to which these elements could be combined.

If Anati's study of Derrynablaha ignored the distinctive character of the carvings, it also ignored their placing in the landscape. That is a remarkable oversight, for Avril Purcell has shown that the petroglyphs were not located haphazardly. They are found at the head of a valley close to the only crossing point through the mountains of Iveragh.

Some of the carvings overlook that valley, whilst others are directed towards the pass. The rock that Anati studied in such detail is orientated on a lake (A. Purcell, pers. comm.). Whatever else we can say about the carved rocks of Derrynablaha, this is landscape architecture of a high order.

We can draw two lessons from this example. If we are to study the wider relations of Irish petroglyphs, it is essential that we compare entire compositions, rather than the elements from which they were constructed. Since they are such simple geometric motifs, the right approach would be to consider the rules according to which these features were combined. It seems clear that we must also pay more attention to the setting of these carvings in the landscape. This is not an entirely new approach (Johnston 1989), but if there were any regularities in the siting of carved rocks, they could provide a further basis for comparisons between different regions. Are the rock carvings in Ireland found in the same situations as those in other areas?

It is essential that we compare like with like. There are two main groups of open air rock art. Cups and rings are found in Ireland, Scotland, northern England and Galicia, with occasional examples in western France, northern and central Spain, Portugal and the Pyrenees. What dating evidence there is suggests that they were created between about 3000 and 2000 BC (Bradley, forthcoming, chapters 3 and 4). Simple cup marks predominate in northern Scotland, Wales, south-west England and north-west France and may have a longer history (*ibid.*). Such simple motifs cannot be studied in isolation, and in this paper I shall concentrate on those areas with a more varied repertoire.

The basic rules of composition depend on the embellishment of cup marks by a growing number of rings (Pl. 26). The most common design is a cup with a single ring and the rarest is a cup with no fewer than ten. As the number of rings increases, these designs appear less often. The art in several areas has a very similar character. In Co. Donegal the proportions of the different circular motifs are exactly the same as they are in Northumberland (van Hoek 1987 and 1988; Beckensall 1991 and 1992), and the figures from the Dingle peninsula match those in West Yorkshire (Cuppage 1986; Ilkley Archaeology Group 1986). Such comparisons extend over a larger area too, and the statistics in Johnston's study of Irish rock art (Johnston 1989) show a similar distribution of motifs to those on the border between Portugal and Spain (Costas 1984). The abstract motifs from Co. Donegal appear in practically the same proportions as they do in Galicia as a whole (van Hoek 1987 and 1988; Costas and Novoa 1993). Fig. 32 compares the evidence from these two areas with the well recorded rock art of Mid Argyll (Royal Commission on the Ancient and Historical Monuments of Scotland 1988).

The central cup mark is often linked to the surrounding area by a radial line and in some cases these lines extend across the carved surface and join different motifs together. This is more likely to happen where the designs include several concentric rings. The published figures from Ireland are unsuitable for

Pl. 26. The main group of motifs at Derrynablaha, Co. Kerry. The figure interpreted by Anati as an 'anthropomorph' is towards the far end of the carved surface and the supposed 'shield' occupies the detached rock in the foreground. (Photo courtesy of Dept. of Archaeology, UCC).

detailed analysis, but in northern England we can show that this pattern is statistically significant. Among the rock carvings in Northumberland, motifs with three or more concentric rings are likely to be linked together (Bradley 1995). The same arrangement can also be recognised in Galicia, where there is only one chance in a thousand that it could have happened by chance. In the rock art of Pontevedra 54% of the motifs with one or two concentric rings are linked to other designs. The figure rises to 81% of those with three or four rings and to 93% of those with five or six (Bradley, forthcoming, chapter 12).

When different motifs are linked to one another, the process seems to be attended by simple rules. Generally speaking, circular motifs are joined together in a series of 'chains'. The point of origin is generally a group of concentric circles, and normally these are connected to equivalent or progressively simpler motifs. In some cases chains with very different origins can be kept entirely separate, so that a series of motifs starting with four concentric circles, for instance, may be distinguished from one whose point of departure is a simpler design. When circular motifs abut one another, they tend to observe a similar hierarchy, so that designs with fewer rings may be joined

onto those with more. Once again it is clear that similar conventions were followed in all three areas with cup and ring carvings: Ireland, northern Britain and Galicia. Anati's 'anthropomorph' at Derrynablaha is a typical example of this type of composition (Fig. 33).

In most cases the abstract carvings share a preference for flat or gently sloping surfaces, and they were rarely created on the most conspicuous rocks (Morris 1981; Johnston 1989). With certain exceptions, where the surface does slope the radial lines run downhill. In Ireland and Britain they usually extend towards the south and east (*ibid.*; Bradley, forthcoming, chapter 5); in Galicia there was a greater emphasis on the south (*ibid.*, chapter 12). But there are important exceptions to all these observations, and these help to distinguish the art of different areas. In northern Britain there are a few carvings on cliffs, and these contain motifs that are usually associated with megalithic tombs (*ibid.*, chapter 8). In the same way, in Galicia few major carvings are found on vertical and steeply sloping surfaces, but these drawings include a significant proportion of weapons (Bradley, Criado and Fábregas 1995).

Galician art is chiefly distinguished from Irish and

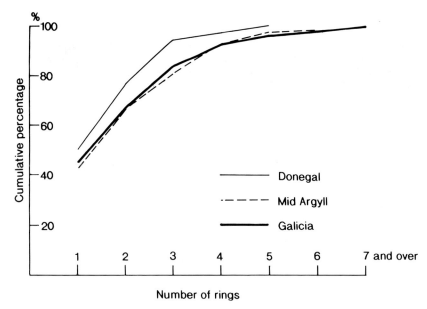

Fig. 32. The distribution of circular motifs on rock sites in Donegal, Mid Argyll and Galicia. The figures for Donegal and Mid Argyll are calculated from the illustrations in van Hoek (1987 and 1988) and Royal Commission on the Ancient and Historical Monuments of Scotland (1988) respectively. Those for Galicia are provided by Costas and Novoa (1993, 247).

British rock art by the presence of three kinds of motifs. The first are drawings of weapons, which depict two types of artefact with a wider distribution: daggers, which have been compared with those in Wessex (Peña 1979); and halberds, which are normally identified with finds in north Portugal and south-east Spain (Peña 1980), although 40% of the halberds in Bronze Age Europe have been discovered in Ireland (Harbison 1969). The second group of motifs are described as idols (Almagro 1973), and here an Irish connection is equally apparent. These drawings seem to represent artefacts that are found at Copper Age sites close to Lisbon, yet objects of rather similar form have been excavated in the Boyne Valley, leading George Eogan (1990) to postulate a direct connection between these two areas. The third group are drawings of animals, which are often found in the higher part of the distribution of Galician rock carvings. Here the question of long distance contacts does not arise, as wild animals are a consistent feature of Neolithic and Bronze Age art in the Iberian peninsula.

Taken at face value, it would seem as if the range of abstract motifs that MacWhite defined as Galician rock art may have formed part of an international style rather like Maritime Beakers and could provide evidence of an Atlantic axis that connected Ireland with the north-west part of Spain (cf. Case, this volume). Such connections may have formed during the development of passage tombs as the abstract motifs have more in common with Irish megalithic art than with anything found on the Continent. The depictions of recognisable artefacts in England, Scotland and Spain suggest that these links retained their importance when metalwork was adopted. The area further to the south experienced a rather different development and is characterised by a separate style of rock carvings (Gómez 1993). It was only in Portugal that fortified settlements were established dur-

ing the Copper Age (Jorge 1993). Further north, in Galicia, there is no evidence of a similar development, and here, as in Ireland and Britain, prehistoric settlements left little trace until the Later Bronze Age. In both regions there are cases in which carvings were slighted during the construction of hill forts (Bradley 1995; García and Peña 1980; Costas and Novoa 1993).

That raises the second major issue. MacWhite's Galician style of rock carvings is identified by images that were created at quite specific places in the landscape. How far did the local character of the rock art reflect the locations in which it was made?

The rock art of Ireland and Britain is found in four kinds of location. Its organisation in the landscape makes considerable use of the contrast between cup-marks and cups with rings, as well as the more subtle gradation between simpler and more complex motifs. In most areas it is associated with tracts of fertile land, but it is generally found around its outer limits where resources might have come under pressure. Sometimes the simpler designs are on lower ground than the rest. This is where settlements could have been established and these are the only carvings to be found near to concentrations of artefacts. The more complex designs are generally higher up and are often situated at viewpoints. In the two cases in which suitable information is available they are found on or beyond the outer edges of the distribution of worked flint. In contrast to the distribution of cup marks and other simple motifs, these images may have been on the boundary of the settled landscape. Although these comments are based on fieldwork in Scotland and north-east England (Bradley 1995), Susan Johnston's work has shown that Irish sites are located in similar positions (Johnston 1991).

Rock carvings are also associated with Neolithic and Early Bronze Age monuments. The motifs used to

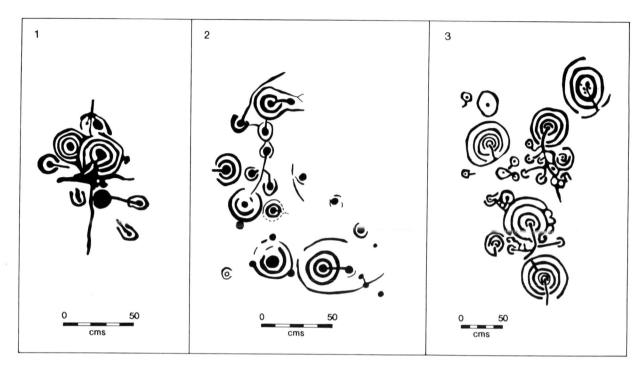

Fig. 33. Examples of the 'chains' of circular motifs in Irish and Galician rock art. 1 is the 'anthropomorph' at Derrynablaha, Co. Kerry, as recorded by Anati (1963); 2 depicts a series of motifs at Kinard East, Co. Kerry (Cuppage 1966); and 3 illustrates a series of curvilinear designs at Laxa do Outeiro do Cogoludo, Pontevedra, Galicia (García and Peña 1980).

decorate these sites are generally similar to those in the surrounding landscape, and this connection is emphasised by the concentrations of carvings around their entrances (Bradley 1993, 62-6). But there are certain cases in which natural surfaces close to major groups of monuments were decorated in a more elaborate style. In some cases these carvings seem to follow the routes leading towards monument complexes and may even become more ornate closer to those sites (Bradley, forthcoming, chapter 7). Examples of this pattern include the Kilmartin valley and Clydebank in Scotland, the Milfield Basin in northern England and possibly the concentration of carvings and earthwork enclosures around Dundalk. Such areas also include motifs which resemble those in megalithic art.

The distribution of rock carvings extends to other routes across the landscape, as we saw in the case of the mountain pass at Derrynablaha. It also includes routes along major valleys, gorges and waterways (Bradley, forthcoming, chapter 8). A good example is the site at Mevagh in Co. Donegal which overlooks an estuary leading between the Atlantic and a series of inland lakes (van Hoek 1988). As if to emphasise its strategic location, there is a modern beacon just below the site. In north-east England, the locations with carved rocks are sometimes intervisible so that one could move from one site to another in a prescribed sequence (R. Saunders, pers. comm.).

They provide a series of thresholds along the main route leading towards the Milfield Basin, and each new group of carvings commands a different view.

There are fewer carvings on the most prominent features of the landscape, suggesting that the significance of those places was already so obvious that it did not need to be emphasised. But certain locations were selected for this kind of treatment, including some conspicuous outcrops, cliffs and occasional rock shelters. A few carvings are also found near to waterfalls (Bradley, forthcoming, chapter 8). More rarely, entire hilltops might be delimited by a fringe of carvings, as happens in north-east England. In Ireland a variant of this pattern occurs on Doagh Island whose southern shoreline is embellished by a series of carvings which look across a narrow channel towards the mountains of Donegal (van Hoek 1987).

Fragments of carved rock could also be removed from these locations and taken to other sites, where they might be reused in the construction of monuments (Bradley 1992). This is particularly true of Early Bronze Age cist slabs. In other cases burial cairns could be built on top of already carved surfaces or their visual impact might be enhanced by the addition of further motifs just outside the kerbstones (Bradley and Mathews, in preparation). In south-west England this tradition extended to the deposition of cup-marked stones in Middle Bronze

Age houses, where occasional examples were buried beneath the hearths (see, for instance, Nowakowski 1991, 155). But that is the latest context in which this style of rock art played any role.

Much the same chronology would be appropriate for the rock carvings in Galicia, which is the only other area where the art is sufficiently varied for its distribution to be studied in detail. In some ways it resembles the distribution of Irish sites, whilst in others it seems very different. The closest links with Ireland and Britain are in the coastal region where the rock art is predomiantly abstract (García and Peña 1980). The main concentration of animal drawings is in the foothills further to the east, in between the fertile coastal region and the high ground where most of the burial mounds occur. In this case there seems to be an important link between the siting of the abstract art around fertile valleys and basins and the location of settlement sites, although these have left little structural evidence behind them and may not have been occupied continuously (Peña and Rey 1993). In some cases the distinction between cup-marks and cups with rings seems to have been quite important, but the relationship found in Britain appears to have been inverted, so that cup-marks can be found on higher ground than any of the other motifs. They also extend further inland and can be associated with barrow cemeteries (Villoch 1995).

With certain exceptions, the animal art is found in the foothills and is generally combined with the same range of abstract motifs as we find on the coast. The majority of these drawings depict red deer at different stages in their life cycle. The distribution of these carvings focuses on a number of small upland basins which provide the only significant source of moisture during the summer drought. The petroglyphs are distributed around the edges of these basins and also along the sheltered valleys leading between them (Bradley, Criado and Fábregas 1995). Red deer are extinct in this part of the country today, but in the summer free-ranging horses congregate in precisely these areas. Again there is evidence of settlement sites near to the carvings (*ibid.*).

Galician rock art is closely related to the distribution of water, shade and fertile soils, and for the most part it commands these areas at the expense of the wider landscape. This means that the carvings rarely occupy particularly conspicuous positions, and there are many cases in which a nearby rock would have provided a view over a much larger area than the one that was actually chosen (*ibid.*). This emphasis on paths and places is reflected in the contents of the art, which sometimes show groups of animals moving around or between the major circular motifs, as if they stood for particular locations in the landscape.

Occasionally lines of hoofprints also run towards them. This reflects the situation in the uplands even now for the animals depicted in the rock carvings follow the same axis as the paths used by horses today (Bradley, Criado and Fábregas 1994).

We can compare the placing of the circular motifs in the Galician landscape with the distribution of similar designs in Ireland and Britain, but we have to be cautious in doing so. In all three areas there is a close relationship between the distribution of rock art and the prehistoric pattern of land use, but this can be overemphasised. The distribution of rock art in Ireland may reflect the settlement pattern in some areas, but it need not do so in others. Nor can we take the naturalistic images in Galicia at face value. It is most unlikely that the uplands were used entirely for hunting, yet the drawings are chiefly concerned with the behaviour of wild animals. There is a regular association between human figures and mature stags, the latter drawn at a larger scale than any of the other animals. This suggests that these scenes provided an image of masculinity. It seems likely the drawings highlight the concerns of just one part of society, and that only certain people may have been allowed to view them (Bradley, forthcoming, chapter 13).

There is another reason for resisting such a simple explanation. Unlike the open air rock carvings in Galicia, the motifs found in Ireland are entirely abstract and echo some of the designs in passage tombs; in Britain they are also associated with other kinds of specialised monument. In view of such connections we should not assume that their meanings were accessible to everyone. Similarly, the drawings of weapons and idols in Galicia stand out from the remaining motifs. They occupy a different position in the landscape, on steeply sloping rocks which command an extensive view. Both these designs evoke connections with far distant areas, and if the echoes of Irish megalithic art are any more than a coincidence, these would have carried similar connotations. Indeed the fact that Ireland was so far away would have added to the power of those images. Again knowledge of their full significance might not have been freely available.

I began by referring to the problem of scale in studies of the European Bronze Age and observed how styles of fine pottery and metalwork could be widely distributed whilst they were actually employed in very different ways. Any distinction between the sacred and profane would be meaningless here. I suggest that Atlantic rock art may be another example of this kind of phenomenon, even though it is poorly dated and has rarely been studied in detail. It provided another symbolic resource that could be deployed in a variety of distinctive contexts, from the embellishment of ceremonial centres to the definition of agricultural land. That diversity may appear to be a source of frustration, but it adds significantly to the richness of our information. Rock art is almost the only medium which links both monuments and landscapes. In a period in which the evidence for ritual life eclipses everything else it provides an opportunity for research that we cannot refuse. Fifty years after MacWhite, the study of rock art has earned a place at the heart of Irish archaeology.

References

Almagro Gorbea, Ma. J. 1973. *Los idolos del Bronce 1 hispánico.* Madrid.

Anati, E. 1963. New petroglyphs at Derrynablaha, Co. Kerry, Ireland. *Journal of the Cork Historical and Archaeological Society* 68, 1-15.

Anati, E. 1993. *Rock Art – the Primordial Language.* Capo di Ponte.

Beckensall, S. 1991. *Prehistoric Rock Motifs of Northumberland,* volume 1. Hexham.

Beckensall, S. 1992. *Prehistoric Rock Motifs of Northumberland,* volume 2. Hexham.

Bradley, R. 1992. Turning the world – rock carvings and the archaeology of death. In N. Sharples and A. Sheridan (eds), *Vessels for the Ancestors,* 168-76. Edinburgh.

Bradley, R. 1993. *Altering the Earth. The Origins of Monuments in Britain and Continental Europe.* Edinburgh.

Bradley, R. 1995. Learning from places. Topographical analysis of northern British rock art. *Northern Archaeology* 13.

Bradley, R. forthcoming. *Signing the Land. Rock Art and the Prehistory of Atlantic Europe.*

Bradley, R., Criado, F. and Fábregas, R. 1994. Rock art research as landscape archaeology: a pilot study in Galicia, north-west Spain. *World Archaeology* 25, 374-90.

Bradley, R., Criado, F. and Fábregas, R. 1995. Rock art and the prehistoric landscape of Galicia. *Proceedings of the Prehistoric Society* 61.

Bradley, R. and Mathews, M. forthcoming. Rock carvings and round cairns on the Northumberland sandstone.

Burgess, C. 1990. The chronology of cup- and cup-and-ring marks in Atlantic Europe. *Revue Archéologique de l'Ouest, supplément* 2, 157-71.

Coles, J. 1965. A rock carving from south-west Ireland. *Proceedings of the Prehistoric Society* 31, 374-5.

Costas Goberna, F. J. 1984. *Petroglifos del litoral sur de la Ria de Vigo.* Vigo.

Costas Goberna, F. J. and Novoa Alvarez, P. 1993. *Los grabados rupestres de Galicia.* La Coruña.

Cuppage, J. 1986. *Archaeological Survey of the Dingle Peninsula.* Ballyferriter.

Eogan, G. 1990. Irish megalithic tombs and Iberia. Comparisons and contrasts. *Probleme der Megalithgräberforschung,* 113-37. Berlin.

García Alén, A. and Peña Santos, A. 1980. *Grabados rupestres de la Provincia de Pontevedra.* Pontevedra.

Gómez Barrera, J. 1993. Manifestaciones de la facies esquemática en el centro y norte de la Península Ibérica. *Espacio, Tiempo y Forma* 5, 231-64.

Harbison, P. 1969. *The Daggers and Halberds of the Early Bronze Age in Ireland. Prähistorische Bronzefunde,* 6.1, Munich.

Ilkley Archaeology Group 1986. *The Carved Rocks on Rombalds Moor.* Wakefield.

Johnston, S. 1989. *Prehistoric Irish Petroglyphs: their Analysis and Interpretation in Anthropological Context.* Ann Arbor.

Johnston, S. 1991. Distributional aspects of prehistoric Irish petroglyphs. In P. Bahn (ed.), *Rock Art and Prehistory,* 86-95. Oxford.

Jorge, S. O. 1993. O povado de Castelo Velho (Freixo de Numão, Vila Nova de Foz Coa) no contexto da pré-historia recente do norte de Portugal. *Actas de 1° Congresso de Arqueologia Peninsular* vol. 1, 179-221. Porto.

MacWhite, E. 1946. A new view on Irish Bronze Age rock-scribings. *Journal of the Royal Society of Antiquaries of Ireland* 76, 59-80.

MacWhite, E. 1956. On the interpretation of archaeological evidence in historical and sociological terms. *American Anthropologist* 58, 3-25.

Morris, R. 1981. *The Prehistoric Rock Art of Southern Scotland.* Oxford.

Morris, R. 1990. Cup and ring mark dating. *Glasgow Archaeological Journal* 16, 374-5.

Nowakowski, J. 1991. Trethellen Farm, Newquay: the excavation of a lowland Bronze Age settlement and Iron Age cemetery. *Cornish Archaeology* 30, 5-242.

Peña Santos, A. 1979. Notas para una revision de los grabados rupestres de 'O Castriño' en Conxo. *El Museo de Pontevedra* 33, 3-32.

Peña Santos, A. 1980. Las representaciones de alabardas en los grabados rupestres gallegos. *Zephyrus* 31, 115-29.

Peña Santos, A. and Rey García, J. 1993. El espacio de la representación. El arte rupestre galiaco desde una perspectiva territorial. *Revista de Estudios Provinciais* 10, 11-50.

Royal Commission on the Ancient and Historical Monuments of Scotland 1988. *Argyll,* vol. 6. Edinburgh.

Shee, E. and O'Kelly, M. 1971. The Derrynablaha shield again. *Journal of the Cork Archaeological and Historical Society* 76, 72-6.

Tilley, C. 1991. *Material Culture and Text: the Art of Ambiguity.* London.

Van Hoek, M. 1987. The prehistoric rock art of County Donegal (part 1). *Ulster Journal of Archaeology* 50, 23-46.

Van Hoek, M. 1988. The prehistoric rock art of County Donegal (part 2). *Ulster Journal of Archaeology* 51, 21-47.

Van Hoek, M. 1990. The rosette in British and Irish rock art. *Glasgow Archaeological Journal* 16, 39-54.

Villoch Vázquez, V. 1995. Análisis de emplazamiento tumular en Galicia: el caso de le necropolis de Saídos das Rozas (Campo Lameiro - Pontevedra). *Actas de XXII Congreso Nacional de Arqueología,* Vigo, vol. 1, 373-8.

New Research on Irish Early Bronze Age Cemeteries

Charles Mount

Abstract

The burials of the Early Bronze Age show a wide degree of variety which reflected the social variations within Irish Bronze Age society. An overview of the burial practices of the period is attempted by analysing the evidence from south-east Ireland. The burials are examined in relation to their distribution and siting and the effects of post-depositional factors such as ploughing and quarrying as agents of discovery are assessed. The composition of cemeteries is examined and it is suggested that the mixed cemetery with combinations of cists and pits as well as a range of pottery types was more common than previously thought. The cemeteries at Edmondstown, Co. Dublin, and Keenoge, Co. Meath, are examined in greater detail and the demographic and social patterns noted at these two sites are then sought in the rest of south-east Ireland. An outline of the organisation of Early Bronze Age society is presented and on the basis of this analysis it is suggested that this society was socially differentiated, with a proportion of high ranking individuals who were primarily adult males, often marked out from the rest by more elaborate funerary treatment.

Introduction

New work is changing the way we look at Irish Early Bronze Age burials. These were for a long time considered to represent a 'single grave' culture which contrasted with the communal rites of the Neolithic, but continuing analysis is demonstrating that widespread cremation and communal or collective burial continued from the Neolithic and that true 'single burial' was accorded only to a social élite. During the Irish Early Bronze Age both simple or stone lined circular and oval pits and more substantial slab lined rectangular and polygonal cist graves were constructed and in some instances cists assumed sub-megalithic proportions (Waddell 1990). The human remains were prepared for burial in a variety of ways. Some individuals were placed in extended position into large pits, or in contracted and flexed positions in smaller pits and cists. There is evidence that some individuals were bound or tied before burial. On occasion the remains might be stored until the flesh had decayed enough for the bones to separate or disarticulate, and were then interred. The majority of individuals were either partially or completely cremated on a funeral pyre. The remains were then collected, and sometimes after further crushing or cleaning were placed into the grave. The remains were often accompanied by decorated pottery vessels and less often with objects of stone or bronze. The burials were frequently placed in cemeteries, which might be either flat or under stone cairns or earthen barrows.

This paper looks at the period as one of developing complexity reflecting the social variations within Irish Bronze Age society, accounting for the proliferation in pottery styles as well as the complex variations in the burial record which are apparent from the broad overlapping of the various pottery and burial types. This aims to achieve an explanatory overview of the burial practices of the period by discussing the burial evidence from south-east Ireland, an area roughly corresponding to the southern portion of the province of Leinster and including seven counties: Carlow, Dublin, Kildare, Kilkenny, Laois, Wexford and Wicklow (Fig. 34). This area includes a wide range of topographical formations ranging from coastal and riverine locations to areas of lowland and upland, with a variety of soil types. The data concerning the 225 documented burial sites from this region forms the basis of parts 1 and 3 of this paper.

Part 1: The nature of the evidence

Cemeteries and single burials

In view of the scheme that will be advanced later it will be argued that any single burial has the potential to be a cemetery but for this discussion a cemetery will be defined as two or more graves.

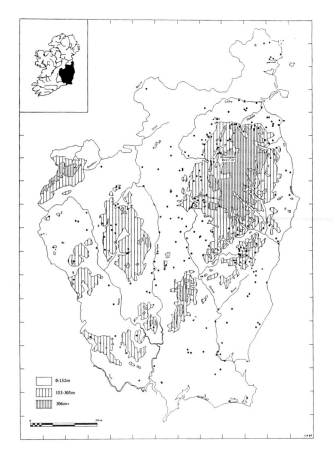

Fig. 34. Distribution of burial sites in south-east Ireland.

The manner of discovery

Exact details of discovery are recorded for 166 sites in south-east Ireland, or 74% of the total of 225 (Mount 1989, 37-8). Ploughing was responsible for the uncovering of forty-six sites (20%), while quarrying produced fifty-four sites (24%). Excavation and other activities accounted for only sixty-six sites (29%), and a further fifty-nine sites (26%) have no recorded details. Omitting the not knowns, ploughing and quarrying were the primary agents of discovery, responsible for 60% of the sites with known details of discovery (Fig. 35). As ploughing and quarrying are the most common agents of site discovery one might expect that as land use has intensified, especially in the second half of the century, the number of site reports would have increased. But this has not been the case. In the counties closest to Dublin the rate of site reporting has decreased and differing local conditions, the presence of archaeologists, local societies and institutional policies have resulted in variations of the overall pattern (Mount 1989, 44-5).

Site discovery and grave type

The agencies of discovery have also had an influence upon the types of grave uncovered. Details of both the manner of discovery and the individual grave type are available for 361 (88%) of the total of 412 graves (Mount 1989, 39-40). Sixty-three of these graves

Manner of site discovery

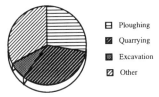

Fig. 35. Relative proportions of the manner of site discovery excluding unknowns. Ploughing and quarrying have clearly been the most important means of uncovering burials.

were found as a result of ploughing and of these, fifty-three (84%) were cists, while only ten pit burials (16%) were noted (Fig. 36). In contrast to this, 118 of these graves were found in quarries, fifty-six of which were cists (47%) and fifty-five were pit burials (47%), seven graves (6%) lacked precise details of type. This tendency for pit burials to be found in quarries in equal proportions to cists was primarily a result of the method of extraction, stripping sod and taking material by hand from a section face, that prevailed until after the Second World War and before the introduction of mechanisation. The exposure of pit burials in section in quarry faces made them much more noticeable, whereas ploughing tended to disturb

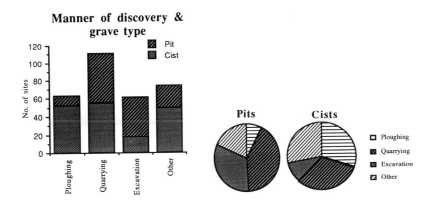

Fig. 36. The influence of the manner of discovery on grave type demonstrates that ploughing has tended to uncover more cists and quarrying more pit burials.

the burial without bringing much evidence to the surface. This problem has been enhanced with the increase in agricultural mechanisation, the tractor now dragging the plough behind, making one less likely to notice a disturbed pit burial. The much higher rate of pit burials found during archaeological excavation, forty-two (65%), compared with eighteen cists (28%), is a compelling argument that pit burials are largely under-represented in the archaeological record. The great numbers of pit burials occurring on cemetery sites, for example Edmondstown (Mount and Hartnett 1993), with a ratio of at least fifteen pit burials to three cists, Greenhills (Waddell 1990, 83) with four pit burials to two cists, Scarawalsh (Rynne 1966) with five pit burials to one cist or the cemeteries at Oldtown and Ploopluck (Waddell 1990, 99) which were composed entirely of pit burials, emphasise the point. On the larger and better preserved cemetery sites, pit burials outnumber cists. This strongly suggests that pit burial was the more common grave type of the period and that the use of cists was restricted to a minority.

Grave depth

The manner of site discovery has not only influenced the type of graves recovered but has had an influence on the number of graves and type of cemeteries. This influence can be assessed by examining the depths at which graves have been found. For the purpose of this paper, grave depth was defined as either the distance to the top of the capstone of a cist or the covering stone of a pit burial or the top of a pottery vessel, in an unprotected pit. Details of depth are only known for 129 graves, just over a third of the total (38%) (Mount 1989, 40-3) (Fig. 37). A further 214 (62%) are said to have been found below ground surface. If these are omitted and the remaining sites divided into six depth ranges, then the majority (73%) were found at less than 74cm in depth,

with more than a third at less than 25cm and 14% at more than 1m in depth. This is an interesting pattern, with an apparent decrease in graves at greater depths, but nevertheless a significant number, eighteen in all, at more than 1m in depth. The question is, does this accurately reflect the depths at which Bronze Age people buried their dead, or have other factors contributed to this pattern?

A cross tabulation of the graves for which there is information concerning the depth and manner of discovery reveals that 119 (92%) also have details of the manner of discovery (Table 3). The important factor is the complementary nature of the depths of discovery of graves found through ploughing and quarrying. At the shallower depths, ploughing was the dominant agent of discovery, accounting for 41% of the graves at less than 24cm, compared to 28% in quarries. Ploughing accounted for 41% of graves found between 25cm and 49cm, compared to 32% from quarries. But at the depth of 50cm to 74cm, 45% of the graves were found in quarries, compared to only 23% by ploughing. This relative increase in the percentages of graves found by quarrying is more pronounced at the greater depth to 99cm, where it accounted for 80%. There were no graves found by ploughing at more than 1m in depth. Therefore, there is a marked tendency for graves to be found at shallower depths through ploughing with only one found deeper than 75cm, and 83% at less than 50cm. In contrast graves are found at greater depths during quarrying with 61% found at depths greater than 50cm. The conclusion is that ploughing has tended to bias the discovery of Bronze Age graves, by uncovering mostly those buried at less than 50cm in depth. This factor has important consequences for the discovery of cemeteries.

If we look at the types of site found by ploughing or quarrying a complementary pattern is again evident. Of the forty-two sites found by the plough,

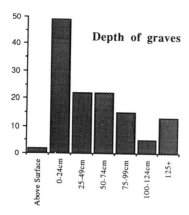

Fig. 37. Depth of graves below ground surface. Graves are most often found at the shallower depths and especially above 25cm.

thirty-three (77%) were single graves, and most of those were cists (Table 4). Only seven cemetery sites (16%) have been found as a result of ploughing. This contrasts with quarries, which out of a total of fifty-six sites have produced twenty-four flat cemeteries (43%), over three times as many as were found by ploughing. Fifty-one sites have been found by other means, twenty-seven (53%) were single flat and eighteen (35%) were either flat cemeteries or cemetery mounds. Therefore ploughing has led to the discovery of cists rather than pits at shallower depths, and has tended to uncover primarily single graves. It appears likely that many of these single graves are components of cemeteries.

The Composition of Cemeteries

The fifty-nine documented cemeteries in the southeast represent less than one third of all the known sites (Mount 1989, 78-9). The average number of graves occurring in a cemetery is four, and three is the most common number (Fig. 38). Twenty-nine cemeteries (49%) consisted entirely of cist graves, twenty-five (42%) contained both cists and pit burials, and five sites (8%) were exclusively pit cemeteries. The average number of graves occurring in a cist-only cemetery is three, the most common number is three and the range is between two and six. Waddell (1981, 166) has noted that the majority of burial sites with more than one grave had either two or three, and that sites with four or more graves were much less common. This is because many of the two or three grave sites are cist-only cemeteries. In contrast the smaller number of mixed cemeteries average five graves, with the most common number between two and three, but with a range from two to more than twenty. The average number of graves in an exclusively pit cemetery is more than six, the most common number is six and the range is from two to ten. Both the average number and range of graves in the exclusively cist cemeteries is lower than the means of the other

two cemetery types, and the average of all the cemeteries. The affects of grave type on burial discovery would appear to account for the greater number of cisted rather than mixed cemeteries and the fewer number of graves in the cisted cemeteries in comparison to the mixed cemeteries. Therefore a number of the cisted cemeteries are likely to represent the remnants of mixed cemeteries from which the pit burials have not been recovered. The consequence of this is that the true picture of the cemeteries has been obscured and mixed cemeteries would probably have been the more common cemetery site type of the period, rather than cist-only cemeteries. The two types of grave are mixed not only on the same site but occasionally within the same grave. At Killinane (Moore 1984) the cremated remains were placed into a pit in the floor of the cist and at Carrig (Grogan 1990) two of the cists had secondary pit burials inserted into them. The early dating of the bowls, which are closely related to the cists, allows one to speculate that for many cemeteries the construction of a cist grave commenced the formal mortuary use of a cemetery site. Although this cannot yet be determined stratigraphically, at Edmondstown

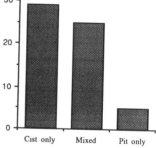

Fig. 38. The composition of cemeteries. Mixed cemeteries are almost as common as cist only.

(Mount and Hartnett 1993) the three cists were situated in a central position in relation to the pit burials which were grouped around and in some cases over them. This suggests that cist 1 or 2, which contained inhumations, one of an adult male accompanied by a bowl food vessel, would have initiated the use of the site. In order to assess the place of cemeteries an ongoing project of analysis has been taking place.

Part 2: Cemeteries

Edmondstown, Co. Dublin

The cemetery consisted of four cist burials and a minimum of seventeen to nineteen pit burials which contained at least 27 individuals (Fig. 39). Thirteen

Table 3: Cross tabulation between the manner of discovery and the depth of burial. Quarrying has uncovered burials at greater depths than ploughing

	Plough	Quarry	Excav	Other	Not Known
Above Surface	1	–	1	–	–
Below Surface	14	29	16	20	8
0-24cm	20	14	5	8	2
25-49cm	9	7	1	4	1
50-74cm	5	10	–	4	3
75-99cm	–	12	1	1	–
100-124cm	–	3	1	–	1
125-149cm	–	8	2	3	–
Not Known	10	25	15	29	31
Total	59	108	42	69	46

Table 4: Cross tabulation of manner of discovery by burial mode. Ploughing tends to uncover more single burials and quarrying more flat cemeteries

	Plough	Quarry	Excav	Other	Not Known
Single Flat	33	24	3	27	32
Single Mound	2	4	2	5	6
Flat cemetery	7	24	3	8	9
Cemetery Mound	–	2	6	10	6
Not Known	–	2	–	1	11
Total	42	56	14	51	64

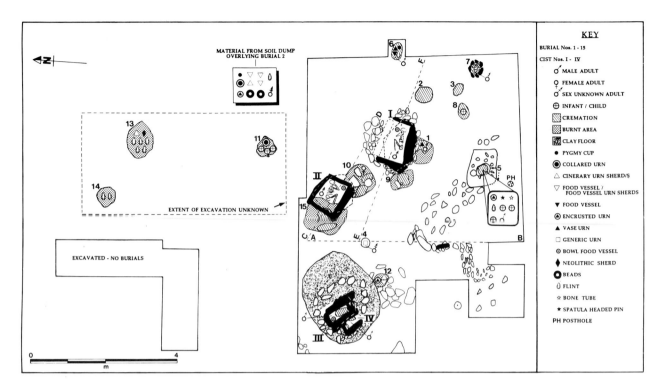

Fig. 39. The cemetery at Edmondstown, Co. Dublin.

of the graves contained pottery and three contained bone and/or flint artefacts. The finds consisted of remains of up to twenty complete or partially complete vessels, including three bowl food vessels, three sets of food vessel sherds, four or five vase urns, three encrusted urns, two collared urns, one plain coarse and one missing urn, two pygmy cups, a possible Neolithic sherd, three disc beads, bone pin and tube, one flint knife, six flint scrapers, three other flints and some quartz.

Human Remains

i. Condition of the cremations

Thirteen quantities of cremated bone were available for analysis and the colour, bone size and proportions of body parts were noted. All of the bone was well cremated and usually white to grey in colour, with the exception of the male in cist II, whose bone was white or light brown in colour with portions of the back and leg bones less intensely burnt and blue/grey in colour. The male in pit burial 6 was also less efficiently burnt.

With the exception of pit burials 1 and 12, the bone does not appear to have been crushed after its removal from the pyre. Four burials had evidence of inefficient collection of body parts. Pit burial 2 contained only a small quantity of bone and not all the body parts were present. The amount of bone in pit burial 7 was also small as were pit burials 12 and 13. These are very small quantities in comparison to the bone in cist III and would appear to be only token deposits.

This has been noted at other sites. At Glasnamullen, Co. Wicklow (NMI Record), only *c.* 15% of the bone appeared to have been collected from the funeral pyre and placed under the collared urn in burial 2.

There is some variation in the condition of the cremated bone. The heavier cremations, which were less well burnt, not crushed and represented by larger numbers of bones, were identified as male. At the other end of this scale was the bone from pit burial 12 where the individual bones were not only efficiently cremated and well crushed but were few in number. Overall the female and undifferentiated adult cremations tend to be somewhat lighter, although they did not necessarily contain fewer fragments.

ii. Age and sex

About 27 individuals are represented and these include four adult males, one adult female and six unsexed adults, four children, three to four infants and eight quantities of bone which were either unavailable for analysis or were too small for identification. The small quantities of bone in pit burials 12 and 13 indicate that these remains were only token deposits. Of the identified adults, males clearly predominate at 80%; however, a proportion of the unsexed adults may be female (Fig. 41). Children represent between 37% and 42% of the aged remains, which is a little below the ratio of 45-52% one would expect in a pre-industrial subsistence society (Weiss 1973).

Similar patterns have been noted at other cemeteries

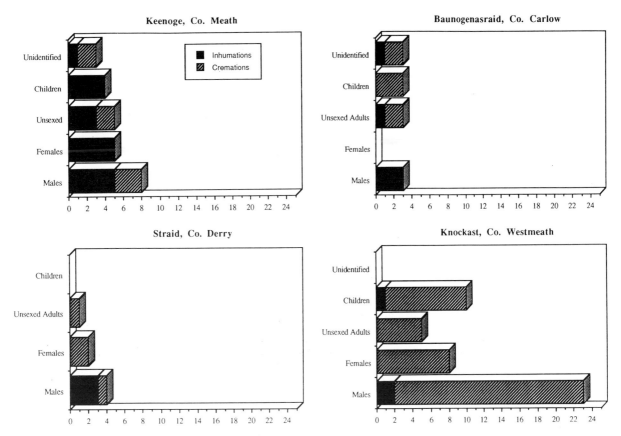

Fig. 40. Age and sex characteristics of individuals at Keenoge, Co. Meath; Baunogenasraid, Co. Carlow; Straid, Co. Derry; and Knockast, Co. Westmeath.

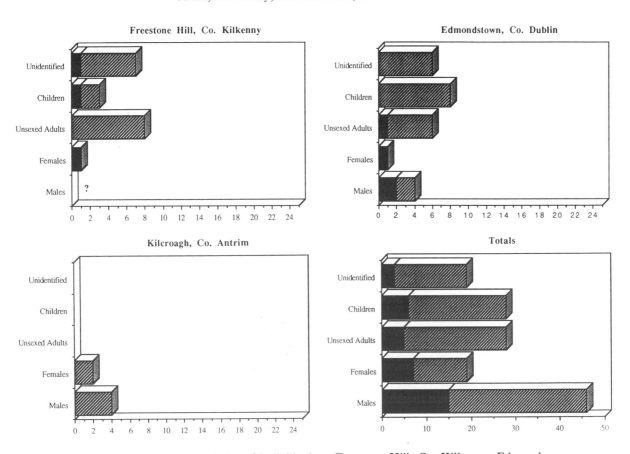

Fig. 41. Age and sex characteristics of individuals at Freestone Hill, Co. Kilkenny; Edmondstown, Co. Dublin; Kilcoagh, Co. Antrim and totals of Figs 40 and 41.

that have been analysed. At Knockast, Co. Westmeath (Hencken and Movius 1934) adult males clearly predominated with 23 males to 8 females, and children were less than 25% of the identified remains (Fig. 40). At Freestone Hill, Co. Kilkenny (Raftery 1969) children were also under-represented in comparison to adults and at Baunogenasraid, Co. Carlow (Raftery 1974) adult males were identified in greater numbers than females and all adults predominated over children (Figs 40-41).

All of the interments in the cists at Edmondstown were adults, and only the individual in cist II, because of his or her youth, cannot be positively identified. These men were the only individuals associated with bowl food vessels and two of these were the only inhumations on the site. This treatment contrasts with that of women and children who were all cremated. Similarly at Knockast all the females and children, with one exception, were cremated (Fig. 40). The tendency for adult males to be associated with bowls and in cists in greater numbers than females and children (Mount 1989, 103; 1991, 21-3) is discussed below.

Of the nineteen graves at Edmondstown, ten contained single individuals and three were multiple burials, two were not available for analysis and three more were token burials. Multiple burials represented nearly 16% of the recovered burials from the site. They have been noted in just over 11% of the graves in south-east Ireland (Mount 1989, 99) and between 31% and 40% of the graves in the south-west (Doody 1987, 17). The individuals in multiple burials were mostly children and infants. In two cases they were buried with adults, one of whom may be male, and in the third case two children and an infant were buried together. There is also a single child buried on its own in pit burial 8. As over 80% of the children were buried communally it appears that this was their usual method of burial at this site. Therefore there appears to have been a principle underlying the selection of those individuals who were buried on the site and the manner in which they were interred, with adult males singled out for special treatment while women and children received less elaborate care.

Keenoge, Co. Meath

This flat cemetery consisted of six cist burials and eight to ten pit burials, which contained at least 26 individuals (Fig. 42). At least seven of the graves contained pottery and one contained bronze and flint artefacts. The finds consisted of remains of up to twelve complete or partially complete vessels, including nine complete bowl food vessels, one or two vase urns, one encrusted urn, a jet necklace of forty beads, one bronze razor knife, one flint scraper, and

a number of other flints (Mount and Mahr, in press).

Human Remains

i. Condition of the cremations

Six quantities of cremated bone were available for analysis. Almost all of the bone was well cremated and usually white in colour, although a few fragments were blue to black. With the exception of graves 4 and 14 the bone was not crushed after its removal from the pyre. Four burials had evidence of inefficient collection of body parts. Graves 3, 4 and 13 contained only a small quantity of bone and not all the body parts were present. The cremations in graves 3 and 4 contained few skull fragments while half the fragments in grave 5 were of skull. This has been noted at other cemeteries. There is some variation in the condition of the cremated bone. The three heavier cremations from graves 5, 8 and 14 were identified as male and only the remains of the male in grave 14 were crushed. The lighter cremations were identified as adult and a number of these may represent women. It appears that the effort expended by the mourners in collecting the remains from the funeral pyre was not the same for each individual and more time was spent in recovering the remains of men.

ii. Age and sex

A minimum of twenty-six individuals are represented in the cemetery; these include eight adult and one mature adult male, four adult and one young adult female, four unsexed adults and five children and infants as well as three quantities of bone which were either unavailable for analysis or were too small for identification. The small quantities of cremated bone in grave 13 suggests that this was only a token deposit. Adults males were most common at 64% of the sexually identified adults, however a proportion of the unsexed adults may be female (Fig. 40). Children and infants together represent just under 22% of the aged remains, which is far below the ratio of 45-52% one would expect in a pre-industrial subsistence society (Weiss 1973). These large numbers of adult males in comparison to women and children have been noted at other cemeteries (Figs 40-41) and the results from Keenoge further reinforce the patterns noted at Edmondstown, Co. Dublin (Mount and Hartnett 1993, 54-6), Knockast, Co. Westmeath, Freestone Hill, Co. Kilkenny, Baunogenasraid, Co. Carlow and Straid, Co. Derry (Brannon *et al.* 1990). They suggest that only a portion of any given community was granted a formal burial, indicating a high degree of social differentiation. The contrasts in the treatment of those individuals who were interred was also indicative of this social differentiation (Mount 1991, 21-3).

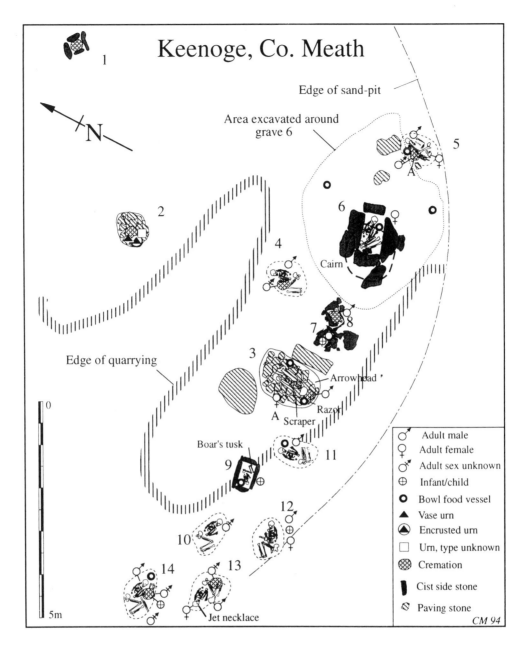

Fig. 42. The cemetery at Keenoge, Co. Meath.

The interments in the cists were varied, consisting of an adult male, adult female, unsexed adult and two children. But this is not a complete picture as the remains in graves 1 and 2 are lost. The woman in grave 6 is notable as she was buried in a well-built cist with a bowl food vessel, which is often a male accompaniment (Mount 1989, 103; Mount and Hartnett 1993, 57-8). This burial parallels the young adult woman who was buried in a cist at Ballybrew, Co. Wicklow. She was accompanied by a tripartite bowl, a lignite bead, round scraper and flint flake and had been placed on a matting of rushes (Martin *et al.* 1935-7, 255-70). At Keenoge eight of the nine men, four of the five women and three of the five children and infants were buried in pits – thus only a minority received burial in a cist. Twice as many men were associated

with bowls as women and one child was associated with a bowl. The tendency for men to be associated with bowls is known from other cemeteries including Edmondstown, Co. Dublin, Straid, Co. Derry (Brannon *et al.* 1990), and Haylands, Co. Wicklow (Price and Walshe 1933). There is also a strong possibility that the majority of the children associated with bowls were male as well. Sixty-seven percent of the men were inhumed and 33% were cremated, while 100% of the women were inhumed and 80% of the children and infants were inhumed. This treatment contrasts markedly with Edmondstown, Knockast and Straid where nearly all the women and children were cremated. Undoubtedly the men of the Keenoge community were more often favoured with formal burial than their wives, mothers, sisters and children, but when the women of the community were granted a formal burial they received equal or in some cases superior treatment. Therefore social status within the Keenoge community was not solely a male accomplishment and other aspects, perhaps inheritance or kin relationships, would have had a part to play in the acquisition of social status. Perhaps the woman in grave 6 rose to the leading position in her family, either through the death of her husband or through her own accomplishments.

The mixture of inhumed and cremated remains within a single grave is striking. Five of the twelve burial deposits available for analysis had a mixture of inhumed and cremated remains. It is unlikely that the interments in the multiple graves were all made simultaneously and there would have been a number of successive burials in each grave. This pattern has been noted at Carrig, Co. Wicklow (Grogan 1990) where cist D had up to five successive burials and is known from other sites. In grave 3 at Keenoge the placement of the cremated male into the grave appears to have disturbed the female inhumation. In any case the association with the razor would tend to indicate that he was a later insertion. However the other cremations would not have necessarily followed the inhumations. At Straid, Co. Derry, Brannon noted that the cremation had probably been placed into cist 3 before the inhumation (Brannon *et al.* 1990, 34). As the currency of inhumation and cremation were clearly contemporary there must have been an important symbolism attached to each rite. The principles underlying the selection of cremation or inhumation for a particular individual would have reflected fundamental divisions within the contemporary society.

At Keenoge only a minority of the individuals were cremated. This contrasts with the evidence from south-east Ireland (Mount 1991) where more than two thirds were cremated and other cemetery sites at Edmondstown, Freestone Hill and Knockast where most of the individuals were cremated. At the Mound of the Hostages at Tara all but one of the burials was a cremation (Waddell 1990, 128). In this respect Keenoge is paralleled by the pit cemeteries at Oldtown and Ploopluck in Co. Kildare where inhumations were associated with bowls in pits (Waddell 1990, 99). The emphasis on inhumation at Keenoge may hint at a differing social structure from the communities who used Edmondstown, Freestone Hill and Knockast, although the possibility that unaccompanied cremations from Keenoge were missed should be borne in mind.

Of the fourteen graves at Keenoge, only five contained single individuals, nine were multiple burials and two more were not available for analysis. Multiple burials represented 69% of the recovered burials from the site. They have been noted in just over 11% of the graves in south-east Ireland (Mount 1989, 99) and between 31% and 40% of the graves in the south-west (Doody 1987, 17). Analysis of Keenoge, together with Edmondstown and other sites, is changing the way we look at Early Bronze Age burials. These were for a long time considered to represent a 'single grave' culture (Herity and Eogan 1977, 133) but ongoing analysis is demonstrating that communal or collective burial continued from the Neolithic and that true 'single burial' was accorded to only a minority of individuals.

The graves and especially the pits at Keenoge may have been used as family plots, which were opened for successive burials, and it is tempting to view the individuals in these graves as closely related, perhaps members of a single family unit. The group in grave 12, a man, woman and child might represent a single family and the man and woman in grave 3 might, if we were willing to accept the bowl and razor as contemporary, have been husband and wife, as could conceivably be the couple in grave 4. But other criteria may have applied to the inclusion of individuals in graves. In grave 14 two men were buried with a juvenile and child. Could these have been brothers, or father and son? The better preservation of the infant cremation in grave 7 in comparison to the adult may indicate that the child's burial occasioned the disturbance of the adult. Alternately the adult's burial may simply have represented a token or symbolic burial of a small portion of their remains, with the remainder left on the pyre, buried elsewhere or scattered. The small amount of the cremation in grave 3 might also represent a token burial. The small number of women and children represented indicates that wives and children did not automatically have the right to burial with their husbands, fathers and brothers and their remains were disposed of in a different manner. Perhaps they were cremated and scattered into the river that was so conveniently close.

The variations in the treatment of the men at Keenoge is interesting (Fig. 40). They were buried in a number of ways ranging from crouched inhumation to uncrushed and crushed cremation. This range of burial rite was not reflected in the women's burials as they were all apparently inhumed. This may indicate a range of social status within the male community reflecting each man's particular occupation and role in society. The artefactual evidence from Ireland at this period is pronounced enough to indicate that some men were taking time from subsistence farming to concentrate on metal-working, flint acquisition and production and ceramic production (Herity and Eogan 1977, 137-42). Some men must

Minimum individuals

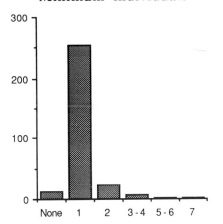

Fig. 43. The minimum number of individuals per grave. Only a few graves appear to have had multiple burials but this pattern will probably change with further research.

also have been involved in articulating a political structure and overseeing the smooth re-distribution of agricultural resources which would have made such a system possible, either as family or clan leaders. It can be tentatively suggested that the differences in the treatment of the men at Keenoge, and other cemeteries, may represent the various grades of social status ascribed to each of these individuals. The richness of the land in the Keenoge region (Mount and Mahr, in press) would have provided enough of a surplus to support specialists in a number of fields and the control of this resource would also have been a basic factor of social differentiation.

Part 3: Demography

The patterns noted at Edmondstown and Keenoge can help us to examine burials on the larger scale.

The minimum number of individuals

Three hundred of the 412 individual graves known from the south-east (73%) have details of the number of individuals they contained (Mount 1989, 91) (Fig. 43) and 255 graves (85%) contained a minimum of one burial. But a significant number of these burials are represented by quantities of cremated bone, many of which have not been examined by palaeopathologists, therefore a number represent multiple interments. Eleven percent of the graves contained more than one burial, and of these, twenty-three (8%) contained two burials, seven (2%) contained between three and four burials, two (0.7%) contained between five and six and one (0.3%) contained seven interments. Martin Doody (1987, 17) noted that in Munster 32% of the cremation deposits and 40% of

the inhumed burials were found to represent more than one individual. If the situation in the south-east is similar then the number of multiple burials may be under-represented by more than one third.

Cremation and inhumation

There are a minimum number of 364 individuals represented in the study area, of which 112 (31%) were inhumed and 233 (64%) were cremated, with a further nineteen (5%) whose burial rite is not recorded (Mount 1989, 92-5). The number of cremated individuals is more than twice that of inhumed, but the figure for cremated individuals is a minimum estimation. Another important factor is the under-representation of pit burials noted earlier. This would have contributed to a reduction in the overall number of recovered cremations. Therefore the percentage of cremated individuals should be higher.

The question of the relationship between inhumation and cremation in Early Bronze Age burial practices is important. In the past they have been viewed in chronological terms simply as customs, with cremation replacing inhumation over time. But as discussed earlier both cremations and inhumations have been found within the same grave. Cremation was the more common burial rite but for much of the period people would have had a choice. Why did they choose one option over another?

In some social groups it may have been important to preserve the bones of some individuals, while the majority were incinerated. Rowlands (1980, 51) has suggested that this illustrates a contrast between the burial rites of individuals of high and low rank. The survival of the bones symbolised the perpetuation of the body and status of the individual. This would have allowed the body to become an organic monument or a symbolically charged relic, reminiscent of the medieval cult of relics. In our own era the importance of preserving the remains of prominent males continues and Napoleon, Lenin, Stalin, Mao, Ho Chi-Minh and Kim Il Sung amongst others have all been embalmed and provided with symbolic mausolea. In recent times some of these individuals have, in death, been reduced in status, for example Demitrov of Bulgaria, whose remains were removed from his mausoleum and cremated. This act has clearly reduced his status in death and has removed the ability of the old ruling order to rally around his relics.

This hypothesis indicates the sociology that lay behind the inhumation of a minority of the population, who were primarily, though not exclusively, adult males while the majority were cremated. The occurrence of cremated remains in the same graves as inhumations, but often in a secondary or perhaps inferior position can be interpreted as implying a secondary status. At Ballyhacket Upper (Waddell 1990, 53) a quantity of cremated bone was overlain by the walling of a cist which contained an inhumation. The cursory treatment of the cremation may indicate that it was less important than the inhumation. Where cremations are primary in a grave inhumations were rarely placed in after. Sometimes a small quantity of cremated bone might be placed onto an inhumation as at Oldtown (Waddell 1990, 99), almost like a token offering.

Cremations were not simply placed into the grave, but were often crushed and pounded, as at Haynestown (Manning 1977-86) and Carrig (Grogan 1990), and placed into the grave in handfuls. At Haynestown, a number of individuals were mixed in a single deposit. This minimised the physical remains of the individual, reducing them almost to powder, and in cases of multiple interments, mingled their remains with those of a group. This paralleled the collective burials of the Neolithic and may indicate some continuity of the structures that underlay the Neolithic traditions.

Within the rite of inhumation there were also contrasts. At least twenty-two inhumations were disarticulated. The remains had been defleshed before their interment and in some cases only a portion of an individual might be buried. At Dillonsdown (Waddell 1990, 160) the long bones and skull of an individual were absent, and at Newtownmacabe (Waddell 1990, 99) an adult male was accompanied only by the skull of an adult female. These individuals had been stored for some time before they were buried. Of the fourteen disarticulated burials that have been aged it is interesting that seven (50%) were children. This represents about 20% of the identified children's remains from the south-east.

A number of inhumations show evidence of *post mortem* binding. Ryan (1974, 23) noted that the contracted adult male from Sliguff, Co. Carlow, must have been tightly bound in order for him to be placed into the cist in such a closely contracted position. At Whitestown, Co. Dublin (Waddell 1990, 86) an adult inhumation had been placed into the cist on its back, and its legs had been probably tied into a contracted position. The contracted male from Glassamucky, Co. Dublin (Waddell 1990, 83) must also have been tightly bound. This binding and the defleshing noted above are examples of a range of activities that formed part of the funerary rituals accompanying burial of which little evidence remains. In these cases some time must have elapsed between the death of the individual and their final interment and the funeral ritual may have taken place in a number of stages, involving the preparation and temporary storage of the body. Indeed the construction of special mortuary houses, like

the one excavated at Ballyveelish, Co. Tipperary (Doody 1987, fig. 1.11), may have served this purpose.

Kinnes (1976, 26) suggested that the increasing size of the megalithic tombs, or proliferation of chambers in Britain, did not involve an extension of the privilege of burial, but rather an increased diversity in the range of deposits. The practice of constructing individual cist and pit burials in the Bronze Age would have allowed a wider range of burial deposits, without the need to invest large amounts of labour in tomb construction. This would have suited small kin based groups who might have cooperated in the construction of ceremonial monuments, henges, timber and stone circles, but who each possessed their own cemetery. The expansion in the range of deposits corresponds with the proliferation of pottery types noted at this time. These more common formal burials may have been expressing a social ethos in opposition to the restricted rite of inhumation, which may be linked to the aspirations of lower sub-groups who sought to improve their position in society. While this may be only dimly perceived in the material sphere at this time it may be symbolised through the development of new burial forms. This would explain the range of burial rites at Keenoge. Indeed the wealth of the Keenoge community may have provided the conditions for junior or peripheral members of the lineage to increase their influence. This process of social advancement may have resulted in the abandonment of cists and inhumation altogether as the technologically advanced metal owning society of Late Bronze Age Ireland developed and social display moved away from the burial sphere, the realm of the *ancien régime*, to the control of metal production and distribution.

The ages of the individuals

About 160 individuals have been broadly identified as adults or sub-adults. Of these 128 were adults (80%), while only thirty-two were sub-adult (20%) (Mount 1989, 96-7). Morris (1987, 58) in his study of burial and society in Iron Age Attica divided the burials in his sample into two age classes, adult/youth and child/infant, arguing that this simple binary division took advantage of the most reliable contrast in the evidence. On the basis of life expectancy tables for pre-industrial agricultural societies published by Acsadi and Nemeskeri (1970), and Weiss (1973). Morris calculated that the graves should contain about 45.2-51.8% infant/children under ten years, and 48.2%-54.8% youth/adults over ten years. Comparing this age profile to the general situation prevailing in the study area, sub-adults should represent about half of the aged remains, or somewhere in the range of eighty individuals. However, with only thirty-two individuals, sub-adults are under-represented in the burial record by more than half, indicating that only a minority of children received formal burial. If only a portion of the deceased children of the period were finding their way into formal burials, the remainder must have been disposed of in a manner which has left little trace. The corollary of this is that not all members of a community received formal burial. If some children were entitled to the privilege of interment in formal burial sites, and others not, then there must have been a principle underlying this selection. If the society was socially differentiated, then this criterion would have been the rank or status of the child. As it is unlikely that a child would achieve status in its own right, then a position of prestige must have been inherited. If one portion of society was excluded then others must have been similarly excluded.

The sexes of the individuals

The sexes of fifty-one (14%) adults have been established (Mount 1989, 98-9). Thirty were males (59%), with three possible males, and sixteen were females (31%). Adult females would appear to have been under-represented in formal burial in comparison to adult males. Glenn (see Clarke *et al.* 1985, 152) has examined the Early Bronze Age burials in Scottish cists. From her sample 137 individuals could be aged and sexed. Of these eighty-two (59.9%) were male, thirty-eight (27.7%) were female and seventeen (12.4%) sub-adult (neo-natal to adolescent). She also found that males had a higher average age of 36.7 years, in comparison to 28.8 years for females. Fifteen percent of the males were older than forty-five years, while the eldest female was in her mid forties. Glenn suggested that the age and sex proportions of her sample were not representative of a general population, but must reflect a restricted sub-group. If we divide Glenn's figures into the two categories of age and sex so that they can be compared to the ones from the south-east they show that in Scotland sub-adults represented 12.4% of the burial population, and males represented 68.3% of the sexed adults in comparison to 31.7% females. These figures are in broad agreement with those from south-east Ireland, demonstrating that adult males were more likely to receive formal burial than females at this period, and only a small proportion of sub-adults were interred.

The nature of the interments

There are a total of 112 interments (39%) of single individuals (Table 5) (Mount 1989, 99-102). A further 143 quantities of cremated bone (49.7%) must represent at least one, or a portion of one individual.

However, a proportion are also likely to represent more than one individual. In the present state of analysis multiple interments have been found in just over 10% of the graves.

Seventy-five of the single interments have been aged. Sixty-six of these (88%) were adults, and the remaining nine individuals (12%) were children. Twenty-three of the single interments have been sexed, a sample of just over 20%. The sexes of the identified single interments break down as sixteen adult males (70%) and seven adult females (30%). Males were about twice as likely to be buried on their own as females, while children received this treatment in only a small percentage of cases. It is also of note that in two of the four cases where children were buried with adult males, as at Ballybrew (Waddell 1990, 159), they were placed into the grave first and the male subsequently interred. There are twenty-three examples of double burial (8%). In twelve cases adults were associated with other adults (4%), and in eleven cases were associated with one child (4%). In these combinations the numbers of identified males and females, although statistically very small, are equal while males tend to be associated with children more often than females. Also the percentage of the total number of forty-six individuals from double burials represented by children (23.9%) is more than double that in single burials, and slightly higher than the children's percentage of all aged individuals. It would appear that children were more than twice as likely to receive admission to a formal burial if they were accompanied by an adult. Or to put it another way, they rarely received such treatment in their own right. This supports the idea that they may have inherited the right to formal burial.

Ten graves contained more than two individuals (3%). Three contained adults associated with other adults, and seven graves contained combinations of adults and children. The average number of individuals in these multiple burials is four, with the most common number three, and a range from three to seven. If the multiple and double burials together represented as much as 30% of the total, as they did in Munster, then we could estimate that roughly the same numbers of individuals were represented in the total multiple graves as in the total individual graves. However, confirmation of this must await a thorough examination of the skeletal material from the study area.

In those multiple burials containing children their percentages, which range between 33% and 66%, begin to assume the proportions that one might expect in a pre-industrial agricultural society. The overall percentage ratio of females to males of 60% to 40% is also higher than that noted in the single

Table 5: Identified grave groups

	Frequency	Percent
Single individual	37	12.8
Minimum 1 adult	143	49.7
Single adult	43	14.9
Single male	16	5.6
Single female	7	2.4
Single child	9	3.1
Two individuals	3	1.0
Two adults	1	0.3
Two males	2	0.7
Male & other adult	2	0.7
Two females	1	0.3
Female & other individual	1	0.4
Male & female	2	0.7
Male & child	4	1.4
Female & child	1	0.3
Adult & child	6	2.1
Three adults	1	0.3
Male, female & child	1	0.4
Female & 2 children	1	0.3
Adult & 2 children	1	0.3
Male, female & 2 adults	1	0.3
Four individuals	1	0.4
Two adults & 2 children	1	0.3
Three females & 2 children	1	0.3
Four adults & 2 children	1	0.4
Two males, 2 adults & 3 children	1	0.3
Total	288	100.00

burials. Of course it must be acknowledged that the small size of this sample leaves any conclusions open to question, but it is tempting to suggest that these multiple interments, with their high proportions of children and females, are more representative of a typical population than the single burials, and are complementary. Another way of viewing this is that we may be seeing a proportion of the females and children, who did not merit their own individual graves but did have the right of formal burial, accorded a communal burial. Another interesting aspect is that most of these multiple interments were cremations. It has been suggested that cremation may sometimes be interpreted as a sign of lower rank. Its link in this instance with the communal burial of the members of society who were most often excluded

from formal burials may be significant. Another factor is the absence of pottery from these larger multiple interments.

The interments and their pottery associations

Of the sixty-one bowl food vessels with details of association, fifty (82%) were associated with single burials (Mount 1989, 103-6). Thirty-two of these single burials have been aged, twenty-nine were adults (90%), and three were children (10%). Of these adults nine have been sexed, six were males (67%) and two were females (33%). To put it another way, 38% of the singly interred adult males in the sample were associated with bowl food vessels, in comparison to 29% of the females. Notably, more than 30% of the nine individual child burials were also associated with bowl food vessels. It is interesting that at Kilgraney, Co. Carlow (Cahill 1986) the child who was accompanied by two adults had been provided with its own undecorated bowl. Once again we must be wary of the small size of the sample, but while adult males are found more frequently with bowl food vessels than both adult females and children, the percentage of all males with bowls is not significantly higher than that of females or children. It appears that while only a selected proportion of the population had the right to individual burial, and this population may have been dominated by males, the proportion of those males who had a right to a bowl food vessel was only slightly higher than the females or children. Seven bowl food vessels were associated with double burials (11%), but it can be argued that in three of these cases they accompanied males who shared graves with children, and were in effect associated with a single individual. In a fourth case a bowl was placed with each of two males in a grave. There were also five bowls (8%) associated with four multiple burials. In two cases these were associated with adults, and in the other two with adults and children.

Detailed analysis of the bone material associated with vase food vessels is largely lacking. This is primarily because this pottery type, like the cinerary urns, was usually associated with cremations. All that can be said is that in four cases they have been found in association with adults, twice with two adults and once with a single individual. There are fifteen cases in which vases were associated with quantities of cremated bone which can only be described as representing a minimum of one individual.

Thirty-one quantities of cremated bone and thirty-nine single individuals were accompanied by no pottery. Of these, thirty-two have been aged and divide into twenty-seven adults (84%) and five children (16%). Eleven have been sexed and represent eight males (73%) and three females (27%).

Conclusion

I have argued in part 1 that the types of sites and graves discovered have been influenced by the manner of discovery and it was concluded that both pit burials and mixed cemeteries were under-represented. In part 2 the cemeteries at Edmondstown and Keenoge were examined and complex social structures suggested. Finally in part 3 the demography of south-east Ireland was examined. Adult males are represented more often than females, and both occur in greater numbers than children. This indicates that only a portion of the general population was receiving formal burial. This pattern is typical of a socially differentiated society where formal burial is the right of rank. A complementary pattern was observed between the single interments, which had a high percentage of adult males, and the multiple burials, which were dominated by the remains of women and children. It was suggested that these burials may represent the remains of those not considered to merit formal burial individually but did receive it as a collective group. The association of bowl food vessels with a small segment of the population, which was often inhumed and dominated by adult males, was outlined. On the basis of this analysis it appears that Early Bronze Age society was socially differentiated, with a proportion of high ranking individuals, who were often marked out from the rest by more elaborate funerary treatment.

Acknowledgements

This paper is based in part upon research carried out for a Masters Thesis in the Dept of Archaeology, University College, Dublin, and I would like to express my gratitude to the Head of the Department, Professor George Eogan, and to my supervisor Dr Gabriel Cooney who both provided consistent encouragement, many hours of discussion and helpful suggestions both during my time at UCD and since. The analysis of the human remains from Edmondstown and Keenoge was carried out by Dr Laureen Buckley to whom thanks are due. All figures are by the author, with the exception of Fig. 39, by Roddy Moynihan and reproduced from Mount and Hartnett (1993).

References

Acsadi, G. and Nemersiki, J. 1970. *History of Human Life Span and Mortality*. Akadémiai Kiado, Budapest.

Brannon, N. F., Williams, B. B. and Wilkinson, J. L. 1990. The salvage excavation of Bronze Age cists, Straid Townland, County Londonderry. *Ulster Journal of Archaeology* 53, 29-39.

Cahill, M. 1986. Kilgraney. In C. Cotter (ed.) *Excavations 1986*, 12. Dublin.

Clarke, D. V., Cowie, T. G., and Foxon, A. 1985. *Symbols of Power at the Time of Stonehenge*. Edinburgh.

Doody, M. G. 1987. Early Bronze Age burials, Ballyveelish 3, Co. Tipperary. In R. M. Cleary, M. F. Hurley and E. A. Twohig (eds), *Archaeological Excavations on the Cork-Dublin Gas Pipeline (1981-2)*. Cork.

Grogan, E. 1990. Bronze Age cemetery at Carrig, Co. Wicklow. *Archaeology Ireland* 4 (4), 12-14.

Hencken, H. O. and Movius, H. L. 1934. The cemetery-cairn of Knockast. *Proceedings of the Royal Irish Academy* 41C, 232-84.

Herity, M. and Eogan, G. 1977. *Ireland in Prehistory*. London.

Kinnes, I. A. 1976. Monumental function in British Neolithic burial practices. *World Archaeology* 7, 15-29.

Manning, C. 1977-86. A cist at Haynestown. *Journal of the Kildare Archaeological Society* 16, 484-91.

Martin, C. P., Price, L., and Mitchell, G. F. 1935-37. On two short cist interments found at Ballybrew, Co. Wicklow. *Proceedings of the Royal Irish Academy* 37C, 255-70.

Moore, F. 1984. A Bronze Age burial at Killinane, Near Bagenalstown, Co. Carlow. *Old Kilkenny Review* 3 (1), 64-8.

Morris, I. 1987. *Burial and Ancient Society*. Cambridge.

Mount, C. 1989. Early Bronze Age burials in southern Leinster. Unpublished M.A. thesis, University College, Dublin.

Mount, C. 1991. Early Bronze Age burials - the social implications. *Archaeology Ireland* 5 (2), 21-3.

Mount, C. and Hartnett, P. J. 1993. Early Bronze Age Cemetery at Edmondstown County Dublin. *Proceedings of the Royal Irish Academy* 93C, 21-79.

Mount, C. and Mahr, A. (in press). Early Bronze Age cemetery at Keenoge, Co. Meath. *Proceedings of the Royal Irish Academy*.

Price, L. and Walshe, P. T. 1933. Stone and Bronze Age antiquities of the Barony of Lower Talbotstown, Co. Wicklow; with a description of the excavation of Haylands Mote, near Blessington. *Journal of the Royal Society of Antiquaries of Ireland* 63, 6-67.

Raftery, B. 1969. Freestone Hill, Co. Kilkenny: an Iron Age Hillfort and Bronze Age Cairn. *Proceedings of the Royal Irish Academy* 68C, 1-108.

Raftery, B. 1974. A prehistoric burial mound at Baunogenasraid, Co. Carlow. *Proceedings of the Royal Irish Academy* 74C, 277-312.

Rowlands M. 1980. Kinship, alliance and exchange in the European Bronze Age. In J. Barrett and R. Bradley (eds) *Settlement and Society in the British Later Bronze Age*, Bar British Series 83 (i), Oxford. 15-55.

Ryan, M. 1974. Cist-burial with Food Vessel from Slyguff Townland Nr. Bagenalstown, Co. Carlow. *Carloviana* 23, 21-4.

Rynne, E., 1966. Bronze Age cemetery at Scarawalsh,

County Wexford. *Journal of the Royal Society of Antiquaries of Ireland* 96, 39-46.

Waddell, J. 1981. The antique order of the dead, cemeteries and continuity in Bronze age Ireland. In D. Ó Corráin (ed.), *Irish Antiquity*, 163-71. Cork.

Waddell, J. 1990. *The Bronze Age Burials of Ireland.* Galway.

Weiss, K. M. 1973. *Demographic Models for Anthropology.* Memoirs of the Society for American Archaeology, No. 27.

Structure and Deposition in Irish Wedge Tombs: An Open and Shut Case?

Paul Walsh

Abstract

This paper considers the architecture of one of the four main classes of Irish megalithic tombs, the wedge tomb, with a view to examining whether the monuments were built so as to allow recurrent access. The architecture, while exhibiting a unity in form, shows diversity in execution. It is possible to suggest that the main chambers at some sites were sealed. In certain instances it is clear that we are looking at the final result of what may have been a varied series of activities which, in the light of recent radiocarbon determinations, points to the ongoing use of some of these monuments in a way that is archaeologically invisible.

In this paper sites are referred to by their townland name followed (in brackets) by the two letter abbreviation for the counties used in the volumes of the *Survey of the megalithic tombs of Ireland* (de Valera and Ó Nualláin 1961; 1964; 1972; 1982; Ó Nualláin 1989). Where a site plan and description have been published the appropriate megalithic survey number or reference is appended.

Introduction

It is now generally recognised – though with varying degrees of acceptance – that megalithic tombs were not simply burial structures *per se* but, as monuments, may have served a variety of functions within the cultural context of both the societies that built and used them and those that came later (e.g. Bergh 1994; Bradley 1993; Cooney 1983; 1990; Hodder 1984; 1989; McMann 1994; Renfrew 1976, 1981). It may be said that they were as much 'monuments for the living' as 'monuments for the dead'. In that regard, one of the trends in recent archaeological writing has been the attempt to offer alternative interpretations of these structures in terms of how individuals might have 'physically' encountered them (e.g. Thomas 1991; 1992; Richards 1992). Although this could lead to a certain theatricalisation of the past, nonetheless, by introducing a different way of looking at the existing evidence it has facilitated much positive re-evaluation. An intriguing aspect of the study of megalithic tombs is the question of the placement of the mortuary deposits within them. Was this done as a single operation and the tomb sealed or was the monument left open or, at least, rendered re-accessible for successive depositions or ritual? With this in mind I propose to look at the design of one particular tomb type, the wedge tomb, and to consider how access might have been gained to these monuments.

Wedge tomb morphology

Wedge tombs form the most numerous class of megalithic tombs in Ireland accounting for some 505 (33%) of the total of 1,535 identified to date. The essential characteristics of this series are well known (Shee Twohig 1990; Ó Nualláin 1991). In summary, the tombs comprise a gallery composed of side walls either roughly parallel or wedge-shaped in plan and usually orientated on a general north-east to south-west axis (Fig. 44). It is often accompanied by at least one outer revetment of walling which may be closely set though, in many cases, this especially accentuates the pronounced wedge-shaped plan of the monument as a whole. Its eastern end, more often than not, is closed by a single slab and there are instances where a small chamber is present at this end, e.g. Ballyedmonduff (Du., Ó Ríordáin and de Valera 1952).

Evidence for gallery segmentation is found at many sites where the main chamber is commonly preceded by a short antechamber or 'portico',[1] the demarcation being effected in the majority of cases by a transversely-set stone, occasionally by jambs, or more rarely by sills. In the majority of examples the roofstones rest directly on the side walls of the gallery. In general, there is a gradual decrease in height from the western to the eastern end of the monument and this further enhances the overall 'wedge' appearance; one that echoes, if in a somewhat miniature and

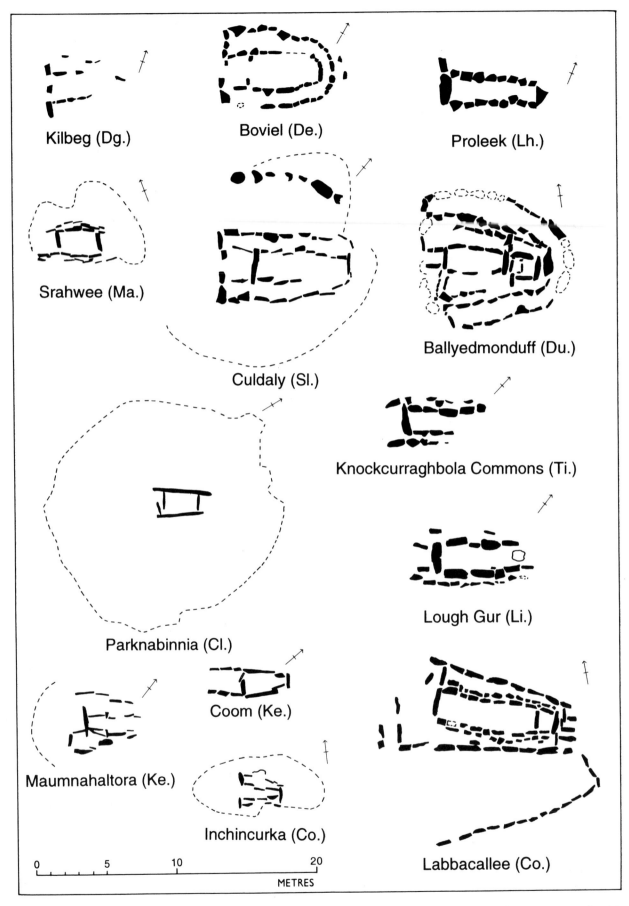

Fig. 44. Wedge tomb plans: roofstones omitted. Surveys by Archaeological Branch, Ordnance Survey, except: Boviel (after Herring 1940), Ballyedmonduff (after Ó Ríordáin and de Valera 1952), Lough Gur (after Ó Ríordáin and Ó hIceadha 1955) and Labbacallee (after Leask and Price 1936).

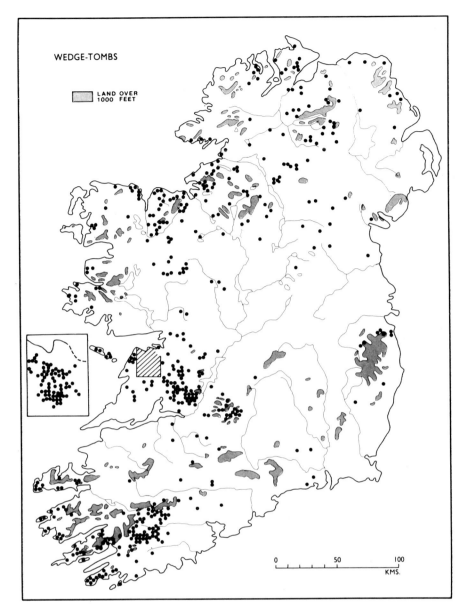

Fig. 45. Distribution of wedge tombs.

truncated form, the trapezoidal configuration of many long barrows. There are often some remains of mound or cairn present at most sites though it is impossible now to be certain if all the structures were ever intended to be completely covered. Unlike the court and passage tombs where the employment of corbels necessitated a substantial counterbalancing cairn, the placing of the roofstones directly on the sidewalls would not have required such elaborate cairn construction at wedge tombs. In many cases, the outer-walling may have marked the outer limits of the cairn. The cairn or mound outline that is visible today may mark only the final stage in a succession of events at individual sites and it may well be that the surviving different forms (round, heel-shaped, etc.) reflect local ritual preferences expressed in a variety of ways at different times.

The distribution of this tomb type evinces a marked western bias with notable concentrations in the north and south Munster regions respectively accounting for 56% of the total (Fig. 45). While the multiplicity of identical dots on the distribution map suggests a significant degree of uniformity throughout the series such a perception is somewhat illusory. Wedge tombs come in a variety of shapes and sizes and, in certain cases, their design undoubtedly was influenced by the local geology. For example, the availability of large limestone flags in the Burren region of Clare and the easily quarried slabs of sandstone in south-west Cork and Kerry have facilitated the construction of neat, regular chambers. And yet, though there are certain standard design principles adhered to in the construction of these tombs, each monument is different in some detail. They exhibit a unity in conceptual form but diversity in individual execution. Small sites such as Reananiree (Co.) are quite efficient containers, if such indeed is all they were ever intended to be (Pl. 27). This miniature example has all the essential

Pl. 27. Reananiree, Co. Cork. Scale: 50cm interval.

characteristics of the series but is only 1.5m long by *c.* 0.75m wide and is little more than 0.4m high at its taller south-western end. Four monuments of this size would fit comfortably on the floor of the main chamber of Labbacallee (Co. 3, Leask and Price 1936) which is 6.2m long and averages 1.7m wide. This latter structure was clearly intended to be seen as more than just a convenient repository for the dead and it is ostensibly monumental in character (Pl. 28). Both of these sites, within the same county, represent the extreme ends of the scale in terms of construction.

Western component

In the best preserved examples the western end of the monument usually incorporates the largest stones and, more often than not, is the most imposing and monumental part of the structure. This end is further enhanced by having a flat or, more rarely, slightly concave facade. It may be said that the architecture contrives to invite you to this end of the monument. It is here that we would expect to gain access and, likewise, it is here that we might expect the original builders to have congregated to deposit the remains. This hypothesis may seem to have a lot to offer but it falls short when practical considerations of access are taken into account at individual sites. Nevertheless, the evidence from excavations - exiguous as it is - points to multiple and successive burials taking place and some tombs have morphological details suggestive of western entrance features. It is necessary, therefore, to examine the architecture of the series as a whole to try and establish whether there is any secure basis on which to base such inferences.

Pl. 28. Labbacallee, Co. Cork: view from south-east.

There are two factors that must be considered at the outset. If it was intended that repeated access to these monuments should be possible then we would expect, firstly, that they would be of sufficient proportions so that one could physically get into them and, secondly, at the very least, possess some form of doorway or entrance feature. Superficially, the tombs may be divided on the basis of chamber size into two groups: single wedge-shaped, box-like constructions and long low galleries. The former are typical of those found in north-west Clare, e.g. Parknabinnia (Cl. 67; Pl. 29) and south Munster, e.g. Altar (Co. 61) and though the latter are found principally in the northern half of the country, e.g. Tamybuck (An.); Burren (Cv. 5); Lisduff (Ma. 93); Proleek (Lh., Buckley and Sweetman 1991, 34), examples do occur elsewhere, e.g. Knockcurraghbola Commons (Ti. 13); Maumnahaltora (Ke. 6). The important difference between the two groups from the viewpoint of access is the height of the chamber. It would be possible to enter the interiors of many of the tombs with box-like galleries. However, in the case of the long, low galleries access to the rear could only be gained with considerable difficulty and, in certain cases, possibly not at all, e.g. Gortacullin (Cl.) and Killakee (Du; Ó hEailidhe 1978).

Directing our attention to the western end of wedge tombs we find considerable variation in the design here. These variations may conveniently be listed under five headings. In setting out these headings a distinction must be borne in mind between segmented and unsegmented galleries; i.e. between those that have a 'portico' and main chamber and those where there is no evidence for such. The five headings are as follows:

1. Galleries closed by slabs that imply some form of door structure.

2. Galleries segmented by jambs/sills or other elements in which access can be gained to both 'portico' and the main chamber.

3. Galleries segmented by a septal stone in which access can be gained to the 'portico' but not to the main chamber.

4. Galleries sealed by a single large stone that do not appear to allow for access.

5. Open unsegmented galleries with no evidence for closure.

These five headings are employed for the sake of convenience as they highlight significant differences between the monuments. Comparison of the basic elements of construction is naturally hindered by the state of the surviving remains and there is such variation in the form exhibited that it is sometimes difficult to decide under which heading a monument should be treated. For example the gallery at Srahwee (Ma. 91) is divided by a stone that could be interpreted either as a high sill, a narrow septal stone or an extra large jamb; it is included under heading 2. Likewise, destruction has removed much of the western end of the monument at Labbacallee (Co. 3) but the extension of the outer walling beyond the northern and southern sides of the gallery is taken here to suggest that there might have been some form of 'portico' formerly present; it is included under heading 3.

Galleries closed by slabs that imply some form of door structure

At least twelve tombs in the Burren region of northwest Co. Clare exhibit a distinct form of closure which is suggestive of a possible door structure. It is effected by two slabs, one blocking approximately three quarters of the width and the other set outside it (de Valera and Ó Nualláin 1961, 104), e.g. Gleninsheen

(Cl. 15), Parknabinnia (Cl. 67) and Ballyganner South (Cl. 38). The jamb-like arrangements outside the west end of the galleries at Baur South (Cl. 26), Carncreagh (Cl. 52) and Tyredagh Lower (Cl. 98) and those within the chamber at Corbehagh (Cl. 91) are probably related to these.

Mention of three other sites which have evidence for multiple closing stones at the west end is relevant here. At Streedagh (Sl. 8) three overlapping stones (one probably not *in situ*) stand inside the line of the gallery walls and seal its west end. At Aghamore (Le.) and Meenkeeragh (Dg.) the facade stones overlap to close this end. These are reminiscent of the configuration at Clogherny (Ty.) where the gallery was closed by two stones set almost back to back. Here, excavation revealed that the inner stone was not set in a socket but rested on three wedge stones (Davies 1939a, 37). The arrangement of slabs at these sites suggests that they could have allowed for the periodic opening of these tombs by removal of one of a number of relatively small facade stones.

Pl. 29. Parknabinnia, Co. Clare. Scale: 20cm interval.

Galleries segmented by jambs/sills or other elements in which access can be gained to both 'portico' and the main chamber

In certain cases the gallery is divided into a 'portico' and main chamber by jambs and/or sill-stones (Fig. 46a). Given the ruined condition of many tombs and the fact that the galleries often contain considerable amounts of fill, evidence for sill-stones is meagre. The only certain example of a sill occurs at Island (Co. 6) where it was flanked by a jamb-like upright at the east (O'Kelly 1958). Other likely instances include Poulaphuca (Cl. 20), Carrowcrom (Ma. 60), and Killsellagh (Sl. 28). Mention should also be made of the segmenting element at Caherdowney (Co. 8) where a high slab, centrally set between the side walls with a small gap at each end, is flanked at the east by two jamb-like pillar stones. This cannot be considered as a sill-stone proper.

Jamb segmentation, likewise, is not common but is especially evident at the excavated sites; Largantea (De., Herring 1938), Boviel (De., Herring and May 1940), and both Loughash tombs (Ty., Davies 1939b; Davies and Mullin 1940). They are also present at Sheshnan (Le. 10), Crohane (Ke. 14), Coumaclavlig (Co.) and at the destroyed site Clogh (Sl. 17). Another form of jamb segmentation occurs at Wardhouse (Le. 1), Cabragh (Sl. 89), Meenformal (Dg.), Carrowmore or Glentogher (Dg.) and probably Carrowgarve South (Ma. 53) where single jamb-like stones project from the sidewalls of the galleries. An unusual type is found at Coom (Ke. 16). Here a single stone blocks more than half of the opening between the 'portico' and main chamber and is overlapped by a second stone. A somewhat similar arrangement occurs at Beardiville (An.). Mention has already being made of the atypical segmentation at Srahwee (Ma. 91).

Where there is no evidence for clear segmentation the architecture sometimes suggests a differentiation between a western 'portico' and the remainder of the gallery. This may be manifested by a distinct broadening, e.g. Cahernaglass (Ga. 15), or narrowing, e.g. Carmoney (Dg.) of the western end of the gallery and/or by the use of two well matched opposing stones as at Caltragh (Sl. 54) and Killybeg (Fe., eastern site). These stones stand in marked contrast to the stones used in the remainder of the gallery and leave little doubt but that some form of 'portico' was probably present. In all these cases it would be possible, at least theoretically, to gain access to the main chamber.

Galleries segmented by a septal stone in which access can be gained to the 'portico' but not to the main chamber

The importance of differentiating a western component from the main chamber has been noted above

and at seventy-eight sites (15%) this is marked by a septal stone (Fig. 46b). These stones are usually the largest stones in the monument and are well selected with good surfaces and flat tops and, in the majority of cases, the stones are inset in the side walls and reach to the full height of the gallery, e.g. Burren (Cv. 5), Meenagulleen (Ke. 15). A small number of septal stones are of enormous proportions, e.g. Toorclogher (Ga. 20), Ardaragh West (Co. 54)) and would have protruded well above the gallery roofstones, e.g. also Gurteendarragh (Le. 5), Usna (Ro. 4). The lower portions of many of these stones are frequently concealed but some, at least, do not appear to have been set in sockets, e.g. Burren (Cv. 5), Drumeague (Cv. 29), Aghadrumgowna at Calf Field (Cv. 25), Gortakeeran (Sl. 87), and probably Kilhoyle (De.) and Baurnadomeeny (Ti. 6). This does not imply that they were movable but rather that their sheer bulk and weight, together with the fact that they are inset in the side walls of the gallery, probably did not necessitate the digging of sockets. At a few sites the septal stone is set between the side walls of the galleries and is usually not as massive as some of the inset examples, e.g. Formoyle More (Cl. 115), Cabry (Dg.), Gransha (Dg.), and Scrahallia (Ga., Cooney 1985-6). In ten cases the gallery roofstones rest directly on the septal or there is evidence that the 'portico' itself was roofed; Aghadrumgowna at Calf Field (Cv. 25), Burren (Cv. 5), Ballycrom (Cl. 95), Barbane (Cl. 126), Carrownaganonagh (Dg.), Altore (Ro. 9), Moytirra West (Sl. 103), Gortakeeran (Sl. 87), Baurnadomeeny (Ti. 6), and Knockcurraghbola Commons (Ti. 10). Nonetheless, in all instances where definite septal stones occur the main chamber is effectively sealed off from western access. This is particularly evident at Knockcurraghbola Commons (Ti. 10), (Pl. 30).

It is clear that the septal stone functioned both as a closing and segmenting element within the overall design and it is noteworthy that they are found in association with jambs at Cabragh (Sl. 86), Killybeg (Fe., western site), Greenan (Fe.) and Maumnahaltora (Ke. 6). In the case of the first three mentioned sites the jambs flank the septal stone; to the west at Cabragh and Killybeg and to the east at Greenan. The two stones flanking the north end of the inset septal stone at Burren (Cv. 5) could be interpreted as jambs though they do not project into the gallery as such. At Maumnahaltora the jambs are set 1m to the east of the septal stone.

Galleries sealed by a single large stone that do not appear to allow for access

There are forty-nine (10%) sites where a large slab closes the western end of the gallery, e.g. Garranbane (Li., Shee Twohig 1988) (Fig. 46c). As with the septal

Pl. 30. Knockcurraghbola Commons, Co. Tipperary. Scale: 20cm interval.

stones noted above many of these slabs are substantial and often are the largest stones in the monument. They are similar to those used as septal stones and it may be that in certain cases some of these sites originally possessed 'porticos'. For example, if the surviving northern sidestone of the 'portico' at Lackamore (Ti. 1) was removed the gallery would give the appearance of being closed by a single stone. Likewise, two of the three tombs at Ballycrom (Cl. 93 and 95) and one of the two tombs at Cloonyconry More (Cl. 113) have 'porticos' but Ballycrom (Cl. 94) and Cloonyconry More (Cl. 114) do not. In these two instances one can readily imagine how the stones forming the sides of 'porticos' might have been removed and leave no trace. Nevertheless, there is strong evidence to suggest that some sites that are now closed by a single stone never possessed such a feature, e.g. Ballinphunta (Cl. 90); Kilcatherine (Co. 48), Magheranaul (Dg.), Loughbrack (Ti. 11) and Proleek (Lh.), (Pl. 31). A possible example occurs at Munmahoge (Wa.; Ó Nualláin and Walsh 1986, 28).

Open unsegmented galleries with no evidence for closure

There are very few well-preserved wedge tombs and most sites simply exhibit features that enable them to be classified as such. It could be argued that the western end of the main chamber of every monument was once sealed in some fashion or marked off by a 'portico' and that this 'closing' evidence lies concealed in the fill of many galleries or has been removed. There are some tombs, however, where the overall preservation can be considered as reasonably good but possess no evidence for any closing element. In these cases it is worth questioning if it ever existed. It is likely that the open galleries at Tamybuck (An.) and Aghnacally (Cv. 13) once possessed closing stones or some similar feature though no evidence for such now survives. There are twelve sites where jambs are found at the western end of galleries where no evidence for segmentation or other closure survives, e.g. Culleens (Sl. 50), Laghtneil (Co. 32). At five of these sites in south-west Munster longitudinally-set jambs stand inside the line of the gallery walls at the west end: Crossoge (Co.), Derree (Co.), Cooldaniel (Co.) and probably Derryriordan South (Co. 33) and Knocknagoun (Co. 9).

The use of jambs without any apparent closing element does suggest that at these sites a definite entrance feature was intended. There are at least seven other tombs in this region that should be considered in this

Pl. 31. Proleek, Co. Louth.

context: Carrigonirtane (Co. 13), Inchincurka (Co. 42), Keamcorravooly (Co. 24), Killberrihert (Co. 19), Lackabaun (Co. 38) and especially Altar (Co. 61) and Toormore (Co., O'Brien 1994, 214-19). If there was a closing stone present at the first five mentioned sites then it probably was not substantial. It seems reasonable to suggest that the prostrate slab discovered outside the western end of Coumatloukane (Ke. 17, Herity 1970) was a closing or segmenting stone and one could imagine a similar arrangement at Inchincurka (Co. 42). The evidence from the excavated sites of Altar (Co. 61) and Toormore (Co.) will be considered below.

Discussion

It is clear that certain constructional elements exhibit distinct distributional patterns, e.g. the use of double closing stones in north-west Clare. It is reasonable to suggest that such regional variations reflect certain local preferences for particular architectural styles or were a response to specific ritual fashions. There seems little reason to doubt but that it was intended as a door structure as it is invariably found in tombs composed of single side stones and roofstones. One would have expected that if it were intended that these be sealed compartments then the western end would also have comprised a single slab. It may, of course, be incorrect to assume that the door element was intended for repeated use of the tomb but was simply the penultimate constructional phase prior to the primary deposition of the remains; the site then being sealed by the smaller overlapping slab. As the gallery side walls normally project a little to the west of the closing slabs in this region it is possible that the recess so formed could have fulfilled the function of a 'portico' but, in these instances, there is no definite architectural evidence for such. There are only three sites in the north-west Clare area where the presence of 'porticos' seems likely: Ballyganner South (Cl.), Faunarooska (Cl. 5) and Cappaghkennedy (Cl. 42).

It would be possible in the case of tombs with jamb/sill segmentation, e.g. Loughash 'Giant's Grave' (Ty.) to gain repeated access to the main gallery from the 'portico', albeit with some considerable difficulty considering the low size of these monuments. It is a noteworthy feature of the distribution of sites that have jamb segmentation that it is found at only five sites in the southern half of the country and is almost totally absent from the Clare and north Tipperary concentrations (Fig. 46a). Despite the variation in execution the evidence clearly indicates the importance of segmentation in the overall construction of a number of these monuments. It can be estimated that about one fifth of the tombs possessed some form of 'portico' and, though the evidence is not conclusive, it appears that where they survive their western ends more often than not are open or, at least, are capable of being entered. This suggests that it was intended that they be repeatedly used, or at least, could be easily accessed. Although the plan of Baurnadomeeny (Ti. 6; O'Kelly 1960) gives the impression of a sealed 'portico' its western edge, however, is demarcated by sill-like stones. Similar sill-stones were found at the entrance to the 'portico' at Largantea (De., Herring 1938) and Loughash 'Giant's Grave' (Ty., Davies 1939b). Sometimes the opening is narrowed either by having façade stones project slightly across it in jamb-like fashion, e.g. Burren (Cv. 5), Culdaly (Sl. 114), or by the insertion of a single stone at one side, e.g. Ballyedmonduff (Du., Ó Ríordáin and de Valera 1952), Kilhoyle (De., Herring and May 1936-7) and possibly Moylisha (Wi., Ó hIceadha 1946). At fifteen sites this opening is divided by an orthostat, e.g. Gortakeeran (Sl. 87), both Loughash tombs (Ty.), Baurnadomeeny (Ti. 6). This particular feature occurs predominantly in the northern part of the country (Fig. 46d). There are four other sites where no evidence for a 'portico' survives that also have divided entrances; Tobercurry (Sl. 117), Kilbeg (Dg.) and possibly Aughrim (Cv. 14). A probable example will be found in the south at Ballyhoneen (Ke. 1) and the single pillar stone standing within the west end of Glantane East (Co. 7) may also be relevant in this context. All in all, the evidence demonstrates that some significance was attached to incorporating a chamber at the western end of the monument and that this may have been left open on purpose seems clear. The presence of cists within these 'porticos' at Kilmashogue (Du., Kilbride-Jones 1954), Lough Gur (Li., Ó Ríordáin and Ó hIceadha 1955), Largantea (De., Herring 1938), and Baurnadomeeny (Ti., O'Kelly 1960) may be pertinent with regard to the possible reuse of these sites though at Baurnadomeeny the excavator considered it to be an original feature.

I have already noted above that it is probable that some of the sites with large western closing stones may have once possessed 'porticos'. Taken together the evidence from those sites with septal and closing stones (25% of the sites) indicates that the main chamber was sealed at the western end by a large stone. It is reasonable to suggest that the incorporation of this stone, either as a septal or closing element, and which is fully integrated into the overall design, indicates that once the monument was erected, its contents placed within, and the whole roofed over, it was not intended that further access should be gained to the main chamber at least. It may be that in these instances it was never intended that anyone, other than those for whom the monument was conceived in the first place, should be interred there. But as we know from the history of our own western Christian tradition, that has never stopped others – be they contemporaries or successors – from appropriating the rite of formal burial within structures, even to the detriment of the architecture. In general, the distribution pattern of both these closing elements are similar and fairly widespread throughout the series though the single closing stones are not especially common in the north and both types notably are absent from the south Munster area (Fig. 46b and c).

In as much as access to the main chamber effectively was obstructed by either a septal or closing stone then it could be argued that, in these instances, the tombs were entered from the east end as Shee Twohig (1990, 53) has suggested for some of the sites in the west Tipperary and east Clare region. This hypothesis gains some support from the excavations at Baurnadomeeny (Ti. 6, O'Kelly 1960) and Lough Gur (Li. 4, Ó Ríordáin and Ó hIceadha 1955) where no evidence for east end closure was found, though at the latter site a likely displaced closing stone occurred in the upper levels at this end. Nevertheless, this evidence must be balanced with that from other tombs in the same area and from the series as a whole where definite east end stones are present, e.g. Loughbrack (Ti. 11), Corderry (Ti. 17), Gortakeeran (Sl. 87), Culdaly (Sl. 114). It should also be borne in mind that the east end of many of these monuments, being composed of smaller stones, is sometimes concealed and is especially vulnerable to destruction. This is not to deny that subsequent users of the monuments may have gained access via the east end. It may have been the easiest way into some of the main chambers. We would expect this to be done at sites where the western closing stone or septal is massive and an east end stone is of sufficient size to allow entry.

If the burial evidence from the gallery at Labbacallee (Co. 3) is taken as indicating successive deposition, and the radiocarbon determinations would appear to support this (Brindley and Lanting 1991-2, 21), then the question of how access was gained at this and similar sites is most pertinent. The excavators concluded that once the basic structure had

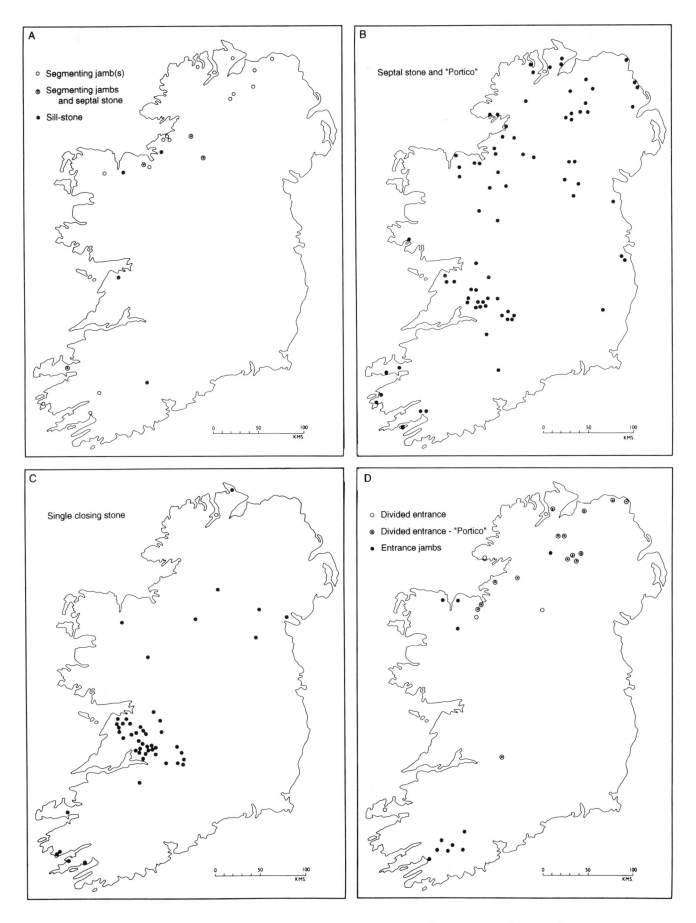

Fig. 46. Distribution maps: (a) Jamb/sill segmentation; (b) Septal stone and 'portico';
(c) single closing stone; (d) divided entrance and entrance jambs.

been erected and the massive western roof stone placed in position, access to the main chamber and small east chamber was probably effected by leaving the latter's roofstone to one side so that the burial deposits could be placed in both chambers (Leask and Price 1936, 81). This may well have been the manner in which subsequent burials also were deposited within the tomb. Indeed, it may be suggested that this was another method employed by those who reused this and other monuments where the western end is sealed by either a septal or closing stone. Such a hypothesis has been suggested by Case to account for the Beaker material at West Kennet (1995, 10).

The employment of a large stone as a closing or segmenting element contrasts sharply with many other examples where there is no surviving evidence for either segmentation or for closure. The absence of septal and single closing stones has already being noted for the south Munster group of monuments. At Toormore (Co.) sockets were recovered for the fallen side and end stones but there was none demarcating the western end (O'Brien 1990; 1994, 217-22). It is clear that a simple slab leaning against the uprights would have effected closure and the former presence of such a stone would leave no archaeological trace. A similar arrangement may have existed at Altar (Co. 61) where a low kerb of stones was discovered at this end of the chamber. The excavator considered that this may have provided the footing for a moveable slab (O'Brien 1993, 24). But even allowing for this type of closure, and I certainly do, it stands in marked contrast to the full and complete sealing achieved by the septal arrangement.

It may be that those who built many of these monuments did not perceive them as having an entrance as such, or for that matter, a front and rear as we see them. Their objective may have been simply to erect a monument for the dead which conformed to a particular conceptual pattern or paradigm. The degree to which there was some agreed concept of architectural design, or how such a concept evolved or was communicated, are difficult questions. The evidence indicates that there were no hard and fast rules regarding the specific size and details of construction. The builders clearly had certain ideas but the chosen form was open to reinterpretation and allowed for variations in execution. These were probably dictated as much by the local geology as by changing fashion or individual whim. Although working within convention the builders of these monuments were not imprisoned by it. The development and retention of the conceptual design must have been due to the ongoing construction of these monuments on a regular basis.

But just because we find evidence for variation in form should we expect, therefore, the same ceremonial/burial/liturgical practices to have taken place at each and every monument? Surely, as Barber has stated, 'only the last sites built will reflect a single liturgical tradition; all the earlier sites will present a palimpsest, a conflation, of the formal accommodations of the several liturgies in vogue during the currency of their use and subsequent re-use' (1992, 31). The implications of the different architectural forms used throughout the series – forms that undoubtedly were modified and revised – seem to me to be that we are witnessing the results of a number of strands of a ritual tradition; one that expressed itself in an assortment of liturgies which necessitated differences in the application of the basic elements of construction.

Some twenty-three tombs (5%) have been excavated since 1930 though finds are known to have been recovered from at least eleven others. Radiocarbon determinations of thirty-two samples from six of these sites (Brindley and Lanting 1991-2) provide evidence that these monuments were being used for burial by *c.* 3800 BP. The dates do not support pre-Beaker use of these tombs though this does necessitate a reinterpretation of the Neolithic material from Boviel (Herring and May 1940; Brindley and Lanting 1991-2, 25). The results also highlight the recurrent use of some of these monuments, e.g. Altar (Co. 61) in a way that is archaeologically invisible and this has implications for the interpretation of some other sites, e.g. Island (Co., *ibid.*, 21). There is clear evidence for continuity of burial at a number of sites both in the gallery and/or in secondary pits and cists, e.g. Bowl food vessels at Loughash 'Cashelbane' (Ty.), Kilhoyle (De.), Largantea (De.), Lough Gur (Li.) and Kilmashogue (Du.); vase urn at Kilmashogue (Du.); encrusted urns at Craigarogan (An.), Lislane (Ty.), Loughash 'Giant's Grave' (Ty.); cordoned urn at Largantea (De.) (Brindley and Lanting 1991-2; Kavanagh 1973; 1976; Ó Ríordáin and Waddell 1993). This is very important in the context of distinguishing between the period when these tombs may have been built 'as compared with the period in which activity was focused on them' (ApSimon 1985-6, 11-12).

Court, portal and passage tombs

A brief comment on the implications of this study for the three other recognised traditions of Irish megalithic tombs might not be out of place here. It is clear that there is no structural, sealing element present at the entrance to the chambers at the majority of court tombs. It seems to me that the incorporation of a definite entrance feature as typified by the use of jambs and lintel accompanied sometimes by a low sill – in effect, an open door – did not simply allow for possible re-entry, but was contrived so that access could repeatedly be gained to the chambers within. Richards (1992) has been led to similar conclusions regarding the stalled arrangement in the Orkney-Cromarty chambered cairns. This is not to deny that such entrances could not be temporarily blocked or finally sealed, e.g. Annaghmare (Ar., Waterman 1965, 11). In contrast to this, it is difficult to determine how repeated access could be gained to many portal tombs, especially those with tall 'doorstones' (Herity 1982, 290; O'Donovan 1993); if such, indeed, was ever intended by the original builders. It would not be possible to move many of the doorstones, e.g. Drumanone (Ro. 3), Kilmogue (Kk.), Haroldstown (Cw.) without the whole structure collapsing. Clearly this stone was an integral stabilising structural component of the design and not simply a closing element; though it also performs this function. Notwithstanding this, it can be argued that access to a number of these chambers might have been gained by removing the sidewalls which often are not set in the ground but lean against the portals and backstone. In the case of passage tombs, particularly those in the Boyne Valley and Lough Crew cemeteries, the architectural evidence indicates that in the majority of instances the presence of kerb stones would, at the very least, have hindered repeated access and may well have been intended as an important element in the final sealing of the monument; denying entry to the chambers. In the Lough Crew cemetery it is only at Cairn T that the kerb directly articulates with the side stones of the passage. It is a noteworthy feature of the tombs in this cemetery, as indeed, of the great mound of Newgrange as well, that the passages do not extend as far as the kerb stones but stop short some distance behind them. And the passage itself sometimes is sealed by one or more closing stones (McMann 1994, 530, fig. 6; O'Kelly 1982, 98). One must pose the question, therefore, as to how long these monuments remained open for communal/successive burial and/or ritual and whether or not the builders ever envisaged them being reused? The evidence suggests to me that as in the case of some, at least, of the portal tombs it would appear that while re-entry was possible and did occur it was not intended, once the closing or sealing elements had been placed in position.

Conclusions and questions

On the basis of the available evidence it is reasonable to suggest that the majority of wedge tombs were single phase constructions. That is, they were conceived and executed as complete entities. Assuredly, some were altered or adapted to conform with changing interpretations and rituals and they continued to be recognised by succeeding peoples both as centres for burial and ritual. It is over thirty years since de Valera and Ó Nualláin considered the implications of whether there was 'a significant difference between closed tombs, i.e. those which provide for no functional entry to the main chamber, and those which would provide for periodic opening without considerable demolition' (1961, 104-5). The examination of the architectural evidence outlined above suggests that there is a clear impression given by some of the surviving examples that some form of ongoing access was intended and such access may have involved recurrent burial. In others a 'portico' was left open but the main chamber was completely sealed. The evidence clearly testifies to the importance of this particular design and it must reflect the formal requirements of some liturgical aspect of the ceremonies performed either at the initial burial deposition or intended for subsequent ritual.

It may be no more than semantics to state that we should now begin to consider tombs as being built within the wedge tomb 'tradition' rather than as belonging to the wedge tomb 'class', as Bergh (1994, 12) has suggested for passage tombs. We might also question whether the narrowing of our focus on the class as a whole has not coloured our perceptions of those we envisage as having built and used them? Are we correct in our inferences that the adoption of a distinctive architectural form is but a monumental expression of a cohesive social group or, for that matter, corresponds with fundamental social transformation? In other words, was there a specific 'wedge tomb' people? The answers to these questions lie outside the scope of this particular study and cannot reasonably be hoped to be resolved from the evidence of the architecture alone. Nevertheless, I hope that the approach adopted in this paper will help enlarge the focus of our enquiries into this monument type and allow an even greater appreciation of what was a well-developed and sophisticated architectural tradition: a tradition that has so many implications for our understanding of life and death in Bronze Age Ireland.

Acknowledgements

This paper is based on my work as archaeologist in the Ordnance Survey and I wish to thank the Director of Operations for permission to publish it. Without the detailed work of Ruairdhí de Valera and Seán Ó Nualláin this paper could not have been written.

I wish to dedicate it to Seán O Nualláin, the former senior archaeologist at the Ordnance Survey, in grateful thanks for the many stimulating discussions at numerous sites over the years. The maps and plans are the work of Vincent Steadman, Ordnance Survey. My special thanks to John Channing for providing me with information on his excavations at Aughrim, Co. Cavan. I am grateful to my colleague, Eamon Cody, for his comments on a draft of this paper.

Note

1. The term 'portico' has been used in the volumes of the *Survey of the Megalithic Tombs of Ireland* to describe the small chamber at the western end of wedge tombs. Its application to sites that have large inset septal stones is, to a certain extent, a misnomer as in ordinary context the word implies that access could be gained through it to the larger chamber beyond. The same objection can be applied to the term 'antechamber'. As portico has gained wide acceptance in the literature it is retained here but placed in inverted commas so as not to give a false impression of its significance.

References

ApSimon, A. 1985-6. Chronological contexts for Irish megalithic tombs. *Journal of Irish Archaeology* 3, 5-15.

Barber, J. 1992. Megalithic architecture. In N. Sharples and A. Sheridan (eds), *Vessels for the Ancestors: essays on the Neolithic of Britain and Ireland in honour of Audrey Henshall*, 13-32. Edinburgh.

Bergh, S. 1994. *Landscape of the monuments. A study of the passage tombs in the Cúil Irra Region*. Stockholm.

Bradley, R. 1993. *Altering the earth. The origins of monuments in Britain and continental Europe*. Edinburgh.

Brindley, A. L. and Lanting, J. N. 1991-2. Radiocarbon dates from wedge tombs. *Journal of Irish Archaeology* 6, 19-26.

Buckley, V. M. and Sweetman, P. D. 1991. *Archaeological survey of County Louth*. Dublin.

Case, H. 1995. Some Wiltshire Beakers and their contexts. *The Wiltshire Archaeological and Natural History Magazine* 88, 1-17.

Channing, J. 1992. Aughrim. Wedge tomb. In I. Bennett (ed.), *Excavations 1992*, 4. Dublin.

Chart, D. A. (ed.) 1940. *A preliminary survey of the ancient monuments of Northern Ireland*. Belfast.

Cooney, G. 1983. Megalithic tombs in their environmental setting, a settlement perspective. In T. Reeves-Smyth and F. Hammond (eds), *Landscape archaeology in Ireland. British Archaeological Reports, British Series* 116, 179-94. Oxford.

Cooney, G. 1985-6. An unrecorded wedge-tomb at Scrahallia, Cashel, Connemara, Co. Galway. *Journal of the Galway Archaeological and Historical Society* 40, 134-7.

Cooney, G. 1990. The place of megalithic tomb cemeteries in Ireland. *Antiquity* 64, 741-53.

Davies, O. 1939a. Excavations at Clogherny. *Ulster Journal of Archaeology* 2, 36-43.

Davies, O. 1939b. Excavations at the Giant's Grave, Loughash. *Ulster Journal of Archaeology* 2, 254-68.

Davies, O. and Mullin, J. B. 1940. Excavation of Cashelbane cairn, Loughash, Co. Tyrone. *Journal of the Royal Society of Antiquaries of Ireland* 70, 143-63.

De Valera, R. and Ó Nualláin, S. 1961. *Survey of the Megalithic tombs of Ireland, Vol. I, Co. Clare*. Dublin.

De Valera, R. and Ó Nualláin, S. 1964. *Survey of the Megalithic tombs of Ireland, Vol. II, Co. Mayo*. Dublin.

De Valera, R. and Ó Nualláin, S. 1972. *Survey of the Megalithic tombs of Ireland, Vol. III, Cos Galway, Roscommon, Leitrim, Longford, Westmeath, Laoighis, Offaly, Kildare, Cavan*. Dublin.

De Valera, R. and Ó Nualláin, S. 1982. *Survey of the Megalithic tombs of Ireland, Vol. IV, Cos Cork, Kerry, Limerick, Tipperary*. Dublin.

Herity, M. 1970. The prehistoric peoples of Kerry: a programme of investigation. *Journal of the Kerry Archaeological Society* 4, 3-14.

Herity, M. 1982. Irish decorated Neolithic pottery. *Proceedings of the Royal Irish Academy* 82C, 247-404.

Herring, I. J. 1938. The cairn excavation at Well Glass Spring, Largantea, Co. Londonderry. *Ulster Journal of Archaeology* 1, 164-88.

Herring, I. J. and May, A. McL. 1936-7. The Giant's Grave, Kilhoyle, Co. Londonderry. *Proceedings of the Belfast Natural History and Philosophical Society*, 34-48.

Herring, I. J. and May, A. McL. 1940. Cloghnagalla cairn, Boviel, Co. Londonderry. *Ulster Journal of Archaeology* 3, 41-55.

Hodder, I. 1984. Burials, houses, women and men in the European Neolithic. In D. Miller and C. Tilley (eds), *Ideology, power and prehistory*, 51-68. Cambridge.

Hodder, I. 1989. Post-modernism, post-structuralism and post-processual archaeology. In I. Hodder (ed.), *The meaning of things*, 64-88. London.

Kavanagh, R. 1973. The Encrusted Urn in Ireland. *Proceedings of the Royal Irish Academy* 73C, 507-617.

Kavanagh, R. 1976. Collared and Cordoned Cinerary Urns in Ireland. *Proceedings of the Royal Irish Academy* 76C, 293-403.

Kilbride Jones, H. E. 1954. The excavation of an unrecorded megalithic tomb on Kilmashogue Mountain, Co. Dublin. *Proceedings of the Royal Irish Academy* 56C, 461-79.

Leask, H. and Price, L. 1936. The Labbacallee megalith, Co. Cork. *Proceedings of the Royal Irish Academy* 43C, 77-101.

McMann, J. 1994. Forms of power: dimensions of an Irish megalithic landscape. *Antiquity* 68, 525-44.

O'Brien, W. 1989. The Altar, Altar. Wedge tomb. In I. Bennett (ed.), *Excavations 1989*, 14.

O'Brien, W. 1993. Altar tomb and the prehistory of Mizen. *Mizen Journal* 1, 19-26.

O'Brien, W. 1990. Toormore. Wedge tomb. In I. Bennett (ed.), *Excavations 1990*, 20-1. Dublin.

O'Brien, W. 1994. *Mount Gabriel. Bronze Age mining in Ireland.* Galway.

O'Donovan, E. 1993. Full doorstones in Portal Tombs, precluding successive burial. *Trowel* 4, 12-18.

Ó hEailidhe, P. 1978. An unrecorded wedge-tomb at Killakee, County Dublin. *Journal of the Royal Society of Antiquaries of Ireland* 108, 101-3.

Ó hIceadha, G. 1946. The Moylisha megalith, Co. Wicklow. *Journal of the Royal Society of Antiquaries of Ireland* 76, 119-28.

O'Kelly, M. J. 1958. A wedge-shaped gallery grave at Island, Co. Cork. *Journal of the Royal Society of Antiquaries of Ireland* 88, 1-23.

O'Kelly, M. J. 1960. A wedge-shaped gallery-grave at Baurnadomeeny, Co. Tipperary. *Journal of the Cork Historical and Archaeological Society* 65, 85-115.

O'Kelly, M. J. 1982. *Newgrange. Archaeology, art and legend.* London.

Ó Nualláin, S. 1989. *Survey of the Megalithic tombs of Ireland, Vol. V, Co. Sligo.* Dublin.

Ó Nualláin, S. 1991. The megalithic tomb builders. In M. Ryan (ed.), *The illustrated archaeology of Ireland*, 55-9. Dublin.

Ó Nualláin, S. and Walsh, P. 1986. A reconsideration of the Tramore passage-tombs. *Proceedings of the Prehistoric Society* 52, 25-9.

Ó Ríordáin, B. and Waddell, J. 1993. *The Funerary Bowls and Vases of the Irish Bronze Age.* Galway.

Ó Ríordáin, S. P. and de Valera, R. 1952. Excavation of a megalithic tomb at Ballyedmonduff, Co. Dublin.

Proceedings of the Royal Irish Academy 55C, 61-81.

Ó Ríordáin, S. P. and Ó hIceadha, G. 1955. Lough Gur Excavations: the megalithic tomb. *Journal of the Royal Society of Antiquaries of Ireland* 85, 34-50.

Renfrew, C. 1976. Megaliths, territories and populations. In S. J. de Laet (ed.), *Acculturation and Continuity in Atlantic Europe*, 198-220. Bruges.

Renfrew, C. 1981. Introduction: the megalith builders of western Europe. In J. D. Evans, B. Cunliffe and C. Renfrew (eds), *Antiquity and man: essays in honour of Glyn Daniel*, 72-81. London.

Richards, C. 1992. Doorways into another world: the Orkney-Cromarty chambered tombs. In N. Sharples and A. Sheridan (eds), *Vessels for the Ancestors: essays on the Neolithic of Britain and Ireland in honour of Audrey Henshall*, 62-76. Edinburgh.

Shee Twohig, E. 1988. A wedge-tomb at Garranbane, Murroe, Co. Limerick. *North Munster Antiquarian Journal* 30, 50-2.

Shee Twohig, E. 1990. *Irish megalithic tombs.* Princes Risborough.

Thomas, J. S. 1991. *Rethinking the Neolithic.* Cambridge.

Thomas, J. S. 1992. Monuments, movement, and the context of megalithic art. In N. Sharples and A. Sheridan (eds), *Vessels for the Ancestors: essays on the Neolithic of Britain and Ireland in honour of Audrey Henshall*, 143-155. Edinburgh.

Waterman, D. 1965. The court cairn at Annaghmare, Co. Armagh. *Ulster Journal of Archaeology* 28, 3-46.

Ideas, People and Things: Ireland and the External World during the Later Bronze Age

George Eogan

Abstract

Principally at two stages during the Late Bronze Age, the Bishopsland and Dowris Phases, Ireland had significant contacts with the outside world. During the Bishopsland Phase Ireland was strongly influenced from southern England, especially the Somerset region. In turn Ireland may have contributed to the Taunton Phase possibly through the export of metal. Ireland's external contacts were strengthened during the Dowris Phase. A range of new metal types was introduced. These had a background in two principal areas, Britain (largely tools and weapons and sheet bronze making) and south Scandinavia (largely ornaments or non-utilitarian objects). Conversely the products of the Irish industry were welcomed abroad. These include bag-shaped axes but especially gold ornaments, notably pennanular bracelets. Raw metal may also have been exported.

A feature of Ireland throughout prehistory is the evidence for contact and interchange with external regions, this includes both receiving and giving not only objects but also knowledge and ideas. At some periods such contacts were more intense than at others but throughout they served as an enriching factor for cultural development, for the Later Bronze Age this is particularly so. It is overwhelmingly metal objects that serve as source material but the presence of amber and jet as well as wooden objects, notably notched shield moulds, demonstrates that metal pieces are only part, albeit a significant one, of the material that formerly existed. This paper will concentrate on artefacts that throw light on imports and exports but the wider context and background to contemporary developments will also be taken into account. Geographically Ireland is an Atlantic land and as a result shares features with some other Atlantic lands. However, the 'Atlantic Bronze Age' is not a cohesive and closely integrated complex but one whose components varied with time but also regionally as is for instance shown by the distribution of different forms of metal torcs that were current in different regions at the beginning of the Later Bronze Age (Fig. 47). However, the importance of the 'Atlantic' contexts, especially in the south, may have been over-emphasised in the past. Relationships eastwards to Britain and northwards to north-west Germany and south Scandanavia were more important.

It is hardly necessary to say that in prehistoric Europe, especially from Neolithic times onwards, there is clear evidence for long-range contacts. Their nature and causation are not always clear. They could be due to several factors such as movements of people, to trade or commercial contacts, to the spread of ritual practices or simply to gift exchange. It is a fact that during the Bronze Age internationalisation developed further and in order for metal industries to flourish in some parts of Europe the acquisition of raw materials from outside became a necessity. A clear example of this was the rise of an outstanding Nordic Bronze Age in an area that did not have natural supplies of copper, tin or gold. But another factor that should be taken into account is the rise of parallel or contemporary complexes. These might be identified by having closely related ritual practices, such as the Armorican and Wessex Early Bronze Ages (Briard 1965, 51-77; Piggott 1938). Some objects were more favoured than others in particular regions, a good example being segmented faience beads in Armorica and Wessex during the later part of the Early Bronze Age. These indicate a spread of a personal fashion although they may have had a wider social significance, for instance as a replacement for gold ornaments. Other items can represent acquisitions from higher centres such as Mycenaean objects outside the Mycenaean world (Schauer 1984) or the sharing of a common industrial heritage. Classic examples of the latter occur on both sides of the English Channel during the Later Bronze age, initially with the Penard Phase and subsequently with the Wilburton-Saint-Brieuc-des-Iffs and with the carp's tongue sword complexes (Burgess 1968).

In discussing contacts between Ireland and external regions during the Later Bronze Age evidence is restricted; it is almost exclusively confined to metal

Fig. 47. Main areas of occurrence of bar torcs. Top right: bronze torcs. Top left: gold bar torcs. Bottom left: Berzocana type torcs.

types. There is no indication that new grain crops or animals were introduced and this also applies to architecture. While information on domestic dwellings is limited the round house seems to be the leading type and structures of that form were in use during previous stages, even back in early Mesolithic times (Woodman 1985, 129-42). However, that need not indicate continuity over centuries or millennia. Conversely there is no evidence that Ireland contributed in the sphere of domestic architecture to external areas.

As will be argued more fully there is evidence for contact between Ireland and the external world. A key factor in its stimulation may have been Ireland's natural resources of copper and gold in particular; both raw materials as well as finished objects could have been exported. But Ireland was also at the receiving end from the metal point of view and that involved techniques as well as types. As Ireland is an island all external contacts involved sea-crossing and that implies boats. A boat consisting of a hide covered wooden frame, like the present day curraghs of the west of Ireland, could have been adequate for open sea journeys. On the other hand more substantial

wooden boats could have been used as evidence from the south of England shows (Muckelroy 1981). Not only for Ireland but for other parts of Europe, boats were significant for Bronze Age communities. In this connection it is relevant to recall that representations of boats were the dominant images in Later Bronze Age rock carvings of Sweden (Coles 1994, 10; Thrane, this volume) and other parts of southern Scandinavia.

As has for long been established, cultural affinities were a feature of many parts of Europe during the Bronze Age. For the West, as it has already been mentioned, it has been considered that there was an Atlantic Bronze Age (Savory 1949) which shared many features in common and which constituted a vast province that extended from the south of Spain to northern Scotland. Within this area there were interchanges but this does not mean that there was uniformity or that a culturally cohesive community existed. Not only did the composition of the components vary from time-to-time but equally important there were geographical differences. There is no reason to assume that the Atlantic complexes were later or inferior to other regions. They were not an appendix to central European complexes, in fact in the Europe of the day a series of parallel cultural developments took place, these reflect regional inspiration but also regional interchange. A feature of the Atlantic zones of Europe is, therefore, regional innovation and expression rather than a cohesive complex extending for about one thousand five hundred miles in length as the crow flies.

During the Killymaddy Stage ('Middle' Bronze Age) Ireland had a flourishing bronze industry as is demonstrated by the number of artefacts – 'palstaves', rapiers of Classes 1 and 2 and ribbed kite-shaped spearheads – but also by evidence for their manufacture as is provided by double-piece stone moulds (Eogan 1993, 94-5). The scale of the production is demonstrated if we take the number of rapiers as an example. The work of Burgess and Gerloff (1981, 6-46) has shown that one hundred and eighty rapiers of Groups I and II are known from Ireland whereas the figure from the much larger geographical area of Britain is one hundred and forty examples. This provides clear evidence for large-scale bronze production in Ireland. Examples of other leading metal types, haft flanged axes (Smith 1959) and ribbed kite-shaped spearheads have also been found in Britain (Rowlands 1976, map 14) with related spearheads occurring as far away as Brittany (Briard 1965, fig. 25). The Killymaddy mould evidence suggests that the first bronze sickles were also introduced at this time (Herity and Eogan 1977, fig. 62, C-G). This evidence clearly demonstrates that during this stage Ireland was not a culturally isolated island – but one that had external contacts. The people were undoubtedly hard working but the absence of personal ornaments may indicate a puritanical streak.

It is clear that during the Killymaddy stage Ireland's external contacts were limited but around the 13th century BC, a time of major changes throughout Europe, Ireland's foreign connections strengthened and significant changes took place (Herity and Eogan 1977, 167-82). This could be due to an increase in the prosperity of farming communities in southern England who were able to acquire more metal but did not have it locally. For that they could have turned to Ireland and in doing so passed on new tool types (such as axes and chisels) and technologies (such as twisting). Gold ornaments also became a feature as was the technique of manufacturing them from both bar and sheet gold. In this connection the distribution pattern of gold bar torcs is of interest. This demonstrates that in the middle area of the Atlantic zone (eastern Ireland, southern Britain and north-western France) a creative industry arose with gold as its most spectacular manifestation (Eogan 1994, 42-79). But simultaneously, in the south and north, equivalent industries were emerging. In Iberia

the neckings are represented by the Berzocana type, again in gold, while in the north, in the west Baltic area, the twisted bronze necking was the preferred type (Fig. 47).

On the available evidence Ireland had only limited contact with external regions during the equivalent to the Early Urnfield period (roughly the southern English Penard-Wilburton stages), but that is also the situation in northern England and in Scotland. During this time Irish industrial production was more restricted than previously, personal ornaments went out of use, there was, however, some enrichment from the southern English industries, notably the introduction of the first swords from the Penard industry and further weaponry during the Wilburton stage.

An important aspect of the Bishopsland Phase was new developments in farming practices as well as in metal-working but of considerable significance was the incorporation of Ireland into the wider external world, a world that over large parts of Europe was in a state of economic and ritual change. It was a time when disparate communities were being transformed into a homogeneous civil society that shared many common elements but also a society that may have been centred around prominent families with an overall leader. This does not appear to have been a time of strains or stress or of catastrophes but a time of spontaneous creative combustion that positively affected many aspects of life – economic, social and ritual. The changes took different forms in different regions. New opportunities opened up in continental Europe, where sufficient resources, land and people, existed to take advantage of new circumstances and the assimilation of new codes and practices. For middle and northern Europe in particular the most revolutionary change was in the sphere of innovations in communications and transport. The emergence of the multiple spoked wheel and greater use of the harnessed horse was a significant event, an event that led not only to the fast dissemination of knowledge but of goods and people likewise.

As was independently pointed out many years ago by Margaret Smith (1959) and Jay Butler (1963) southern England, at this time was in receipt of invigorating impulses from Continental Europe. The established trans-channel and trans-North Sea connections were strengthened, this may have been due to trade but immigrants may also have played a role as transmitters of change. For southern England in particular a new stage of the Bronze Age emerged, a feature of which was the presence of enterprising native rulers and confident and energetic people. But it also appears that some people of Continental origin arrived. This would have exposed the locals to foreign ways, they may even have become privy to foreign intentions. One way that that could have been brought about was by the acquisition of foreign wives by Englishmen. It could have been such a person that was buried – the rite was inhumation – in a chalk-cut pit grave at Hollicondane, near Ramsgate, Kent and accompanied by bronze ornaments – a broad ribbed bracelet and three incised decorated penannular bracelets (C. M. Piggott 1949, 118-21). The homeland of this *'fremde Frau'* (Jockenhövel 1991) would have been at least as far north at Lüneburg, northern Germany (cf. Jacob-Friesen 1963, 275, Abb. 267). As her burial rite and grave goods were alien it can be considered that she was not totally assimilated into the manners and customs of her adopted land.

But this person did not stand alone, apparently there were others, as will presently be demonstrated, but we must also consider foreign things. Novel metal objects were also a feature of the emerging Beer-hackett-Taunton Phase. It is clear from their distribution that regional groupings emerged. One such region, Sussex with its distinctive ornaments, Sussex loops, shows this while the gold hoard from Mountfield (Eogan 1967, 151-2; 1994, fig. 21, 1-2) may suggest the presence of a magnate. Such evidence indicates local innovation and production but more importantly the emergence of consumption areas which probably reflect regional social groups.

Another such group, and one that is most relevant from the Irish point of view, occurs in Somerset (Fig. 48). The evidence for this is provided by a concentration of metal types while the personality of the area is demonstrated by the virtual restriction to it of four bronze ornament types – ribbed bracelets, penannular bracelets with body of lozenge-shaped or round cross-section and unexpanded terminals and torcs, and one tool type, the non-socketed sickle of Fox's Group II B and C (1941, 142). It may be assumed that sickles indicate that agrarian innovations were also taking place. In this connection it should be noted that examples of the relevant bronzes have been found at farmsteads in the same general area such as South Lodge Camp (Dorset) and Thorny Down (Wiltshire). Indeed, it may well be that the bulk of the Deverel-Rimbury sites date to this stage. Sickles may have had a wider significance than just agrarian tools. At least for northern-middle Europe Sommerfeld (1994) has put forward the view that sickles represent wealth, indicators of a 'monetary' structure. A further significant feature of Somerset at this time is the presence of hoards of metal objects, both of bronze and gold. Hoards have, of course, a distribution throughout the south of England but if we take those with the more or less exclusive Somerset type ornaments and the relevant sickle types they may help us with interpretation. I suggest that the hoards might be considered

as representing territorial foci, each of which could have been presided over by a leader. If that was the case the postulated local leaders need not have been autonomous but subject to a central authority. But if that was the case what is the evidence? Right in this region there is a tell-tale piece – a fragmented disc of sheet gold mounted on a copper backing which, together with pottery, accompanied the cremated remains of an individual that was interred underneath an earthen mound on Lansdown Hill close to the city of Bath. This was probably the remains of another north European – at least the decoration on the disk as reconstructed (Eogan, 1994, pl. 5) suggests a background in the Danish region, such as the gold disc from Jaegersborg, north of Copenhagen (Eogan 1981, 156-7). It is relevant to note that the Danish discs accompanied the inhumed remains of individual males who were buried with considerable pomp and ceremony indicating that during life they had access to wealth and were probably persons that wielded authority and held power. One may, therefore, speculate that the Lansdown burial constitutes a memory of a final farewell to a foreign 'fief', a *'fremde Mann'*.

The west of England and Wales had now become an important region, for instance as Peter Northover has shown (1989) it is in this region that the heaviest gold bar torcs are found. But the west had more; there must also have been a significant fiefdom at Mold as the material from another barrow burial indicates (Powell 1953). The sheet gold object could have been worn on the body as was the earliest sheet bronze armour at this time as in the warriors' grave at Čaka, Slovakia (Točik & Paulík 1960) but the Mold object being of gold was much more glorious but equally important it was much more civil. This lavish use of sheet gold is without precedent in Britain or Ireland. It, therefore, must have had a Continental background but where is not certain. The cones of west central Europe were the only objects that utilised large quantities of sheet gold (Schauer 1986) but the amber beads would be west Baltic in origin. Like the finds from Hollicondane (Ramsgate) and Lansdown perhaps the background to Mold is also north European.

We must now consider the overall role of the Lords of Lansdown and Mold. I have already indicated that they were civil leaders but that may also include external commitments of a commercial nature. Their places of burial could be significant, both are close to the Irish Sea, one just off the Bristol Channel and the other not far away from the estuary of the River Dee. There are copper deposits at Great Orme near Llandudno (Dutton and Fasham 1994) so perhaps the Mold fief was involved with industrial exploitation. At this time southern England had a vigorous metal

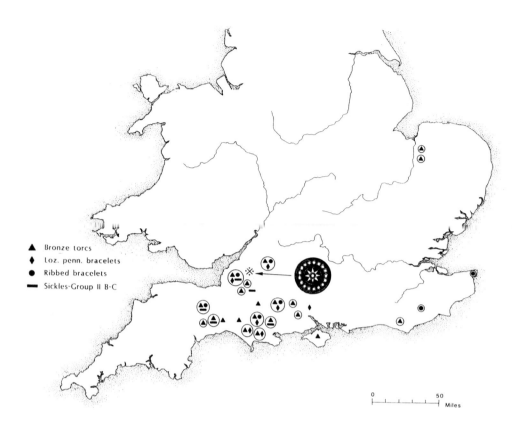

Fig. 48. Distribution of Taunton Phase bronze objects that concentrate in the Somerset region and the find place of the Lansdown disc.

industry but native supplies of copper and gold were non-existent. Therefore, importation would have been a feature and Ireland could have been a main source. Control of such supplies could have been within the role of the chiefs of Mold and Lansdown. To the south an equivalent role may have been played by the owner of the hoard of gold bar torcs and bracelets found at Towednack in Cornwall. Instead of having been placed in a grave this regalia could have been committed to the earth as a memorial to an outstanding tin lord.

During the Bishopsland Phase Ireland's external connections may have accrued from the export of gold and copper, possibly mainly in a raw state, to southern Britain. Coupled with an industrial expansion there may have been a farming expansion as is indicated by the sickle from the Bishopsland hoard. Spiritually new beliefs may also have emerged. Wealth was a feature of this changing society, at least gold was plentiful as is clear from the two bar torcs from Tara, Co. Meath, which between them weigh about forty ounces (Armstrong 1933, 59). It is interesting that both bar torcs and the hoards of gold objects have a similar distribution, largely eastern. As has been suggested by way of explanation for the Somerset hoards the Irish hoards might represent territorial foci, the approximate place where prominent families lived and grew in wealth due to improved farming condi-

tions or as a result of direct or indirect trade in metal export.

Apart from the introduction of possibly new ritual practice and social change it is certainly clear that Ireland was in receipt of new metal types and technologies from the Beerhackett-Taunton complex. The technique of twisting seems to have been one; the working of sheet gold may have been another. But of particular significance was the introduction of new tool types such as the first socketed axes, socketed hammers, engraving tools, anvils and clamps. These objects could have been used in metalworking and in woodworking, two crafts which were now expanding and developing. External influence also contributed to the emergence of the practice of manufacturing and wearing personal ornaments. As has for long been recognised the Bishopsland Phase was a time of change in Ireland, for its rise external stimulus, largely emanating from the Somerset region, was significant.

At a time coinciding with changes in Britain and on the continent the Bishopsland Phase came to an end. As a result Ireland's external contacts were reduced. Industrially Ireland reverted to a stage where local production had a priority and where traditional types were playing a leading role. Amongst these were spearheads with protected openings in the blade, spearheads with lunate openings in the blade, and Class 4 rapiers. Socketed axeheads with broad flat collar around mouth and body of rectangular cross-section, Class 2-4 (Eogan, forthcoming) indicate not only local industrial activity but also local innovation. But contacts with the external world were not totally eliminated. The Penard Phase was the source of the earliest swords, Class 1 (Eogan 1965, 5-9) and the open ended socketed sickle. Later the Wilburton Phase contributed the first flange-hilted swords, Classes 2 and 3 (Eogan 1965, 9-10).

The internationalisation of the European Bronze Age grew apace during the later Bronze Age. After 1000 BC Ireland's external connections once more expanded, an array of new types emerged while export was also a feature. External influence came from two main sources – 'carp's-tongue' – Ewart Park, Britain (probably the southern area) and the west Baltic area during Period 5. Only a small number need be imports, what existed was the acquisition of external knowledge which provided the inspiration to produce local versions which were, in some cases, considerably modified versions of the prototype. Britain was the main donor area and the objects fall into two categories, weapons and tools. The weapons and associated equipment are represented by Class 4 swords, short tongue-shaped chapes, purse-shaped chapes, plain leaf-shaped spearheads, and bronze shields. Introduced tool types consisted of socketed axeheads of Class 5-8, socketed hammers, socketed knives of Thorndon, Dungiven and Kells types, tanged chisels (kite-shaped blade or blade with concave sides and having either a lateral projection to each side or an evenly expanded collar), socketed chisels (body long or short but rectangular cross-section, body with rounded cross-section and splayed cutting edge), socketed gouges, buckets and Class A cauldrons, flesh forks, and socketed sickles. In addition to tools and weapons elements of horse harness (rattle pendants and phalerae) and at least one personal item (the developed Class 2 razor) have a British background as has the technique of sheet bronze working.

The contribution from the west Baltic area consisted of amber, disc-headed pins with both straight and bent stem, 'dress-fasteners', annular bracelets with circle, toggle, horns, and possibly gold bowls and boxes, the Lattoon disc, gorgets, 'sleeve-fasteners' and U-notched shields. The origin of penannular bracelets with evenly expanded terminals presents a problem. They could represent an Irish development of the bracelets with unexpanded terminals of the Bishopsland Phase or they could have been stimulated by the British Form 9 bracelets (Eogan 1994, 85) or even by the West Baltic 'oath rings'. It may also be

that some artistic features found on Irish objects, especially concentric circles and conical projections, although widely used in Late Bronze Age Europe, also have their background in the Nordic region.

A puzzling aspect of the incoming features is that, as already mentioned, the artefacts fall into two main groups with a different geographical background to each. The British group consists of 'useful' objects, tools and weapons and the important technique of sheet bronze working. The Scandinavian contribution consisted of non-utilitarian objects, mainly items of personal or ceremonial embellishment. As appears to have been the case during the preceding Bishopsland stage the need for metal by certain foreign communities may have been a factor in the initiation of contacts. This could have led to the establishment of trade routes.

The distribution of some Irish types tends to back up such a view although the main item, metal, could remain invisible as it would have been melted down. As previously mentioned the linear distribution of 'lock rings' at least in north Britain suggests a route (Eogan 1969, fig. 2) between the Firth of Tay and north Munster or vice-versa involving north-eastern England, the Mersey and north Wales. While having a sparse distribution in Britain 'dress-fasteners' and thick penannualar bracelets, both definite Irish types, nevertheless, have a distinctive distribution. In the south of Britain this is the coastal region from Cornwall in the west to Norfolk in the east and it is across to the North Sea, at Gahlstorf not far from the mouth of the river Weser that the only example of either, a thick penannular bracelet, was found (Eogan 1994, figs 39, 40). It is interesting that these distributions to a large extent coincide with the distribution of the British Form 1 gold bracelet (Eogan 1994, 85, fig. 38), with an example in bronze occurring in the Ty Mawr hoard, Anglesey (Lynch 1970, 210, fig. 69: 7) and a linear distribution between there and Norfolk. There is an equivalent distribution from Cornwall and the Bristol channel area eastwards. Perhaps Form 1 bracelets constituted a 'badge' that was worn by British traders or middlemen (Eogan 1994, 106-7). Taken with the already mentioned 'lock-ring' distribution these two distributions seem to link Ireland to the North Sea. On a broader frame it may be speculated that the distributions represent transit routes through which Irish produce bound for west Baltic lands passed or by which west Baltic influences reached Ireland. In contrast the penannular bracelets with evenly expanded terminals while being generally coastal are found to the north in the areas bordering the north Irish Sea (Anglesey) and western Scotland with an extension up to Great Glen (Eogan 1994, fig. 39).

The external influences need not all have arrived simultaneously or in the same region. On geographical grounds we would expect that influences from Britain would have been stronger in the eastern parts. The limited distribution of socketed axes of Classes 6 and 7 (Eogan, forthcoming) in the north-east indicates that this was an area of direct contact for at least some British types. Class 8 axes with their greatest distribution in the midlands suggest east coast connections. The north-east may also have been an area that initially received south Scandinavian types, at least the primary form of disc-headed pins are more numerous in that area and so are 'sleeve-fasteners'.

In addition Ireland was once more drawn into the wider sphere of connections, while within the country regional preferences were emerging. In contrast to the Bishopsland stage parts of the west of the country became important areas. A core area emerged in the lands bordering the lower Shannon valley. This area is characterised by spectacular gold ornaments – especially 'lock-rings' and gorgets. As was visualised for the Somerset hoards of the Taunton Phase perhaps the 'lock-rings' and gorgets and the gold hoards of the area pinpoint social foci, with the great gold hoard from Mooghaun representing the core of the lordship north of the river, while to the south of the river, Cullen fulfilled an equivalent role. At first glance this North Munster province suggests that an opening to the Atlantic took place but the absence of foreign types in the area or North Munster types in coastal Atlantic lands prohibits us from considering North Munster as an Atlantic emporium or trading centre. On the contrary the distribution of the 'lock-rings' suggests land connections eastward.

It is of course true that in Atlantic lands considerable development was taking place as the 'carp's tongue sword complex' testifies. But connections between Ireland and the western continental lands were limited. The V-notched shields could indicate influence from Iberia while the penannular bronze bracelet from an unrecorded find place near Oporto demonstrates Irish penetration southwards (da Silva 1986, 185, fig. 99: 7). Class B cauldrons may also be relevant. At the opposite end of this geographical area there is amongst the clay mould debris from the Jarlshof workshop in the Shetlands part of a mould for casting a sunflower pin with a prominent central conical boss, a distinctive Irish type (Hamilton 1956, 24, fig. 14: 1; Eogan 1974, 92-3, categories F and G).

In Britain objects of Irish origin are mainly confined to the west as the distribution of 'dress-fasteners' and penannular bracelets with evenly expanded terminals shows. As already noted influence also extended to eastern England and beyond the North Sea to Gahlstorf in the Bremen area (Hawkes, in Hawkes and Clarke 1963, 195-204). In addition to ornaments some other British objects have an Irish background. A Class A cauldron (Tulnacross Type) from Hackenknowe, Peebleshire, may have been, in Gerloff's view, imported from Ireland. It is also interesting that it was part of a cauldron of similar type that was found at Abildholt in Jutland. The Tulnacross type cauldron is an almost exclusively Irish type. However, as Gerloff has noted the handle ring on the Abildholt example may resemble the English ring variant so it may have been exported from that country (Gerloff 1986, 96-7, 107). Another Irish form found in England is the bag-shaped axe. These are mainly found in northern England and Scotland but with the largest numbers coming from eastern Scotland (Schmidt and Burgess 1981, pl. 127). All this implies transport. Britain has provided evidence for wagons with multiple spoked wheels as well as evidence for the harnessed horse. In Ireland there is only limited evidence, provided solely by some evidence of pieces of horse harness. But a relevant item comes from Caergwrle in North Wales, the model of a boat, wooden but with sheet-gold overlay decorated with concentric circles (Savory 1980, 69).

The evidence is abundantly clear that Ireland's external contacts during the Dowris Phase were vigorous even if geographically restricted. As a result a productive Dowris Phase emerged but in turn influences from Ireland enriched British communities and to a lesser extent Continental people. This mutual enrichment represents one of the significant aspects of the Late Bronze Age in western Europe.

Conclusions

For the later Bronze Age Ireland's external connections were strongest during the initial (Bishopsland) and final (Dowris) stages. The emergence of the Bishopsland Phase owes a great deal to stimulus from southern Britain, especially Somerset in the west. During the Roscommon Phase external contact was considerably reduced, however limited contacts existed during the Penard and Wilburton stages. During the Dowris Phase external connections once more became significant. Britain was an important donor area but so was southern Scandinavia. As the relevant Scandinavian types do not occur in Britain a system of direct trade routes must have existed and, as has been argued, these could have passed through Britain. In its turn Ireland influenced external developments, especially in the use of gold bracelets and some tool types in parts of Britain and then northwards to the south-western zone of the *Nordischer Kreis*.

In any study of international connections metal objects are of significance but what is difficult to detect – the export of copper and gold from Ireland – may have been the most significant of all. As has been previously mentioned Ireland is an Atlantic land but yet Ireland did not receive or give to distant Atlantic communities. The area of Ireland's external connections were limited, Britain being the main one and, for the Dowris Phase, south Scandinavia in addition. There is no evidence that an integrated trading network or other contacts existed then extending from Andalucía to Shetland. On the contrary Ireland's connections were mainly eastwards.

References

Armstrong, E. C. R. 1933. *Catalogue of Irish gold ornaments in the collection of the Royal Irish Academy.* Dublin.

Briard, J. 1965. *Les Dépôts Bretons et l'Age du Bronze Atlantique.* Rennes.

Burgess, C. 1968. The later Bronze Age in the British Isles and North-Western France. *The Archaeological Journal* 125, 1-45.

Burgess, C. and Gerloff, S. 1981. *The Dirks and Rapiers of Great Britain and Ireland.* Prähistorische Bronzefunde, 4.7. Munich.

Butler, J. J. 1963. Bronze Age Connections across the North Sea. *Paleohistoria* 9, 1-286.

Coles, J. 1994. *Rock Carvings of Uppland.* Uppsala.

Dutton, A. and Fasham, P. J. 1994. Prehistoric copper mining on the Great Orme, Llandudno, Gwynedd, *Proceedings of the Prehistoric Society* 60, 245-86.

Eogan, G. 1965. *Catalogue of Irish Bronze Swords.* Dublin.

Eogan, G. 1967. The associated finds of Gold Bar Torcs. *Journal of the Royal Society of Antiquaries of Ireland* 97, 129-75.

Eogan, G. 1969. 'Lock Rings' of the late Bronze Age. *Proceedings of the Royal Irish Academy* 67C, 93-148.

Eogan, G. 1974. Pins of the Irish late Bronze Age. *Journal of the Royal Society of Antiquaries of Ireland* 104, 74-119.

Eogan, G. 1981. Gold discs of the Irish Late Bronze Age. In D. Ó Corráin (ed.), *Irish Antiquity: Essays and studies presented to Professor M. J. O'Kelly,* 147-62. Cork.

Eogan, G. 1981. Gold vessels of the Bronze Age in Ireland and beyond. *Proceedings of the Royal Irish Academy* 81C, 345-82.

Eogan, G. 1990. Possible connections between Britain and Ireland and the east Mediterranean region during the Bronze Age. *Orientalisch-Ägäische Einflusse in der Europäischen Bronzezeit.* Bonn. Monographien 15. Römisch Germanisches Zentralmuseum. Mainz.

Eogan, G. 1993. Aspects of metal production and manufacturing systems during the Irish Bronze Age. *Acta Praehistorica et Archaeologica* 25, 87-110.

Eogan, G. 1994. *The accomplished art: Gold and Gold working in Britain and Ireland during the Bronze Age.* Oxford.

Eogan, G. forthcoming. *The Socketed Bronze Axehead in Ireland. Prähistorische Bronzefunde.* Munich.

Fox, C. 1941. The non-socketed Sickles of Britain. *Archaeologia Cambrensis* 96, 136-56.

Gerloff, S. 1986. Bronze Age Class A Cauldrons: Typology, Origins and Chronology. *Journal of the Royal Society of Antiquaries of Ireland* 116, 84-115.

Hamilton, J. R. C. 1956. *Excavations at Jarlshof, Shetland.* London.

Hawkes, C. F. C. and Clarke, R. R. 1963. Gahlstorf and Caister-on-sea: Two finds of Late Bronze Age Irish Gold. In I. Ll. Foster and Leslie Alcock (eds), *Culture and Environment: Essays in honour of Sir Cyril Fox,* 193-250. London.

Herity, M. and Eogan, G. 1977. *Ireland in Prehistory.* London.

Jacob-Friesen, K. H. 1963. *Einführung in Niedersachsens Urgeschichte, II Teil, Bronzezeit.* 4th edition. G. Jacob-Friesen (ed.). Hildesheim.

Jockenhövel, A. 1991. Räumliche Mobilität von personen in der mittleren Bronzezeit des Westlichen Mitteleuropa. *Germania* 69, 49-62.

Lynch, F. 1970. *Prehistoric Anglesey.* Llangefni.

Muckelroy, K. 1981. Middle Bronze Age Trade between Britain and Europe. *Proceedings of the Prehistoric Society* 47, 275-97.

Northover, P. 1989. The gold torc from Saint Helier, Jersey. *Annual Bulletin Société Jersiaise* 25, 112-37.

Piggott, C. M. 1949. A late Bronze Age hoard from Blackrock in Sussex and its significance. *Proceedings of the Prehistoric Society* 15, 107-21.

Piggott, S. 1938. The early Bronze Age in Wessex. *Proceedings of the Prehistoric Society* 4, 52-106.

Powell, T. G. F. 1953. The Gold ornament from Mold, Flintshire, North Wales. *Proceedings of the Prehistoric Society* 19, 161-79.

Rowlands, M. J. 1976. *The production and distribution of metalwork in the Middle Bronze Age in Southern Britain.* British Archaeological Reports 31. Oxford.

Savory, H. N. 1949. The Atlantic Bronze Age in south-west Europe. *Proceedings of the Prehistoric Society* 15, 128-55.

Savory, H. N. 1980. *Guide Catalogue of the Bronze Age collections in the National Museum of Wales.* Cardiff.

Schauer, P. 1984. Spuren Minoisch-Mykenischen und orientalischen Einflusses in atlantischen Westeuropa. *Jahrbuch des Römisch-Germanischen Zentralmuseums* 31, 137-86.

Schauer, P. 1986. *Die Goldblechkegel der Bronzezeit.* Bonn.

Schmidt, P.K. and Burgess, C. 1981. *The Axes of Scotland, and Northern England.* Prähistorische Bronzefunde, 9.7. Munich.

Silva, A. da. 1986. *A Cultura Castreja No Norosete de Portugal.* Paços de Ferreira.

Smith M. A. 1959. Some Somerset Hoards and their place in the Bronze Age of Southern Britain. *Proceedings of the Prehistoric Society* 25, 144-87.

Sommerfeld, C. 1994. *Gerätegeld Sichel: Studiem in Monetären Struktur bronzelicher Horte in nördlichen Mitteleuropa. Vorgeschichtliche Forschungen* 19. Berlin.

Točik, A. and Paulík, J. 1960. Vyskum Mohyly Čaka (Die Ausgrabung eines Grabhügels in Čaka). *Slovenska Archaeologie* 8, 59-124.

Woodman, P. 1985. *Excavations at Mount Sandel 1973-77.* Belfast.

Ireland and Spain in the Bronze Age

Martín Almagro-Gorbea

Abstract

The relationship between Ireland and Iberia in the Bronze Age can be considered a rewarding topic for study. The geographical situation of these two countries explains contacts from Megalithic and Bell Beaker times and through the Bronze Age, mostly attested by metallurgical and gold elements. The relationships attested by some prestige elements are particularly interesting: shields and a ritual 'banquet set' of Oriental origin spread from the eastern Mediterranean to the Atlantic in the Late Bronze Age. The common Celtic roots of Ireland and Iberia are also analysed. The Celtic culture of Iberia is the result of a long formative process in the Atlantic Bronze Age, but sporadic movements of people are not excluded. This early origin of the Celts of Iberia helps to explain the affinities between all Atlantic Celtic peoples, whose roots date back, both in Ireland and in Iberia, to a very ancient period of the Bronze Age.

The relationship between Ireland and Iberia in the Bronze Age can be considered as a profitable subject for study, particularly since the pioneering work of Eoin MacWhite (1951) at the beginning of the 1950s.

The geographical situation of these lands at both ends of western Europe provides an explanation for the contacts that are so very important to our understanding of the cultural development of Atlantic Europe. Such contacts are obvious because Ireland offers a similar environment to that of north-western Iberia and also has similar metallurgical resources, copper and gold in particular, which played such an important role in the cultural development and in the relationships of the Bronze Age.

To understand these relationships, the common cultural trends affecting Ireland and Iberia in this period must also be assessed. Ireland relates firstly with central northern Europe through Britain, and secondly, with Brittany and western France. Iberia, north of the Ebro, relates with central Europe through the south of France. The Mediterranean is of prime importance and continuity, and has always represented a cultural crucible and an important means of contact. Lastly, the third line is the Atlantic, whose presence is mainly felt in the most western regions and which is facilitated by a similar environment, relating the Mediterranean with the western regions of Europe to the North Sea (Almagro-Gorbea 1986, 344 ff).

First contacts already date back to the Atlantic Megalithic world (Eogan 1990). Certain megalithic peculiarities cannot be explained by mere cultural convergence, for example the big stone basins in the chamber of some great passage graves or the development of an abstract geometric megalithic art (Shee Twohig 1981), which point to a similarity in social organisation and ideological beliefs.

The appearance of Beaker elements represents a new development that appears quite contemporaneously in both areas. Beakers documented in Ireland and Iberia are not identical, but they have a common origin in Central Europe and, from a cultural point of view, they denote an identical social and ideological structure, perhaps even associated with a similar people. Beakers in Atlantic Europe represent a cultural substrate which strengthened the common trends present since the megalithic period and explain some similar characteristics emerging in Bronze Age cultures both in Ireland and Iberia (Harrison 1980, 70 ff, 126 ff).

Possible contacts from the middle of the third millennium could be deduced from the common presence of All-Over-Cord Beakers (Fig. 49A). But AOC are moreover rare in Ireland (Harrison 1980, fig. 5) and they only appear in north-east Iberia with a non-Atlantic distribution that denotes their arrival across the Languedoc and the Rhone Valley (Harrison 1977, 13, fig. 3).

Maritime Beakers with their characteristic herringbone pattern have a very wide distribution throughout western Europe (Fig. 49B), because they extend from the Rhine to the Atlantic and from Scotland and Ireland to Iberia (Harrison 1977, 13, fig. 1; 1980, fig. 6). These Maritime Beakers confirm the presence of contacts, even though indirect ones, ever since the second half of the third millennium

BC. In Ireland, they must be considered to have arrived via Britain, whereas the concentration of Maritime Beakers in western Iberia points to an intermediary role by Brittany where these types are well represented and associated with tanged daggers, V-perforated buttons and wristguards (Fig. 49C). Both in Ireland, Brittany and western Iberia, Beakers appear in megalithic graves, confirming their association with the local substrate, although certain Breton cists, like Kerouaren (Plouhinec, Morbihan) and Penker (Plozevet, Finistère), may represent individual graves of Beaker people (Harrison 1980, 111).

Beaker people disseminated a characteristic metallurgy, well documented in Iberia and Ireland, with tanged copper daggers and awls. Palmela points are, in due course, associated with Beakers in Iberia, but this element reached Brittany and not Ireland. More than 350 wide butt axes (Type A) have appeared in Ireland, where arsenical copper halberds are also characteristic (Burgess 1979; Gerloff 1975), and similar types are also known in Iberia. These tanged daggers, axes and halberds, although considered to be derived from Central European types, would soon be developed as an Atlantic metallurgy, which raises the possibility of a triangle formed by the Carpathians, Iberia and Ireland evidently related through the new metallurgy and through their emerging élites. Another common feature are wristguards (Fig. 49C), most likely originating from the Carpathians (Sangmeister 1964) and, like tanged daggers, associated with Maritime Beakers. In addition, V-perforated buttons are related to socially distinctive dress, a tradition continued in Iberia in the Early Bronze Age (Harbison 1976; Harrison 1977, figs 35-37; Naranjo 1984, 66 ff.).

It could be interesting also to compare the Irish copper mines of Ross Island (O'Brien 1994, 229; this volume) and Mount Gabriel, Co. Cork (O'Brien 1994), to that of Albarracín, Teruel (Almagro-Gorbea and Collado 1981), associated with Beaker pottery. They all have narrow, shallow corridors, dug in the rock, following small seams of minerals. These mines, the appearance of the first metal hoards and the use of arsenical copper metallurgy show a parallel technological development which will give rise to the Bronze Age.

Gold of alluvial origin and worked by beating is also characteristic (Fig. 50A). Gold working traditions are sometimes related in Ireland and Iberia, from the Early to the Late Bronze Age (Pingel 1992; Eogan 1994). In the Early Bronze Age gold sun-discs and lunulae represent the most characteristic elements in Ireland, whereas in Iberia there is a predominance of wristguards and bands but there are also some sun-discs and lunulae which point to Irish influence (*infra*).

Socio-ideological changes should be considered highly important. They are reflected in the disappearance of the collective burials of the megalithic tradition and in the appearance and diffusion of individual burials. This new cultural component is already documented in Ireland in the Late Neolithic, where it has been considered of Nordic origin (Herity and Eogan 1977, 81ff) and is an immediate precedent for its subsequent widespread use when the custom is burial in a crouched position, generally placed in a pit or cist.

The Beaker tradition continued in Ireland and Iberia into the Early Bronze Age, explaining the continuity in metallurgy, copper and gold working and also in the practice of single burial. But this continuity has been exaggerated and its chronology must be revised, particularly in Iberia (Almagro-Gorbea, unpublished). In Ireland, single burials continued with the Food Vessel people associated with individual graves in a pit or cist (Herity and Eogan 1977, 133 ff; Megaw and Simpson 1981, 178 ff). In Iberia tanged daggers and wristguards are also associated with non-decorated Beaker-shaped vessels representing the transition to the Bronze Age, in cist burials widespread from Atios, in the north-west (de la Peña 1985), to the Ferradeira group and Chichina, in the south-west, and the big cists of El Argar A can be included in this tradition (Almagro-Gorbea, unpublished). V-perforated buttons and wristguards, some of them luxury ones, persist in this phase, like that of Agua Branca, Portugal, comparable to those from Driffield, Yorkshire, and Culduthel Mains, Inverness. But most of the Irish wristguards are later, with two perforations and concentrated in Ulster and related to the Food Vessels (Harbison 1976, 20; Harrison 1980, fig. 36).

Other characteristic common metal items are halberds and axes. Iberian Atlantic 'Carrapatas' halberds are very similar, and probably derive from Irish prototypes (Harbison 1969a; Schubart 1973). Thin-butted axes with curved sides cast in univalve stone moulds are common in Ireland and Atlantic Iberia (Harbison 1969, 24 ff; Monteagudo 1977; Herity and Eogan 1977, 139, fig. 54). Some riveted daggers can be related to them (Harbison 1967; Ruiz Gálvez 1984, 226). Some rock art elements have been related to Food Vessel people, as cup and rings, labyrinths and field patterns. Their heaviest concentration in west Cork and south Kerry and the similarity of patterns with 'Galician rock-art' have suggested an Iberian origin (MacWhite 1951, 33 ff). But their origin would rather be in an artistic and ideological common Atlantic world (Bradley, this volume), strengthened by contacts and relations confirmed by common elements in material culture and by ships as depicted in the Anta dos Cebros, Pontevedra (Alonso Romero 1974; 1994).

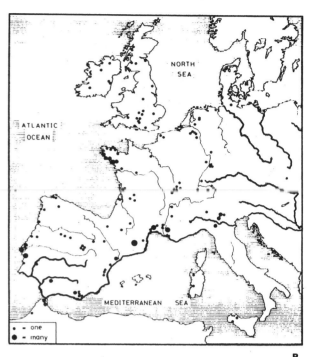

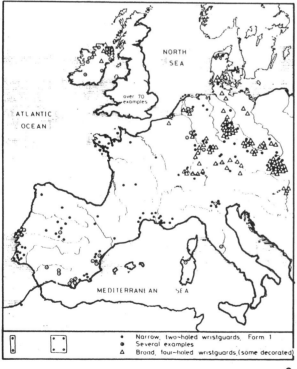

Fig. 49. A: Distribution of AOC Beakers.
B: Maritime Beakers. C: archers' wristguards
(after Harrison 1980).

★ ★ ★

The Bronze Age in Iberia began in the Montelavar-Carrapatas Phase, with Beaker metallurgy of arsenical copper but no Beaker pottery (Ruiz Gálvez 1979; Jorge 1990). Wristguards and Palmela points continue, as in the horizon of Ferradeira, in the Portuguese Algarve (Schubart 1975, 115 ff, fig. 26), probably until the appearance of the first tongued 'swords' (Almagro-Gorbea 1977). Undecorated Beaker vessels appear in single graves in cists under barrows as at San Pedro de Bruriz, Lugo, at Los Pasos, Zamora, or the cists of Villalmanzo, Burgos, with a long tanged dagger (Delibes 1977, 30, 72). Characteristic of this phase are the Carrapatas halberds (Senna 1994) with prototypes in the Early Bronze Age of Ireland, within relations with Wessex I and the First Series of the Armorican Barrows (Briard 1965, 68, fig. 18; Harbison 1969a; Ruiz Gálvez 1984, 223). Carrapatas halberds are associated with Iberian tanged daggers, as in some rock engravings (MacWhite 1951, pl. 33; Peña and Vázquez Varela 1992, 81 ff) and in the warrior stele from Longroiva (Almagro 1966, fig. 30) with halberd, bow and a tanged dagger. Some daggers have rivets and grooves, as in the hoards from Sabero, León, and Gumial, Asturias, the cists of Carnota and Sta. Comba, Coruña, and of Quinta da Agua Branca, Portugal (Ruiz Gálvez 1984, 226). These details appear on certain long Irish daggers as in the Killaha hoard, Co. Kerry, precisely accompanied by a halberd related to the Carrapatas type and with thin-butted axes, within the same complex of Atlantic metallurgy related to the Food Vessels in Ireland (Herity and Eogan 1977, 139, fig. 55).

After the Montelavar phase appear the first tongued 'swords', such as those from Pinhal do Melos and Santiago or the more developed one from Cuevallusa I, with a wide and grooved blade characteristic of the Early Bronze Age (Almagro-Gorbea 1976). These weapons, concentrated in north-western Iberia, are related to Breton 'swords' corresponding to Wessex I and the First Series of the Armorican Barrows (Briard 1965, 68, fig. 18; Harbison 1969a). Although these 'swords' are not documented in Ireland, some of their characteristics, such as rounded butts and grooved edges, are common to the Killaha and Redondas IX daggers (Harrison 1974, fig. 4), which recall the Snowshill type of the end of Wessex I (Gerloff 1975, 115 ff). Some large axes with rounded sides and trapezoidal shape can also be attributed to this era (Monteagudo 1977, type 2C), which recall the Irish Ballyvalley types (Harbison 1969), like the axe from Santa Cruz, Bajo Alemtejo, or La Iglesuela, Teruel (Monteagudo 1977, types 9A, etc.).

The evolution in ornaments demonstrates contacts which can be explained by the wealth of gold in both regions and by an élite with a common origin in the Beaker tradition. Gold spirals are typical of early Atlantic Iberian gold-working (Pingel 1986, figs 7-8). Lunulae are a characteristic Irish ornament (Taylor 1970, 56 ff; *id.* 1980; Eogan 1994, 33); over sixty with incised geometric decoration are known from Ireland, six from Scotland, one from Wales, four from Cornwall and twelve from Brittany and Normandy in north-western France (Eogan 1994, 123-7), but the southern-most known lunula, possibly of local manufacture, appears in the Cabeceiras de Basto hoard, Portugal, associated with two gold sun-discs (Cardozo 1930; MacWhite 1951, 50; Hernando 1980, 90 ff, fig. 1, 3-4). Sun-discs are another characteristic ornament of the beginning of gold-working in Ireland (Eogan 1994, 19), documented in Iberia in Cabeceiras de Basto and in the Museum of Oviedo, but there are references to others in Condeixa-a-Veilha y Bensafrim, Portugal (MacWhite 1951, 50, pl. 8; Hernando 1980, 113; Coffyn 1985, fig. 1, 2-3). These relations are confirmed by some paddle torques, like those from El Viso, Cordoba, with double-axe terminals like some Irish lunulae (Hernando 1980, 88 ff, fig. 1, 1), and from the Kerivoa hoard, Brittany, containing a silver diadem, a lunula and a paddle torque in a box (Eluère 1982, 56 ff). Also a bronze box with a large hoop and various gold spirals was found at Antas de Ulla, Pontevedra (Ruiz Gálvez 1979, 161) and some Irish ornaments have been found in boxes, as the lunula from Newtown, Co. Cavan (Eogan 1994, fig. 12). Basket earrings, another typical ornament of early Irish gold-working (Eogan 1994, 15) and related to paddle torques, are known in Iberia, at Ermegeira, Cova de Moura and Estremoz (Hernado 1980, 100 ff, fig. 5, 3), always in late Beaker contexts.

The last phase of the Early Bronze Age is represented by the Cuevallusa II-III 'swords' (Almagro-Gorbea 1976), related to the Saint-Brandan type of Brittany (Gaucher and Mohen 1972), of the transition to the Middle Bronze Age, weapons not documented in Ireland. However, the axe from Albá, Lugo, is considered a possible Lough Ravel type import (Monteagudo 1977, 11, C1). In ornament, the treasure of Caldas de Reyes, Pontevedra (Ruiz Gálvez 1978) represents the Early to Middle Bronze Age transition with numerous Breton contacts, paddle torques, necklaces in strips, solid bracelets and in particular gold bell-shaped vessels with a traditional decoration and function, but whose shape belongs to the Second Series of Armorican Barrows, at the beginning of the Middle Bronze Age.

In the Middle Bronze Age, direct contacts between Ireland and Iberia do not seem so evident, although there are common components like bronze anvils and flanged axes, the earliest palstaves without loops and Atlantic rapiers, etc. (Ruiz Gálvez 1984). But these types, found both in Ireland and Iberia, can more readily be explained by common British and Breton parallels, rather than by direct contacts between Ireland and Iberia, although they are all part of the same Atlantic relationships.

* * *

From the Late Bronze Age, swords, axes, sickles, etc., reveal interesting correlations within the Atlantic Bronze Age, and the Iberia-Ireland contacts become more evident (Ruiz Gálvez 1984; Coffyn 1985).

In the Bishopsland Phase contacts are intensified, although Brittany and the west of France seem to have continued to play an important intermediary role. At this stage gold bar torcs, ornaments of evident Irish origin (Eogan 1994, 50 ff, 127 ff), reached extensive areas of Iberia (Fig. 50B), like the six unfinished specimens from the treasure from Bodonal, Badajoz (Almagro-Gorbea 1974) (Fig. 50C), and a new example from Castrojeriz, Burgos (Delibes *et al.* in press). These torcs probably arrived through western France, where this type is also documented (Eluère 1982, 79 ff; Eogan 1994, 129-30, fig. 32). The Spanish distribution of these ornaments, the fact that the Bodonal treasure is the heaviest one with specimens half finished and made with a circular (not twisted) bar and the fact that the Iberian torques had geometric decoration makes us suppose a local production, perhaps by itinerant artisans which would explain their spread throughout the entire Atlantic area, from Scotland to southern Iberia.

Other ornaments of the Late Bronze Age could explain other gold-working relationships between Ireland and Iberia. An incised decorated gold necking, a characteristic ornament of south-western Iberia, found in a hoard at Downpatrick, in the north-east of Ireland (Eogan 1994, fig. 26, 12, fig. 29, fig. 31), and a disk from Extremadura, now in the National Archaeological Museum of Madrid (Almagro-Gorbea 1977, pl. XI, 1; Pereda 1991, 126), recall the so-called hair ornaments ('lock-rings') that are so common in Ireland for their technique with welded threads (Eogan 1994, 89, fig. 42).

The Late Bronze Age can be considered a new era in Atlantic relations because of the increase in contacts. In this period new influences reached Iberia from the Eastern Mediteranean (Almagro-Gorbea 1989; 1992), which could explain the appearance of trunnion axes (Coffyn 1985, map 49) and open socketed sickles (*id.*, map 56) and other implements

with tubular shafts characteristic of the Late Bronze Age in Britain and Ireland (Herity and Eogan 1977, fig. 73, 5-7; Megaw and Simpson 1981, fig. 6.25: 11, fig. 6.40: 12). In Ireland there is a double looped palstave from Ballincollig, Co. Cork (Coffyn 1985, map 48, 1), some single faced palstaves (Chitty 1936), originally from the centre of Portugal (Coffyn 1985, map 41), and carp's tongue swords, from the Tartesian area (Ruiz Gálvez 1984; Coffyn 1985).

Other elements which document the relations of Iberia with Ireland in the Late Bronze Age can be interpreted as objects of prestige and symbolic value which help us to understand the social structure and ideology of these areas, and also the mechanisms of these relations. Among these objects we must include the V-notched shields (Coles 1962, 157 ff; Herity and Eogan 1977, 197), well represented in the 'Extremadura stelae', and also in the Ebro Valley and in southern France (Almagro 1966, 156 ff; Almagro-Gorbea 1977, 159 ff; Galán 1993, 93 ff, figs 22-24). In Ireland they are documented in Clonbrin, Co. Longford, and in the moulds from Churchfield and Kilmahamogue, dated to the Dowris Phase. In addition, U-notched shields come from Cloonlara, Co. Mayo, and Annandale, Co. Leitrim, which makes Ireland an interesting point of contact for both types.

These objects were weapons of prestige of the Atlantic élite of the Late Bronze Age to reinforce their status among society, a process that would lead to the gradual formation of a warrior élite as a social class and explain their wide dissemination. Their association with fibulae, chariots, combs, etc., on the Iberian stelae points to the hypothesis of an eastern Mediterranean origin related to the pre-colonial Phoenician-Cypriot colonisation (Almagro 1966; Almagro-Gorbea 1989).

Objects related to feasting also became characteristic of this Atlantic élite warrior society (Schubart 1961; Almagro-Gorbea 1989; 1992; Gomez de Soto 1991; Delibes *et al.* 1993), most likely of heroic type, similar to the Aegean and Central Europe ones: drinking bowls, cauldrons, meat hooks and spits and ritual chariot-stands, etc. (Coffyn 1985, 55 ff; Almagro-Gorbea 1992). This assemblage, documented in Ireland by cauldrons and flesh hooks (Fig. 51) (Jockenhövel 1974; Herity and Eogan 1977, 202 ff, fig. 68, 18, fig. 76b, fig. 84; Gerloff 1986), evidences the presence of the customary ritual banquet between the social élite of the Atlantic area, most likely of heroic type. Their use represents an innovation in culinary techniques, but in particular represents the ritualisation of the banquet as a social and political act, judging from the use of specialised implements. Thus their relations with similar customs documented by written references from both the Orient (1 Sam. 2, 13-14) and pre-classical Greece (Bruns 1970) can

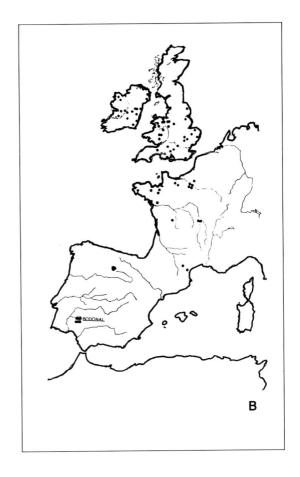

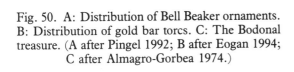

Fig. 50. A: Distribution of Bell Beaker ornaments. B: Distribution of gold bar torcs. C: The Bodonal treasure. (A after Pingel 1992; B after Eogan 1994; C after Almagro-Gorbea 1974.)

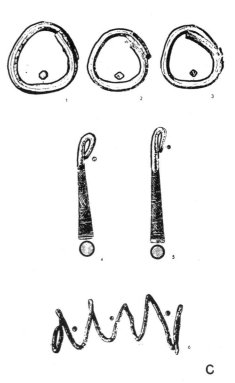

be understood as a sign of the transformation of the way of life among the social élite in the Late Bronze Age, because no precedents are known from earlier periods in the Atlantic area.

These objects are of great interest if we are to undertand the 'pre-colonial' relations between the eastern Mediterranean and the Atlantic through the Iberian peninsula during the Late Bronze Age (Almagro-Gorbea 1989, 1992).

Cauldrons were originally considered to be of Mediterranean origin, Greek (Leeds 1930) or Oriental (Hawkes and Smith 1957), although most of the Oriental cauldrons known date back to the Geometric Cypriot III, 850 BC, as most of the Oriental representations indicate. But there are earlier representations, like a cauldron on a tripod on the obelisk of Asurnasirpal I, 1047-1029 BC, and biblical references confirm the use of cauldrons and hooks at least in the 10th century BC (1 Sam. 2, 13-14). However, cauldrons of type A are the oldest in the Atlantic world and they are considered Irish because they have a north Atlantic distribution with a strong concentration in Ireland and south-east England and they date back to the beginning of Late Bronze Age I (Gerloff 1986), as do the oldest flesh or meat hooks with only two teeth, characteristic of the Bishopsland hoard (Eogan 1983, fig. 10, 17; Jockenhövel 1974), a type also found in Iberia (Delibes *et al.* 1993). These objects seem to have a probable Mycenaean origin and to be derived from prototypes of Middle Cypriot I (Catling 1964, fig. 4, 7-8) arriving through the Danube region and Central Europe with items of Hallstatt A and B (Hundt 1953; Jockenhövel 1974) along with the cauldrons of type A (Gerloff 1986).

But this proposed origin for the Atlantic cauldrons and banquet items might be partially reconsidered, because they could have reached the Atlantic by two routes. One was from the Mycenean world via the Danubian area, which would explain the origin of Irish Type A cauldrons and simple hooks. But there is a close association of cauldrons with other banquet utensils, such as hooks, spits, chariot-stands, etc., all of them of eastern Mediterranean origin, as proven by the spit from Amatunte, dated *c.* 1050-950 BC (Karageorghis and Lo Schiavo 1989), and the bronze vases from the Guia (da Silva 1986) and Berzocana hoards (Almagro-Gorbea 1977, 243 ff, fig. 6, 3), proof that they reached the Atlantic west also via Iberia before Late Bronze Age II. The Iberian hooks from the Solveira and Senhora da Guia hoards (Delibes *et al.* 1993), the latter decorated with spirals, evidence its definite origin in the eastern Mediterranean. But its hollow tubes with rings are similar to English and Irish specimens, like those of Monalty Lough, Co. Monaghan (Jockenhövel 1974). The Guia hook is

associated with a spit, five decorated bronze vessels and two ritual chariot-stands (da Silva 1986) similar to Sardinian tripods (Lo Schiavo *et al.* 1985, fig. 14) derived from Syrian-Phoenician-Cypriot prototypes of the 13-12th century BC (Catling 1964, pl. 37; Mattäus 1985, 322 ff), which make us suppose that all these objects formed part of a 'banquet set' of Oriental origin spread thoroughout the Mediterranean to the Atlantic in the Late Bronze Age.

Some of these elements show bird figures which are considered an Atlantic component (Jockenhövel 1974; Mohen 1977). But birds and protoms of bulls and goats form part of the common decorative repertoire of this technical-ornamental complex of the Canaan-Cypriot workshops of the Late Bronze Age (Mattäus 1985, fig. 127b, 5), together with rings for suspension, explaining the similar decoration of the Sa Idda spit in Sardinia and other Atlantic specimens, from Cachouda in Portugal, to Compiègne in France and Dunaverney, Co. Antrim, in Ireland (Delibes *et al.* 1993). Rings decorate the Oriental tripods of Ugarit, Beth Shan, Cyprus, etc., dating from Late Cypriot IIC and exported to the Aegean and Italy in the 13-12th centuries BC to disappear around the year 1000 BC replaced in the Aegean by specimens of local production (Mattäus 1985), which let us suppose a parallel process in the west. The Sardinian tripod from Oristano, associated with birds (Lo Schiavo *et al.* 1985, fig. 14, 1-2), and the chariots and stands of the central and western Mediterranean can be considered to come from Cyprus (Almagro-Gorbea 1992), like the chariots of Guia, and the Atlantic hooks and spits with rings for suspension at the end of the piece. This type of ring also appears on Cypriot banquet implements, like those from the founders' hoard, Enkomi (Catling 1964, 278 ff, pl. 10, c-e; Mattäus 1985, pl. 123, 3-4), or from grave 523 from Amatunte (Karageorghis and Lo Schiavo 1989). The twisted wires of the meat hooks from Cantabrana, in Iberia, Thoringné, in Brittany, and Argyll, in Scotland (Delibes *et al.* 1993), seem to have the same origin. This decorative component appears on the support from Tel Nami, Palestine, in the Late Bronze Age, *c.* 13th century BC (Wolf 1994, 490, fig. 8), and on palettes of Late Cypriot III from Enkomi and Cape Gelidonia (Bass 1967, 94) imitated also in Sardinia (Lo Schiavo *et al.* 1985, fig. 10, 2).

All the technological and ornamental features described consequently form part of a technological and decorative complex applied to the banquet assemblage, which explains the characteristics of the Atlantic specimens. Their origin is not central European as had been supposed (Mohen 1977), nor Atlantic, because there are no precedents in this zone, but must be considered eastern. This thesis helps to

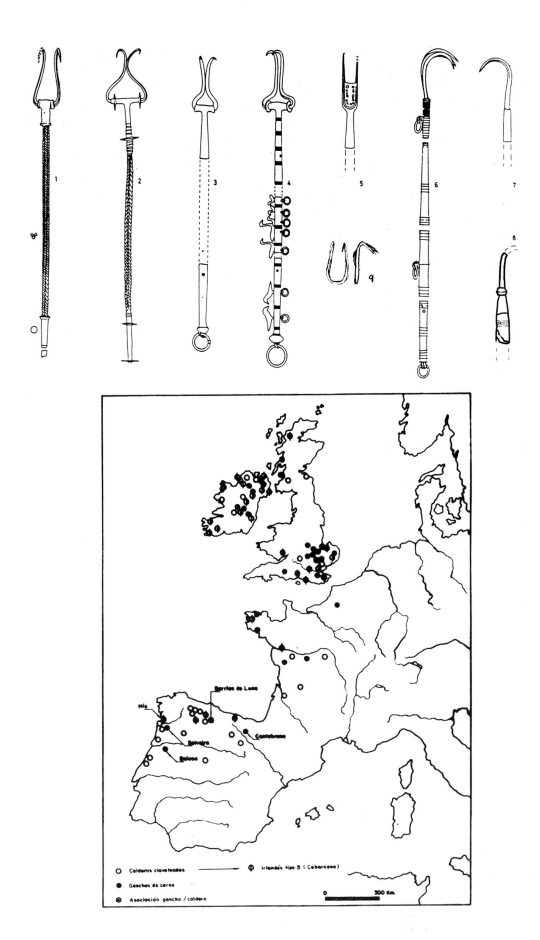

Fig. 51. Meat hooks of Atlantic type and distribution of cauldrons and meat hooks (after Delibes *et al*. 1993).

explain how the tradition of a sumptuous banquet assemblage, documented in pre-classical Greece as reported in the Iliad (Bruns 1970), reached the Atlantic regions from the eastern Mediterranean, in rituals possibly associated with hospitality to improve contacts and exchanges. The role of Iberia in its diffusion could be explained because these traditions would crystallise in the Orientalising period of Tartessos and, with good reason, the iconography of the banquet in the Orient is associated with regal settings due to their political function and ritual character, as indicated in biblical allusions (Ex. 38.3; Lv. 6.21; 1 Sam 2. 13-14; Jr. 52, 17-19; Miq. 3,3; Zac. 14, 20-21; Job. 41,12; etc.).

By way of conclusion, cauldrons and vessels, 'ritual' chariot-stands, spits and meat hooks, etc., evidence the custom of the sumptuous banquet that is witnessed in the Late Bronze Age throughout the Atlantic west from Ireland to Iberia, where these traditions crystallised in the hierarchies of the Orientalising period of Tartessos, from where some customs would irradiate to the more northerly areas of the Atlantic world as early as the beginning of the Late Bronze Age. Their origin is difficult to explain without influence from the eastern Mediterranean, where there was a deeply rooted tradition of ritual banquets, well documented by biblical traditions, etc. But the greatest importance of these objects, from a historical point of view, is that they evidence the contacts between the Atlantic world and the pre-colonial world of the Mediterranean, now well documented since the Late Bronze Age.

★ ★ ★

One last point of interest that may appear polemic should be considered when analysing relations between Ireland and Iberia, this is their common Celtic roots in the Bronze Age.

The traditional hypothesis was that Iberian Celts derived from the Iberian Urnfield Culture, found in north-eastern Iberia (Ruiz Zapatero 1985) and not coinciding with the Celtic area according to the historic texts, nor with the linguistic evidence well documented in central and western areas of Iberia (Tovar 1961; Almagro-Gorbea 1993).

All these areas had a cultural substrate of Atlantic tradition, well attested in north-western Iberia, from the valley of the Ebro to the Guadalquivir and encompass social, linguistic, ritual and ideological components, whose relationship helps to document their origin and high chronology in the Bronze Age (Almagro-Gorbea 1993). Indeed, the most certain Celtic cultural evidence comes from the central areas

of the Spanish peninsula, the ancient 'Celtiberia' after Strabo (III, 4, 13), Pliny (III, 5, 24-26) and Ptolomeus (II, 6, 53-57). In the Bronze Age, in the middle of the second millennium BC, this zone appears occupied by the Cogotas Culture, with Beaker roots and with metal elements of the Atlantic Bronze Age (Almagro-Gorbea, in press). In the first millennium BC, elbow fibulae, Huelva-type swords and round huts evidence south Atlantic influences from the Tartesian area (Almagro-Gorbea 1994). These cultural substrate elements can be considered 'pre-Celtic' because they show highly primitive characteristics, closer to the Indo-European world, although already related with the later Celtic culture. But their archaism points to the Bronze Age, and it cannot then arise from the Celtic cultures of the Hallstatt and La Tène (Almagro-Gorbea 1993; Ruiz Zapatero 1993).

This substrate includes ritual rock 'altars' and 'saunas' or *Schwitzbaden* (Almagro-Gorbea and Alvarez 1993) which confirm the reference by Strabo (III, 3, 6) to warrior initiation rituals. It also includes water offerings known since the Bronze Age (Almagro-Gorbea, in press) and maintained among Cantabrians until the Roman era (Suet., *Galba*, 7, 12), and the Urnfield incineration ritual is never documented. Water deities, a symbol of life and death and related to the Otherworld, are also documented. Some of their pre-Celtic names are found in hydronyms, like *Deva, Navia, deo Salamati* (de Hoz 1963), and their cult is evidenced in inscriptions, myths and, perhaps, in the water offerings.

These people had physiolatric cults evidenced by rock 'altars', like those of Ulaca (Avila), Axtroki (Basque Region) or Peñalba de Villastar (Teruel), associated to a *Lug* Celtic inscription (Marco 1986). Throughout all the western areas there are very archaic divinities of non-anthropomorphous conception and associated with rocks, with names beginning with *Bandu-, Cosu-, Navia-, Reve-* or *Treba-* (García Fernández and Albalat 1990, map 6).

Band- was a divinity etymologically related with magical cohesion (from **bhendh-* to bend = to link). It has been interpreted as a divinity of brotherhoods and of their relationship with their chief through *devotio* (id., 109 ff., 181 and 340). Their epithets, *Aetobrigus, Lanobrigae,* etc., and their iconography as *Fortuna-Tyché* confirm that it was a divinity of the whole community, guarantor of their union and survival. Their warrior connotations explain their association with Mars and their relationship with Celtic warriors, like the Irish *fianna* and other similar warrior groups. Another of these divinities, *Cossus,* was a warrior god associated with omphalic rocks related to Celtic cosmic conceptions. Its epithet *Oenaecus* confirms its relationship with a legal-religious assembly, the Irish *oenach*, similar to other Indo-European ones, as the Germanic *Ghilde* or the Italic *curia* (*id.*, 266).

Strabo (III, 3, 6) records that these warriors' panoply included 'bronze' spear-heads (*tinès dè dórati chrôntai 'epidoratídes dè chálkeai*), a fact that can be explained by having preserved ancestral rituals of Bronze Age society, as the *salii* in Rome. That also explains how they were organised in age groups, with brotherhoods and initiation rituals which included frugal meals and baths or 'saunas', the so-called 'pedras formosas' of the north-west and the Meseta, related to an Irish tradition perhaps documented in the *fulachta fiadh* (the 'cooking places of the *fianna*') (Buckley 1990) and the triple initiating bath of Cú Chulainn (Almagro-Gorbea and Alvarez 1993).

These warlike brotherhoods practised the *ver sacrum* and young people would leave their 'castros' or hill forts and live as *latrones* (Diod. V, 34, 6; Str. III, 3, 5-8; Almagro-Gorbea 1994, 46). This warlike organisation is comparable to the *fratrias* of other Indo-European pre-urban peoples like the *Harii*, the infernal army of the *Germani*, or the *fianna* from Ireland. The oldest Irish epic (*Cycle of Finn*) documents how the *fianna* were devoted to warlike and hunting activities and they had to undergo tests of initiation and lived on the fringes of society, led by *Finn*, a chief or hero with magic powers to whom they owed absolute obedience and were bound by *devotio*, as the *Lusitani* and *Celtiberi* in Iberia (García Fernández and Albalat 1990).

Other customs help us understand the socio-economic organisation of these 'pre-Celtic' people, who lived in 'castros' or hill forts (Almagro-Gorbea 1994). Women worked in the fields and men received the dowry and the daughters would inherit the land (III, 4, 18), as among the Picti. Justinus (44, 3, 7) observes that '*feminae res domesticas agrorumque administrant, ipsi armis rapinis serviunt*', which permits the structure of this primitive society to be reconstructed; the women worked in the fields and house and the men were engaged in war, hunting and cattle raising; this is a warlike structure characteristic of the Bronze Age. It implies an archaic social structure of Indo-European origin with collective exploitation of the land, documented among the *Vaccei*.

The *origo* of the peoples of western Iberia documented in Roman epigraphy also confirms these customs because it alludes to the *castella* or 'castros' or hill forts documented by archaeology that defended their territory (Albertos 1988; Untermann 1987). This *origo* is prior to the Celtiberian one with a genitive plural alluding to their familial structures. This onomastic distinction probably differentiates a primitive pre-gentile socio-economic organisation of

the 'pre-Celtic' substrate in western and northern Iberia from the gentile 'Celtic' peoples located in the east of the Meseta and in the highlands of the Iberian system, better known as Celtiberians, although that proto-Celtic western substrate was in part absorbed by the expansion of the Celtiberian Culture (Almagro-Gorbea 1993).

The primitive rituals and customs recorded by Strabo (III, 3, 5-8) and Justinus (XLIV, 3, 7) permit the identification of a very ancient cultural substrate, formed by Lusitans, Galaics, Asturs, Cantabrians, etc., which Strabo (III, 4, 20) distinguished from the 'Celtic' populations (Celtiberians) and which should be considered to originate prior to the Celtic world as presently identified in central Europe.

This substrate is confirmed by linguistic data, because of the Celtic etymology of toponyms, ethnonyms, anthroponyms and teonyms, which confirm the linguistic personality of western Iberia, specially documented by the so-called 'Lusitanian'. This language is of western Indo-European type and has a more archaic character and is closer to Indo-European than any other documented Celtic language. It is disputed whether it is pre-Celtic (Tovar 1985; Schmidt 1985, 338; de Hoz 1983; Gorrochategui 1985; Villar 1991), or Celtic (Untermann 1987; Prosdocimi 1989). Its distribution in north-western Iberia coincides with the ritual 'saunas', rock altars and water hoards, belonging to the same pre-Celtic Atlantic cultural substratum preserved in the western areas of Iberia until Romanisation.

This alternative explanation considers the Celtic culture of Iberia to be of a very long formation, because its components have been merged in a framework of acculturation and evolution from the Atlantic Bronze Age, although without excluding sporadic movements of people (Almagro-Gorbea 1993). This explanation would explain the origin of the Celts of Iberia without resorting to invasions from the Urnfield, Hallstatt or La Tène cultures, a thesis which has never been able to establish the place of origin or the arrival routes of these elements.

This hypothesis would better explain also the affinities between all Atlantic Celtic peoples, whose roots seem to date back, both in Ireland and in Iberia, to a very ancient period of the Bronze Age (Waddell 1991, 1992; Almagro-Gorbea 1993). These affinities could also explain the mythical traditions about ethnic migrations between Iberia and Ireland (Waddell 1978; Harbison 1979).

All these theories could help us to better understand, from an overall perspective, the relations between Ireland and Iberia throughout almost two thousand years. In particular, they may help us to explain the origin of their Celtic peoples which form an essential part of their ethnic and cultural roots, partially preserved until today only in those remote areas of the Atlantic 'Far West'.

References

Albertos, M. L. 1988. Sobre los castella del NO. peninsular. *Actas del I Congreso Peninsular de Historia Antigua* 2, 191 ff. Santiago.

Almagro, M. 1966. *Las estelas decoradas del Suroeste Peninsular.* Madrid.

Almagro-Gorbea, M. 1974. The Bodonal de la Sierra Gold Find. *Journal of the Royal Society of Antiquaries of Ireland* 104, 44-51.

Almagro-Gorbea, M. 1976. La espada de Entrambasaguas. Aportación a la secuencia de las espadas del Bronce en el Norte de la Península Ibérica. *XL Aniversario del Centro de Estudios Montañeses*, 453-77. Santander.

Almagro-Gorbea, M. 1977. *El Bronce Final y el Período Orientalizante en Extremadura. Bibliotheca Praehistorica Hispana 14.* Madrid.

Almagro-Gorbea, M. 1986. El Bronce Final y el inicio de la Edad del Hierro en la Península Ibérica. *Historia de España I, Prehistoria*, 341-532. Madrid.

Almagro-Gorbea, M. 1989. Arqueología e Historia Antigua: El proceso protoorientalizante y el inicio de los contactos de Tartessos con el Levante mediterráneo. *Homenaje al Prof. S. Montero (Anejos de Gerion II)*, 277-88. Madrid.

Almagro-Gorbea, M. 1992. Intercambios culturales entre Aragón y el Mediterráneo en el Bronce Final. *Aragón/Litoral mediterráneo. Intercambios culturales durante la Prehistoria. Homenaje a J. Maluquer de Motes*, 633-58. Zaragoza.

Almagro-Gorbea, M. 1993. Los celtas en la Península Ibérica: orígen y personalidad cultural. In M. Almagro-Gorbea and G. Ruiz Zapatero (eds), *Los Celtas: Hispania y Europa*, 121-73. Madrid.

Almagro-Gorbea, M. 1994. El urbanismo en la Hispania Céltica: castros y oppida en la Península Ibérica. In M. Almagro-Gorbea and A. Mª Martín (eds), *Castros y oppida de Extremadura (Complutum Extra 4)*, 13-75. Madrid.

Almagro-Gorbea, M. In press. Sacred places and cults of the Late Bronze Age tradition in Celtic Hispania. *Archäologische Forschungen zum Kultgeschichten in der jüngeren Bronzezeit und frühen Eisenzeit Alteuropas.* Regensburg 1993.

Almagro-Gorbea, M. In press. L'Età del Bronzo nella Penisola Iberica. *Absolute Chronology. Archaeological Europe 2500-500 BC (Acta Archaeologica 67 (1996)).*

Almagro-Gorbea, M. and Alvarez, J. 1993. La 'Fragua' de Ulaca: saunas y baños de iniciación en el mundo céltico. *Cuadernos de Arqueología de la Universidad de Navarra 1*, 177-253.

Almagro-Gorbea, M. and Collado, O. 1981. La Loma de las Tejerías. Un asentamiento minero campaniforme en Albarracín (Teruel). *Teruel* 66, 87-105.

Alonso Romero, F. 1974. Hallazgo de un petroglifo con representaciones esquemáticas de la Edad del Bronce. *Zephyrus* 25, 295-308.

Alonso Romero, F. 1994. Un petroglifo con representación de una nave de la edad del Bronce en Anta dos Cebros, Pontevedra. *XXI Congreso Nacional de Arqueología. Vigo 1993.* Zaragoza.

Bass, G. F. 1967. *Cape Gelidonya: a Bronze Age Shipwreck, Transactions of the American Philosophical Society* 57, 8. Philadelphia.

Briard, J. 1965. *Les dépôts bretons de l'Age du Bronze atlantique.* Rennes.

Bruns, G. 1970. Küchenwessen und Mahlzeiten. *Archäologia Homerica Q.* Göttingen.

Buckley, V. (ed.) 1990. *Burnt offerings. International Contributions to Burnt Mound Archaeology.* Dublin.

Burgess, C. 1979. The background of early metal-working in Ireland and Britain. In M. Ryan (ed.), *The Origins of Metallurgy in Atlantic Europe. Proceedings of the Fifth Atlantic Colloquium*, 207-14. Dublin.

Cardozo, M. 1930. *Joias arcaicas encontradas em Portugal.* La Coruña.

Catling, H. W. 1964. *Cypriot Bronzework in the Mycenaean World.* Oxford.

Chitty, L. F. 1936. Single faced palstaves in Portugal and Ireland. *Proceedings of the Prehistoric Society* 2, 236-8.

Coffyn, A. 1985. *Le Bronze Final atlantique dans la Péninsule Ibérique.* Paris.

Coles, J. M. 1962. European Bronze Age shields. *Proceedings of the Prehistoric Society* 28, 156-90.

Delibes, G. 1977. *El Vaso Campaniforme en la Meseta Norte Española. Studia Archaeologica 46.* Valladolid.

Delibes, G. *et al.* 1993. Nuevos 'ganchos de carne' protohistóricos de la Península Ibérica. *Tabona* 8, 2, 417-34.

Delibes, G., Elorza, J. C., Castro, B. In press. El torques de oro de Castrojeriz. *Homenaje al prof. D. Juan José Martín González.* Valladolid.

Eluère, C. 1982. *Les ors préhistoriques (L'âge du bronze en France 2).* Paris.

Eogan, G. 1983. *Hoards of the Irish Later Bronze Age.* Dublin.

Eogan, G. 1990. Irish megalithic tombs and Iberia: Comparisons and contacts. *Probleme Megalithgräberforschung. Vorträge zum 100 Geburstag von Vera Leisner (Madrider Forschungen 16)*, 113-37. Berlin.

Eogan, G. 1994. *The Accomplished Art. Gold and Gold-Working in Britain and Ireland during the Bronze Age (c. 2300-650 BC).* Oxford.

Galán, E. 1993. *Estelas, paisaje y territorio en el Bronce Final del Suroeste de la Península Ibérica (Complutum Extra 3).* Madrid.

García Fernández and Albalat, B. 1990. *Guerra y religión en la Gallaecia y la Lusitania.* La Coruña.

Gaucher, G. and Mohen, J. P. 1972. *Typologie des objets métalliques de l'Age du Bronze en France, I. Epées.* Paris.

Gerloff, S. 1975. *The Early Bronze Age Daggers in Great Britain, Prähistorische Bronzefunde 6.2.* Munich.

Gerloff, S. 1986. Bronze Age Class A cauldrons: typology, origins and chronology. *Journal of Royal Society of Antiquaries of Ireland* 116, 84-115.

Gomez de Soto, J. 1991. Le fondeur, le trafiquant et les cuisiniers. La broche d'Amathonte de Chypre et la chronologie absolue du Bronze Final Atlantique. In C. Chevillot and A. Coffyn (eds) *L'Age du Bronze Atlantique. Actes du 1er Colloque de Beynac*, 369-73. Beynac.

Gorrochategui, J. 1985. En torno a la clasificación del Lusitano. *Actas del IV Coloquio sobre Lenguas y Culturas Paleohispánicas*, 7-91. Vitoria.

Harbison, P. 1967. Mediterranean and Atlantic elements in the early Bronze Age of Northern Portugal and Galicia. *Madrider Mitteilungen* 8, 100-22.

Harbison, P. 1969. *The Axes of the Early Bronze Age in Ireland, Prähistorische Bronzefunde* 9.1. Munich.

Harbison, P. 1969a. *The Daggers and Halberds of the Early Bronze Age in Ireland, Prähistorische Bronzefunde* 6.1. Munich.

Harbison, P. 1976. *Bracers and V-perforated buttons in the Beaker and Food Vessel Cultures of Ireland (Archaeologia Atlantica. Research Report 1)*. Bad Bramstedt.

Harbison, P. 1979. Celtic migrations in Western Europe. *II Coloquio de Lenguas y Culturas prerromanas de la Península Ibérica. Tübingen 1976*, 225-35. Salamanca.

Harrison, R. J. 1974. Ireland and Spain in the Early Bronze Age. *Journal of the Royal Society of Antiquaries of Ireland* 104, 52-73.

Harrison, R. J. 1977. *The Bell Beaker Cultures of Spain and Portugal*. Harvard.

Harrison, R. J. 1980. *The Beaker Folk. Copper Age Archaeology in Western Europe*. London.

Hawkes, C. F. C. and Smith, M. A. 1957. On Some Buckets and Cauldrons of the Bronze and Early Iron Ages. *The Antiquaries Journal* 37, 131-98.

Herity, M. and Eogan, G. 1977. *Ireland in Prehistory*. London.

Hernando, A. 1980. La orfebrería durante el Calcolítico y el Bronce Antiguo en la península Ibérica. *Trabajos de Prehistoria* 40, 85-138.

Hoz, J. de, 1963. Hidronimia antigua europea en la Península Ibérica. *Emerita* 31, 227-42.

Hoz, J. de, 1983. Las lenguas y la epigrafí prerromanas de la Península Ibérica. *Unidad y pluralidad del mundo antiguo. Actas del VI Congreso Español de Estudios Clásicos*, 351-96. Madrid.

Hundt, H. J. 1953. Uber Tüllenhaken und Gabeln. *Germania* 32, 145-55.

Jockenhövel, A. 1974. Fleischhaken von den Britischen Inseln. *Archäologisches Korrespondenzblatt* 4, 329-38.

Jorge, V. Oliveira, et al. 1990. *Portugal das origens á romanizaçao*. Lisboa.

Karageorghis, V. and Lo Schiavo, F. 1989. A west Mediterranean obelos from Amathus. *Revista Studi Fenici* 17, 15-29.

Leeds, E. T. 1930. A Bronze Cauldron from the River Cherwell, Oxfordshire, with notes on Cauldrons and other Bronze Vessels of Allied Types. *Archaeologia* 80, 1-36.

Lo Schiavo, F., McNamara, E., Vagnetti, L. 1985. Late Cypriot Imports to Italy and their Influence on Local Bronzeworks. *Papers of the British School in Rome* 53, 1-71.

MacWhite, E. 1951. *Estudios sobre las relaciones atlánticas de la Península Ibérica en la Edad del Bronce*. Madrid.

Marco, F. 1986. El dios céltico Lug y el santuario de Peñalba de Villastar. *Homenaje a A. Beltrán*, 731-59. Zaragoza.

Matthäus, H. 1985. *Metallgefässe und Gefässuntersätze der Bronzezeit, der Geomettrischen und Archaischen Periode auf Cypern, Prähistorische Bronzefunde* 2.8. Munich.

Megaw, J. V. S. and Simpson, D. D. A. 1981. *Introduction to British prehistory*. Leicester.

Mohen, J.-P. 1977. Broches à rôtir articulées de l'Age du Bronze. *Antiquités Nationales* 9, 34-9.

Monteagudo, L. 1977. *Die Beile auf der Iberischen Halbinsel, Prähistorische Bronzefunde* 9.6. Munich.

Naranjo, C. 1984. El Castillo de Cardeñosa. Un yacimiento de los inicios de la Edad del Bronce en la Sierra de Avila. *Noticiario Arqueológico Hispano* 19, 35-84.

O'Brien, W. F. 1994. *Mount Gabriel. Bronze Age Mining in Ireland*. Galway.

Peña, A. de la. 1985. Las cistas de Gandón (Cangas de Morrazo, Pontevedra). *Museo de Pontevedra* 39, 79-99.

Peña, A. de la, and Vázquez Varela, J. M. 1992. *Los petroglifos gallegos* (2 ed.). La Coruña.

Pereda, A. 1991. *Orfebreria prerromana. Arqueología del oro*. Madrid.

Pingel, V. 1986. Zum Beginn der Goldmetallurgie im Westen der Iberischen Halbinsel. *Marburger Studien zur Vor-und Frühgeschichte* 7, 193-211.

Pingel, V. 1992. *Die vorgeschichtlichen Goldfunde der Iberischen Halbinsel. Eine archäologische Untersuchung zur Auswertung der Spektralanalysen (Madrider Forschungen 17)*. Berlin.

Prosdocimi, A. 1989a. La iscrizione gallica de Larzac e la flessione dei temi in -a,-i, -ja. Con un excursus sulla morfologia del Lusitano: acc. *crougin*, dat. *crougeai*. *Römisch-Germanische Forschungen* 94, 190-205.

Ruiz-Gálvez, M. 1978. El tesoro de Caldas de Reyes. *Trabajos de Prehistoria* 35, 173-92.

Ruíz Gálvez, M. 1979. El Bronce Antiguo en la fachada atlántica peninsular. *Trabajos de Prehistoria* 36, 151-172.

Ruiz Gálvez, M. 1984. *La Península Ibérica y sus relaciones con el Círculo Cultural Atlántico*. Madrid.

Ruiz Zapatero, G. 1985. *Los Campos de Urnas del NE. de la Península Ibérica*. Tesis Doctoral de la Universidad Complutense 83/85. Madrid.

Ruiz Zapatero, G. 1993. El concepto de Celtas en la Prehistoria europea y española. In M. Almagro-Gorbea and G. Ruiz Zapatero (eds) *Los Celtas: Hispania y Europa*, 23-62. Madrid.

Ryan, M. (ed.). 1979. *The Origins of Metallurgy in Atlantic Europe. Proceedings of the Fifth Atlantic Colloquium*. Dublin.

Sangmeister, E. 1964. Die schmallen 'Armschutzplatten'. *Studien aus Alteuropa* 1, 93-122.

Schmidt, K. H. 1985. A Contribution to the identification of Lusitanian. *Actas del III Coloquio sobre Lenguas y Culturas Paleohispánicas, Lisboa 1980*, 319-41. Salamanca.

Schubart, H. 1961. Atlantische Nitenkessel vom der Pyrenäenhalbinsel. *Madrider Mitteilungen* 2, 35-54.

Schubart, H. 1973. Las alabardas tipo Montejícar.

Homenaje al Prof. Luis Pericot, 247-69. Barcelona.

Schubart, H. 1975. *Die Kultur der Bronzezeit im Südwesten der Iberischen Halbinsel (Madrider Forschungen 9)*. Berlin.

Senna-Martínez, J. C. de. 1994. Subsidios para o estudio do Bronze Pleno na Estremadura atlántica: A alabarda de Tipo 'Atlantico' do habitat das Baútas (Amadora). *Zephyrus* 1994, 161-80.

Shee Twohig, E. 1981. *The Megalithic Art of Western Europe*. Oxford.

Silva, A. Coelho Ferreira da. 1986. *A Cultura Castreja no Noroeste de Portugal*. Paços da Ferreira.

Taylor, J. J. 1970. Lunulae reconsidered. *Proceedings of the Prehistoric Society* 36, 38-81.

Taylor, J. J. 1980. *Bronze Age Gold Work of the British Isles*. Cambridge.

Tovar, A. 1961. *The Ancient Languages of Spain and Portugal*. New York.

Tovar, A. 1985. La inscripción de Cabezo das Fraguas y la lengua de los lusitanos. *Actas del III Coloquio sobre Lenguas y Culturas Paleohispánicas, Lisboa 1980*, 227-53. Salamanca.

Untermann, J. 1987. Lusitanisch, Keltiberisch, Keltisch. *Actas del IV Coloquio sobre Lenguas y Culturas Paleohispánicas, Vitoria 1985*, 57-76.

Villar, F. 1991. *Los indoeuropeos y los orígenes de Europa. Lenguaje e Historia*. Madrid.

Waddell, J. 1978. The Invasion Hypothesis in Irish Prehistory. *Antiquity* 52, 121-8.

Waddell, J. 1991. The Celticization of the West: an Irish Perspective. In C. Chevillot and A. Coffyn (eds), *L'Age du Bronze Atlantique. Actes du 1er Colloque de Beynac*, 349-66. Beynac.

Waddell, J. 1992. The Irish Sea in Prehistory. *The Journal of Irish Archaeology* 6, 29-40.

Wolf, S. R. 1994. Archaeology in Israel. *American Journal of Archaeology* 98, 481-519.

Penultima Thule: The Bronze Age in the Western Baltic Region as an Analogy to the Irish Bronze Age

Henrik Thrane

Abstract

As an introduction to the immanent question behind my invitation to this conference the problems facing the prehistoric mariners wanting to cross the North Sea are examined. Recent work seems to indicate that direct sailing was extremely rare or perhaps nigh impossible before the introduction of the sail. A brief outline of current knowledge about Bronze Age settlement in South Scandinavia is presented and some similarities or differences between the Irish and the Nordic Bronze Ages are indicated. It is finally suggested that a study of parallel developments in Europe may enrich our understanding of the genuine European elements of our Bronze Ages.

The theme of the first conference in the European Council programme was 'The Identity of Bronze Age Europe'. Behind this title lay of course a concern about modern Europe's identity. Are we less European on the outer isles than in the ancient core area of the Mediterranean – or vice versa? If anyone came to that conference with the idea that there ever was a common European identity in the Bronze Age, they left London disappointed. It was not all that easy to identify which elements were common to all European Bronze Ages cultures – beyond the trivial.

Here Professor Almagro and I are meant to cover the length and breadth of the European continent and I am sure that we have one thing in common, we look upon our native Bronze Age as something special.

NAVIGATION

Far and few, far and few,
Are the lands where the Jumblies live;
Their heads are green, and their hands are blue,
And they went to sea in a Sieve.

Edward Lear

I wonder whither an ancient Irish navigator would turn his vessel looking for contacts? Without maps how did he choose which way to go and when to set off? How did he prepare for the journey and how could he estimate its length and duration?

Scandinavia and the British Isles have the North Sea in common. What is now the sewer of the Continent and Britain used to be the hunting ground of Mesolithic hunters and remains the main supplier of amber to us Danes. Whether the North Sea was regarded as a friendly or hostile ocean, I doubt if the prospect of crossing it directly had much appeal

before the Vikings adapted the sail to their clinker built vessels. One result of that invention was the city of Dublin, needless to say at a conference in the moat of Dublin Castle. But Charles Green (1988, 104) felt that 'except by accident of weather or ignorance, no direct passage from North Schleswig to England was ever made at this time.'

The doyen of maritime archaeology in the Baltic, Ole Crumlin-Pedersen, suggested some ten years ago (1983; 1985) that pre-Viking navigation differed radically from Viking sailing. We know the Nydam type of large clinker built rowing boat quite well (Crumlin-Pedersen and Rieck 1988) and something of its successors (Evans and Bruce-Mitford 1975; Christensen 1995) but even these seaworthy vessels had to make long journeys in short trips, hugging the coast, going ashore for the night, travelling only during periods of sufficiently long daylight, i.e. between April and September. As you cannot go on rowing for many hours, a system of watches must have been the norm. In calm waters this length of rowing would probably move the vessel at an average of three knots (Green 1988). In the Baltic, regularly spaced shore stations in historical Sweden seem to reflect this ancient day by day sailing (Westerdahl 1991) and even as late as the 13th century the coastal route seems to have been preferred (Crumlin-Pedersen 1983, Abb. 62, 1). On the other hand, crossings of open water to a coast below the horizon may have been done overnight, navigating by the stars and arriving within sight of the journey's end at dawn (Ellmers 1981) which would be relevant for the Channel and the Irish Sea.

Green gives much pertinent information on the difficulties of the coastal waters along the Frisian coast. His estimate of the journey from Jutland to Kent or East Anglia having lasted up to two months (1988, 106) may seem pessimistic, but reflects the magnitude of the undertaking. If the hazards were this great for the Migration period, what are we to expect for the Bronze Age with its sewn vessels of the Dover-Ferriby-Hjortspring family (Jensen *et al.* 1989; Wright 1990; McGrail 1990)? These vessels are not regarded as fit for crossing the Channel (Marsden 1995), but the Channel was crossed, as the lost cargoes at Dover etc. are direct witnesses of.

Norwegian colleagues, inspired by the curraghs (McGrail 1990), imagined that sewn skin boats actually crossed from Norway to Scotland, which would certainly stretch not only the evidence to its limits but also the abilities of crew and vessel (Marstrander 1963; Fett and Fett 1979; but also Rausing 1984). Sewn skin boats would be much lighter (not according to Rausing 1984) and easier to paddle (proper oars belong to vessels with a solid gunwhale) but would drift easier for wind, current and tide without a heavy keel.

Detlev Ellmers (1995) reads the rock carvings as clear signs of crews of 10-24 paddlers in the larger vessels (Fig. 52) with extra helmsman and bow watch – and for special purposes (only?) additional high status persons. Were all the crew paddling all the way, that would imply quite short trips of at most 8-10 hours. For longer journeys we must imagine boats at least as big as the Hjortspring vessel with its ten 'thwarts' (seats for 20 paddlers).

If we are to follow the idea of Westerdahl (1995) that ships were adapted to the waters they were meant to sail, we must envisage a whole range of specialised vessels, some for coastal sailing in the Baltic, and quite different ones for the North Sea and Skagerak crossings (Westerdahl 1995, figs 7-8). The Scandinavian rock carvings with the ship as the dominant figural motif actually show a wide range of boat sizes (Fig. 53).

Little is known of the actual night resting places or landing sites, apart from those which during the Late Roman period developed into seasonal settlements serving more important inland centres like Gudme (Nielsen *et al.* 1994). It has, however, been suggested that the mouths of the small Nordic rivers, like small bays and the many islands in the southern Danish archipelagos and the Swedish 'skärgard' would have been well suited at all times. Even regular night stops may, however, leave very little tangible archaeological evidence (Crumlin-Pedersen 1995). Coastal settlements are known from the Bronze Age, but they reveal more of fishing and hunting activities than about relations with distant societies (e.g. Hasmark and Bulbjerg: Müller 1919).

We have only one way of probing this question, which is the old-fashioned approach of looking at distribution maps of bronzes (e.g. Thrane 1975, figs

131-32). The distribution of imported Late Bronze Age metalwork beyond Denmark is significantly restricted to the Swedish coasts (Fig. 54).

The kind of seafaring sketched here would leave little opportunity for direct voyages across the North Sea and that agrees with the evidence of the metalwork. There is very little evidence of proper imports from the British Isles into Scandinavia, even in Denmark (a few flat axes, the odd spearhead, sword or palstave, the remarkable Late Bronze Age shield Sørup 2 (Harbison 1970; Butler 1963; Coles 1962; Thrane 1975, fig. 40b) and the Abildholt cauldron so out of place in the Danish Bronze Age (Becker 1949; Thrane 1979)). The shield would have more congenial surroundings in Central Sweden where rock carvings of British shield types are frequent (e.g. Fredsjö 1981).

With even the most positive attitude this material will not support the idea of any intensive trade or exchange across the North Sea, not to mention beyond the land barrier of Britain, to Ireland. The other western imports, socketed axes mainly, are equally rare and the whole complex could be interpreted as the end result of sporadic contacts along the Continental coast, most of the objects having been sucked up by people in the Netherlands and northwest German coastal zones.

If we interpret the metal objects found outside their home range as the evidence of exchange (one way or the other: Thrane 1975) emanating from the home area, it will be logical to propose that the end of the distribution reflects the end of the exchange chain. The next conclusion will be that Central European products were exchanged (down the line) as far north as the Bottnian Bay (Meinander 1954) and Scotland (Coles 1960, 48ff) while the Nordic bronzes generally stop east of the Rhine and west of the Vistula with the odd outlier in France, Switzerland or Roumania (Thrane 1975, 260ff, fig. 128 – if they are Nordic *sensu strictu*).

The implication of this distribution pattern is that the expeditions from Denmark ended even before the major navigational hazards at the island of Texel where three tidal circles may make navigating pretty desperate (Green 1988, 111). Around Drouwen in the Drenthe province the Nordic and Mittelelbe products seem to stop (Butler 1988). The climax of this Nordic connection appears to be contemporary with the great centres of wealth in Denmark (Thrane 1994).

Objects from France and southeast England seem only rarely to cross the Ijsselmeer and the river Ijssel which may have functioned as a sort of barrier – immediately east of Texel (O'Connor 1980; Butler 1989). The inhabitants of the Frisian islands would probably have taken over any further exchange westwards and

Fig. 52. Manned boat (first and last man with raised paddle) depicted on a
late Bronze Age rock carving at Smörsten, Bohuslän (after Asmus).

similarly in Normandy and Brittany?

The clusters of Bronze Age barrows, which remain the best source for Bronze Age settlement in Scandinavia, tend to follow the coasts too, maybe even regularly spaced at *c.* 5 km intervals (Stjernquist 1983; Olausson 1992). The suggestion that the major barrows and cairns on the coasts served as guides for the navigators is an old one (Johansen 1979; Wigren 1987).

One point which should be borne in mind, however, is that it was the sea which linked Bronze Age settlement together in the Baltic region. The settlement in eastern Denmark is generally restricted to a rather narrow zone along the coasts, no more than 4-5 km wide, of course following the shores into the fjords (Stjernquist 1983; Olausson 1992). Further inland the settlement tends to group along the major waterways, lakes and rivers - much like the Neolithic settlement, by the way. This does not only reflect a dependance upon maritime resources like fishing but certainly, and even more so, the need for and the importance of communication.

Nordic Bronze Age

In Scandinavia we only talk of the Early and Late Bronze Age. The (post Beaker) Dagger period is not normally included in the Bronze Age proper, which only begins at 1800 BC (Hvass and Storgaard 1993).

Denmark (in the sense before 1648 - i.e. including Scania, Halland, Blekinge and Bohuslän) is the richest part of Bronze Age Scandinavia with the only decent agricultural potential and with direct access to the Continent over land or by short distance across the Baltic. The Early Bronze Age finds are being published *in toto* in a magnificent series from 1972-2005 (Aner and Kersten 1972 ff) while for the Late Bronze Age you still have to rely on Evert Baudou's seminal work from 1960.

Denmark is also the region of the earthen barrows and of the concentration of gold and bronze work. The main expressions are:

1. The ubiquity of Bronze Age barrows characterises the whole region (Fig. 55). Their sheer number for the whole Nordic culture area probably

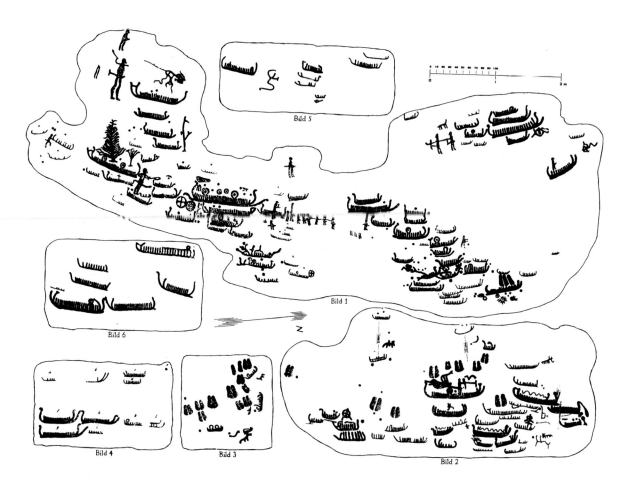

Fig. 53. Rock carving from Lökeberg, West Sweden (after Baltzer).

exceeds 150,000 (estimated at 50,000 in Denmark alone). Innumerable cooking pits and hundreds of cooking stone cairns mark the Bronze Age settlement in Sweden (Wigren 1987) and even down into Denmark as the Nordic parallel to the pyrotechnology evidenced by the Irish *fulachta fiadh.*

2. The continuity in the burial record from the corded ware period to Montelius Period II and the cremation burials from Period III to the Roman Iron Age (400 AD). The burial rite is probably the most European aspect with remarkable agreements between the Homeric rites and the actual graves. The famous log coffins give a floating dendrochronology (Hvass and Storgaard 1993), the urns are normally ordinary settlement pottery. It is still debated what the relationship of living population to the burials in the mounds really was.

3. The absurd wealth of metalwork. Counted per square km I doubt if any other European landscape will be able to compete with the central Danish landscapes for number (or weight) of bronze and gold objects. This is a paradox, as we must maintain that all metal had to be imported, traditionally from Central Europe (in spite of the existence of copper on Heligoland and in Central Sweden: Hjärthner-Holdar

1993). The abundance, diversity and associations of the metalwork mean that chronology is well founded, pottery and flints being the weak spots.

4. The diversity but also the continuity of votive hoarding through the Bronze Age into the opening generations of the Early Iron Age.

5. The ever more obvious continuity of the settlement evidence from middle Neolithic through to the late Middle Ages. While 40 years ago the situation was so bad that pastoralism and nomadic ways of living were resorted to as explanations for the absence of proper houses we now find the same general type of longhouses appearing even in North Scandinavia. The evolution of the main house type may be followed uninterrupted from 2500 BC to 1200 AD (Fig. 56) and the innovation may be seen to follow general trends in the North European lowland zone (Larsson *et al.* 1992).

From this list you may pick the elements which you will regard as common to the Nordic and the Irish Bronze Ages. I doubt whether there is much for you. As I see it we have in common the hoarding of metalwork, swords, tools and ornaments in bogs and that sort of place plus the making and use of great bronze horns (Pl. 32).

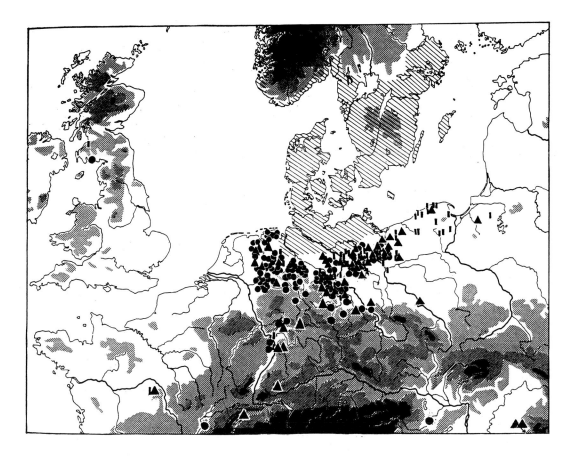

Fig. 54. The Nordic Bronze Age during Periods IV-V (hatched area) with Nordic objects found outside their presumed area of origin, I - swords, triangle - ornaments, dots - other types (after Thrane 1975, fig. 128).

One thing the Bronze Age did to people all over Europe was to teach them chemistry and to increase the communication across the Continent, even to the remotest parts, like subarctic Scandinavia. Whatever the local hunters may have imagined when they received a bronze sword or pin, it must have opened their eyes to the diversity of human experience outside their own woods.

This is how I would present a picture of a typical Danish or South Scandinavian Bronze Age settlement (referring to the recent statements in Hvass and Storgaard 1993 and in Larsson *et al.* 1992 and Tesch 1993 for further references):

A group of two to four families formed a sort of community, if not a closed village, rather an open hamlet/Weiler type of settlement, with two to four long houses spread out, each with its four-poster hayloft or granary next to it. The site would have been picked on high sandy ground. Fortified or even enclosed settlements are unknown with the exception of Vistad (Larsson 1993; see now Olausson 1995).

This group would have its ancestral tombs in a group (or groups) of barrows on high land in the vicinity. The landscape would be rather open - at least around the settlement with plenty of pasture. Pollen analyses show an increasingly open landscape and

heaths were already created in the early Bronze Age on the sandy soils of Jutland. Forest was certainly present and necessary for the timbers of the huge oak coffins and the substantial house constructions.

The long houses were three-aisled with living space in the west and sometimes with a stable in the other end (Tesch 1993). We know next to nothing of the interior arrangements.

The fields were quite small, ploughed with the ard and mainly used for growing wheat, barley and millet. The significance of the grain is indicated *inter alia* by fragments of bronze sickles found in many urn graves.

The relevance of the appearance of hulled barley in the Late Bronze Age as evidence of manuring of the fields is being discussed currently (Berglund 1991). Cattle probably played a more important role than just providing energy, meat and leather, certainly this was the case at the major site of Kirkebjerg on Funen. Pig and sheep were important, while the horse was kept more for status purposes than for labour.

The large permanent settlements produced enormous amounts of stone refuse from the cooking pits and this could be placed in cooking stone cairns. The average settlement was, however, less permanent, indeed rather labile, moving the houses probably every

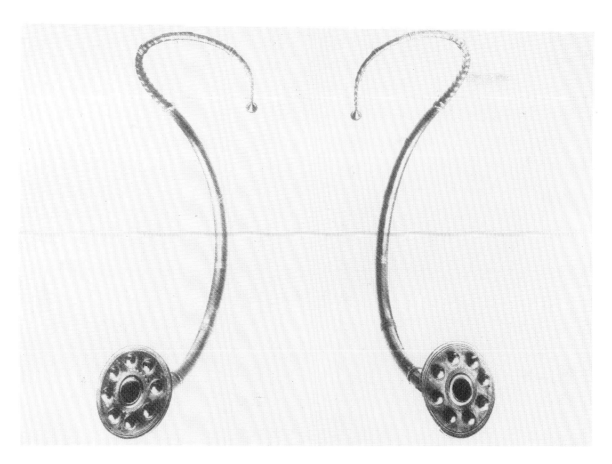

Pl. 32. Pair of lurs from Tellerup, Funen, Denmark, 900-700 BC. (Photo: National Museum, Copenhagen).

generation or so. This displacement of the actual settlement site was only short, keeping within the traditional territory of the individual group.

This territory bounded by natural borders like rivers and bogs would be *c.* 2-4 square km (Thrane 1991; Tesch 1993). The territory held more than the houses and fields, ritual places are known to us by sitting stones with cup marks, never far from the settlements themselves and by the hoards.

I assume that the primary settlements were grouped into larger, political units ruled by central authority, i.e. a chief. We only have evidence of this structure in the richer and more monumental graves but perhaps also in some of the very large houses. A hierarchy of settlement is indicated in Sweden as well as in Denmark.

Centres of power and prestige begin to loom large in current research (Thrane 1994). Ritual monuments like henges are absent from Scandinavia. Instead we have the rock carving sites along the North Baltic coasts and in Central Sweden. The major rock carving sites may well have functioned as regional ritual places, perhaps marking important borders in the communication routes, and are in some ways the best examples of central sites.

The individual chiefdoms probably functioned in a sort of network with other chiefdoms, neighbours

and further afield. The supply of metal and other valuables for the benefit of the chiefs and for the common good would be one important *raison d'être* for the chiefs and would probably drain quite a lot of resources from the local production. This of course implies a surplus production as well as a redistributive system.

The absence of military installations is remarkable, while the presence of swords, axes and spearheads is an eyecatcher right from the beginning of the Bronze Age proper (Period I). I hesitate to imply the existence of warrior retinues of the Tacitus type since much of the 'military' equipment is clearly symbolical; shields, helmets, ritual axes, swords with weak joints etc. would not have been much use except in mock fights. The substitute of a dagger for a sword in a full length scabbard from Muldbjerg (Boye 1896, pl. 10) implies not only a pious fraud but, perhaps more interesting, an interest in the inheritance of swords. Other metalwork implies not only high quality casting but also status and ritual (Pl. 32).

The contacts with foreign chiefs were presumably ritualized and would certainly have been organised traditionally in order to avoid unnecessary tension. I imagine summer expeditions across the Baltic with the initiative coming just as much from the North as from the East or the South.

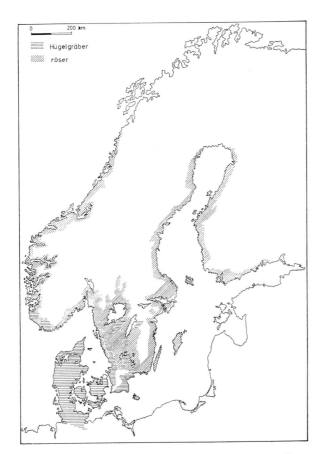

Fig. 55. Distribution of Bronze Age tumuli (Hügelgräber) and cairns (röser) in Scandinavia (after Hoops *Reallexikon der germanischen Altertumskunde* 3, p. 522).

The crucial issue at this stage of our deliberations is the same as usual all through the Nordic Metal Ages: what was supplied in exchange for all the metal? Was it an equal exchange, goods for goods? Somehow I doubt that we will ever find these goods. The amber trade which de Navarro institutionalised by his amber route map may be part of the phenomenon but I very much doubt whether it was more than that.

Through the contacts across the Baltic the continuing innovation which is such a characteristic feature of the Nordic Bronze Age was maintained with a remarkable ability to follow the trends of Central Europe.

Twenty years ago I characterised the Nordic Late Bronze Age thus: 'In nearly every aspect of South Scandinavian culture there is some foreign element at one stage or the other. The essence of the Nordic Bronze Age and that which makes it unique is the talent for transforming every foreign impulse into something special marked by the hallmark of local tradition' (Thrane 1975, 263).

I admit that this was perhaps influenced by my attitude to the then European Community and I cannot escape that contemporary bond now in 1995. I think, however, that there may be an historical truth

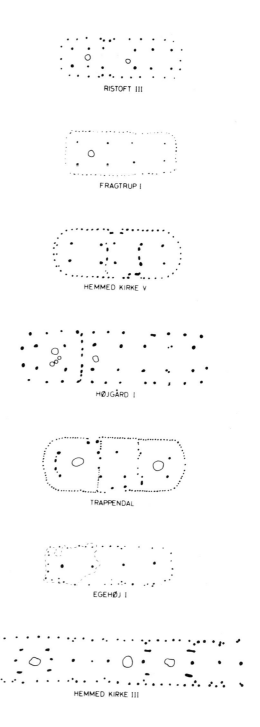

Fig. 56. House plans from Denmark, lower four are Periods II-III, the upper three Late Bronze Age Periods IV-VI (after Hvass and Storgaard 1993, 137).

in it too. You may call it the Nordic mental attitude: we are quite good at adapting ourselves to new impulses and demands and challenges. This may be seen not only at home but also when we expand - look at England, but kindly forget Sicily and Russia, where the natives swallowed us.

In a European context it may be just as relevant to look at parallel developments as the traditional examination of metalwork movements from one region to the other. I have found much inspiration in this conference presentation of recent Irish Bronze Age research and am convinced that there may be a lot more to learn from the study of various European Bronze Ages than from comparisons with exotic ethnographic cultures.

References

Aner, E. and Kersten K. 1972. *Die Funde der älteren Bronzezeit des nordischen Kreises in Dänemark, Schleswig-Holstein und Niedersachsen I.* Neumünster.

Baudou, E. 1960. *Regionale und chronologische Einteilung der jüngeren Bronzezeit im Nordischen Kreis.* Stockholm.

Becker, C. J. 1949. An Irish Bronze Cauldron found in Jutland. *Acta Archaeologica* 20, 265-70.

Berglund, B. E. (ed.). 1991. The Cultural Landscape during 6000 Years in Southern Sweden. *Ecological Bulletins* 41.

Boye, V. 1896. *Fund af Egekister fra Bronzealderen i Danmark* [also in French]. København. New edition 1986. Aarhus.

Butler, J. J. 1963. Bronze Age connections across the North Sea. *Palaeohistoria* 9. Groningen.

Butler, J. J. 1988. Drouwen: the end of a 'Nordic' rainbow? *Palaeohistoria* 28, 133-68.

Butler, J. J. 1989, Bronze Age Connections: France and the Netherlands. *Palaeohistoria* 29, 9-34.

Christensen, A. E. 1995. Boat Fragments from Mangersnes. In Olsen *et al.* (eds), 73-80.

Coles, J. M. 1960. Scottish Late Bronze Age Metalwork. *Proceedings of the Society of Antiquaries of Scotland* 93, 16-134.

Coles, J. M. 1962. European Bronze Shields. *Proceedings of the Prehistoric Society* 28, 156-90.

Crumlin-Pedersen, O. 1983. Schiffe und Seehandelsrouten. *Lübecker Schriften zur Archäologie und Kulturgeschichte* 7, 229-37.

Crumlin-Pedersen, O. 1985. Havne og søfart i romersk og germansk jernalder. *Skrifter fra historisk institut, Odense Universitet* 33, 68-92. Odense (In German in *Frühmittelalterliche Studien* 21, 101-23).

Crumlin-Pedersen, O. (ed.). 1995. *Atlas over Fyns kyst i jernalder, vikingetid og middelalder.* Odense.

Crumlin-Pedersen, O. and Rieck, F. 1988. *Både fra Danmarks Oldtid.* Roskilde.

Ellmers, D. 1981. Der Nachtsprung an eine hinter dem Horizont liegende Gegenkünste. *Deutsches Schiffartarchiv* 4, 153-67.

Ellmers, D. 1995. Crew Structure on Board Scandinavian Vessels. In Olsen *et al.* (eds), 231-40.

Evans, A. and Bruce-Mitford, R. 1975. The Ship. In R. Bruce-Mitford (ed.), *The Sutton Hoo Ship Burial*, 345-435. London.

Fett, E. Nissen and P. Fett. 1979. Relations West Norway-Western Europe documented in Petroglyphs. *Norwegian Archaeological Review* 12, 65-107.

Fredsjö, Å. 1981. Rock-carvings Kville härad Kville

Parish (County of Bohuslän). *Studies in North European Archaeology* 14/15, Gothenburg.

Green, C. 1988. *Sutton Hoo: The Excavation of a Royal Shipburial.* London.

Harbison, P. 1970. Irish Early Bronze Age Exports found on the Continent and their Derivatives. *Palaeohistoria* 14, 175-86.

Hjärthner-Holdar, E. 1993. *Järnets och järnmetallurgins introduktion i Sverige.* Uppsala.

Hvass. S. and Storgaard, B. 1993. *Digging into the Past.* Allingåbro.

Jensen, J., Sørensen, J. N., Rieck, F. and Aistrup, M. S. 1989. *Hjortspringbåden genopstillet, Nationalmuseets Arbejdsmark,* 101-14.

Johansen, E. 1979. Utsyn og innsyn fra Kjøkøyvasden. *Universitetets Oldsaksamling 150 År*, 88-95. Oslo.

Larsson. L., J. Callmer and B. Stjernquist (eds). 1992. The Archaeology of the Cultural Landscape. *Acta Archaeologica Lundensia series in 4o.* No. 19.

Larsson, T. B. 1993. Vistad kring en befast gård i Östergötland och östersjökontakter under yngre bronsålder. *Studia Archaeologica Universitatis Umensis* 4. Umeå.

McGrail, S. 1990. Boats and boatmanship in the late prehistoric southern North Sea and Channel region. In S. McGrail *et al.* (eds). *Maritime Celts, Frisians and Saxons*, 32-48. London.

Marsden, P. 1995. Early Ships, boats and ports in Britain In Olsen *et al.* (ed.), 167-74.

Marstrander, S. 1963. *Østfolds jordbruksristninger. Skjeberg.* Oslo.

Meinander, C. F. 1954. *Die Bronzezeit in Finland. Finska Fornminnesförenings Tidskrift* 54. Helsinki.

Müller, S. 1919. Bronzealderens Bopladser. *Aarbøger for nordisk Oldkyndighed og Historie* 1919, 35-105. København.

Nielsen, P. O., K. Randsborg and H. Thrane (eds). 1994. *The Archaeology of Gudme and Lundeborg.* Odense.

O'Connor, B. 1980. *Cross-Channel Relations in the Later Bronze Age. British Archaeological Reports International Series* 91. Oxford.

Olausson, D. 1992. The Archaeology of the Bronze Age Cultural Landscape. In Larsson *et al.* (eds), 251-82.

Olausson, M. 1995. Det inneslutna rummet. *Arkeologiska undersökningar Skrifter* nr 9. Stockholm.

Olsen, O., J. Skamby Madsen and F. Rieck (eds), 1995. *Shipshape, Essays for Ole Crumlin-Pedersen.* Holbaek.

Rausing, G. 1984. *Prehistoric Boats and Ships of Northwestern Europe.* Lund.

Stjernquist, B. 1983. Gravarna som källa till kunskapen om den yngre bronsälders bebyggelse i Skåne. In B. Stjernquist (ed.), *Struktur och förändring i bronsålderns samhälle, 130-40. University of Lund Institute of Archaeology Report Series* no. 17. Lund.

Tesch, S. 1993. *Houses, Farmsteads, and Long-term Change.* Lund.

Thrane, H. 1975. *Europaeiske forbindelser. Nationalmuseets skrifter arkaeologisk-historisk raekke* 16. Odense.

Thrane, H. 1979. Fremde Bronzegefässe in südskandinawischen Funde aus der jüngeren Bronzezeit (Period

V). *Acta Archaeologica* 49, 1-36.

Thrane, H. 1991. Territoriality in a Bronze Age Landscape. In K. Jennbert *et al.* (eds), *Regions and Reflections, Acta Archaeologica Lundensia series in 8°*, 20, 119-128. Lund.

Thrane, H. 1994. Centres of Wealth in Northern Europe. In K. Kristiansen and J. Jensen (eds), *Europe in the First Millennium BC*, 95-110. Sheffield.

Westerdahl, C. 1991. Norrlandsleden: The Maritime Cultural Landscape of the Norrland Sailing Route. In O. Crumlin-Pedersen (ed.), *Aspects of Maritime Scandinavia AD 200-1200*, 105-20. Roskilde.

Westerdahl, C. 1995. Traditional Zones of Transport Geography in Relation to Ship Types. In Olsen *et al.* (eds), 213-30.

Wigren, S. 1987. *Södermanländsk bronsåldersbygd, Theses and Papers in Nordic Archaeology* 16. Edsbruk.

Wright, E. 1990. *The Ferriby Boats – Seacraft of the Bronze Age*. London.

Celts, Celticisation and the
Irish Bronze Age

John Waddell

Abstract

It is argued that the emergence of a Celtic language in Ireland was the culmination of a long process of social and economic interaction between Ireland and Britain, and between these islands and adjacent parts of Continental Europe. For Ireland, the Irish Sea was one crucial factor in this process, facilitating contact and enabling this island to share in the European phenomenon of the creation of the larger speech communities of later prehistory. This model of 'becoming Celtic-speaking' demands that we should examine even more closely the nature and the degree of contact between Ireland and Britain and the Continent. However, the archaeological data needs to be studied in its own right, free of ethnic 'Celtic' labels and preconceptions. Presumptions about a modern common Celticity have tended to impose a similar and equally questionable construction on the ancient 'Celtic World'. Celticisation, becoming Celtic-speaking, was a Bronze Age process.

The title of this contribution might be considered doubly unfortunate: the 'Bronze Age' is claimed to be an out-moded concept, useful perhaps as a general chapter heading but no longer an indication of an important theme in prehistory (Barrett 1994). 'Celticisation' may mean, in the narrow sense employed here, 'becoming Celtic-speaking' but, like the name Celt, it inevitably raises a plethora of cultural, ethnic and other issues.

To complicate matters further, the question of 'who spoke what?' in prehistory is, of course, one inherently incapable of resolution and most sensible prehistorians do not succumb to the temptation to speculate. But the question is important nonetheless because it forces us to confront the essence of human communication on a particular and on a general level. It also forces us to examine many aspects of society, such as structure, demography, trade and exchange, and the problem of ethnic identity. Archaeology is equipped to address some of these issues and if we cannot conclusively answer the general question, at the very least we can attempt to harmonise the archaeological and the linguistic models employed.

What language was spoken in Neolithic Ireland? According to Colin Renfrew (in his 1987 *Archaeology and Language*) it was an Indo-European tongue disseminated with the demographic changes associated with the transition to an agricultural economic system; it was a pre-Indo-European language according to J. P. Mallory's 1989 *In Search of the Indo-Europeans* in which the traditional view of a late Neolithic or early Bronze Age dispersal of Indo-European folk is

cogently argued. There are alternative views of course: one compromise is offered by Zvelebil and Zvelebil (1988) and to a great extent, one or other solution to the two extremes is acceptable depending on the primacy given to either the linguistic or the archaeological evidence (Yoffee 1990). Whatever solution is adopted, there is general agreement that some Indo-European language or languages could have been spoken in these islands, and indeed over a much wider area of Europe, at the beginning of the Bronze Age.

We should probably envisage a complex mosaic of interacting mono- or bilingual communities (some Indo-European, some non-Indo-European), but all interlinking linguistically in various ways with their neighbouring communities. This early prehistoric picture is not a static one – but one of constant and dynamic flux. The dynamic nature of linguistic interaction needs to be stressed and this is well illustrated in modern sociolinguistics, in the study of dialect chaining and various forms of language mixing. However, according to the traditional Neo-grammarian historical linguistic model, language groups such as Common Germanic, Slavonic, and Common Celtic emerged in time from the parent Indo-European. Common Celtic (or Proto-Celtic), ancestral to Brittonic, Goidelic and other Celtic languages such as Hispano-Celtic (or Celtiberian) and Gaulish, developed in a Continental 'homeland' from whence the Celtic languages spread to various parts of 'the Celtic World' including Britain and Ireland (Fig. 57). This is an enduring belief, as one writer recently put it: 'that the Celts arrived in Britain and Ireland from the mainland of Europe can be taken as certain, but there is a great deal of uncertainty about the circumstances in which they arrived' (Price 1987, 6). Or as another has said: 'the Celts of the Hallstatt and particularly the La Tène period spread over the whole of Europe . . .' (Schmidt 1992, 44). Indeed McCone (1994, 63) believes the first speakers of a Celtic tongue arrived in Ireland as late as about 200 BC. Maps like Fig. 57 showing homelands and varying directions of Celtic expansion figure in recent works such as *Celtic Art* (Megaw and Megaw 1989, fig. 2), *Art of the Celts* (Laing and Laing 1992, fig. 10) and *The Celtic World* (Green 1995, xxiv).

The genetic, family tree, model of linguistic reconstruction, which implies divergence as the significant factor in language change (Fig. 58a), has supported and has been supported by migrationary archaeological theories. The inevitable equation of attested Celtic languages such as Goidelic or Brittonic with a people such as 'Q-Celts' and 'P-Celts' or with a material culture has had a long history. In Ireland, various writers have, in the past, equated 'the coming of the Celts' with the introduction of such archaeological phenomena as the knowledge of iron or a La Tène art style. This prolonged and convoluted debate has been summarised in Waddell (1991, 1991a). In 1928, for example, R. A. S. Macalister stated in his *Archaeology of Ireland* that the Celts came to Ireland at the inception of the Iron Age *c*. 400 BC; they were few in numbers but subdued the pre-Celtic aborigines with their superior iron weapons. The notion of Bronze Age Celts, however, is not a new one. In 1889 Sir John Rhys suggested that the round barrows of the British Bronze Age were the work of invading Celts, a view also proposed by Lloyd in his *History of Wales* in 1911 and by Hubert in his 1932 *Les Celtes et l'expansion celtique*.

Others in the 1920s and 1930s attributed early Celticisation to the late Bronze Age 'sword-bearers'. O. G. S. Crawford published an influential paper in 1922 in which he argued that 'towards the close of the Bronze Age the British Isles were invaded by the first wave of Celtic-speaking peoples bringing with them leaf-shaped bronze swords, many other new types of bronze objects, and at least two types of pottery new to these islands'. A few years later, in 1930, Estyn Evans, influenced by the work of Cyril Fox, suggested that in the Highland Zone of Britain and in Ireland the new language was acquired by a process of absorption: 'it is not unlikely that with this absorption, and without any important movement of peoples, the first Celtic language brought by the invaders from the Celtic Cradle may have reached the west, replacing a primitive tongue of pre-Aryan type'.

Here we have an early recognition that the archaeological record in this island did not offer convincing evidence for intrusive Celts on any scale.

In the late 1960s Myles Dillon, who had studied Indo-European elements in early Irish tradition, reverted to older notions of early Bronze Age Celts and suggested that they might even be identified with the 'Beaker Folk' around 2000 BC (Dillon and Chadwick 1967; Dillon 1968). He was aware that most scholars dated the first Celtic settlements in Britain as late as 600 BC but he argued that the great archaism of Irish tradition in language, literature and social organisation made such an early date a probability. Today such wide linguistic disagreement seems to be a thing of the past; now, at least in this one area, a measure of consensus is evident: these islands became Celtic-speaking in later prehistoric times (MacEoin 1986; Schmidt 1994). But how this came about is still the subject of some disagreement in both archaeological and linguistic circles.

The saga of controversy and argument as to how Ireland became Celtic-speaking has been a long one but the recent debate on the origins of the Irish may be firmly blamed on J. P. Mallory who initiated a conference on this subject in Belfast in 1984. There was general agreement then that Celtic emerged in the last millennium BC and some consensus that this could not be explained satisfactorily without some reference to an intrusion of people though this was not recognisable in the archaeological record of either the later Bronze Age or the Iron Age. My suggestion that a prestige goods economy reflecting the interaction of regional élites may have been a primary factor in the emergence of an insular Celtic language was not received with great enthusiasm. However, alternative models of language diffusion were at least being canvassed. Piggott (1979, 1983) had suggested that prestige gift exchange formed a mobile upper class archaeology and that the transmission of the Celtic languages might have occurred in this way too. Koch (1986, 16) agreed: 'given the importance of metal weapons and ornaments for the tribal hierarchs to superordinate and define themselves, the *koiné* of the metal trade might naturally have become a prestige speech which distinguished the upper strata from a peasantry whose limited means excluded them from this cosmopolitan market'.

In 1987 Renfrew proposed a convergence model of Celtic linguistic development and adapted Christopher Hawkes' concept of 'cumulative Celticity' which ascribed the Celticisation of Britain and Ireland to the continuing accumulation of new, upper class, Celtic-speaking masters. Renfrew suggested that peer polity interaction contributed to the emergence of the Celtic languages from generalised Indo-European

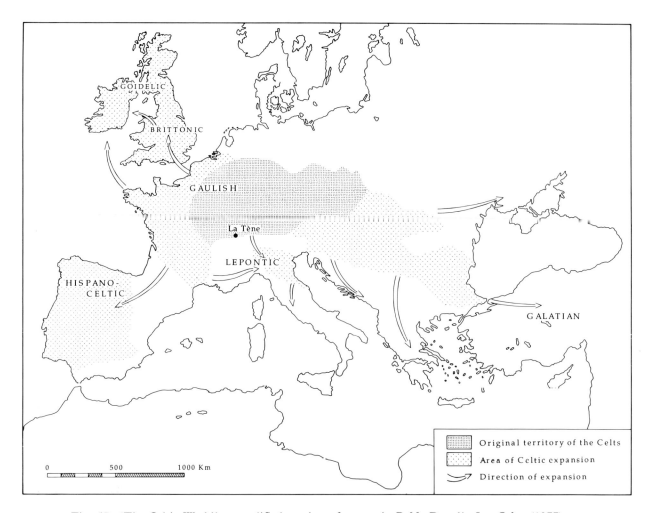

Fig. 57. 'The Celtic World': a modified version of a map in P.-M. Duval's *Les Celtes* (1977).

'essentially in those areas where their speech is later attested' there being no one localised Celtic 'homeland'. The homelands of the Celts would be constituted by the full extent of the area where Celtic languages came to be spoken (always excluding such later offshoots as Galatia). He envisaged a process of parallel development precipitated by the élite elements of ranked societies.

There are alternatives to the phylogenetic linguistic model which are more in keeping with a processual archaeological approach. Robb (1993), for instance, has proposed a non-genetic model of the prehistory of European languages in which the rate of the creation and demise of languages (due to a variety of social processes) will change through time. Large language areas would have been a feature of the Palaeolithic and Mesolithic and throughout this long period the small number of language families would probably fluctuate around an average (represented by the vertical line in Fig. 58b). Increasing sedentism and population growth in the Mesolithic and earlier Neolithic, and the formation of small, self-sufficient territorial groups would have produced a considerable increase in the number of languages spoken. Language proliferation would have halted and then declined in the later Neolithic and throughout the Bronze Age with the gradual formation of fewer, larger language groups.

The emergence of a Celtic language or languages in later prehistory would be due to an intensification of a complex series of processes operating across parts of Europe since the 3rd millennium BC: these would have included economic intensification, increasing polity size, developing gender and social stratification, and increasingly active trade along coasts and rivers. Factors such as a vertical social continuum (perhaps represented by some form of clientship) allowing for reciprocal linguistic contacts at every level in a hierarchical society, may have been important too. Koch (1991, 18) sees the developments in the later Irish Bronze Age from about 1300 BC as significant in this respect. The more aristocratic and warlike nature of society, the conspicuous display in fine weaponry and ornament and the deposition of fine metalwork in pits and in watery contexts (a shift towards a chthonic religion) all find parallels in Britain

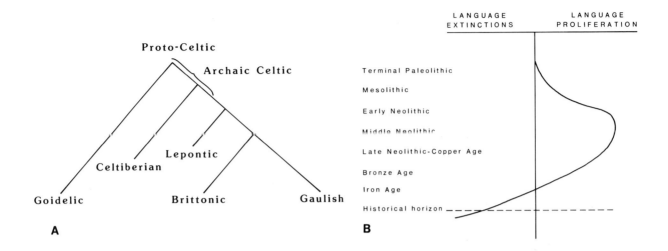

Fig. 58. a: Phylogenetic model of the Celtic language family (after Schmidt 1992a).
b: Hypothetical trajectory of prehistoric European languages (after Robb 1993).

and on the Continent and reflect a social and cultural reordering 'in all respects recognisably Celtic'. Marisa Ruiz-Galvez (1991) has argued that the Atlantic seaways of the Iberian peninsula may have been important vectors of linguistic change and development. She suggests that Lusitanian in western Iberia developed as a pre-Celtic trade language on the Atlantic coasts of the peninsula and became the dominant language between the Tagus and the Douro. The status of Lusitanian is debated – some believe it to be pre-Celtic as she claims, but others have argued that it is a Celtic dialect related to Hispano-Celtic. In any event, the development of stable settlement, of technological improvements including complex ship-building techniques and of long distance exchange were all significant factors in the process of its development. Changes in social structure, including greater ranking and greater social complexity were equally important. She emphasises that, as history demonstrates, intense and continuous trade contacts imply the arrival and establishment of small groups of people who are immensely influential and active in the communities in which they find themselves.

There is abundant sociolinguistic evidence to illustrate the importance of trade and sea-borne contact in the spheres of language change and development: among the conditions which determine the nature and outcome of language contact, new language needs and consequent patterns of use 'those of the economic environment play a crucial role' (Coulmas 1992, 154).

While, as elsewhere, Ireland had its own regional idiosyncrasies, there is good evidence that it participated at an élite level in wider European fashions in the later Bronze Age. This evidence consists of a

range of metal types and some items, notably bronze spears and shields, and finely decorated or crafted objects of gold or bronze, of various dates, are justifiably seen as prestigious possessions, some probably for ostentatious display. There is some evidence too that social stratification became more marked in the later Bronze Age. There are significant gaps in the archaeological record but the broad picture is a fairly consistent one.

I suspect that the intensity of Ireland's contacts with Britain, across that relatively modest body of water, the Irish Sea, has been underestimated. A multitude of small craft must have plied both Irish rivers and coastal waters throughout prehistory. The high seas would rarely have been used, long distance travel by sea was the exception rather than the rule until relatively recent times. Brief sea voyages which rarely, if ever, took the seafarer out of sight of land were the norm. On the coast a variety of boats would have hugged the land and provided a labyrinthine network of contacts around these shores and across the Irish Sea. Fernand Braudel's evocative picture of the ancient Mediterranean with voyagers 'moving crab-like from rock to rock, from promontories to islands and from islands to promontories' may be applied to this part of the world as well. The archaeological evidence suggests that the Irish Sea, far from being a barrier to communication, may have been a focal area for interaction and exchange, displaying evidence for recurring cycles of contact over long periods of time.

There is no shortage of distribution maps of Bronze Age material to illustrate this point (Waddell 1992, figs 2ff.). For the earlier Bronze Age, the distribution of a characteristically Irish type of early Bronze Age pottery vessel, the Irish Bowl, suggests a significant pattern of contact with south-west Scotland, and to a lesser extent with the Isle of Man and south-west Wales. A limited amount of analysis suggests that most pottery vessels of this sort were made of more or less local clays and, in all probability, were not exported any great distance. But how pottery fashions themselves were transmitted over wider areas is not at all clear. Since these bowls come mainly from burials, it is possible that we are witnessing the spread of some ritual rather than something like the exogamous movement of female potters. Whatever the transmission mechanism, the distribution of a pottery fashion is very likely to be an indication of an integrated social network at some level.

The Cordoned Urn is an Irish-Scottish type (Waddell 1995) and most examples come from funerary contexts, invariably with cremated burials, but finds from coastal sandhills in northern Ireland and in Scotland are a reminder that the exploitation of coastal resources was part of the spectrum of economic activity of the makers of these vessels. Island finds are particularly interesting, besides the Isle of Man, urns are recorded from Aran, on the Atlantic coast in the west of Ireland, Arran and Bute in Scotland and Anglesea in north Wales. It is a possibility that the makers of cordoned urns were among the important middlemen in the transmission of the products of the copper workshops of the south-west of Ireland to the north-east of that island and across the North Channel to Scotland. The concentration of these urns in Counties Antrim and Down is noteworthy; this was an area of important metal workshops. The distribution of the Collared Urn Tradition may imply a more extensive use of the Irish Sea basin. Here, however, an essentially English phenomenon impinges mainly on the eastern half of Ireland. The widespread distributions of both these Urn Traditions are particularly difficult to explain. Older notions of the migration of various 'Urn Folk' seem less than adequate today but the significant degree of standardisation in burial rite and general pot shape, which transcend the regional differences that do exist, imply something more than the mere diffusion of a pottery fashion. Once more, a possible explanation may lie in an extensive and intricate system of interaction between communities, this complex pattern of communication serving to impose and maintain a measure of uniformity sufficient to publicly demonstrate participation in a symbolic activity which conferred some measure of social approbation. Clearly the networks of relationships and the social imperatives were both sufficiently strong and compelling to allow their material expression to cover great distances and to traverse the Irish Sea.

The pottery fashions instanced here disappear from the archaeological record at the end of the earlier Bronze Age but the contacts they represent were only a part of a wider spectrum of activity which must have included some of the contemporary metal exchanges; these presumably continued and intensified in the later Bronze Age.

New patterns of interaction do seem to have developed from about 1300 BC, novel gold and bronze types appear and there are significant developments in weaponry. Many of these innovations indicate long distance exchange networks and it has been plausibly argued that élite elements of ranked societies were now major participants in the exchange process and that their political power and status rested to some degree on their ability to control the distribution and value of certain prestigious objects. A whole range of material indicates that Ireland shared in the social transformations taking place elsewhere, both in Britain and on the Continent. Gold objects like the ornate neck-rings called bar torcs are generally believed to have been the prestigious possessions of such a social élite. Though mainly an Irish-British fashion, a significant number of these torcs have been found in France, mostly in the north-west. Their insular distribution implies that they may have been a limited element in a pattern of alliances across the North Channel but a significant feature of traffic across the southern half of the Irish Sea with north Wales playing a central role (Fig. 59).

One of the earliest types of bronze sword in these islands is the Ballintober sword type and it seems to be a weapon form favoured for some reason in the northern half of Ireland and the southern half of England. The type may have been first developed in the Thames Valley which was clearly an important area of sword manufacture as well as being a crucial link with the Continent (Fig. 60). Though the nature of the alliances postulated is not at all clear, it is tempting to speculate that a scatter of dots like this may conceivably be an echo of the competing ambitions of a network of major and minor chiefs. Significant imports are rare but the Kurd buckets from the Dowris hoard and from Nannau in Wales may be instanced: they had a profound effect on subsequent sheet bronze vessel production. Sabine Gerloff (1986) places them at the head of the insular series of buckets and cauldrons.

The identification of regional assemblages has proved difficult in Ireland but George Eogan has demonstrated two significant concentrations of fine metalwork in his Dowris Phase, one in the region of the Shannon Estuary, the other in the north-east of the country. The Shannon assemblage, which includes distinctive gold gorgets, so-called hair ornaments and bowls also of gold, and some bronze horns or trumpets, illustrates the real difficulty in identifying possible routes of long distance exchange (Eogan

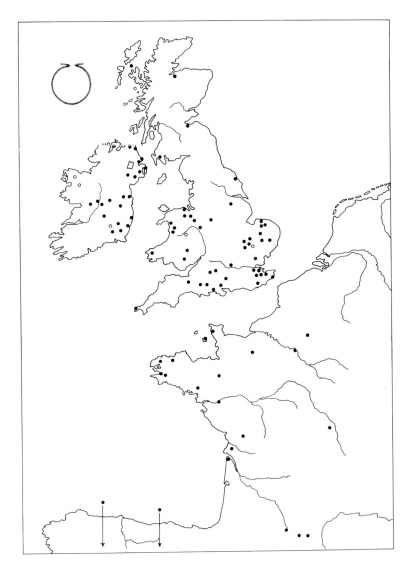

Fig. 59. Distribution of gold torcs (after Logan 1994).

1993). However, Kristiansen (1993) has demonstrated how this may be done in other circumstances with the identification of a series of interacting élite centres stretching from northern Europe to northern Italy in the 8th century BC.

The Irish-British examples of the bronze Gündlingen sword, in use at the beginning of the Iron Age, show that mutual contact continued, as indeed did Continental contacts, for the form is a variant of a wider European sword type. Apart from once again noting the importance of the Thames Valley, the scattered distribution elsewhere in these islands provides few clues as to how the fashion was actually disseminated. As with the earlier Ballintober swords it would be wrong to imagine a uniform weapon type distributed across both islands. Minor typological details occasionally permit the identification of Irish pieces in Britain and vice versa, as Colquhoun and Burgess (1988) have shown. Again what is important, however, is not so much where the type originated, or where a particular sword was made and how far

it may have been transported, but the general impression the distribution map presents of a shared fashion and the communication this implies some time in the middle of the last millennium BC.

Numerous other types of artefacts also demonstrate the importance of the Irish Sea in the Bronze Age: pottery, including Beaker and some Vase Tradition pottery as well as Trevisker ware, and a whole range of other metal types. Iron Age material should be considered too, these patterns of contact did not cease with the end of the Bronze Age. The demise of the bronze industry at this time is as dramatic a transformation as the disappearance of those burial practices of the earlier Bronze Age almost a thousand years before, and it has prompted catastrophic explanations. If, as seems likely, bronze had an important role in the maintenance of status relationships, then iron working may well have disrupted this structure and precipitated a decline in associated customs like hoard deposition. It does not necessarily follow that there was a wider socio-economic collapse since bronze was

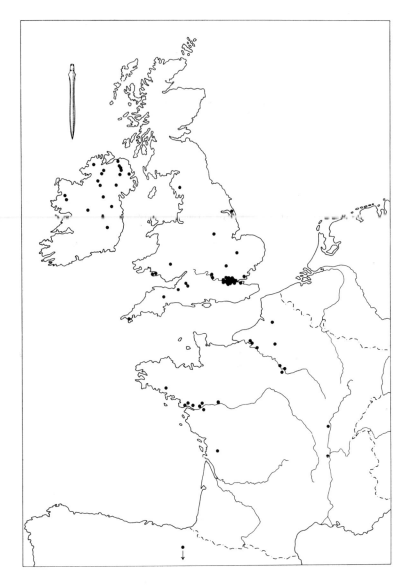

Fig. 60. Distribution of Ballintober and related swords (after Eogan 1965 and Colquhoun and Burgess 1988; Continental distribution after Gomez 1987).

probably just one element, admittedly a prestigious one, in a wider spectrum of activity. Cooney and Grogan (1994, 180) have have argued convincingly that there is considerable continuity in other spheres in the period in question from about 600 to about 300 BC. If there was some disruption, then the hiatus was to prove a temporary one for a whole series of artefacts, from beehive querns to decorated bronzes, demonstrates a wide range of contacts across the Irish Sea before and after the turn of the millennium (Raftery 1984).

What sort of picture may we now have of prehistoric contact between the two islands? Is it in fact a picture of varying and sporadic connections as sometimes claimed, or is it possible to suggest another pattern? It has to be admitted that the interpretation of archaeological distribution maps is fraught with difficulty. It is not easy to identify the mechanisms which produced a particular distribution and many factors may distort the issue. These difficulties have been

recently considered by Needham (1993) who suggests that such maps should be called maps of recovery, given that they are the products of various possible taphonomic processes and at a minimal level they reflect the 'displacement' of goods, exchange being but one aspect of displacement. No doubt various forms of displacement await identification in the series of maps I have referred to. Consideration of how material finds its way into what we call the archaeological record raises the question of the prior 'life-cycle' of the objects themselves. Needham points out that 'a life-cycle takes place between the acts of production (or extraction) and deposition; these two points, or "nodes", alone being capable of archaeological definition, account for the set of data in a map of recovery. Yet it is life-cycles that are the key to the definition of exchange and other forms of transmission, in order to get beyond mere recognition of displacement'.

Thus some of the patterns recorded on our maps

may well be the visible expression at a particular time for a particular reason, of a deeper rooted and longer lasting network of relationships, the dots being just the archaeologically visible elements of a much more intricate pattern of social interaction. Some may reflect a web of communities, perhaps linked by kinship over a period of many centuries. This sort of interaction may have been a perennial feature of the Irish Sea region and I would argue that its constancy has been underestimated. The prehistoric reality may have been a constant pattern of communication, the Irish Sea and its hinterlands being a focal area for interaction and exchange over the 'longue durée' of almost two millennia of the Bronze Age. It is even possible that the degree of traffic of people and kin across the North Channel, for instance, may have been sufficiently regular to constitute a 'migration stream' in both directions. In the Irish Sea region in general, the patterns of contact may have shifted from time to time, and different regional systems of interrelationships may have operated in different places, perhaps making the term 'culture province' inappropriate, but constantly recurring cyles of contact over such a long time span must have had interminable consequences in many spheres not least in terms of linguistic developments.

The degree to which the island of Ireland participated in this pattern of socio-economic interaction is probably one of the difficulties uppermost in the minds of many Irish historical linguists and archaeologists. Koch (1991) however would agree that proto-Celtic was consolidated in the prestige economies of the late Bronze Age (*c.* 1300-600 BC) 'in which an Atlantic Zone with centres in Armorica, south-east England, south Wales, Ireland, and later on Iberia, was in a continuous close contact with, and generally followed the cultural lead of, Urnfield/Hallstatt C west-central Europe'. He has also argued that invasion is not 'at the heart of the social process of Insular Celticisation which depended rather upon the spread of heroic values through exchange and competition within a stable network, and not upon overwhelming force or population replacement'. But other historical linguists may well ask if the supposed contacts were sufficiently constant and intense to initiate and maintain the linguistic developments envisaged here. Evans (1992, 9) would consider any attempt to mate a processual view of archaeology with an assumed processual view of Celtic linguistic formation 'an especially hazardous exercise'.

Many would probably agree with Koch (1991, 17) that 'by any reckoning the Celticisation of the British Isles was one of the great events of Insular prehistory' but would still believe, in some form, in 'the coming' of at least some Celts (Mallory 1989, 1991, 1992;

Warner 1991). It is interesting, in this regard, to note that Barry Raftery's recent study of the Irish Iron Age, *Pagan Celtic Ireland*, which deals only briefly with this problem, concludes that 'it seems almost heretical to conclude that a Celtic invasion of Ireland never happened' (1994, 228).

This is not the place to pursue the argument that the role of maritime contacts in precipitating language development may be underestimated. However, one of the main vectors for language spread is trade, whatever the conditions of the exchange and the form of goods traded (up to and including people, in which case the 'commodity' can actually become an agent of change). It would in fact be surprising if, in what may well have been a multilingual environment, the level of material displacement evidenced by archaeological research had not resulted in some pattern of language spread and the adoption of a *lingua franca*, particularly in coastal regions of early Europe and, of course, particularly in islands with extensive coastlines such as Ireland and Britain.

The debate about how these islands became Celtic speaking will undoubtedly continue and progress will be made - not merely in the realm of archaeological research but also in the promising field of molecular genetics which may help to untangle some ancient ethnic knots (Bodmer 1993).

As mentioned at the beginning of this paper the term 'Celticisation' presents difficulties. Like 'Celt' it has more than linguistic significance for many people and like the phrase 'the Celtic World' it may seem to suggest a degree of cultural homogeneity which is, to say the least, disputable. It is not surprising that the widespread distribution of linguistic evidence or of elements of material culture like sword, fibula or art style should inspire the idea that 'in early times the Celts (whether or not they were themselves aware of the fact) were an ethnically identifiable group' (Price 1992, 2). Such perceptions and the extent to which 'common factors in material culture, and rural economy, no less than in social institutions and language' (to use Powell's phrase: 1958, 65) were characteristic of 'the Celtic World' as a whole is now the subject of some healthy scrutiny. Old myths, like the notion of a 'Celtic church', are being re-evaluated (Davies 1992). To date, however, greater attention has been paid to more recent Celtic mythologies: for example Sims-Williams (1986) on the racial stereotype of the visionary Celt, McDonald (1986) on the creation of modern Breton Celticity, Dietler (1994) on Celtic identity in both France and the European Union, Leerssen (1994) on the west of Ireland as part of the 'Celtic Fringe', and particularly Chapman (1992) who examines the question of Celtic ethnic identity past and present. Chapman points out that the common modern definition of the ancient Celts is a scholarly and retrospective one with limitations that are not always recognised; there is no evidence that the Celts of the last millennium BC considered themselves to be Celts and had a unitary language. It may be added that even if there was a significant degree of linguistic unity between adjacent regions, as may have been the case, the presence of a broadly common language in a series of geographical locations does not of itself imply shared ethnic identity or even a *sense* of shared identity.

Celtic identities are in great measure a nineteenth and twentieth-century construct and the investigation of these concepts is important because they have shaped modern scholarship. Modern presumptions about a common Celticity have tended to impose a similar vision on the past. Naive or exaggerated ideas about cultural and racial integrity have inevitably produced a bogus historiography which has hindered archaeological analysis. Self-stereotypes are not peculiar to modern 'Celts' of course but some of the quainter misconceptions are well known and include, for instance, a belief in 'the good people', in such engaging qualities as a special loquaciousness and in the existence of a 'Celtic approach to life' (Severy 1977, 619).

Fortunately there is a growing body of archaeological work which is beginning to delineate the many problems posed by 'Celtic' archaeology particularly in the realms of settlement, social structure, religion and art. Champion (1987) has remarked that 'Iron Age studies have been hijacked by a special concern with the Celts deeply rooted in nineteenth century thinking' and Hill (1989, 1995) has called for a different approach to this period, one untrammelled by Celtic labels (and with less emphasis on the exciting bits such as Mediterranean contacts, princely graves and oppida). Champion has also examined the question of Celtic migrations (1980), the written sources for the wider Iron Age (1985), and the variegated nature of 'Celtic society' in time and space (1995). Collis (1986) would reject the idea that certain cultural assemblages can be labelled 'Celtic' and has also has remarked upon the different sorts of contemporary societies 'with different social organisations and settlement patterns, and presumably ideologies' which have been considered Celtic – a term which when 'linked with concepts such as "Hallstatt" and "La Tène" will inevitably warp our conceptual framework. . .' (1994, 32). He has noted the contrasting types of Iron Age society, ranging from the urbanised societies of Gaul in the first century BC to the decentralised societies of the Pennines. In attempting to understand what is evidently a most complicated situation, we should be aware that 'the written

sources may be as much a snare and delusion as a guide'. Even the image of Celtic intemperance has not escaped some reassessment: Dietler (1990) has studied the social role of alcohol and the prejudices of Classical authors have been examined by Chapman (1992, 166).

The subject of Celtic religion is a vast and unwieldy one but a good illustration of how the interpretation of a remarkable body of archaeological data is coloured by an equally impressive corpus of literary material. However, the Romano-Celtic evidence is not as revealing or as reliable as has been thought (Webster 1995). Much of the Irish and Welsh literature is, of course, of considerably later, medieval, date and coupling it with earlier evidence gives a misleadingly timeless image (Fitzpatrick 1991). Moreover, we now know that some of the later Irish tales were 'pasts dreamt of, artefacts of past glories' to quote Barrett's (1981, 217) expressive phrase: they are at best a very opaque window on the Iron Age, at worst no window at all (see Koch 1994 and references to the work of Aitchison, McCone and Mallory in particular). As far as the archaeological evidence for ritual and religion is concerned, at one level there are great regional differences and, at another, some remarkable similarities across a wide geographical area, both of which deserve careful and impartial analysis. For example, there must be few representations of a human head, a horned figure or a pig that have not received a Celtic label. The 'cult of the head' . . . 'a persistent theme throughout all aspects of Celtic life' (Ross 1967, 61, 126) is questioned by Chapman (1992, 287) who describes it as one example of a 'creative scholarly invention'. Horned figures (Ross 1967, 127) or antlered figures (Green 1989, 86) are widely named Cernunnos and Powell's caveat (1971, 202) is equally widely ignored: writing on the well-known antlered figure on the Gundestrup cauldron, he described how it had 'become a sure target for every Celtic mythologizer, but there is no ground for believing, on the strength of a single defective inscription in Paris, that every Celtic horned god should be called "Cernunnos" nor that this is certainly the true form of the name'. The image of the pig was obviously of major cultic importance in some parts of 'the Celtic World' (Green 1989, 139; Ford 1990). But it had a wider and variable currency (Foster 1977) and why a bronze statuette of a boar from Liechtenstein and a figurine of a depressed-looking pig from far-away Bulgaria should be included in various catalogues of Celtic material (Megaw 1970, 129; Pauli 1980, 246; Moscati 1991, 481) must be a puzzle to those uncertain as to how to assess their 'Celticity'. The literature on what is invariably termed Celtic art or La Tène art is enormous and complicated by ambiguity at every turn. These two terms are sometimes synonymous, as in Megaw and Megaw (1995), and sometimes not and few writers have adequately addressed such fundamental questions as definition or ethnic attribution (Taylor 1991). In assuming that Celtic speakers produced La Tène art, there has been a tendency to attribute to the art style the elaborate, paradoxical, mysterious and ambiguous characteristics supposedly possessed by the Celts themselves (Merriman 1987). The correlation of La Tène art and Celts has been questioned by various writers and obviously, given its discontinuous distribution, some Celts had no use for it. It is also possible that some non-Celts may have adopted it: because the evidence is so scanty, the distribution of Celtic speaking peoples on the 'Celtic fringe' in Central Europe is uncertain and whether La Tène material there represents a Celtic presence is unclear (Barford 1991; Cumberpatch 1995; for the linguistic evidence see Evans 1979). It may have been a status symbol, rapidly emulated but used in radically different ways from region to region (Champion and Champion 1986, 64; Champion 1987, 105). The potential magical charge of the motifs may also explain their widespread use (Kruta 1985, 92). According to Megaw and Megaw (1994) La Tène art is a 'Europe-wide visual language linking together related but not necessarily identical groups of people'. For Jope (1987), however, Celtic art is more than just a product of people who spoke Celtic languages, it has a coherence which spans more than two millennia and may represent an equally coherent ethnicity.

It may seem foolhardy to attempt to separate insular 'Celticisation' and 'Celts' but it is surely time to try. The emergence of a Celtic language in Ireland was, I would argue, the culmination of a long process of social and economic interaction between Ireland and Britain, and between these islands and adjacent parts of Continental Europe. For Ireland, the Irish Sea was one crucial factor in this process, facilitating rather than inhibiting contact, and enabling this island to share not just in the European phenomenon of the creation of the larger speech communities of later prehistory but in wider systems of fashions and beliefs as well. This model of Celticization, 'of becoming Celtic-speaking', should force us to examine even more closely the nature and the degree of contact between Ireland and Britain and the Continent. However, the archaeological data deserves to be studied in its own right, free of ethnic labels and preconceptions, and if linguistic and archaeological models can be harmonised, so much the better. The process as envisaged does not see Ireland just as a recipient nor does it exclude the possibility of movements of people – as we know only too well these are difficult to detect in the archaeological record. If such movements did occur in the Bronze Age or in the Iron Age, then they only gave added impetus to a diachronic dynamic long underway. For the island of Ireland, to paraphrase Koch (1991, 19), Celticization, *as an instance of language shift*, was not an event but a process, and a Bronze Age process at that.

References

Barford, P. 1991. Celts in Central Europe and beyond. *Archaeologia Polona* 29, 79-98.

Barrett, J. 1981. Aspects of the Iron Age in Atlantic Scotland. A case study in the problems of archaeological interpretation. *Proceedings of the Society of Antiquaries of Scotland* 111, 205-19.

Barrett, J. 1994. The Bronze Age. In B. Vyner (ed.), *Building on the Past. Papers celebrating 150 years of the Royal Archaeological Institute*, 103-22. London.

Bodmer, W.F. 1993. The Genetics of Celtic Populations. *Proceedings of the British Academy* 82, 37-57.

Champion, T.C. 1980. Mass Migration in Later Prehistoric Europe. In P. Sörbom (ed.), *Transport Technology and Social Change*, 33-42. Stockholm.

Champion, T.C. 1985. Written sources and the European Iron Age. In T. C. Champion and J. V. S. Megaw (eds), *Settlement and Society: aspects of West European prehistory in the first millennium BC*, 9-22. Leicester.

Champion, T. C. 1987. The European Iron Age: assessing the state of the art. *Scottish Archaeological Review* 4, 98-107.

Champion, T. C. 1995. Power, Politics and Status. In M. Green (ed.), *The Celtic World*, 85-94. London.

Champion, T. C. and S. Champion. 1986. Peer Polity Interaction in the European Iron Age. In C. Renfrew and C. F. Cherry (eds), *Peer Polity Interaction and Socio-Political Change*, 59-68. Cambridge.

Chapman, M. 1992. *The Celts. The Construction of a Myth.* Basingstoke.

Collis, J. 1986. Adieu Hallstatt! Adieu La Tène! In A. Duval and J. Gomez (eds), *Actes du VIIIe Colloque sur les Ages du Fer*, 327-30.

Collis, J. 1994. Reconstructing Iron Age Society. In K. Kristiansen and J. Jensen (eds), *Europe in the First Millennium BC*, 31-9. Sheffield.

Colquhoun, I and C. Burgess. 1988. *The Swords of Britain. Prähistorische Bronzefunde*, 4.5. Munich.

Cooney, G. and E. Grogan. 1994. *Irish Prehistory: a social perspective.* Dublin.

Coulmas, F. 1992. *Language and Economy.* Oxford.

Crawford, O. G. S. 1922. A Prehistoric Invasion of England. *Antiquaries Journal* 2, 27-45.

Cumberpatch, C. G. 1995. Settlement and Economy in Late Iron Age Slovakia, southern Poland and Trans-Danubian Hungary. In J. D. Hill and C. G. Cumberpatch (eds), *Different Iron Ages: Studies on the Iron Age in Temperate Europe*, 195-217. British Archaeological Reports, International Series S602. Oxford.

Davies, W. 1992. The Myth of the Celtic Church. In N.

Edwards and A. Lane (eds), *The Early Church in Wales and the West*, 12-21. Oxford.

Dietler, M. 1990. Driven by Drink: the Role of Drinking in the Political Economy and the Case of Early Iron Age France. *Journal of Anthropological Archaeology* 9, 352-406.

Dietler, M. 1994. 'Our Ancestors the Gauls': Archaeology, Ethnic Nationalism, and the Manipulation of Celtic Identity in Modern Europe. *American Anthropologist* 96, 584-605.

Dillon, M. 1968. The Coming of the Celts. In F. G. Thompson (ed.), *Maintaining a National Identity*, 85-8. Annual Book of the Celtic League. Dublin.

Dillon, M. and N. K. Chadwick 1967. *The Celtic Realms*. London.

Duval, P.-M. 1977. *Les Celtes*. Paris.

Eogan, G. 1965. *Catalogue of Irish Bronze Swords*. Dublin.

Eogan, G. 1993. The Late Bronze Age: Customs, Crafts and Cults. In E. Shee Twohig and M. Ronayne (eds), *Past Perceptions: the Prehistoric Archaeology of South-West Ireland*, 121-33. Cork.

Eogan, G. 1994. *The Accomplished Art. Gold and Goldworking in Britain and Ireland during the Bronze Age*. Oxford.

Evans, D. E. 1979. The Labyrinth of Continental Celtic. *Proceedings of the British Academy* 65, 497-538.

Evans, D. E. 1992. Celticity, Identity and the Study of Language. *Archaeologia Cambrensis* 140, 1-16.

Evans, E. E. 1930. The Sword-bearers. *Antiquity* 4, 157-72.

Fitzpatrick, A. P. 1991. Celtic (Iron Age) Religion - Traditional and Timeless?, *Scottish Archaeological Review* 8, 123-29.

Ford, P. K. 1990. A Highly Important Pig. In A. T. E. Matonis and D. F. Melia (eds), *Celtic Language, Celtic Culture: a Festschrift for Eric P. Hamp*, 292-304. Van Nuys. California.

Foster, J. 1977. *Bronze Boar Figurines in Iron Age and Roman Britain. British Archaeological Reports* 39. Oxford.

Gerloff, S. 1986. Bronze Age Class A Cauldrons: Typology, Origins and Chronology. *Journal of the Royal Society of Antiquaries of Ireland* 116, 84-115.

Gomez, J. 1987. Les Épées du Cognacais (Charente) et la Chronologie des Épées du Type Chelsea-Ballintober en France. In J. C. Blanchet (ed.), *Les relations entre le Continent et les Iles Brittaniques à l'age du bronze*, 125-32. Amiens.

Green, M. 1989. *Symbol and Image in Celtic Religious Art*. London.

Green, M. (ed.). 1995. *The Celtic World*. London.

Hill, J. D. 1989. Re-thinking the Iron Age. *Scottish Archaeological Review* 6, 16-24.

Hill, J. D. 1995. How should we understand Iron Age societies and hillforts? A contextual study from southern Britain. In J. D. Hill and C. G. Cumberpatch (eds), *Different Iron Ages: Studies on the Iron Age in Temperate Europe*, 45-66. British Archaeological Reports, International Series S602. Oxford.

Hubert, H. 1932. *Les Celtes et l'expansion celtique*. Paris.

Jope, M. 1987. Celtic Art: expressiveness and communica-

tion through 2500 years. *Proceedings of the British Academy* 73, 97-124.

Koch, J. T. 1986. New Thoughts on *Albion, Ierné*, and the Pretanic Isles. *Proceedings of the Harvard Celtic Colloquium* 6, 1-28.

Koch, J. T. 1991. Ériu, Alba and Letha: When was a language ancestral to Gaelic first spoken in Ireland? *Emania* 9, 17-27.

Koch, J. T. 1994. Windows on the Iron Age: 1964-1994. In J. P. Mallory and G. Stockman (eds), *Ulidia. Proceedings of the First International Conference on the Ulster Cycle of Tales*, 229-42. Belfast.

Kristiansen, K. 1993. From Villanova to Seddin. The Reconstruction of an Elite Exchange Network during the Eighth Century BC. In C. Scarre and F. Healy (eds), *Trade and Exchange in Prehistoric Europe*, 143-52. Oxford.

Kruta, V. 1985. *The Celts of the West*. London.

Laing, L. and J. Laing. 1992. *Art of the Celts*. London.

Leerssen, J. 1994. The Western Mirage: on the Celtic Chronotope in the European Imagination. In T. Collins (ed.), *Decoding the Landscape*, 1-11. Galway.

Lloyd, J. E. 1911. *A History of Wales*. London.

Macalister, R. A. S. 1928. *The Archaeology of Ireland*. London.

McCone, K. 1994. An tSean-Ghaeilge agus a Réamhstair. In K. McCone *et al.* (eds), *Stair na Gaeilge in ómós do Pádraig Ó Fiannachta*, 61-219. Maynooth.

McDonald, M. 1986. Celtic Ethnic Kinship and the Problem of being English. *Current Anthropology* 27, 333-47.

MacEoin, G. 1986. The Celticity of Celtic Ireland. In K. H. Schmidt (ed.), *Geschichte und Kultur der Kelten*, 161-74. Heidelberg.

Mallory, J. P. 1984. The Origins of the Irish. *The Journal of Irish Archaeology* 2, 65-9.

Mallory, J. P. 1989. *In Search of the Indo-Europeans*. London.

Mallory, J. P. 1991. Two Perspectives on the Origins of the Irish. *Emania* 9, 53-8.

Mallory, J. P. 1992. Migration and Language Change. *Peregrinatio Gothica III. Universitetets Oldsaksamlings Skrifter, Ny rekke*, 14, 145-53.

Megaw, J. V. S. 1970. *Art of the European Iron Age*. Bath.

Megaw, R. and V. Megaw. 1989. *Celtic Art. From its beginnings to the Book of Kells*. London.

Megaw, R. and V. Megaw. 1994. Through a window on the European Iron Age darkly: fifty years of reading early Celtic art *World Archaeology* 25, 287-303.

Megaw, R. and V. Megaw. 1995. The Nature and Function of Celtic Art. In M. Green (ed.), *The Celtic World*, 345-75. London.

Merriman, N. 1987. Value and motivation in prehistory: the evidence for 'Celtic spirit'. In I. Hodder (ed.), *The Archaeology of Contextual Meanings*, 111-16. Cambridge.

Moscati, S. (ed.). 1991. *The Celts*. Milan.

Needham, S. 1993. Displacement and Exchange in Archaeological Methodology. In C. Scarre and F. Healy (eds), *Trade and Exchange in Prehistoric Europe*, 161-9. Oxford.

Pauli, L. (ed.). 1980. *Die Kelten in Mitteleuropa*. Salzburg.

Piggott, S. 1979. South-west England - North-west Europe: contrasts and contacts in prehistory. In V. Maxwell (ed.), *Prehistoric Dartmoor in its Context*, 10-20. Devon Archaeological Society.

Piggott, S. 1983. The Coming of the Celts. The Archaeological Argument. In G. MacEoin (ed.), *Proceedings of the Sixth International Congress of Celtic Studies, Galway 1979*, 138-48. Dublin.

Powell, T. G. E. 1958. *The Celts*. London.

Powell, T. G. E. 1971. From Urartu to Gundestrup: the agency of Thracian metalwork. In J. Boardman *et al.* (eds), *The European Community in Later Prehistory. Studies in honour of C. F. C. Hawkes*, 183-210. London.

Price, G. 1987. *Ireland and the Celtic Connection*. The Princess Grace Irish Library Lectures 4. Gerrards Cross.

Price, G. 1992. The Celtic Languages. In G. Price (ed.), *The Celtic Connection*, 1-9. Gerrards Cross.

Raftery, B. 1984. *La Tène in Ireland. Problems of Origin and Chronology*. Marburg.

Raftery, B. 1994. *Pagan Celtic Ireland. The Enigma of the Irish Iron Age*. London.

Renfrew, C. 1987. *Archaeology and Language. The Puzzle of the Indo-Europeans*. London.

Rhys, J. 1889. *Early Britain. Celtic Britain*. London.

Robb, J. 1993. A Social Prehistory of European Languages. *Antiquity* 67, 747-60.

Ross, A. 1967. *Pagan Celtic Britain. Studies in Iconography and Tradition*. London.

Ruiz-Galvez, M. 1991. Songs of a Wayfaring Lad. Late Bronze Age Atlantic exchange and the building of the regional identity in the west Iberian peninsula. *Oxford Journal of Archaeology* 10, 277-306.

Schmidt, K. H. 1992. The Celtic Problem. Ethnogenesis, location, date? *Zeitschrift für Celtische Philologie* 45, 38-65.

Schmidt, K. H. 1992a. Celtic Movements in the First Millennium BC. *The Journal of Indo-European Studies* 20, 145-178.

Schmidt, K. H. 1994. Insular Celtic: P and Q Celtic. In M. Ball (ed.), *The Celtic Languages*, 64-98. London.

Severy, M. 1977. The Celts. *National Geographic* 151, 5, 582-633.

Sims-Williams, P. 1986. The Visionary Celt: the Construction of an Ethnic Preconception. *Cambridge Medieval Celtic Studies* 11, 71-96.

Taylor, T. 1991. Celtic Art. *Scottish Archaeological Review* 8, 129-32.

Waddell, J. 1991. The Celticization of the West: an Irish Perspective. In C. Chevillot and A. Coffyn (eds), *L'Age du Bronze Atlantique. Actes du Ier Colloque de Beynac*, 349-66. Beynac.

Waddell, J. 1991a. The Question of the Celticization of Ireland. *Emania* 9, 5-16.

Waddell, J. 1992. The Irish Sea in Prehistory. *The Journal of Irish Archaeology* 6, 29-40.

Waddell, J. 1995. The Cordoned Urn tradition. In I. Kinnes and G. Varndell (eds), '*Unbaked Urns of Rudely Shape*'. *Essays on British and Irish Pottery for Ian Longworth*, 113-22. Oxford.

Warner, R. B. 1991. Cultural Intrusions in the Early Iron Age: some notes. *Emania* 9, 44-52.

Webster, J. 1995. Translation and Subjection: Interpretatio and the Celtic Gods. In J. D. Hill and C. G. Cumberpatch (eds), *Different Iron Ages: Studies on the Iron Age in Temperate Europe*, 175-83. British Archaeological Reports, International Series S602. Oxford.

Yoffee, N. 1990. Before Babel. A Review Article. *Proceedings of the Prehistoric Society* 56, 299-313.

Zvelebil, M. and K. V. Zvelebil. 1988. Agricultural transition and Indo-European dispersals. *Antiquity* 62, 574-83.